THE CAMBRIDGE
COMPANION TO THE
ARTHURIAN LEGEND

EDITED BY
ELIZABETH ARCHIBALD AND AD PUTTER

CAMBRIDGE
UNIVERSITY PRESS

CAMBRIDGE UNIVERSITY PRESS
Cambridge, New York, Melbourne, Madrid, Cape Town, Singapore, São Paulo, Delhi

Cambridge University Press
The Edinburgh Building, Cambridge CB2 8RU, UK

Published in the United States of America by Cambridge University Press, New York

www.cambridge.org
Information on this title: www.cambridge.org/9780521677882

First published 2009

Printed in the United Kingdom at the University Press, Cambridge

A catalogue record for this publication is available from the British Library

Library of Congress Cataloguing in Publication data
The Cambridge companion to the Arthurian legend / [edited by]
Elizabeth Archibald and Ad Putter.
p.   cm.
Includes bibliographical references and index.
ISBN 978-0-521-86059-8
1. Arthurian romances – History and criticism.   2. English literature – Middle English,
1100–1500 – History and criticism.   3. Romances, English – History and criticism.
I. Archibald, Elizabeth, 1951–   II. Putter, Ad.   III. Title.
PR328.C36 2009
820.9′351–dc22
2009020686

ISBN 978-0-521-86059-8 hardback
ISBN 978-0-521-67788-2 paperback

CONTENTS

CONTENTS

ACKNOWLEDGEMENTS

Our greatest debt is to our contributors, who responded admirably to our request to describe such rich material so succinctly. Norris Lacy also gave us useful editorial advice. We are grateful to Amanda Hopkins for copy-editing an advanced draft of this book, to Cory Rushton for help in compiling the further reading section, to Gareth Griffth for producing the index, and to the University of Bristol for supporting their work through awards from the Arts Faculty Research Fund and the Tucker-Cruse Fund. We thank Linda Bree for commissioning this volume; she and Maartje Scheltens supplied much valuable advice and support, and Tom O'Reilly oversaw the production most efficiently. We are grateful to David Cox for producing the map of Arthurian Britain. Geraldine Stoneham was the ideal copy-editor, and saved us from many infelicities and inconsistencies.

We dedicate this volume to the memory of Derek and Elisabeth Brewer, both distinguished Arthurians.

ELIZABETH ARCHIBALD
AD PUTTER

ELIZABETH ARCHIBALD is Professor of Medieval Literature in the English Department at the University of Bristol. Her publications include *Apollonius of Tyre* (1991), *Incest and the Medieval Imagination* (2001), and *A Companion to Malory*, co-edited with A. S. G. Edwards (1996). She is currently working on macaronic literature and on bathing in the Middle Ages.

JOHN BURROW is Fellow of the British Academy and Emeritus Professor at the University of Bristol. He is the author of many studies of medieval English literature, including *A Reading of 'Sir Gawain and the Green Knight'* (1965), *Medieval Writers and Their Work* (1982) and most recently *The Poetry of Praise* (2008).

JANE GILBERT is Senior Lecturer in French at University College London, and a comparatist working in English, French, and modern theory. She is currently completing a monograph on the interface between life and death in medieval French and English literature.

ROB GOSSEDGE is a Lecturer in English Literature at Cardiff University. He has recently published articles on Welsh modernism and the reception of Arthurian literature in the post-medieval period. He is currently finishing a book on British rewritings of the Matter of Britain in the nineteenth and twentieth centuries.

RONALD HUTTON is Professor of History at the University of Bristol, and author of twelve books, including *Witches, Druids and King Arthur: Studies in Paganism, Myth and Magic* (2003).

STEPHEN KNIGHT is Distinguished Research Professor in English Literature at Cardiff University. He has written widely on medieval and modern themes, including King Arthur and Robin Hood; his latest book, *Merlin: Knowledge and Power*, will be published in 2009.

NORRIS J. LACY is the Edwin Erle Sparks Professor of French and Medieval Studies at Pennsylvania State University. He is an Honorary President of the International Arthurian Society and has been knighted by the French government. His many Arthurian publications include *The Craft of Chrétien de Troyes* (1980), *The New Arthurian Encyclopedia* (3rd edn, 1996), *The Arthurian Handbook* (2nd edn, 1997), and *A Companion to Chrétien de Troyes* (2005, co-edited with Joan Tasker Grimbert).

ANDREW LYNCH is Professor of English and Cultural Studies, and Director of the Centre for Medieval and Early Modern Studies, at the University of Western Australia. His publications include *Malory's Book of Arms* (1997) and numerous articles and book chapters on medieval Arthurian literature and its modern afterlives.

PEGGY MCCRACKEN is Professor of French and Women's Studies at the University of Michigan. She is the author of *The Romance of Adultery: Queenship and Sexual Transgression in Old French Literature* (1998) and *The Curse of Eve, the Wound of the Hero: Blood, Gender, and Medieval Literature* (2003).

AD PUTTER is Professor of Medieval English Literature at the University of Bristol. He is the General Editor of the series *Arthurian Literature in the Middle Ages*, and has published widely in the area of medieval literature. His books include *Sir Gawain and the Green Knight and French Arthurian Romance* (1995), *An Introduction to the Gawain Poet* (1996), and (with Judith Jefferson and Myra Stokes) *Studies in the Metre of Alliterative Verse* (2007).

ROBERT ALLEN ROUSE teaches medieval literature and culture at the University of British Columbia. He is the author of *The Idea of Anglo-Saxon England in Middle English Romance* (2005), and co-author with Cory Rushton of *The Medieval Quest for Arthur* (2005). He is currently working on a study of the role of geography in the romance narratives of medieval England.

CORY JAMES RUSHTON is Assistant Professor of English at St Francis Xavier University, Canada. He co-authored *The Medieval Quest for Arthur* with Robert Rouse (2005), and has published numerous articles on the Arthurian legend and romance. He co-edited (with Amanda Hopkins) *The Erotic in the Literature of Medieval Britain* (2007). Forthcoming publications include *A Companion to Middle English Romance* (co-edited with Raluca Radulescu), and *Disability and Medieval Law: History, Literature, Society.*

CORINNE SAUNDERS is Professor in the Department of English Studies in the University of Durham and is the English editor of the journal *Medium Ævum*. She is the author of *The Forest of Medieval Romance* (1993), *Rape and Ravishment in the Literature of Medieval England* (2001), and *Magic and the Supernatural in Medieval English Romance: Ideas and Imaginings* (forthcoming 2009). She has edited and co-edited numerous volumes, including *A Companion to Romance* (2004), *Cultural Encounters in the Romance of Medieval England* (2005), and *A Concise Companion to Chaucer* (2006).

JANE TAYLOR is Emeritus Professor of French at Durham University. An Honorary President of the International Arthurian Society, she has worked extensively on medieval French literature, especially on Arthurian romance and lyric poetry, as well as on translation. Her latest book, *The Making of Poetry: Late Medieval Poetic Anthologies*, was published in 2007.

BARRY WINDEATT is Professor of English in the University of Cambridge, and Fellow and Keeper of Rare Books at Emmanuel College. His research focuses on the imaginative literature, visual culture and contemplative traditions of medieval England in a European context. As Director of the Cambridge 'Medieval Imaginations' Project he has created a website for research and teaching on text and image in later medieval England (www.english.cam.ac.uk/medieval/).

Frequently Cited Sources

The primary texts and critical studies listed below are mentioned so frequently by our contributors that they are cited in both text and footnotes only by author and/or short title, and by page/chapter/line number, as appropriate. When a contributor refers to a different edition of one of these primary texts, full details are given in a footnote. In the case of Malory, where numerous different editions are widely used by scholars and students, Caxton's book and chapter divisions are included after the page numbers in square brackets.

Primary Texts and Translations

Chaucer   Geoffrey Chaucer, *The Riverside Chaucer*, ed. Larry D. Benson (Boston: Houghton Mifflin, 1987; Oxford University Press, 1988)

Kibler   Chrétien de Troyes, *Arthurian Romances*, trans. William W. Kibler (Harmondsworth: Penguin, 1991); this translation is cited by page number. The textual history of Chrétien's romances is complex; for ease of reference, line numbers are taken from the editions of Chrétien's romances in the series Classiques français du moyen âge: *Erec et Enide*, ed. Mario Roques (1981); *Le Chevalier au lion (Yvain)*, ed. Mario Roques (1978); *Le Chevalier de la charrete (Lancelot)*, ed. Mario Roques (1978); *Cligés*, ed. Alexandre Micha (1978); *Le Conte du Graal (Perceval)*, ed. F. Lecoy, 2 vols. (1984)

Lacy   *Lancelot-Grail: The Old French Arthurian Vulgate and Post-Vulgate in Translation*, gen. ed. Norris J. Lacy, 5 vols. (New York and London: Garland, 1993–6)

Lancelot   *Lancelot: roman en prose du XIIIe siècle*, ed. Alexandre Micha, TLF, 9 vols. (Geneva: Droz, 1978–83)

Malory — Malory, Sir Thomas, *The Works of Sir Thomas Malory* [*Morte Darthur*], ed. Eugène Vinaver, 3rd edn rev. P. J. C. Field, 3 vols. (Oxford: Clarendon Press, 1990)

Mort Artu — *La Mort le roi Artu*, ed. Jean Frappier, TLF, 3rd edn (Geneva: Droz, 1964)

Sir Gawain — *Sir Gawain and the Green Knight*, ed. J. R. R. Tolkien and E. V. Gordon, 2nd edn rev. Norman Davis (Oxford: Clarendon Press, 1967)

Tennyson — Alfred Lord Tennyson, *Idylls of the King*, ed. J. M. Gray (Harmondsworth: Penguin, 1983; repr. 1996)

Thorpe — Geoffrey of Monmouth, *History of the Kings of Britain*, trans. Lewis Thorpe (Harmondsworth: Penguin, 1966)

Twain — Mark Twain, *A Connecticut Yankee at King Arthur's Court*, ed. Justin Kaplan (Harmondsworth: Penguin, 1971; repr. 1986)

Secondary Sources

The ongoing series *Arthurian Literature in the Middle Ages*, series editors †W. R. J. Barron and Ad Putter, is indispensable for the study of the Arthurian legend; it updates and expands Loomis's 1957 volume of the same title (*ALMA* – see below). Some if not all of the volumes listed below are relevant to every chapter in this book, and should be consulted for information about editions of primary sources and critical studies of specific texts and topics.

AoE — *The Arthur of the English: The Arthurian Legend in Medieval English Life and Literature*, ed. W. R. J. Barron, Arthurian Literature in the Middle Ages 2 (Cardiff: University of Wales Press, 1999)

AoF — *The Arthur of the French: The Arthurian Legend in Medieval French and Occitan Literature*, ed. Glyn S. Burgess and Karen Pratt, Arthurian Literature in the Middle Ages 4 (Cardiff: University of Wales Press, 2006)

AoG — *The Arthur of the Germans: The Arthurian Legend in Medieval German and Dutch Literature*, ed. W. H. Jackson and S. A. Ranawake, Arthurian Literature in the Middle Ages 3 (Cardiff: University of Wales Press, 2000)

AoW — *The Arthur of the Welsh: The Arthurian Legend in Medieval Welsh Literature*, ed. Rachel Bromwich, A. O. H. Jarman and Brynley Roberts, Arthurian Literature in the Middle Ages 1 (Cardiff: University of Wales Press, 1991)

Other Abbreviations

ALMA   *Arthurian Literature in the Middle Ages*, ed. R. S. Loomis (Oxford: Clarendon Press, 1957)
BBIAS   *Bibliographical Bulletin of the International Arthurian Society*
CFMA   Classiques français du moyen âge
EETS   Early English Text Society
       o.s. Original Series
       e.s. Extra Series
PMLA   *Publications of the Modern Language Association of America*
SATF   Société des anciens textes français
STS   Scottish Text Society
TLF   Textes littéraires français

A SELECTIVE CHRONOLOGY

This chronology of the most important landmarks in the history of Arthurian legend and literature is very selective, especially in relation to post-medieval material (art, music and drama as well as literature), where we have focused on the English tradition. Many dates, particularly in earlier periods, are approximate, and there is great uncertainty about the dating of Welsh Arthurian texts, some of which are believed to have had a long oral tradition before being committed to writing. Fuller overviews and further details about individual entries can be found in the chronological survey chapters of this *Companion*. Readers may also wish to consult reference works such as *The New Arthurian Encyclopaedia*, ed. Lacy, and *The Arthurian Annals*, ed. Nastali and Boardman (see Further Reading).

455–75	Arthur's reign, according to Geoffrey of Monmouth
516(?518)	Date of battle of Mount Badon in *Annales Cambriae*
537(?539)	Date of Arthur's last battle in *Annales Cambriae*
c. 548	Gildas, *De Excidio Britanniae*: mentions battle of Mount Badon
7th century?	*Gododdin*: mentions Arthur
830	Nennius, *Historia Brittonum*: records battles of Arthur
c. 950	*Annales Cambriae*: mentions battle of Camlann where Arthur and Mordred fell
11th century	Probable time of composition of the earliest Arthurian tales from *The Mabinogion* (*Peredur, Culhwch and Olwen*) and Latin saints' lives from Wales
c. 1105	Modena Cathedral archivolt depicting Arthurian scenes
c. 1135	Geoffrey of Monmouth's *Historia Regum Britanniae (History of the Kings of Britain)*: includes account of Arthur's life

c. 1150	Geoffrey of Monmouth, *Vita Merlini* (*Life of Merlin*)
1155	Wace, *Roman de Brut*: translates Geoffrey's *Historia*; first mention of Round Table
c. 1169–81	Chrétien de Troyes, Arthurian romances: first mention of Camelot, Grail, and Lancelot's love for Guinevere
c. 1180–1205	Hartmann von Aue translates Chrétien's romances into German
c. 1185	Andreas Capellanus, *De Amore*: treatise on courtly love with Arthurian episode
c. 1190	Renaut de Beaujeu, *Le Bel Inconnu*: Fair Unknown romance about Gawain's son
1191	Exhumation of Arthur and Guinevere's tomb at Glastonbury Abbey
?later 12th century	*De Ortu Waluuanii*: Latin Gawain romance
later 12th century	Béroul, *Tristan*: Arthur present at trial vindicating Iseut
c. 1210	Laȝamon, *Brut*: first English version of Arthurian history (based on Geoffrey of Monmouth and Wace)
	Guillaume le Clerc, *Fergus*: romance parodying Chrétien, set in Scotland
	Robert de Boron: first cycle of Grail romances
	Wolfram von Eschenbach, *Parzival*: German Grail romance
c. 1215–30	Vulgate Cycle (*Lancelot-Grail* Cycle): vast French Arthurian prose romance-history including *Lancelot*, *Queste del Saint Graal* and *Mort Artu*, later supplemented by *Estoire del Saint Graal* and *Merlin*
c. 1235–40	Post-Vulgate Cycle (*Roman du Graal*): French prose reworking of Vulgate Cycle
c. 1250	Prose *Tristan*: French fusion of Tristan legend with Arthurian stories
c. 1260	Penninc and Pieter Vostaert, *Roman van Walewein*: Dutch Gawain romance
1290	Edward I hosts Round Table tournament at Winchester and commissions Round Table
early 14th century	Dutch *Lancelot*-compilation: part of Vulgate Cycle plus interpolated Dutch romances
c. 1340	*Perceforest*: vast French prose romance merging legends of Alexander and Arthur
	Tavola Ritonda: Italian Arthurian compilation
c. 1380	Alliterative *Morte Arthure* (Middle English)

c. 1390	*Sir Gawain and the Green Knight*
	Geoffrey Chaucer, *Canterbury Tales*: allusions to Arthurian characters
1430s	John Lydgate, *Fall of Princes* (based on Boccaccio and Laurent de Premierfait): includes rise and fall of Arthur
c. 1450	Burgundian prose adaptations of Chrétien's *Erec* and *Cligés*
c. 1457–64	John Hardyng's *Chronicle* (2 versions): includes Grail quest
1469–70	Sir Thomas Malory completes *Le Morte Darthur*
c. 1481–92	Ulrich Fuetrer, *Buch der Abenteuer*: German Arthurian compilation
1485	First printed edition of Malory by William Caxton
1486	Henry VII names eldest son Arthur
1534	First printed edition of Polydore Vergil's *Anglica Historia*: questions historicity of Arthurian legend
1587	Thomas Hughes, *The Misfortunes of Arthur*: Senecan tragedy
1590–6	Publication of Edmund Spenser, *The Faerie Queene*: includes Prince Arthur
1613	Michael Drayton, *Poly-Olbion*: includes Arthurian 'history'
1691	Henry Purcell and John Dryden, *King Arthur: The British Worthy* (opera)
1695	Richard Blackmore, *Prince Arthur*: verse epic
1730–1	Henry Fielding, *Tom Thumb*: satire set at Arthurian court
1765	Percy's *Reliques*: includes Arthurian tales and ballads
1813	Sir Walter Scott, *The Bridal of Triermain*: Arthurian episode
1816	First reprinting of Malory since 1634
1829	Thomas Love Peacock, *The Misfortunes of Elphin*: satire set in sixth-century Wales
1832	Alfred Lord Tennyson, *The Lady of Shalott*: Tennyson's first Arthurian poem
1836–46	Lady Charlotte Guest translates *The Mabinogion*
1848	Foundation of the Pre-Raphaelite Brotherhood
1858	William Morris, *The Defence of Guenevere*
1859–85	Tennyson, *Idylls of the King*

1865	Richard Wagner, *Tristan und Isolde*
1881–98	Edward Burne-Jones, *The Sleep of Arthur in Avalon* (cover illustration and frontispiece)
1882	Wagner, *Parsifal*
1889	Mark Twain, *A Connecticut Yankee in the Court of King Arthur*
1903	Edwin Porter, *Parsifal*: first Arthurian film
1920	Jessie Weston, *From Ritual to Romance*: anthropological study of romance motifs
1922	T. S. Eliot, *The Waste Land*
1923	Thomas Hardy, *The Famous Tragedy of the Queen of Cornwall*
1927	Rodgers and Hart, *A Connecticut Yankee* (musical)
1938	T. H. White, *The Sword in the Stone*; reprinted 1958 as the first part of *The Once and Future King*
1949	International Arthurian Society founded
1958–9	John Steinbeck, *The Acts of King Arthur* (published 1976): retelling of Malory
1960	Lerner and Loewe, *Camelot* (musical)
1967	Joshua Logan, *Camelot* (film)
1970–9	Mary Stewart, The Merlin Trilogy
1965–77	Susan Cooper, The Dark is Rising series
1974	Robert Bresson, *Lancelot du Lac* (film)
1975	Terry Gilliam and Terry Jones, *Monty Python and the Holy Grail* (film)
1978	Thomas Berger, *Arthur Rex*
	Eric Rohmer, *Perceval le Gallois* (film)
1981	John Boorman, *Excalibur* (film)
1982	Marion Zimmer Bradley, *The Mists of Avalon*
1982–5	*Camelot 3000*: sci-fi Arthurian comic strip
1984	Mary Stewart, *The Wicked Day*
	David Lodge, *Small World*
1995	Jerry Zucker, *First Knight* (film)
2004	Antoine Fuqua, *King Arthur* (film)
2005	Eric Idle and John Du Prez, *Spamalot* (musical)

Arthurian Britain

AD PUTTER AND ELIZABETH ARCHIBALD

Introduction

When Laȝamon, a Worcestershire priest, wrote around 1200 (quoting Merlin) that Arthur would be food for storytellers till the end of time, he prophesied more truly than he could have imagined.[1] Eight hundred years later, Arthur still has very extensive name recognition. Continuously from the twelfth century to the present day, authors and artists using various modes – romances, poetry, plays, novels, sculptures, manuscript illuminations, frescoes, paintings, operas, films, graphic novels, cartoons – have produced variations on the basic theme of the great king who saved Britain from enemies at home and abroad, conquered much of the Continent (even Rome, according to some sources), and established a court which became a magnet for the best and bravest knights in the world, only to be brought low by treachery in the end, like many other legendary rulers. Fortune's wheel, such a potent symbol in the Middle Ages, turns inexorably, carrying him up to the very top, and then throwing him down.

The Arthurian legend became one of the dominant narrative themes of the later Middle Ages. According to Jean Bodel, there were three: the Matter of Rome (from the fall of Troy to Æneas' establishment of the Roman Empire), the Matter of France (the deeds of Charlemagne and his lords), and the Matter of Britain (the story of Arthur and his Round Table).[2] The story of Alexander was also very popular, but more often as a cautionary tale of excessive ambition. Although Arthur was a British king, his legend was known and retold much more widely. An early Welsh tradition, partly oral, seems to have underlain the first 'biography', that of Geoffrey of Monmouth. Geoffrey's work circulated widely and its influence was soon felt; the first Arthurian chivalric romances were written in France, quickly followed by German adaptations. The many versions of the legend, in Latin and every western European vernacular, offer a series of kaleidoscopic variations on the main themes, and offer modern scholars a fascinating and inexhaustible series of examples of reception and intertextuality. Medieval writers saw no shame in plagiarism; indeed, it was *de rigueur* in the sense that a text needed to be authorised, in the most literal sense, by having a declared source, whether real or invented.[3] So Arthurian writers draw on earlier sources, but some also introduce major new developments, such as Lancelot's love for Guinevere, or the quest for the Grail, and then later writers choose whether, and how, to respond to these developments.

This intertextuality gives the Arthurian legend a special richness when combined with the remarkable flexibility and infinite expandability of the central story. Other major narratives are limited by the focus on a single hero (Alexander), on a short span of that hero's life (Robin Hood), on a fixed set of locations and cast of characters (the Troy story), or historical context (Charlemagne). Part of the success of the Arthurian legend can be attributed to the shift of focus from Arthur to his knights (or, in some modern versions, to the women associated with his court). The protagonist of an Arthurian romance can be a major figure like Gawain or Lancelot or Tristan, or a new character, a would-be knight like Percival; in modern texts it can also be Guinevere or Morgan.[4] The focus can be on a single protagonist, as in *Sir Gawain and the Green Knight*, or on a group, as in the Grail quest. Established heroes can acquire previously unknown siblings or children. So Arthur's nephews are Gawain and Mordred in Geoffrey of Monmouth, but later they are joined by Agravain, Gaheris and Gareth, and also at least one sister. A sub-genre of Arthurian romance develops in the Fair Unknown stories whose young protagonist usually turns out to be Gawain's son (or brother in the case of Malory's *Sir Gareth*). In *The Secular Scripture*, Northrop Frye points to identity lost and recovered as a crucial romance theme, and it is widely used in Arthurian texts, with accompanying recognition scenes.[5] Such themes may be doubled and patterned: a knight who initially does not know his own identity may later discover that he has a grown son, as both Arthur and Lancelot do (though we never see the first meeting of Arthur and Mordred in any medieval text).

The evergreen popularity of the Arthurian legend across Europe for over a thousand years makes it very hard to cover it comprehensively in a single book. R. S. Loomis managed to cover the whole of the Middle Ages in the seminal volume he edited in 1959, which remained indispensable for many decades (*ALMA*). Now, however, its scholarship is out of date, and it is being replaced by a series of multi-authored volumes (each dedicated to a particular language or in some cases group of related languages); these have become the definitive guides.[6] There are a number of valuable surveys of Arthurian literature which include post-medieval versions, but some are inevitably very selective (for instance, Derek Pearsall's *Arthurian Romance: A Short Introduction* [2003]), and those which aim to be comprehensive are descriptive rather than analytical (for example, Alan Lupack, *The Oxford*

Guide to Arthurian Literature and Legend [2005]). Our aim is to strike a balance between the descriptive and the analytic, so this *Companion* is divided into two parts. The chronological section shows how the legend evolved from the shadowy Welsh tradition through medieval chronicle and romance and post-medieval scepticism to modern novels, cartoons and films. Here we have concentrated on the Latin, French and English traditions for the Middle Ages, and on Anglophone versions for the post-medieval period. In the thematic section we have chosen themes which seem to us to be key to understanding Arthurian literature; all essays in this section deal with both medieval and post-medieval material, though the main focus is medieval.

Many rich areas of Arthuriana have had to be omitted, for instance art and music.[7] Arthurian texts were produced in the Middle Ages in Scandinavia, in Italy and the Iberian peninsula, and even in Hebrew; they add to the rich intertextuality of Arthurian studies, but only a few could be mentioned here. Our aim in the chronological sections is not completeness but an overview of the evolution of the legend in the dominant traditions (Latin, French and English). We cannot do full justice to this remarkable evolution – Norris Lacy notes in Chapter 7 that 'just over 80 per cent of all Arthurian works in English date from the twentieth century' – nor can we treat more than a few of the major Arthurian themes.

Evolution

The evolution of the Arthurian legend from the beginning to the present day is traced in seven chronological chapters. To begin at the beginning is, of course, to ask the question whether or not there ever was an Arthur, and if so, who, what, where and when. This question takes us back to the earliest sources – for it is here that one would hope to discover the footprint of the man before he entered the world of legend. However, as Ronald Hutton shows in 'The Early Arthur', it is an inconvenient truth that Arthur had already entered that world by the time his life-records begin. The earliest sources associate him with the shadowy period around 500, when the Romans who had earlier colonised Britain withdrew and left the native Celtic population (the Britons) vulnerable to attack by Germanic tribes. The language of the new invaders, Anglo-Saxon, is the immediate ancestor of Modern English. In the first chronicle that mentions Arthur, the ninth-century *Historia Brittonum* (sometimes attributed to Nennius),[8] he is already larger than life. Twelve battles by the Britons against the pagan Saxons are said to have taken place under his leadership, and in the one battle that is independently confirmed by other early medieval chronicles, the battle of Mount Badon, Arthur himself is said to have killed 960 men in a single attack. Gildas in his chronicle (*c.* 548), writing shortly after these twelve battles are presumed to have taken place, confirms there was indeed a famous battle at Mount Badon. It happened, he says, in the year he was born, though unfortunately he does not say where Badon is, and makes no mention of Arthur. In the *Gododdin*, a Welsh poem extant in a thirteenth-century manuscript but centuries older in origin, Arthur is already a byword for supreme heroic achievement. The poem praises the prowess of Guaurthur, an excellent warrior 'even though he was no Arthur'. Try as we may, we cannot go back to a pre-mythical Arthur via the earliest sources.

In the cultural renaissance of the twelfth century, the period covered by Ad Putter, some writers were as troubled as we are by the absence of reliable historical sources. William of Malmesbury in his *Deeds of the English Kings* (*c.* 1125) wrote that Arthur is 'the subject of false and dreaming fable' (*fallaces fabulae*) but surely deserves the support of 'true histories' (*veraces historiae*).⁹ A decade later, Geoffrey of Monmouth took up William's gauntlet and produced the *History of the Kings of Britain*, a work that had all the semblance of true history, and included a life of Arthur from his birth to his death. Geoffrey's *History* became the founding text of the Arthurian chronicle tradition, which flourished in the medieval period and beyond: Michael Drayton's *Poly-Olbion* (1613) carried the tradition deep into the Renaissance. In the chronicles Arthur is the king of the Britons, scourge of the Saxons, Picts, Scots and Irish, the conqueror of northern and western Europe, and tragic victim of Mordred's treachery. Needless to say, Geoffrey's *History* was not really a *verax historia* (true history) at all, but medieval readers generally gave credence to it. Shorter synopses of Arthur's biography were soon incorporated into universal histories produced in Britain and on the Continent, and thus Arthur enjoyed, for a while, the unquestionable status of fact. In the Celtic lands of Wales, Cornwall and Brittany, Arthur's destiny as *rex quondam et futurus*, the once and future king, was a matter of regional pride and political importance. The 'Breton hope' was that he would one day return to rid the homeland of all foreign invaders. A commentary on the prophecies of Merlin (attributed to Alain of Lille, 1128–1203) warns readers not to mention Arthur's death when in Brittany: those who do risk being cursed and pelted with stones by the locals.

The *fallaces fabulae* would not go away, however, and later in the twelfth century, when the French poet Chrétien de Troyes composed the earliest surviving Arthurian romances, stories about Arthur and his knights passed from oral into literary art. A world of difference separates the Arthurian romances from the chronicle tradition. If in the latter Arthur is the central hero, a warlike leader whose warriors literally sacrifice their lives in his cause, in romance he often becomes a marginal figurehead, eclipsed in glamour and interest by specific knights of the Round Table, whose adventures in love and chivalry now take centre stage. The focus on the collective interest of Arthur's realm in times of war shifts in romance to the individual hero's self-realisation in times of peace. The 'honest' chronicler, who impresses on us the weighty significance that attaches to historic events, makes way in Chrétien's romances for the self-conscious creator of fiction, who withholds the meaning of events and the identities of characters, and by so doing invites us, like knights-errant, to find out by 'taking the adventure'. In short, the distance between the chronicles and the Arthurian verse romances is vast, and in between it there lay a world of future possibilities.

It was the idea of reconciling these two traditions, romance and chronicle, and of absorbing them into a coherent model of romance-history, that inspired the prose writers of the thirteenth century who are the focus of Jane Taylor's chapter. In the world outside Arthurian fiction, this was the century of the *summa*, the encyclopaedic compendium of theology, philosophy, canon law (or all three combined); and the great Arthurian cycles of the thirteenth century, the Vulgate and Post-Vulgate Cycles and the Prose *Tristan*, could well be described as Arthurian *summae*. In them different romances are harmonised both with one another and with the Arthurian chronicle tradition – with the result that it becomes hard to say whether they were meant to be taken as 'fables' or 'histories'.

English literature lagged behind in these developments by a couple of centuries. As John Burrow remarks in his chapter on the fourteenth century, the heyday of Middle English Arthurian romance was the reigns of Edward III (1322–77) and Richard II (1377–99). The highlight is undoubtedly *Sir Gawain and the Green Knight*. After languishing in obscurity for almost 500 years, *Sir Gawain* was rediscovered in the nineteenth century and is today acknowledged as the great masterpiece of English Arthurian romance, an inspiration to modern writers and artists.[10] The transition to prose also occurred much later in English Arthurian writings than in French. The first Arthurian prose romance is the mid-fifteenth-century Prose *Merlin*, and a couple of decades later Sir Thomas Malory created in his *Le Morte Darthur* (*c.* 1470) a noble and nostalgic Arthurian *summa* in English prose. Since it is Malory who mediated the medieval Arthurian legacy to post-medieval English writers, his importance in shaping the Arthurian tradition can hardly be overstated: he is, and deserves to be, the towering figure in Barry Windeatt's chapter on the fifteenth century.

With some notable exceptions (e.g. Wolfram von Eschenbach's *Parzival*, Malory's *Morte Darthur*), the literature of knighthood was in the Middle Ages the creation of clerics who could read and write at a time when these skills were still rare. Not all churchmen approved of the glorification of chivalry. The theologian Peter of Blois, Chrétien de Troyes's contemporary, worried that audiences everywhere were moved to tears by stories of Arthur, Gawain and Tristan, yet listened stony-faced to stories about God.[11] The Holy Grail in Arthurian romances is the symptom of the tension between the knightly and the godly. The perfect Grail hero, Galahad, combines religious purity with chivalric accomplishment and is rewarded with a vision of the Grail, but he is not for this world, and there are not many other knights in literature who succeed on both chivalric and religious fronts. The attempt by medieval writers to redeem Arthurian chivalry by infusing it with religiosity backfired after the Protestant Reformation. 'The vile and stinking story of the Sangreall' did not go down well with the sixteenth-century puritan Nathaniel Baxter,[12] and even in the nineteenth century, the heyday of the Gothic revival, when the Middle Ages were far enough away to seem exotic and glamorous, the Catholicism of the period and its culture needed exorcising. In the *Idylls of the King*, Alfred Lord Tennyson managed, against the grain of his source, to transmute Malory's episodic histories into concentrated poems. It is a humbling experience to read Tennyson's *Idylls* alongside Malory, and to witness there the poet's persuasive realisation of imaginative possibilities – lyrical beauty, psychological drama, thematic cohesion – that are only glimpsed in Malory. But one also notices prejudice. When Balin enters the room of Pellam (the Maimed King and keeper of the lance with which Longinus pierced Christ), Tennyson describes Balin's Protestant disorientation before Pellam's shrine 'In which he scarce could spy the Christ for Saints'.[13] The anti-Catholic barb is unmistakeable.

Rob Gossedge and Stephen Knight, in their chapter on post-medieval Arthurian literature up to 1900, draw attention to several other factors that changed the face of Arthurian literature. The rise of the nation state, always accompanied by the 'monopolisation of legitimate violence' (in Norbert Elias's phrase), soon turned 'knight-errantry' into a hopeless anachronism. Roger Ascham, tutor of Elizabeth I, condemned Malory's idealisation of knightly adventures (and of course Lancelot's love of Guinevere) as 'open mans slaughter, and bold bawdry',[14] though Mark Twain in *A Connecticut Yankee at the Court of King Arthur* (1889) was able to see some commercial benefit from knights-errant provided they were sent out wearing advertising boards instead of shields. Another important factor in the transformation of Arthurian legend was the gradual evaporation of the belief that Arthur's story as told in the old chronicles had actually happened. The first deadly blow to Arthur's historicity was struck by the humanists, most notably by the historian Polydore Vergil, who being Italian had no particular investment in England's national foundation myth and debunked it in his *Anglica Historia* (c. 1512). Although the book damaged Arthur's historical credentials, it also released him into a world of fantastical history. Edmund Spenser in his *Fairie Queene* did not have to burden 'Prince Arthur' with any more historical baggage than the fact – which even Polydore Vergil conceded was true – that he ruled after his father Uther Pendragon. For the rest of Spenser's allegorical narrative, Prince Arthur is at liberty to disregard his place in historical chronology, to dream of a lady greater than himself, and to go in quest of her: that lady is the Fairy Queen (figuring Elizabeth I). John Dryden's *King Arthur* (1691), in which Arthur competes with the Saxon prince Oswald for the hand of the beautiful Emmeline, could only have been written at a time when writers no longer felt obliged to respect the 'historical facts'.

This dislocation of Arthur from any authoritative master-narratives, be they historical or literary, sums up his fate in the twentieth and twenty-first centuries, which are surveyed by Norris Lacy. So much has happened in this period that it is hard to see the wood for the trees. All we can do here is to single out important new developments. One of these developments, to which this *Companion* belongs, is the rise of Arthurian scholarship. Sir Walter Scott's edition of *Sir Tristrem* (1804), which is still remarkably useful, is an early precurson of this development. A landmark in Arthurian criticism is Jessie Weston's extraordinarily influential study of the Grail legend, *From Ritual to Romance* (1920), which argued – entirely implausibly, it must be said – that the Grail is a remnant of pagan fertility rites, the sacred object that could transform the waste land into plenitude.[15] T. S. Eliot's *The Waste Land* was inspired by Weston's book, and even now she casts her shadow over New Age interest in the 'pagan' Arthur. In Marion Zimmer Bradley's remarkable novel *The Mists of Avalon* (1983), the Grail is the ritual cup of ancient religion – until it is stolen by 'the Merlin' and pressed into Christian service.

Another notable development in the history of Arthurian literature is Arthur's transformation into the hero of children's literature.[16] T. H. White's *The Sword in the Stone* (1938), subsequently reprinted as the first part of *The Once and Future King* (1958), is the great classic of Arthurian children's literature. White's Arthur (the 'Wart') is the open-hearted boy in short trousers, tutored by master Merlin, who is the kind of teacher every pupil dreams of: a teacher who positively encourages youthful adventure and curiosity. The work is one of those surprisingly happy marriages between a modern author's own interests – White was himself a schoolteacher – and those of his source, Malory's 'Tale of King Arthur', where Arthur is still young and has lots to learn, before and after he has been propelled to the throne by pulling the sword from the stone. Through the animated version by Walt Disney (1963), White's *Sword in the Stone* secured a place in the history of film. The Arthur who once triumphed in battles against the Saxons has now conquered the modern media of film, radio, and children's literature: he has proved himself to be indeed *The Once and Future King*.[17]

Themes

As well as engendering a distiguished literary history, the Arthurian legend became a focus for the exploration of heroic and chivalric themes and ideals, some of which are familiar from the legends and folklore of other cultures and centuries: a great warrior leader comes to power and wages many successful wars, but is finally brought low by treachery from within his inner circle. Legendary leaders with bands of outstanding warriors include Agamemnon and Priam at the siege of Troy, Charlemagne with Roland and his comrades, and the Irish hero Fionn MacCumhail (Finn McCool), who not only has an impressive warband, but loses his beautiful young wife Grainne to one of his men, Diarmid (this may be a source for the Tristan and Isolde story which gradually became attracted into the Arthurian sphere).[18] In the early Welsh tradition represented by *Culhwch and Olwen* and in the later romance tradition, Arthur's knights go on quests to find adventure or to rescue people in trouble: other heroes whose adventures involve travel, difficult tasks, or ordeals include Gilgamesh and Enkidu, Jason and Hercules, and Beowulf. Arthur's unexpected ascent of the throne after pulling the sword from the stone, an apparently impossible task, is the stuff of folktale.[19] Arthur's futile attempt to eliminate Mordred, the son fated to destroy him, is reminiscent of many classical stories – for instance, Oedipus and Perseus. In some later medieval versions, Arthur and Mordred kill each other in battle: the duel between father and son is a theme with a long history, though it is unusual for both to be aware of their relationship, and for both to die. But in the Arthurian context, such universal themes take on special resonances, as Jane Gilbert argues in her discussion of Arthurian ethics.

The chronological chapters in this volume attest to the enduring popularity of the legend, and the rich range of intertextual responses to it across Europe over a thousand years. These chapters are of necessity brief surveys. The thematic section of the volume takes a diachronic approach, discussing both medieval and post-medieval responses to the legend. We begin with two chapters on the ways in which Arthurian values have been questioned throughout the evolution of the legend, by setting criticism against idealisation, and on the distinctive ethics of Arthurian texts. The subsequent essays highlight selected aspects of the legend which raise fundamental issues both of literary treatment and of reception: imperial conquest, love and adultery, magic and religion. We end with a chapter on Arthurian geography, a field which has inspired both rigorous and imaginative responses through the ages.

Arthur's court moves around the country, from Caerleon to Carlisle to the mysterious Camelot, and onto the Continent in time of war, but what it stands for does not change. It is a magnet for ambitious knights who want to prove themselves, to establish and increase what Malory calls their 'worship' (honour, repute, standing). Arthur is the supreme warrior and leader, the conqueror of the Saxons and other marauders. In the early Welsh tradition he gathers exceptional warriors around him, some of whom have superhuman powers (see the catalogue in *Culhwch and Olwen*), and this pattern continues with the rise of romance in the twelfth century. Some are his relatives (Gawain, Mordred, Ywain), but others are foreign, whether they come from inside the British Isles (Tristan is Cornish) or from overseas (Lancelot is French, Palomides is a Saracen). Geoffrey of Monmouth, author of the earliest birth to death 'biography' of Arthur (*History of the Kings of Britain, c.* 1135), explains the king's policy and its results:

> Arthur then began to increase his personal entourage by inviting very distin-guished men from far-distant kingdoms to join it. In this way he developed such a code of courtliness in his household that he inspired peoples living far away to imitate him. The result was that even the man of noblest birth, once he was roused to rivalry, thought nothing at all of himself unless he wore his arms and dressed in the same way as Arthur's knights. At last the fame of Arthur's generosity and bravery spread to the very ends of the earth; and the kings of countries far across the sea trembled at the thought that they might be attacked and invaded by him, and so lose control of the lands under their dominion. (Thorpe, ix.11, p. 222)[20]

Geoffrey may be inventing this, though it is clear that by the early twelfth century Arthur's name was already widely known in continental Europe (see Hutton in Chapter 1 and Putter in Chapter 2). If Geoffrey did invent it, he was a very effective spin-doctor; within a few decades romances appeared describing the court and the knights who aspired to be part of it.

Camelot has become a byword for high standards of chivalry, and for courtly ideals and values, but Arthur and his court were not universally admired in the Middle Ages. Some of the earliest references to him occur in saints' lives where the protagonist asserts his authority over the king. The all-conquering warrior of the early tradition, whose biography represented the last great period in British history for Geoffrey of Monmouth, was soon replaced in many romances by a surprisingly passive and ineffective king who stays at court while his knights have adventures and show their prowess. (The television series *Star Trek* offers an interesting analogue: in the first series, Captain Kirk often leaves the Enterprise to save planets, confront aliens, and dally with ladies, but in the second series, *The Next Generation*, the focus widens and Captain Picard frequently remains on the ship while crew members such as Riker take on the adventures.) As we have seen, this somewhat negative characterisation begins with Chrétien de Troyes, widely regarded as the father of Arthurian romance, and continues, through his successors and imitators, up to the present day. Elizabeth Archibald discusses a wide range of texts in which Arthur or his court or Arthurian ideals are questioned and challenged, to varying degrees, through comedy, irony, parody, satire, or open criticism. Often the criticism is implicit and is balanced by praise, but in Marie de France's *Lanval*, the hero leaves Arthur's unfriendly court to accompany the fairy mistress who has saved him from unjust punishment. One might expect Latin Arthurian writers to be more critical than vernacular ones, since romance was often castigated by clerics as frivolous, and many of the pursuits of Arthurian knights go against Christian values (tournaments and the pursuit of renown might be seen as encouraging most of the Seven Deadly Sins other than Sloth). Some criticism is implied in the *De Ortu Waluuanii* or *Rise of Gawain*, a twelfth- or thirteenth-century account of Gawain as a Fair Unknown, and in the Arthurian episode in Andreas Capellanus' treatise on love (late twelfth century).

The introduction of the Grail into the Arthurian world challenges existing values and behaviour: Lancelot is found wanting, whereas his illegitimate son Galahad proves to be a perfect Christian knight, too good for the world. Gawain does particularly badly on the Grail quest, but England showed little interest in Grail adventures until the later fifteenth century, and Gawain remained extremely popular there. *Sir Gawain and the Green Knight* plays with the audience's familiarity with Gawain and the French romance tradition – but does this tantalisingly subtle poem criticise Arthurian values and literature, or vindicate them? Arthurian literature repeatedly raises the issue of heroism, and it seems that in the later Middle Ages there was a fashion for flawed heroes, such as Gawain and Lancelot, and indeed Arthur himself. They were certainly seen as flawed from the sixteenth to the nineteenth centuries, as Chapter 10 by Gossedge and Knight makes clear. Tennyson's Arthur is a return to the early conqueror, rather than the *roi fainéant* of the romance tradition, but Mark Twain's Connecticut Yankee finds much to criticise in Arthur's realm, as do some twentieth- and twenty-first century novelists and film directors.

Though Arthurian ideals and values are sometimes honoured in the breach, and are sometimes mocked or criticised, they are nevertheless part of what makes Arthurian texts distinctive. An account of the legend such as that of

Haydn Middleton, whose novels present a brutal, unjust and much hated Arthur, is deeply unsettling. The Monty Python version of the Grail story is funny because it plays against the audience's expectation of Arthurian conventions – brave knights, virtuous ladies, challenging adventures, high standards of morality and integrity. But are these just the standard trappings of medieval romance? Can we speak of 'distinctive "Arthurian ethics"'? This is the question addressed by Jane Gilbert, who argues that we can, and that the choice to write an Arthurian narrative involves particular 'engagements and directions'. Arthurian texts are peculiarly aware of their status as Arthurian, and are inevitably linked to other Arthurian texts. Gilbert compares the status of the Arthurian world both with the Dreamtime of Australian Aboriginals, and with the currently fashionable online 'virtual worlds'. She distinguishes changing ethical approaches in the centuries from Chrétien to Malory: twelfth-century romancers explore various principles and ideals in non-realistic situations, in a playful and experimental spirit, but thirteenth-century romancers are more didactic, at least in the Vulgate Cycle with the newly incorporated Grail theme, and by the fifteenth century Arthurian romance has become exemplary. In modern versions such as Twain's *Connecticut Yankee* and *Monty Python and the Holy Grail*, she argues, Arthurian discourse can 'interrogate and challenge modernity's moral framework', and 'Arthurian problems show a disturbing propensity to be reborn in modern subjects'. The Arthurian legend's 'food for storytellers' offers not only entertainment but also social and political comment on both past and present.

Fighting and conquest are fundamental aspects of Arthur's story; in the ninth-century *Historia Brittonum* he is enigmatically described as *dux bellorum* or leader of battles, defeating enemies up and down England, Wales and Scotland. Camlann, his last battle, is also an integral part of the tradition, but from Geoffrey's time on it is preceded by a major war against the Romans, the most prestigious available foe. Andrew Lynch addresses the theme of Arthur as imperial conqueror, 'the least popular and least often retold of the main stories about him in medieval literature', which seems problematic to many modern readers. Lynch notes that Arthur's continental conquests in medieval texts are largely symbolic: they had the political benefit of allowing medieval British kings to lay claim to continental territories, but in terms of Arthur's own story, the focus is always on his British realm. Indeed, in some texts the king is regarded as hubristic in attempting to defeat the Roman empire. In the fifteenth century when Malory was writing, England was struggling to retain its French possessions; but Lynch argues that for Malory *imperium* represents not actual territorial empire, but 'the fullness, integrity and limitless potential of power' represented by the Round

Table. Lynch sees Tennyson as carrying on this sense of *imperium*, God-given rather than obtained by conquest, even though nineteenth-century Britain had a vast empire. He goes on to discuss the theme of empire in Twain's *Connecticut Yankee*, in T. H. White (who was opposed to an education system that fostered 'competitive aggression'), in the films *Monty Python and the Holy Grail* and *Excalibur*, and in Marion Zimmer Bradley's *The Mists of Avalon*, where the struggle is between pagans and goddess-worshippers for 'religious *imperium*'. Lynch concludes that giving less attention to continental wars allows modern writers to accept conquest within the British isles as part of the Arthurian story. Arthur as freedom-fighter is more acceptable than Arthur as imperialist invader.

Conquest is central to the seminal early Arthurian texts of Nennius, Geoffrey of Monmouth, and Geoffrey's first adaptors, Wace and La3amon, and it remains central to the chronicle tradition. But Arthur's success at pacifying England and Scotland allowed for a twelve-year period of peace before the continental campaign, according to Geoffrey (ix.11, p. 222), and this space was exploited by writers such as Chrétien de Troyes to allow for the non-political quests and adventures which characterise the romance strand of Arthurian writing. Peacetime allowed for mock battles, tournaments which kept the knights fit: Geoffrey tells us that 'their womenfolk watched from the top of the city walls and aroused them to passionate excitement by their flirtatious behaviour' (ix.15, p. 230). Earlier he had noted that 'women of fashion' wore the same colours as their knights, and 'scorned to give their love to any man who had not proved himself three times in battle. In this way the womenfolk became chaste and more virtuous and for their love the knights were ever more daring' (ix.14, p. 229). The famous opening line of Virgil's *Aeneid*, *arma virumque cano*, 'I sing of arms and the man', is a classic definition of epic literature but needs to be expanded for romance, which tends to sing not just of arms and the man but also of the woman whose love inspires and/or rewards him. Heroic deeds and quests are found in many myths, legends and literatures, but the ennobling effect of romantic love on the hero is a novelty in medieval romance, and Geoffrey is one of the first witnesses of this development. Chaucer summarizes it very clearly in *Troilus and Criseyde*: when the lovesick Troilus is assured by Pandarus that his love will be requited, he becomes supremely friendly, noble, generous, admirable and the best knight of all time, and leaves the bed where he has been tossing and turning to fight enthusiastically and ferociously against the Greeks (i.1079–86). The symbiosis of love and heroism is summed up in Malory's description of Lancelot: he was the top knight, 'Wherefore quene Gwenyvere had hym in grete favoure aboven all other knyghtis, and so he loved the quene agayne aboven all other ladyes dayes of his lyff, and for hir he dud many dedys of armys and saved her from the fire thorow his noble chevalry' (p. 253.15–19 [VI.1]). Lancelot's whole chivalric career from the moment he first sees the queen is coloured by this inspiring and sometimes problematic love.

Other knights, Arthurian and non-Arthurian, are also inspired and rewarded by love, of course, but in the Arthurian context the course of true love cannot run entirely smoothly for the main characters. Conflicts of loyalty abound: Arthurian knights find themselves having to choose between king and queen, lord and mistress, lord and friend, friend and brother, champion and nephew. A knight like Chrétien's Erec, who only stars in one narrative, can win his beloved and in the end live happily ever after with her, but for the central figures of the Round Table, matters are much more complicated. Some marry but apparently continue to live bachelor lives dominated by male camaraderie and fellowship (one might compare James Bond, whose wife is killed only a few chapters after their marriage to allow his career to continue unimpeded). Malory devotes a section of the *Morte Darthur* to Gareth's quest to establish his prowess, in the course of which he falls deeply in love and eventually marries, but after this tale we hear no more of her. In the anonymous *Wedding of Sir Gawain and Dame Ragnell* (c. 1400), Gawain, the eternal lady's man, is said to be devoted to his wife, a hideous hag transformed after marriage into a beauty; but she soon dies and, though various of Gawain's sons star in Fair Unknown romances, marriage plays no further part in his story. Many Arthurian romances focus on the conflict between romantic love and macho fellowship, and love can be represented as interfering with a knight's proper occupation. Early in Malory's *Morte Darthur*, Segwarydes, whose wife has been dallying with Tristram, tells his rival ' "I woll never hate a noble knyght for a lyght lady, and therefore I pray you to be my frende" ' (p. 442.7–8 [VIII.38]). Love may inspire Lancelot, but since it is adulterous, it cannot reward him except intermittently and clandestinely, with ultimately disastrous results.

Love can inspire villainy as well as prowess: in the chronicle tradition, which generally omits Lancelot, the knight who cuckolds and betrays Arthur is Mordred, who is a villain in spite of being closely related to Arthur. This love triangle is retained in many modern versions of the legend, though the identity of the queen's lover varies. Much less well known is the medieval French tradition of Arthur's adultery, the subject of a case study by Peggy McCracken. She focuses on the Arthur of the thirteenth-century Vulgate Cycle, who falls deeply in love on several occasions and does not hesitate to consummate his passion. His lust for his unrecognised half-sister Morgause, which results in the birth of Mordred, has attracted much attention; less familiar to non-specialists are his affairs with the Saxon

Camille and the False Guinevere. Like Lancelot (and sometimes at the same time), Arthur is inspired by the knowledge that his lover is watching him fight; he even goes so far as to repudiate his queen when he is under the spell of the False Guinevere, and continues to love both mistresses after their deaths. McCracken considers the difference between the king's body and the queen's, compares the French account of Arthur's philandering with episodes in Scott's *Bride of Triermain* and Tennyson's *Idylls of the King*, and concludes that the real danger in Arthur's affairs is that the objects of his desire prove treacherous.

Some of Arthur's lovers use magic in seducing the king, and magic is a fundamental part of the Arthurian legend. Merlin facilitates Arthur's conception, and his claim to the throne is based on being the only person who can draw out a sword mysteriously lodged in a stone. Merlin and Arthur never meet in the early chronicle tradition, but in the prose tradition Merlin is at hand in the early years of Arthur's reign to foresee and forestall danger; however, the enchanter is soon trapped in a living death by his own pupil, and the king is left without supernatural help. This may signal that magic is dangerous, and that Arthur and his knights must prove themselves without constant advice and help from magicians. However, Merlin's incarceration does not remove magic from the legend. Knights often encounter it on their quests and adventures, more often in the form of enchantresses than enchanters. Clever women are generally treated as loose cannon in medieval romance. Some enchantresses are well-disposed to the Round Table: the Lady of the Lake raises Lancelot in her underwater palace and instructs him in chivalry, and frequently resolves problems at Camelot. But a constant thorn in Arthur's side is his half-sister Morgan, who was educated in a nunnery and then learned her magic from Merlin himself. Though she takes Arthur away at the end to tend his fatal wound, for most of his life she is hostile to Camelot, and takes every opportunity to ambush and embarrass Arthur, Guinevere and the Round Table knights.

Corinne Saunders explores the uses of both magic and religion in the Arthurian legend, arguing that it 'reflects a Christian world view in which the supernatural is assumed to play a part, and in which religion does not negate the possibility of magic'. Arthurian adventures often begin when the court is assembled for a major Christian feast day; but Celtic legends, in which a supernatural otherworld is close at hand, have contributed considerably to romance plots. The introduction of the Grail (probably derived from both Christian and Celtic traditions) into the Arthurian world produces a new emphasis on spiritual values, and a new version of Merlin's birth: though he is begotten by an incubus as part of a demonic plot, he is baptised and sides with the forces of good. In accounts of the Grail quest, the supernatural is unequivocally Christian, but in other texts it can be more ambiguous; Saunders discusses the case of *Sir Gawain and the Green Knight*, where the status of the Green Knight (human or supernatural?) is unclear. She also draws attention to the surprisingly secular account of Arthur's death – if he does indeed die – in contrast to Lancelot's redemptive end as a hermit. Moving on to post-medieval literature, she notes that in Spenser's *Faerie Queene*, where Prince Arthur plays an important part, black magic is always associated with Catholicism. Tennyson, she argues, found the Grail quest threatening to the combination of secular and sacred which appealed to the Victorians. Loss of faith and spiritual vision is the theme of Eliot's *The Waste Land*, which draws on Arthurian motifs through the anthropological prism of Jessie Weston and others. Saunders sees that thread continuing in later twentieth-century works, which 'tend to detach magic from Christianity', or to set pagan beliefs against Christian ones, as in *The Mists of Avalon*.

The importance of Celtic traditions in the evolution of the Arthurian legend raises the question of Arthurian geography. We will probably never know whether Arthur existed and where, or exactly how his story spread across Britain and onto the Continent. It may have been brought from northern England to Wales by Celts fleeing from the Saxon invasions, but from an early stage his supposed conquests cover a very wide geographical area.[21] Arthurian writers in England and on the Continent wrote confidently about Avalon and Camelot, Badon and Camlann, Joyous Gard and the land of Gorre, Glastonbury and Winchester. English authors tended to include more specific geographical references than French ones, but as Cory Rushton and Robert Rouse argue in their essay on 'Arthurian Geography', political considerations were often more important than geographical precision. Winchester, for instance, seems to have become associated with Camelot in part because of its association with Anglo-Saxon kings. Edward I held a tournament there in 1290, and it was probably for this occasion that he commissioned the Round Table which still hangs there today. He aspired to conquer all of Britain, and must have seen a suitable role model in Arthur. The identification of Tintagel as Arthur's birthplace is not so easy to explain, but this legend seems to have bolstered the imperial ambitions of Richard, brother of Henry III, who rebuilt the castle extensively in the mid-thirteenth century. At Glastonbury, politics had much to do with the discovery of Arthur's supposed grave in the late twelfth century. Rushton and Rouse discuss a surprising number of Arthurian relics, many of which have now disappeared (including his crown and Excalibur). They show that regional rivalry over Arthur has a long history, and is still alive today.

NOTES

1 *Laʒamon's Arthur: The Arthurian Section of Laʒamon's 'Brut'*, ed. W. R. J. Barron and S. C. Weinberg (Harlow: Longman, 1989), lines 9406–12.

2 Jean Bodel, *Chansons des Saisnes*, ed. Annette Brasseur, TLF 369 (Geneva: Droz, 1989), lines 6–10.

3 On the conventions of medieval writing, see John Burrow, *Medieval Writers and Their Work* (Oxford University Press, 1982; rev. edn 1997).

4 Tristan only becomes a knight of the Round Table in the thirteenth-century French prose tradition. The Tristan legend deserves a volume of its own, and will not be discussed in any detail in this *Companion*.

5 Northrop Frye, 'Themes of Descent', *The Secular Scripture: A Study of the Structure of Romance* (Cambridge, MA: Harvard University Press, 1976), pp. 97–126.

6 This series is also entitled *Arthurian Literature in the Middle Ages*, and is published by the University of Wales Press; the volumes published so far are *The Arthur of the Welsh* (1991), *The Arthur of the English* (1999), *The Arthur of the Germans* (2000 – this includes Dutch Arthurian literature) and *The Arthur of the French* (2006).

7 On art, see R. S. and Laura H. Loomis, *Arthurian Legends in Medieval Art* (Oxford University Press, 1938), and Muriel Whitaker, *The Legends of King Arthur in Art*, Arthurian Studies 22 (Cambridge: D. S. Brewer, 1990). On music, see *King Arthur in Music*, ed. Richard Barber, Arthurian Studies 52 (Cambridge: D. S. Brewer, 2002).

8 For convenience we refer to Nennius throughtout, through the date and authorship of the *Histria Brittonum* are both uncertain.

9 William of Malmesbury, *Gesta Regum Anglorum*, ed. and trans. R. A. B. Mynors, R. M. Thompson and M. Winterbottom, 2 vols. (Oxford University Press, 1998), I, pp. 26–7.

10 Examples of indebtedness are James Broughton, 'Gavin and The Green Uncle' in *The Long Undressing* (1971), Iris Murdoch, *The Green Knight* (1993) and Harrison Birtwistle's opera *Gawain* (1994).

11 E. K. Chambers, *Arthur of Britain* (London: Sidgwick and Jackson, 1927), p. 267.

12 Marylyn Parins (ed.), *Sir Thomas Malory: The Critical Heritage* (London: Routledge, 1988), pp. 58–9.

13 *Idylls of the King*, ed. J. M. Gray (Harmondsworth: Penguin, 1983, repr. 1996), Line 403.

14 Roger Ascham, from *The Scholemaster*, in Parins (ed.), *Sir Thomas Malory, The Critical Heritage*, p. 57.

15 Norris J. Lacy (ed.), *A History of Arthurian Scholarship*, Arthurian Studies 65 (Cambridge: D. S. Brewer, 2006), p. 30.

16 Barbara Tepa Lupack (ed.), *Adapting the Arthurian Legends for Children: Essays on Arthurian Juvenilia*, Studies in Arthurian and Courtly Cultures (New York: Palgrave Macmillan, 2004).

17 Roger Simpson, *Radio Camelot: Arthurian Legends on the BBC, 1922–2005*, Arthurian Studies 70 (Woodbridge: D. S. Brewer, 2008); the works by Kevin Harty in the general bibliography provide detailed treatments of Arthurian films.

18 On Fionn, see Hutton, pp. 28–9, and O. J. Padel, 'The Nature of Arthur', *Cambrian Medieval Celtic Studies* 27 (1994), pp. 1–31 (pp. 19–31).

19 See Motif H31 in Stith Thompson, *Motif Index of Folklore*, 6 vols., FF Communications 106–9, 116–17 (Helsinki: Suomalainen Tiedeakatemia, Academia Scientiarum Fennica, 1932–36).

20 Texts frequently mentioned in this volume are referenced in abbreviated form; see pp. xii–xiv.

21 Rachel Bromwich, 'Concepts of Arthur', *Studia Celtica*, 10–11 (1975–6), 163–181; Padel, 'The Nature of Arthur'; and see *AoW* and Hutton's chapter in this volume.

PART I

Evolution

I

RONALD HUTTON

The early Arthur: history and myth

For anybody concerned with the origins of the Arthurian legend, one literary work should represent the point of embarkation: the *Historia Brittonum* or *History of the British*. It is both the earliest clearly dated text to refer to Arthur, and the one upon which most efforts to locate and identify a historical figure behind the name have been based. From it, three different routes of enquiry proceed, which may be characterised as the textual, the folkloric and the archaeological, and each of these will now be followed in turn.

The Arthur of literature

Any pursuit of Arthur through written texts needs to begin with the *Historia* itself; and thanks primarily to the researches of David Dumville and Nicholas Higham, we now know more or less exactly when and why it was produced in its present form. It was completed in Gwynedd, the north-western kingdom of Wales, at the behest of its monarch, Merfyn, during the year 830. Merfyn was no ordinary Welsh ruler of the age, but an able and ruthless newcomer, an adventurer who had just planted himself and his dynasty on the throne of Gwynedd, and had ambitions to lead all the Welsh. As such, he sponsored something that nobody had apparently written before: a complete history of the Welsh people. To suit Merfyn's ambitions for them, and for himself, it represented the Welsh as the natural and rightful owners of all Britain: pious, warlike and gallant folk who had lost control of most of their land to the invading English, because of a mixture of treachery and overwhelming numbers on the part of the invaders. The identity of the author will never be known. There was a later tradition, not recorded before the 1160s, that he was a writer of approximately the right period called Nemnius or Nennius. So he might have been, but no firm evidence survives for this.[1] Whoever he was, he probably came from south-east Wales rather than Gwynedd itself, because of his apparent extensive familiarity with that region. He was also an excellent choice for the job, crafting together a brief and exciting narrative, from a relatively restricted range of materials, which portrayed the Welsh and English exactly as described above, and gave Gwynedd a moral primacy among the Welsh kingdoms.

What has become the most famous section of the entire book follows, without any break, from a description of the growth of numbers of the English in Britain and the succession of a new Anglo-Saxon king of Kent.[2] It opens with the sentence 'Then Arthur fought against them in those days, together with the kings of the British; but he was leader in the battles' (*sed ipse dux erat bellorum*). It then lists twelve battles that he fought, four of them along the same river, the Dubglas or Blackwater. Two of them get special mention: one was at the Guinnion fortress, where he 'carried the image of the holy Mary, the everlasting Virgin, on his shoulders, and the heathen were put to flight on that day, and there was a great slaughter upon them, through the power of the holy Virgin Mary, his mother'. The other was at Mount Badon, or Badon Hill, 'and in it nine hundred and sixty men fell in one day, from a single attack of Arthur's, and no one laid them low save he alone'. The list ends with the comment that 'he was victorious in all his campaigns'. It then resumes its account of the subsequent doings of the English, 'when they were defeated in all their campaigns', in bringing over massive reinforcements from their German homeland to resume their offensive against the native British.

There is no good evidence at all of what source or sources were used for this passage, and responses to the problem have ranged from confident assertions that it was based on a Welsh poem to Nicholas Higham's hypothesis that the whole thing was concocted by the author of the *Historia* himself.[3] Certainly the latter hinted at a known tradition behind it, because he gave the name of one of Arthur's victories, Celidon Wood, in both a Latin and a Welsh version: *silve Celidonis, id est [that is] Cat Coit Celidon*. The implication is that the Welsh name would already be celebrated. It is, indeed, the only battle that we can still locate on a map with any confidence, being the usual medieval Welsh name for the large forest covering much of what became southern Scotland. The sites of all the rest remain a matter for conjecture, so that they could all fall within the bounds of one compact region, or be scattered across Britain. It has long been pointed out that Celidon Wood seems a strange place in which to have been fighting any sort of English, let alone those of Kent, whom neither history nor archaeology has depicted as having got that far north that early. This could mean that the author of the *Historia* was pressing battles that had never involved the English into a piece of propaganda against the latter; but our knowledge of events in this period is so slight that the English might indeed have got anywhere. Nor has there been any more agreement as to what was so significant about Arthur being *dux bellorum*, 'leader in the battles'; it could mean that he was a paramount king, or that he wasn't a king at all, or that he had assumed a former Roman military office, or that he was being likened to the Biblical prophet Joshua (who in the Latin Bible was given the same title), or even that he was being invented in Joshua's image.

The *Historia Brittonum* has, however, more to say about Arthur elsewhere than in this constantly quoted list of battles. This other material occurs near the end of the book, in a section on 'the wonders of Britain' (Chs. 67–74). Most of these are located in south-east Wales, which is why the author is often thought to have come from there. One was in the district of Buellt (modern Builth), and was a cairn of stones with an animal's footprint on top on one near the summit. This was said to have been left by Arthur's dog, Cabal, when Arthur hunted 'the pig Troynt'. Another 'wonder' consisted of a mound in the Ergyng district, which could not be measured because it seemed to keep changing size. It had been raised over the grave of Amr, or Anir, 'son of the warrior Arthur', who was killed by Arthur himself.

There is, or should be, much in the *Historia* to depress anybody in pursuit of a 'real' Arthur. For one thing, it is now clear that we know much less about post-Roman Britain than its author thought that he did. The narrative that he provided has long been rejected as thoroughly unsound, and there is effectively no political and military history of Britain between 407 and 595. Whatever experts in cultural, social, economic and religious affairs may feel, to those interested in specific rulers and their actions, this period is still very much 'the Dark Ages'. It is also very clear that, by the time that the *Historia* was written, Arthur was already long established as a figure of major importance in Welsh memory, credited with actions in settings all the way from mid-Wales to the waist of Scotland. Virtually the whole of this great trove of tradition, extant in the 820s, has been completely lost to us. No other source mentions most of the battles credited to Arthur, or the unfortunate Amr or Anir and the reason for his death. The 'pig Troynt' has probably left a presence in later literature, for it is almost certainly the terrifying wild boar, the Twrch Trwyth, which Arthur and his warband hunt in one of the main episodes of a famous Arthurian story, incorporated during the nineteenth century into the collection of medieval Welsh narratives dubbed by its editor *The Mabinogion*. This is *Mal y Kavas Kulhwch Olwen* (*Culhwch and Olwen*), the tale of Prince Culhwch's wooing of Olwen, and a comparison between it and the *Historia* actually accentuates our problem.

The story of Culhwch and Olwen has traditionally been regarded as the oldest surviving one to feature Arthur, and shows him as already the supreme warlord of all Britain, with a retinue of heroes ready to go on quests and to take on superhuman foes and magicians. It used to be thought that it dated back to the tenth century in its present form; now Rachel Bromwich and Simon Evans have demonstrated that it was written round about 1100, and that details were probably added to it even later. In that sense, it hardly belongs to the world of the 'early Arthur' at all. Kenneth Jackson had already shown how many themes and motifs had been built into it from tales that had been circulating across the Old World for hundreds of years before. It is therefore a sophisticated and elaborate work from the world of high medieval Welsh letters, and this makes it all the more significant that the boar hunt in it is not exactly the same as that (probably) commemorated three centuries before at the cairn in Buellt. Arthur does indeed have a hound here called Cafal, or Cavall, who takes part in the hunt, but as a peripheral character, overshadowed in the story even by other dogs, and certainly not given the prominence warranted by the account of the footprint.

From the *Historia*, the textual trail leads both backwards and forward; but the backward route, alas, does not take us to Arthur, but to the origins of the need for a Welsh history of the sort that the *Historia* represented. These begin with the nearest thing that we possess to an account of the sub-Roman period in Britain written by somebody who was part of it: the work of Gildas, *De Excidio Britanniae*. The people of the high Middle Ages believed that they had a complete and reliable biography of this man: we are now not sure who he was, when he was or where he was. He could have written at any point in the period 490–560, at most places in Britain or Brittany, and might have been a cleric or an educated layman. His purpose was to castigate the native British of his time in general, and a specific set of their kings in particular (all in Wales or south-western Britain) for their sins. In the process he did provide something like an account of British history since the end of Roman rule, but it was sketchy, selective and vague. It was intended to accuse the Britons of being both morally bad and unwarlike, and their defeats by the English as a just punishment by God. He did try to make clear that God had given them a fighting chance, by producing some military heroes and enabling them to defeat the invaders in turn; his point was that they had wasted that chance. The single native British victory that he named was at Mount Badon, which the *Historia* was to credit to Arthur. Gildas, however, never specified who had commanded there, and the only native British general whom he named and extolled was one Aurelius Ambrosius, a man of noble Roman descent. His point here was that his compatriots had needed a Roman to achieve even such success as they had managed. He never mentioned Arthur, even though he seemed to be living at just the right time to do so. This could have been because Gildas disliked him personally, or because his achievements ran counter to the whole argument of the book, or because they were set in a region in which Gildas was not interested. Alternatively, the silence could be because Arthur never existed, or had flourished at a quite different time, or was much less important than later tradition made him out to be.

Next in the textual sequence after Gildas is Bede, the great historian of the early English, writing in the 730s. His purpose was to make out his own people, the English, to be the chosen people of God and the true heirs of the Romans. To justify that view, the native British had to be like the Biblical Canaanites: the low life that got swept aside in the proper implementation of God's plan for Britain. Gildas was an absolute gift to Bede, because he was a native Briton who called his own people a sinful bunch of losers who had deserved all they had suffered at English hands. Bede's history didn't mention Arthur either, but it would hardly have done so, even had he been the great commander portrayed by the *Historia Brittonum*, for two different reasons. One is that until about the year 600 the English had been almost completely illiterate. Almost all that Bede knew about them before then depended on oral tradition, and the kind of oral tradition that tribal peoples preserve tends to consist of epic poetry and song celebrating their own achievements. They are unlikely to have celebrated being trashed by Arthur. The other possible reason why Arthur does not appear in Bede's history is that to do so, as a very successful native British soldier, would have wrecked the entire argument of the book. The same considerations make it even less remarkable that English sources written up after Bede's time, such as the *Anglo-Saxon Chronicle*, do not mention Arthur either.

What is crystal clear is that the *Historia Brittonum*, composed to counteract the effects of both Gildas and Bede and to give the Welsh a heroic self-image as rightful owners of Britain, had a use for Arthur that neither of the earlier two writers had possessed. It is, in fact, the first known work of history to have done so, which is why it should be no surprise that Arthur first features in it. What cannot be deduced from the *Historia* itself is whether there was a 'real' Arthur, and, if there was, how much resemblance he bore to the figure represented in the text; nor are there any other literary works that do anything effective to resolve this problem. In the textual trail that leads forward from the *Historia*, there is only one work, in fact, which contributes anything even very likely to be useful to the matter. This consists of the *Annales Cambriae*, or Welsh Annals, a chronicle apparently put together in south-west Wales during the 950s.[4] It matters because it represents the first attempt to locate Arthur in exact time. For the period before 613 the author had no systematic sequence of native British occurrences. What he did have was an Irish chronicle, now lost, which either already included a total of eleven events set in Britain, or into which he inserted these events. All that have an identifiable location are set in north Wales or further north in Britain, and this northern bias is also apparent in later parts of the chronicle.

Two entries which cannot be located on the map concern Arthur. The earliest is in 516 (or 518, as we are not absolutely sure when the chronicle's base-line begins): 'The battle of Badon, in which Arthur carried the cross of our Lord Jesus Christ on his shoulders [or shield] for three days and nights and the Britons were victors.' The second is in 537 (or 539): 'The battle of Camlann in which Arthur and Medraut perished, and there was death in England and Ireland.' There is some slight evidence that these entries originally derived from different sources, for that on Badon gives the name of the battle, like the rest of the chronicle, in Latin, while that on Camlann gives it in Welsh. They differ also in that the first is harmonious with the *Historia Brittonum* (which the compiler of the chronicle had certainly read), and indeed Nicholas Higham has called it simply a conflation of two of the *Historia*'s battles. The latter is not so harmonious, because it describes a battle not found in the *Historia*, and calls into question the latter's claim that Arthur was victorious in all his campaigns; even if he fell at Camlann while his cause triumphed, this is a qualified success. Nor does the entry give any indication of the relationship between Arthur and Medraut, nor the connection of the battle, if any, with the rest of the annal; 'death' is commonly interpreted as 'plague', but it may mean some other source of mortality.

There is no other literary material that can be universally recognised as at least a reasonably good source for what people thought and said about Arthur before the great watershed of the twelfth century, in which he becomes, or is revealed as, a literary figure of truly international stature. The *Historia* did not, after all, succeed in establishing him immediately as a universally accepted hero amongst the Welsh. The poem *Armes Prydein* had very similar objectives, in calling on Wales to remember its pride as a nation and to resist the English. It can be dated with reasonable confidence to a period just over a century after the *Historia*; and it never mentions Arthur. Some of the lives of Welsh saints – those of Gildas, Cadoc, Carannog and Padarn – give him a prominent role, and have often in the past been taken as evidence for his historical identity. None, however, can be said with certainty to have been written before the twelfth century; it is the same problem as that encountered with the tale of Culhwch and Olwen. There is the enigmatic poem known in modern times as *Preiddeu Annwn, The Spoils of the Underworld* (or *Otherworld*). It apparently describes a disastrous expedition led by Arthur into a supernatural realm, and might well be tenth century; but might equally be 200 years later.

An especially large quantity of ink has been spilled, and continues to flow, over the poem known as the *Gododdin*, one of the classics of early Welsh literature. It purports to describe the almost complete destruction of a band of heroes who set out from what is now south-eastern Scotland to do battle at a place called Catraeth. The period concerned is apparently the late sixth century, a generation or two after the time associated with Arthur in the *Historia* and the *Annales*. One of the warriors concerned, Guaurthur, is compared to Arthur. Now, if the text was put into its present form soon after the actual battle, this is good evidence for Arthur's historical existence, even if it tells us little about him. John Koch has indeed recently published fresh arguments that a sixth- to seventh-century text can be reconstructed from the poem. Even without the major consideration that these have immediately been challenged by other scholars, Koch himself acknowledges that passages were added to the contents in later periods. The latter may extend all the way to the thirteenth century, and the reference to Arthur could well be one of them. What seemed once to be a promising line of enquiry for those primarily concerned with him has therefore got nowhere.

If progressive textual analysis has not been kind to those who had hoped for a better sense of whom the 'original' Arthur might have been, the mood of post-modern literary criticism is no more nurturing. One of the current experts in early Welsh literature, G. R. Isaac, recently reversed the traditional formula that had been applied to it. This had treated it as the creation of the warrior society of a 'Celtic heroic age'. Isaac pointed out that we have no knowledge of such a society other than that afforded by the literature; as far as we are concerned, the latter has created the age.[5] The *Historia Brittonum* did not create Arthur, in the literal sense; when it was written there were already a cairn in Buellt and a tumulus in Ergyng, at the least, which bore witness to the hero's reputation, and probably much else beside. Nor did it create him as an enduring literary figure: the Arthur of the high medieval stories barely overlaps with the deeds and associations of the one in the *Historia*. It is almost certain that the hero of oral tradition would have blossomed into the familiar legendary king even if the *Historia* had never been written. What it did do was to establish the Arthur who has been commonly regarded, ever since the collapse of belief in the later medieval pseudo-histories of Britain, as the 'real' one. Thus the most important feature of this free-floating text is that, although it is apparently the earliest item in the whole Arthurian corpus, it has come to exert a hold on the modern imagination that many of those from later centuries, embodying the most celebrated episodes of the legend, have lacked.

The Arthur of folklore

In addition to the two Arthurs familiar to scholars, the Dark Age warrior and the king of high medieval romance, there has long existed a third. He is written into the native British landscape, as a figure of superhuman might. The capstones of Neolithic tombs in Wales, weighing many tons each, are described in local tradition as pebbles flicked from his shoe, or quoits tossed by him in a game. A substantial Roman temple in Scotland, long destroyed, was supposed to be his oven, while the mountain that looms over Edinburgh was his chair. During the twentieth century, this Arthur was regarded as subsidiary to the others – an example of the exaggeration that folk memory will give to a great human being – but it was not always so. For much of the nineteenth century, it was argued that the original Arthur was a pagan god, probably of the sun, who was turned into a human hero after the coming of Christianity. According to this view, the character who flicks megaliths across counties was the 'true' one, the form from which the others derived. Nineteenth-century scholars were fond of relating traditional heroes to timeless and fundamental forces of nature. Those of the twentieth century, just as strongly affected by a need for imagined reconnection with the past and the land, in an age of rapid change, have preferred to find real people behind the stories. The same contrast has been reflected in attitudes to Robin Hood, Britain's only other legendary figure to achieve enduring international fame.

Recently the essentially mythic status of Arthur has been reasserted by Oliver Padel.[6] His point of departure is, of course, the *Historia Brittonum*, but whereas virtually all other modern commentators have concentrated on the list of battles, he has drawn attention to the physical 'wonders' associated with Arthur later in the book. In his reading, these represent the original, completely imaginary figure behind the legend, a giant associated with magic and with marvellous animals, who was later turned by some traditions into a quasi-historical warrior. The parallel character in Gaelic tradition is Fionn MacCumhail, who likewise commands a picked band of famous warriors in defence of his land, has a particular foe in the form of foreign invaders (the men of Lochlann instead of the English), and has frequent interactions with enchantments and supernatural beings. In Padel's view, both Arthur and Fionn are the same mythical being, a land-protecting superman, deployed in different linguistic regions. This hypothesis has recently been restated at considerably greater length, and in much richer detail, by Thomas Green.[7]

The problem with this hypothesis is that it can cut the other way on both sides of the comparison. The human Arthur of the *Historia* could as readily have turned into the mythical one. As for Fionn, the author of the most recent complete study of his legend to date, Dáithí Ó hÓgáin – on whom both Padel and Green draw – has suggested that behind it lie components of both a historical character, associated particularly with the Laigin people of south-eastern Ireland, and a divine figure symbolising wisdom. Once the two were conflated, the cycle of tales spread out across the whole of the island, drawing in personalities and traditions from other provinces.[8] It is possible that exactly the same happened to the early Arthurian legend. Proponents of a historical Arthur have at times stretched the evidence by taking as proven the earliest possible date for the sources that appear to represent one; conversely, Thomas Green rests much of his case for a mythological hero on assuming the earliest possible date for texts that seem to display such a figure. The arguments made by him and Oliver Padel are, however, as cogent as those for a genuine military leader, and, even if they are wrong, have served two valuable purposes. One is to draw attention to the complementary relationship between the Arthurian and Fionn cycles, the former occupying just the same symbolic space among peoples speaking Brythonic languages as the latter does in the Gaelic-speaking area. The other is to remind us that the assumption of most modern scholarship, that Arthur is in origin purely a Welsh hero, is not necessarily correct: as soon as appropriate records begin, he is found embedded in the traditions of the Cornish, Bretons and southern Scots as well. It is a salutary reminder that only the better survival of early Welsh sources may have caused his particular association with that people, and also – again – of what a large body of information circulating about Arthur in the early Middle Ages has been lost.

A more exotic use of folklore to suggest possible origins for the legend has been made by some American authors, on and off, ever since the 1970s. It focuses on stories collected in the late nineteenth century among the Ossetians, a people living in a remote part of the Caucasus Mountains. These contain motifs that provide apparent parallels to features of the Arthurian cycle, such as a sword set in the earth as a symbol of sovereignty, a marvellous vessel which can only be claimed by a warrior without any moral stain, and a hero who can only die when his sword is thrown into the sea. A mechanism has been found to explain how these traditions could have been transmitted to Britain, in the form of Sarmatian cavalry from the steppes north of the Caucasus, who were employed by the Romans. Some were certainly stationed in Lancashire during the late second century under an officer called Lucius Artorius Castus, one of a tiny number of Romans to bear the Latin version of Arthur's name.[9] This theory of Arthurian origins eventually achieved wide popular currency in 2004 by being built into Jerry Bruckheimer's film *King Arthur*, starring Clive Owen. The problem with it is that none of the parallels lies beyond the possible boundaries of coincidence, or else they could represent different versions of commonly found motifs that had travelled around Eurasia for millennia. As for Castus, he seems to have had nothing remarkable about him except his name, and was duly reposted from Lancashire to Italy: Britain was merely an apparently routine bit of duty in a career that saw service in four different provinces.

More recently a British classicist, Graham Anderson, has located the origins of the legend in archaic Greece. He has found a king of Arcadia called Arktouros, and 104 passages in Greek and Roman literature that appear to refer to characters or episodes from the Arthurian romances. There are also some apparent similarities of names: Gauanes for Gawain, Ganeira for Guinevere, and so on.[10] The same objections, however, occur to this hypothesis as to the Caucasian one, compounded by the fact that Anderson has selected his events and personalities from the whole range of medieval romances, early and late. Had his examples all occurred together in the earliest, then there would have been more mileage to the idea. While respect is due to these 'external' solutions to the problem of Arthur's origins, it still seems as if Britain and Brittany are the best places in which to seek him.

The Arthur of archaeology

For much of the twentieth century, it seemed as if archaeology might succeed in locating a historical Arthur where textual analysis had failed, and for about fifteen intoxicating years – from 1960 to 1975 – many people believed that it was actually doing so. A large part of the traditional appeal of the discipline, since it began to emerge in the late nineteenth century, has been as a quest romance, undertaken to reveal the truth about particular episodes of the human past. Some of the greatest public excitement that it has generated has been when it has appeared to provide evidence to substantiate great traditional stories. Two bodies of these had already been given apparent support by excavation before 1900 – Homer's poems and the Bible – and it was virtually inevitable that the Arthurian romances should eventually get the same treatment. There were three different reasons why they did so in the mid-twentieth century, rather than before or after. One was simply that by then there were many archaeologists available for the work, the result of the full professionalisation of the discipline since the Second World War, and its attachment to university courses. The second was that this supply of personnel was confronted by a problem of funding. Archaeology is hugely more expensive than historical studies, and projects that make a powerful appeal to the popular imagination stand the best chance of raising the necessary money, both from public subscription and from private sponsors. Finally, to a post-war Britain caught in the process of resigning its imperial and Great Power status, and jettisoning most of the attitudes and ideologies left over from its Victorian apogee, the Arthur of the *Historia Brittonum* seemed to be a traditional hero better fitted than most to adapt to changing needs. He was a warrior who had defended his nation with the courage and success of traditional patriotic leaders, while cutting a less stuffy and conventional figure than most. He could be said to belong equally to all the different peoples of Britain and – clad imaginatively but plausibly in the furs, leathers, long hair, trailing moustaches and jewellery of a Celtic warlord – function both as a national icon and a counter-cultural one, an establishment figure and a noble savage.

Between 1930 and 1975, archaeologists had it both ways at once, with huge short-term success. They dug at post-Roman sites, and in search of the figure from the *Historia*, but chose places that were associated with the later, and more generally familiar, high medieval legends. Raleigh Radford dug in Cornwall at Tintagel, which those legends had made Arthur's birthplace, and Castle Dore, the most probable location of King Mark's palace in the story of Tristan. At both places he claimed to have discovered impressive remains of just the right period. He went on to excavate at Glastonbury Abbey, where the twelfth-century monks had proclaimed their discovery of the grave of Arthur and Guinevere, and declare that he had uncovered a native British monastery beneath the English one. Philip Rahtz found a structure on Glastonbury Tor that might be identified with the fortress of King Melwas, captor of Guinevere in another twelfth-century tale. Most spectacular of all seemed to be the achievement of Leslie Alcock, at the hillfort of South Cadbury, which a Tudor legend had held to be the site of Camelot: after a lavish excavation made possible by the maximum possible publicity, he concluded that he had uncovered a stronghold and palace of the correct time. By the end of the 1960s, the decade which saw the projects at Glastonbury and Cadbury, there was a general belief among scholars and public alike that archaeology had proved the existence of the Arthur of the *Historia* and the *Annales*, and so, by implication, permitted belief in much of the rest of the legend.

By 1975 that belief was already evaporating among experts, and by 1980 it had almost wholly gone. In part this reaction was born of disappointment, for at none of these sites was any solid evidence of Arthur's presence, or that of any of his traditional companions, actually found. In part it was the result of overkill, as more sober analysis revealed no trace of post-Roman occupation at Castle Dore or Glastonbury Abbey, while the remains at Tintagel, on the Tor and at Cadbury could all be interpreted in ways that had no relevance to the medieval romances. In part it was due to jealousy, as archaeologists working on productive sites without Arthurian associations felt that their labours were being eclipsed, and starved of funding, by the publicity given to places linked to the legend. In part it reflected the waning of 1960s romanticism and idealism, in the harsher, more cynical and more pessimistic cultural climate of the late 1970s.

It also, however, came about because archaeologists of the post-Roman period no longer needed Arthur. They had revealed a rich and exciting culture that was represented equally at sites that had Arthurian associations and sites that had not, and by the 1980s this could be a focus of interest and study in its own right. It is clear now that during what historically are still the Dark Ages the people of western Britain flourished in a way that they had never done under Roman rule; indeed, once the Romans had officially gone, they appropriated and developed the civilisation of their former masters as their own. They made beautiful and sophisticated artefacts, raised impressive stone memorials to their dead, supported a Church based on monasteries and bishops that was both a powerhouse of piety and a repository of sophisticated, Latin, literacy, and regularly attracted traders who sailed all the way from the Levant. In doing so they created a unique and impressive society, which no longer needs the figure of Arthur to invest it with glamour and interest in the eyes of the present.

Back to the crossroads

Much of what has been said above may induce melancholy in readers who remain primarily interested, after the twentieth-century fashion, in a historical Arthur. There are, however, some consolations to be found for them in the place where this set of reflections started, where literary, folkloric and archaeological approaches to the matter meet and diverge. One is simply that nobody has actually disproved the existence of a 'real' character behind the legend: there remains an Arthur-sized hole in recorded British history.

A second derives from the continuing series of excavations at Tintagel, which have increasingly interpreted it as a high-status secular site – in crude terms a royal or princely headquarters – of the fifth and sixth centuries. Nothing has still been found to link it to Arthur, and the fuss created in non-academic circles in 1998 by the finding of an engraved slate provided another object lesson of the way in which such links could be created without proper evidence. The graffito scrawled on the slate included the name 'Artognou', which has little in common with Arthur, but was immediately treated in some parts of the mass media as though somehow it had. What is really significant about the confirmation of Tintagel's importance during what has been called the Arthurian age is its implications for the power of popular memory. The site was abandoned in the seventh century, and, by the time of Geoffrey of Monmouth, 500 years later, there could have been nothing showing on the ground to indicate its earlier significance. Despite this, he confidently identified it as having played a key part in the story of Arthur. Somehow, tradition had preserved the memory of its former character throughout the intervening half a millennium. This being the case, it is possible that other aspects of the 'developed' Arthurian legend of the central Middle Ages may also have been handed down from an early date, although we lack any means of testing this.

Another consolation for those still in pursuit of an historic Arthur may be provided by the archaeologist Ken Dark, in a recent survey of the material remains now known from sub-Roman Britain. It may be recalled that if the *Historia Brittonum* and *Annales Cambriae* point to any part of the island as especially associated with him, it is to what is now northern England and southern Scotland. The actual, self-conscious, attempt by twentieth-century archaeologists to dig up evidence of Arthur's presence focused instead on sites in the West Country that had later associations with the legend. Now Dark has pieced together a great deal of scattered evidence to conclude that the forts along Hadrian's Wall were renovated, reoccupied and linked anew to the old Roman legionary base at York at some time around the year 500. He commented that this looks as if somebody was making an attempt to revive the late Roman regional command of an officer called the *Dux Britanniarum*. He added that an apparent lack of minor kings in the area, suggested by the absence of reoccupied hill forts of the sort common in the south, reinforces the sense of a single great leader in charge of the whole region at that period. To this he related Gildas's comment that the most important of the monarchs whom he was denouncing, Magloconus, was 'almost' the greatest ruler in Britain of his time. The hint here is that there was a greater elsewhere in the island, and that person could have been the one who possessed the revived jurisdiction of the *Dux*.[11]

Ken Dark has therefore identified archaeological evidence for a figure who corresponds very well to the Arthur of the *Historia*, and in doing so found viable solutions to two classic problems of the texts: Gildas's apparent lack of mention of the hero, and the significance of the *Historia*'s emphasis that he was a *dux* as well as, or instead of, a king. Dark himself, however, never speaks of Arthur in the course of this discussion, and for entirely understandable reasons: as an archaeologist of the present time, he is not interested in the legend, and there is nothing that directly relates it to the data that he is analysing. The implications drawn from his analysis are my own; and I in turn am not attempting to make a case for the 'discovery' of a northern Arthur (by appropriating somebody else's scholarship). What I am trying to do, rather, is show how, just as an Arthur-sized gap still exists in the history of Britain, so an Arthur-shaped figure can still plausibly be detected in the archaeological record. My own vision of the future is that further discoveries made by excavation can be combined with the textual and folk-loric evidence to suggest a number of different possible origins for Arthur. Each of these would be emotionally satisfying, and creatively inspiring, to a different constituency of people interested in a historical figure behind the later medieval legend.

Such an outcome would make a virtue of the obstacles that still stand in the way of any quest for such a figure, and which may otherwise paralyse any conscientious researcher. On the cathedral at Modena in Italy are carv-ings of Arthur and some of his knights, notably Gawain. That would not matter a lot had the sculptures concerned not been firmly dated between the years 1099 and 1109, before the recorded boom in the production of Arthurian romances that is supposed to have made Arthur and his fol-lowers into figures with a pan-European appeal, or at least one common to the whole world of Latin Christianity. In terms of the surviving textual evidence, they shouldn't be there. As it is, they are a further reminder of how little we know and how much we have lost of the early development of the Arthurian legend; solid witnesses to the existence of a mass of spoken and written tradition about Arthur that already extended across western Europe by the year 1100, and of which virtually nothing remains. Some would conclude from this, with good reason, that any attempt either to locate an original Arthur, or even to trace the growth of the legend up to the twelfth century, must be completely futile. It might be possible to argue instead, with equal humility in the face of the loss of evidence, for a mul-tiplicity of plausible interpretations of the sort suggested above. Such an approach would enable individual researchers to choose whether or not they wish to engage with a Dark Age Arthur, and how they wish to do so, while not presenting a general public, still imaginatively fired by the legend, with a complete interpretative void. Such an approach would, furthermore, take up the challenge posed, right at the beginning of our knowledge, by the author of the *Historia Brittonum*, in presenting posterity with a mighty leader who was at once a credible historical person and a figure of myth. Ever since he appears in the record, Arthur has been more than one kind of being, demanding more than one kind of understanding. In that sense, the 'early' Arthur is actually more complex than many of those who have featured in the legend since.

NOTES

1 On one side of the debate, see David Dumville, '"Nennius" and the "Historia Brittonum"', *Studia Celtica*, 10–11 (1975–6), 78–95; on the other, P. J. C. Field, 'Nennius and his History', *Studia Celtica*, 30 (1996), 159–65.

2 *Historia Brittonum*, Ch. 56, ed. and trans. John Morris in *British History and the Welsh Annals*, Arthurian Period Sources 8 (Chichester: Phillimore, 1980), p. 76.

3 Nicholas Higham, *King Arthur: Myth-Making and History* (London: Routledge, 2002), pp. 46–69.

4 John Morris has edited this in the same volume as the *Historia Brittonum*; for the Arthurian entries, see p. 85.

5 G. R. Isaac, 'Gweith Gwen Ystrat and the Northern Heroic Age of the Sixth Century', *Cambrian Medieval Celtic Studies*, 36 (1998), 61–70.

6 O. J. Padel, 'The Nature of Arthur', *Cambrian Medieval Celtic Studies*, 27 (1994), 1–31.

7 Thomas Green, *Concepts of Arthur* (Stroud: Tempus, 2007).

8 Dáithí Ó hÓgáin, *Fionn Mac Cumhaill: Images of the Gaelic Hero* (Dublin: Gill and Macmillan, 1988).

9 C. Scott Littleton and Ann C. Thomas, 'The Sarmatian Connection: New Light on the Origin of the Arthurian and Holy Grail Legends', *Journal of American Folklore*, 91(1978), 512–27; L.A. Malcor, 'Lucius Artorius Castus', *The Heroic Age*, 1(1999), 1–11.

10 Graham Anderson, *King Arthur in Antiquity* (London: Routledge, 2004).

11 Ken Dark, *Britain and the End of the Roman Empire* (Stroud: Tempus, 2000), pp. 193–202.

2

AD PUTTER

The twelfth-century Arthur

King Arthur came into his own in the twelfth century. Around 1135 he acquired a biographer, Geoffrey of Monmouth, and a few decades later a champion poet, Chrétien de Troyes, the pioneer of Arthurian romance. The fame of both these writers, in their own lifetime and beyond, amply justifies their status as the fathers of Arthurian literature. Its mother was an oral tradition about which we know much less. Not many fossils survive, but those that do are so varied and widespread as to leave us in no doubt about the vigour of the popular tradition on which Geoffrey and Chrétien grafted their invention.

If we look across western Europe in the first decades of the twelfth century, we find Arthur and his knights in all kinds of unexpected places. For example, the early twelfth-century archivolt over the north portal of Modena Cathedral in Italy has a sculpture with inscriptions that clearly mark it as Arthurian: a woman, Winloge (Guinevere?), is held captive by a man, Mardoc (Mordred?); to the left, three knights, including Artus de Bretania, attack on horseback; to the right, another three knights, Galvariun, Che (Kay) and Galvagin (Gawain) advance, the latter jousting with Carrado (Curoi?).[1] Around the same time, local charters reveal that Arthurian names were becoming fashionable among the aristocracy. Early examples are *Gualvanus* (Poitiers, 1100), *Vaalauuaynus* (Melle, Belgium, 1118) and *Iwein* (Aalst, Belgium, 1122).[2] In 1125, William of Malmesbury reports in his *History of the English Kings* the discovery of Gawain's grave, 'fourteen feet long':

> It was then [*c.* 1080] that, in the province of Wales called Rhos, they discovered the grave of Gawain (*Walwen*), who was Arthur's nephew … He ruled in the part of Britain still called Galloway (*Walweitha*) and was a knight with a heroic reputation … Arthur's grave, however, is nowhere to be found, whence come the traditional old wives' tales that he may yet return.[3]

In Brittany, too, Arthur's return was keenly awaited, and there is indirect evidence that Arthur and his knights were celebrated in Breton song. The

Old French narrative lays by Marie de France, who was active in England in the 1170s or 1180s, purport to tell the stories behind traditional Breton songs (the *lais* proper).[4] One of Marie's lays, *Lanval*, is about a knight who is neglected at Arthur's court and falsely accused of importuning the queen; he is about to be convicted of treason when his fairy lover whisks him away to Avalon. Unfortunately, none of the songs that inspired Marie's stories have survived from the Middle Ages, and all we now know about the Breton singers is that they were once famous.[5]

Everywhere in Europe, then, there are traces of a vanished tradition, but only Wales can boast a significant body of Arthurian *writing* in the vernacular before Geoffrey and Chrétien. The pre-eminent Welsh story-collection is the *Mabinogion*, the modern name for a group of tales mainly preserved in two fourteenth-century manuscripts.[6] Given the lateness of the manuscripts, it is possible that some of the Arthurian tales in the *Mabinogion* actually draw on Geoffrey and Chrétien. The tales of Geraint and the Lady of the Well appear to derive respectively from Chrétien's *Erec* and *Le Chevalier au lion* (*The Knight with the Lion*) rather than the other way around. Yet even *if* these two tales derive from Chrétien, they are proudly independent adaptations and add much incident and colour drawn from native lore. Thus when Arthur in the tale of Geraint rides out to hunt the White Stag (as in *Erec*), he takes with him his dog Cafal, Arthur's faithful companion in the Welsh tradition and already mentioned in the ninth-century *Historia Brittonum* attributed to Nennius. *The Lady of the Well*, like Chrétien's *Knight with the Lion*, opens with a scene at Arthur's court, but in Welsh such a scene is incomplete without a mention of Arthur's bouncer, Glwelwyd Gafaelfawr (Brave Grey Mighty Grasp), who already appears as doorkeeper in the early Welsh Arthurian poem 'Pa Gur'. In *Peredur*, easily the most independent adaptation of Chrétien (if that is what it is), many adventures are unparalleled in Chrétien's *Le Conte du Graal* (*Story of the Grail*). Here is an example:

> And at dawn Peredur heard a scream. He got up quickly in his shirt and trousers, with his sword about his neck, and out he went. And when he arrived a witch was grabbing hold of the watchman, and he was screaming. Peredur attacked the witch and struck her on the head with a sword until her helmet and mail cap spread out like a dish on her head.
>
> (trans. Davies, pp. 78–9)

When Peredur agrees to spare the woman's life, she takes him to the witches' court at Caerloyw (Gloucester), where he completes his chivalric formation. A touch of the supernatural always helps to set a hero apart from normal men.

These same motifs – Arthur's dog Cafal, the doorkeeper Glwelwyd Gafaelfawr, and a coven of witches – occur in the most impressive Welsh Arthurian story, *Culhwch and Olwen* (c. 1100). This is not based on any known source, and linguistic evidence suggests it pre-dates Chrétien's romances. Culhwch, born in a pig-sty, is cursed by his step-mother: he will never win a woman unless he wins the hand of Olwen, the daughter of the chief giant Ysbaddaden. Culhwch asks Arthur for help. Six of Arthur's knights, including Gwalchmai (Gawain), Cai (Kay) and Bedwyr (Bedivere), ride with Culhwch to meet Ysbaddaden, who makes them feel most unwelcome: "'Where are my good-for-nothing servants and my scoundrels?", he said. "Raise the forks under my eyelids so that I may see my prospective son-in-law"' (trans. Davies, p. 193). To discourage Culhwch further, Ysbaddaden sets him a series of impossible tasks, which Culhwch, aided by Arthur and his men, manages to accomplish. The most difficult adventure is the hunt of the Twrch Trwyth, a magical creature (once king, now wild boar) which leads them a merry dance from Ireland to Wales, and from Wales to Cornwall. In the Cornish sea it disappears from view, leaving behind the comb with which Culhwch has been tasked to groom Ysbaddaden's beard. The action of the tale is wild and wonderful, but the highlights are the set pieces which display, amongst many other fine things, the author's minute knowledge of Arthuriana. From these we learn, for instance, that Arthur was a conqueror of many lands (Africa, India, Greece, etc.); that Cynwyll Sant was one of the Three Who Escaped from Camlann (the site of Arthur's last battle); and – from the sublime to the ridiculous – that Arthur had a servant, Gwelf, who on gloomy days would 'let his bottom lip drop to his navel, and the other would be a hood on his head' (trans. Davies, pp. 187–8). Some of this Arthurian lore was surely meant to be funny.

Another genre of literature from Wales incorporating Arthurian matter is Latin hagiography. In the eleventh- and twelfth-century saints' lives of Gildas, Cadoc, Illtud, Carantoc, and Padarn, Arthur is stereotyped as a local chieftain who bullies the saint before being forced to grovel before him.[7] Arthur is so obviously meant to exemplify the futile exercise of secular power that the presentation of the Arthurian world is of little historical value except for what it tells us about the hagiographers' fancies. To their minds, Arthur was the great powerbroker of Dark Age Wales. Also from Wales come stories of the bard Myrrdin, who went mad after a battle in the north in 585, and lived as a wild man in the forests of Celyddon, where he had prophetic visions of the future. Some of this material dates back to the eleventh century at the latest.

The Celtic tradition is particularly relevant to Geoffrey of Monmouth, a secular cleric and master at the schools of Oxford. His name (sometimes followed by the cognomen *Arthurus*) is found in a number of charters, alongside that of his friend Walter, Archdeacon of Oxford, who, according to Geoffrey, had given him the very old 'British' (Breton or Welsh) book which Geoffrey translated as the *Historia Regum Britanniae* (*History of the Kings of Britain*). Whether the old book really existed is an open question: medieval writers liked to adduce sources and, if they did not have any, they made them up. In 1151 Geoffrey was appointed bishop of St Asaph in North Wales. In all probability he was himself part 'Briton'. One of the many manuscripts of the *History* contains a passage (apparently authorial) in which Geoffrey, a 'bashful Briton', accepts the challenge of translating 'into Latin prose the metrical prophecies that Merlin uttered so sweetly in the British tongue'.[8] Both here and in the epilogue to his *History*, he alleges 'British' sources; and whether or not he invented them, his self-presentation as someone capable of translating them must have been plausible.

Geoffrey is the author of three surviving Arthurian works. The earliest, the *Prophecies of Merlin*, was followed by *The History of the Kings of Britain* (*c.* 1135), Book VII of which incorporates the earlier *Prophecies*; Geoffrey's last work (*c.* 1150) was a long poem in classical hexameters, the *Vita Merlini* (*The Life of Merlin*).[9] The *Prophecies* belong to the once flourishing genre of political prophecy. Geoffrey places Merlin in the period before Arthur's reign. King Vortigern has tried in vain to build a stronghold on Mount Snowdon; since the foundations keep sinking into the ground, his wizards advise him to sprinkle them with the blood of a boy with no human father. The candidate eventually found is Merlin, also called Ambrosius, son of a pious nun and an incubus. Merlin explains to Vortigern why his building keeps falling down: beneath the ground are two lakes, each inhabited by a fierce dragon. When the ground is excavated, Merlin is proved right. The two dragons, one white, one red, attack each other, and Merlin falls into a prophetic trance, forecasting in veiled terms the future of Britain, beginning with the defeat of the Britons (the Red Dragon) by the Saxons (the White Dragon).

Merlin's prognostications do not suit modern tastes, but many early readers took a serious interest in them, for understandable reasons. Merlin is presented as a historical character in the *Historia Brittonum* (*c.* 830), which also contains the story of Vortigern and the boy prophet (named Ambrosius by Nennius). And Geoffrey planted in the midst of Merlin's prophecies several that obviously tally with historical events, thus creating the impression that others will be fulfilled in future. Moreover, Geoffrey made sure that his prophecies were suggestively equivocal. What, for example, might it mean, that 'the balance of trade shall be torn in half, and the half that is left shall be rounded off' (Thorpe, VII.3, p. 174)? (Medieval chroniclers thought the prophecy was fulfilled when King John imposed English coinage on the Irish.) Scholars pored over Geoffrey's prophecies well into the Renaissance – which merely goes to show that the most successful prophecies are those that mean nothing and therefore potentially everything.

Geoffrey's last work, *The Life of Merlin*, fuses the Latin tradition of Ambrosius, Vortigern's prophet in the *Historia Brittonum*, with Welsh stories of Myrddin. In accordance with Welsh tradition, Merlin roams the northern forests, traumatised by the death of his friends in battle, and raves about the past and future. The time-span of Merlin's memory is improbably large, however. Not only does he recall how he prophesied to Vortigern on Mount Snowdon, but he also recounts from personal memory what happened to Arthur, his successor Constantine, and Conan who 'killed the king [i.e. Constantine], and seized the territories over which he now exercises a weak and witless control' (lines 1133–4). The explanation for the impossible longevity of Geoffrey's Merlin is that he is a composite of the Celtic bard Myrddin and the Ambrosius of Nennius.

Geoffrey's crowning achievement is *The History of the Kings of Britain*, which invented a proud past for Britain before the invasions of foreign races. On the face of it, there was nothing much to be proud of. The Celts had been overrun, first by the Romans, then by the Anglo-Saxons, and then again by the Normans. The Norman rulers, to whom Geoffrey dedicated his *History*, naturally took a proprietary interest in the history and culture of their newly acquired lands – an interest leading to the production of numerous histories and descriptions of the British Isles. Bede's canonical *Ecclesiastical History* could not meet the demand, firstly because it was a history of the Church and secondly because it only started with the arrival of St Augustine (597). In Geoffrey, the arrival of St Augustine marks the end of the project rather than the beginning: his *History* thus sought to answer the question of what had happened before recorded history began.

In writing that 'pre-history', Geoffrey relied mainly on his fertile imagination, though he was careful to use accepted methods of historical reconstruction (especially etymology) and to bolster invention by including whatever 'facts' could be garnered from earlier authorities. Geoffrey begins with the foundation of Britain by the Trojan refugee Brutus (hence Britain's name). Many powerful kings follow after, such as Bellus and Brennius (who conquer Rome once they stop fighting each other), Bladud (founder of Bath) and the founder of Leicester, King Leir (Shakespeare's Lear). Arthur comes to the throne as the Saxons threaten to take over Britain following the Roman withdrawal. Like his predecessors, Arthur is above all a conquering hero, and the story of his rule is one of continual territorial expansion. He begins as a fifteen-year-old by regaining control of Britain. The pagan Saxons are driven out with force and crusaders' zeal, and the rebellious Scots, Picts and Irish are ruthlessly subjugated. Next Arthur's ambitions spread outwards, to the north as far as Iceland, and to the south as far as Italy. The values that Geoffrey's Arthur embodies are primarily martial ones: pious patriotism, bravery, generosity. However, Mordred's treacherous usurpation of the throne forces him to retreat just as he is about to cross the Alps and march on Rome. In the final battle, both Mordred and Arthur suffer mortal wounds.

Geoffrey might easily have heightened the drama by having king and traitor kill each other, as happens in later sources,[10] but here as elsewhere he resisted the temptation to over-elaborate, and his factual manner ensured that his life of Arthur became accepted as fact. Although at least one early historian, William of Newburgh, expressed outrage at Geoffrey's 'lies', Geoffrey's *History* established itself as official truth until the sixteenth-century humanists discredited it. Geoffrey's sparse account of Arthur's death illustrates the historian's restraint:

> Arthur himself, our renowned King, was mortally wounded and was carried off to the Isle of Avalon, so that his wounds might be attended to. He handed the crown of Britain over to his cousin Constantine, the son of Cador Duke of Cornwall: this in the year 542 after our Lord's Incarnation.
>
> (Thorpe, xi.2, p. 261)

As Richard Barber writes, 'there is no ambiguity about "mortally" (*letaliter*), for Geoffrey's artistic requirements in the *Historia Regum Britanniae* did not allow him to indulge in romantic possibilities'.[11]

And yet there is a hint of ambiguity surrounding Arthur's end, though the ambiguity is much more subtle than in Geoffrey's *Life of Merlin*. In that work, Arthur is also said to have been injured with a mortal wound (*letali vulnere*, line 1122), but we are nevertheless told of his arrival at an island where it is always spring, and where Morgan promises to look after him until the time of his return. In Geoffrey's *History*, Merlin's prophecy to Vortigern that 'the end of the Boar will be shrouded in mystery' (vii.3, p. 172) promises ambiguity, and Geoffrey's final words about Arthur deliver it: 'mortally wounded' he may be, but he is nevertheless carried off to Avalon 'so that his wounds might be attended to'. Geoffrey's Latin is even more optimistic: Arthur departs 'to have his wounds *healed*' (*ad sananda uulnera sua*).[12]

Geoffrey, in other words, did flirt with 'romantic possibilities', and with the benefit of hindsight it is remarkable how many future directions in Arthurian literature his work glances at: the emphasis on courtliness and love, the change of focus towards the adventures of individual knights and away from the fates of nations and their leaders, a taste for the supernatural, and, finally, the emancipation of story from history and the consequent reorganisation of narrative around thematic principles. Arthur's spectacular conception is auspicious in this regard. His father, Uther Pendragon, falls in love with Ygerna, wife of Cador, the Duke of Cornwall. With Merlin's help, Uther shifts into Cador's shape and so gains access to the Duke's impregnable castle Tintagel. There he sleeps with Ygerna while the real Cador is busy fighting Uther's army. Moments later, messengers arrive at Tintagel to report that Cador is dead. By this contrivance Arthur narrowly escapes the stigma of being conceived in adultery. Merlin's wizardry, too, is prominent, though Geoffrey makes it historically respectable by presenting it not as magic but as science, as a triumph (says Merlin) of 'methods which are quite new and until now unheard-of in your day' (viii.20, p. 206).

Geoffrey's evocations of Arthur's court at peacetime provide glimpses of the chivalric pageantry associated with courtly romance: knights wear their own heraldic colours and flock to Arthur's court, which has become a beacon of courtesy; in what may well be the earliest account of a tournament, Arthur's knights joust with each other 'while their women-folk watched from the top of the city walls and aroused them to passionate excitement by their flirtatious behaviour' (ix.15, p. 230). Readers in search of strange adventures will find it in Arthur's meeting with the monstrous Giant of Mont-St-Michel. Like the knight of romance, Arthur decides to go it alone, and after killing his foe recalls how he once dispatched the Giant Retho, who had challenged him to single combat after Arthur had refused to give him his beard (x.4, p. 240). The tantalising flashback hints at other stories, now lost to memory.

Geoffrey also gave Arthur's history a tragic shape that made it memorable to later writers. When Arthur sails to France, he dreams of a dragon who slays a huge bear (x.3, p. 237). According to his advisors, the dream presages a fight between himself and 'some giant or other' (i.e. the Giant of Mont-St-Michel), but Arthur fondly imagines that the bear represents the Roman Emperor (Leo). For a long time, Arthur lives the dream, but just when he is about to enter Rome, news of Mordred's betrayal forces him to return to England. Arthur's own interpretation of the dream is proved wrong, yet so close does he come to realising it that the story of his rise and fall seems to have been shaped to impress upon us its tragic quality of 'almost-but-not-quite'.

The *History of the Kings of Britain* made an immediate impact on its readers. The respected historian Henry of Huntingdon, who had tried in vain to find material towards an early history of Britain, was given a copy when he visited the monastery of Bec in 1138, and was astounded to find that Geoffrey had succeeded where he had failed. Vernacular translations soon made Geoffrey's Latin *History* accessible to a lay audience. The Jerseyman Wace translated it into French octosyllabic couplets in his *Roman de Brut* (1155), apparently dedicated to Queen Eleanor of Aquitaine.[13] The anticipation of a court audience would explain Wace's refinements of his source. He tones down Arthur's ruthlessness, is enchanted by Guinevere's beauty and exquisite manners, and expands the account of the twelve years of peace, recording (for the first time) the Round Table and mentioning the marvellous adventures that occurred during peacetime and are now celebrated by storytellers. The period of peace comes to an end when the Roman ambassadors arrive at Arthur's court to demand tribute under threat of war. At this point in Geoffrey's *History*, Duke Cador expresses relief that peace and effeminacy are finally over. Wace characteristically adds a lyrical defence of peace, which is put in Gawain's mouth: in peacetime the grass grows greener, knights dally with their lovers and become braver in the process since 'it's for love and their beloved that knights do knightly deeds' (*Brut*, lines 10771–2). Gawain's fine sentiments were no doubt congenial to Wace and the courtiers for whom he was writing, but, of course, Geoffrey's story, which Wace felt obliged to follow, does not really accommodate them, and the peace-loving Gawain is soon back in military action, bashing Roman heads.

Wace was in turn translated into English (*c.* 1200) by Laʒamon, a Worcestershire village priest. Laʒamon translated freely and had more sympathy for the epic qualities of Geoffrey's *History* (which it seems he also knew). His *Brut* is written in a metre reminiscent of Anglo-Saxon poetry, with half-lines typically linked by alliteration. This verse form is not cosmetic but an extension of thought, and it is impossible to read Laʒamon without thinking of Anglo-Saxon heroic verse. Impressive boasts are made before battle, spear-shafts shatter, fated warriors fall in the field, death of kindred is avenged with honour. The Round Table is introduced in Laʒamon as a solution to the tensions that inevitably arise (as in *Beowulf*) when different tribes share the hall. Before acquiring his Table, Arthur must rule by fear, threatening anyone who thinks of breaking the peace with awful consequences: kinsmen will be beheaded, kinswomen will have their noses cut off. Laʒamon's most original contribution to the Arthurian legend may also owe something to Germanic lore. As soon as Arthur is born, he is taken away by elves who endow the child with spells that give him power, longevity and, best of all, generosity. At the end Arthur returns to the elves he came from. In accordance with Merlin's prophecies, he exchanges this world for the otherworld of Avalon, where Queen Argante, a radiant elf, will prepare him for his future return.

Because Wace and Laʒamon believed Geoffrey's account of Arthur's reign to be true, they did not take great liberties with the story they inherited.

It needed a writer who felt no obligations to history to change the face of Arthurian literature: that writer was Chrétien de Troyes. About his life we know little more than what he tells us in his Arthurian romances, *Erec*, *The Knight with the Lion* (*Yvain*), *The Knight of the Cart* (*Lancelot*), *Cligés* and *The Story of the Grail* (*Perceval*).[14] His name suggests he came from Troyes, where the Count and Countess of Champagne (Henry the Liberal and Marie) had their main residence. *The Knight of the Cart* addresses 'my lady Marie', and the unfinished *Story of the Grail* is dedicated to Philip of Alsace, Count of Flanders. After Henry the Liberal's death on crusade in 1181, Philip briefly courted his widow Marie – a period to which Chrétien's dedication of his last romance perhaps belongs. His first romance, *Erec*, probably postdates 1169, when Henry II held a Christmas court in Nantes – an event Chrétien remembered when describing Erec's coronation.[15]

Like Geoffrey and Wace, Chrétien was almost certainly a cleric. In *Cligés*, he lists among his oeuvre a version of the popular story of Tristan and Iseut as well as translations of Ovid. It has recently been argued that Chrétien may have been more of a minstrel than an educated cleric,[16] but while it is true that his romances were primarily meant for public rather than private reading, he himself was supremely literate. His misattribution of two common scriptural quotations (*Cligés*, line 5267, *Conte du Graal*, lines 47–5, Kibler, pp. 188, 381) does not mean he had not read the Bible; it shows, rather, that many Biblical proverbs had begun to lead an independent life – which is why writers with impeccable academic credentials were prone to similar errors of attribution.[17] Chrétien's verbal wit is on display in the prologue to *Erec*, where he distinguishes himself from 'those who try to live by storytelling'. Both he and they work with a 'tale of adventure' (*avanture*), but whereas the storytellers corrupt the story (*li contes*) before kings and counts (*contes*), he fashions it into an artful composition (*conjointure*) 'which will be in memory ... as long as Christianity (*crestiantez*) lasts, of this Chrétien (*Crestiens*) boasts' (Kibler, p. 37). In lesser writers we would call this conceitedness, but Chrétien's boast fulfils itself each time *Erec* is read. Strikingly, Chrétien stakes his claim to fame on his superior art rather than on historical veracity. He is the poet of *conjointure*, which I take to mean the 'art of connecting' both at the level of words (in rhyme and wordplay) and plot.

Having thrown off the shackles of history, Chrétien presents a universe that is self-consciously fictional and obeys its own rules. When he does not want to provide any justification for these rules, he simply calls them 'customs', and it is with a custom that *Erec* begins: Arthur wants to honour the custom of the Hunt of the White Stag. Gawain, who typically appears in Chrétien as the embodiment of good sense, warns Arthur against this:

the man who kills the stag will have to kiss the prettiest girl at court, and each of Arthur's knights is bound to quarrel if his lady is passed over. The king brushes this objection aside: kings must keep their word and customs must be upheld. The motif of the Hunt of the White Stag can be found in many traditional stories where the hunter's pursuit of his quarry leads him to his love.[18] If such stories were known to Chrétien, however, he drastically changed the script. The hero, Prince Erec, does not actually join in the hunt but rides out belatedly to accompany the queen, while Arthur's men chase the stag off-stage. When Guinevere is insulted by a passing knight and his rude dwarf, Erec vows revenge and follows them to a bustling town, where he receives hospitality from an impoverished gentleman and his exquisite daughter. He is told that the offensive knight is the local lord, and that tomorrow is the day of the Sparrowhawk competition, when, according to custom, the knight with the prettiest *amie* wins the hawk. The next day, both the local lord and Erec, who is escorted by the host's daughter, claim the hawk. Erec defeats the lord (Yder) and returns with his *amie* to Arthur's court. The king has in the meantime killed the white stag, but the looming crisis is narrowly averted by Erec's arrival: Erec's lady manifestly outshines all others, so Arthur can safely grant her the kiss. The first 'turn' (*vers*) of the romance concludes with the marriage of Erec and his lady (line 1796, Kibler, p. 60), whose name (Enide) is revealed only now, as she assumes her new social identity.[19] After the wedding, the couple spend a blissful night together, their passion evoked in a double simile: 'The hunted stag who pants from thirst does not so yearn for the fountain, nor does the hungry sparrowhawk return so willingly when called, that they did not come into each other's arms more eagerly' (lines 2027–32, Kibler, pp. 62–3).

This is *conjointure* of the highest order. The lines, alluding to Psalm 42 – 'as the hart longeth for the fountain, so my heart longeth for thee, my lord' – daringly appropriate the language of religious devotion for erotic ends, while the similes of 'the hunted stag' and the 'hungry sparrowhawk' recall and 'conjoin' the two preceding episodes. By following *avanture*, knights reconfigure accident as design and discover the secrets of their own destiny.

In Chrétien's romances, this process of self-realisation typically includes a moment of failure.[20] In *Erec*, the hero is so besotted with his wife that he withdraws completely from chivalric pursuits and loses his honour. Enide notices the complaints of his peers that he has become a *recreant* to arms (lines 2462, 2551, 2801, Kibler, pp. 67–8) but does not dare raise the problem with her husband. One morning she blames herself aloud for his decline, thinking he is asleep. Her reproaches awaken Erec ('de la parolle s'esveilla', line 2507), who insists that she tell him what is troubling her. When she reluctantly speaks up, he commands her to dress herself in her finest apparel, to ride out in front of him, and not to speak unless spoken to. Neither Erec nor Chrétien explains the purpose of this arrangement, and this gives her experiences the character of an ordeal, a test that is all the harder because no reason for it is given.[21]

The poetic justification for the adventures does, however, emerge. Riding ahead, Enide is necessarily the first to see the dangers to her husband (just as she was the first to sense the danger of her husband's *recreantise*), while the prohibition on her speech means that, for Enide, the adventures keep turning on the question of whether to speak or not to speak: should she obey her husband or warn the man she loves? Chrétien expresses Enide's mental anguish in a form he made his own, a quick-fire internal debate in which two conflicting impulses are argued out. For Erec, the adventures are a means to rehabilitation: he is to spend his energies in battle rather than in bed, and if Enide once lured him away from arms, she now functions to lure combatants to him. The end of the ordeal comes when Erec, after defeating two giants, collapses as if dead. The Count of Limors tries to force Enide into marriage, but she protests loudly. Hearing her words, Erec regains consciousness 'like a man who awakes from sleep' (Kibler, p. 96; 'ausi com hom qui s'esvoille', line 4817), just as she wakened him when her ordeal began. The Count's men flee in panic at the sight of a 'dead man walking' and Erec and Enide are reconciled.

On the way home Erec does not miss the opportunity for a final perilous adventure, the 'Joy of the Court'. This adventure is a beautiful example of the mystification that separates chronicle from romance, for even its name is incomprehensible except in retrospect: as Erec is warned, anyone who has undertaken it has come to grief. Erec's intrepid response shows he has absorbed the main moral of the story: retreating would be *recreantise* (line 5606, Kibler, p. 106). He defeats a tall knight in a magical garden, who explains he has been marooned because of a rash promise that he stay there with his *amie* until defeated by a better knight. Erec's victory brings 'joy to the court' and finally restores sense to the adventure's name. Other names and identities are also unveiled: the knight, Mabonograin, was once a squire at the court of Erec's father, and his lady is Enide's niece.

Erec proved a huge success and was translated into many different languages: there is the Welsh *Tale of Geraint*, the Old Norse *Erex Saga* and the German *Erec*, the last by the notable German poet Hartmann von Aue (c. 1155–1210). When French writers turned to prose, some episodes of *Erec* were interlaced with other Arthurian prose material in the thirteenth-century *Erec en prose*, and the whole romance was again prosified in the fifteenth-century Burgundian *Erec*; in the sixteenth century, when Old French became difficult to read, Pierre Sala rendered it into 'modern' French verse. Chrétien's *Knight with the Lion* also became a popular favourite. It, too, was updated by Pierre Sala, translated into German by Hartmann von Aue (*Iwein*), into Old Norse (*Ívens saga*) and Welsh (*The Lady of the Well*), and also into Swedish (*Ivan Lejohnriddaren*) and Middle English *(Ywain and Gawain)*. The romance is gripping from the start, thanks to Chrétien's bold opening gambit, a narrative within a narrative. After Arthur, a pale shadow of his belligerent self in the chronicles, has retreated to the bedroom with Guinevere, the knight Calogrenant tells of his misadventure in the forest of Broceliande (in Brittany), popularly believed to be full of marvels. Wace in his *Roman de Rou* (a mythical history of the Normans) confesses he had been stupid enough to believe the rumours and visited Broceliande in search of marvels, but found nothing: 'As a fool I went and as a fool I returned.'[22] Chrétien wittily gives these same words to Calogrenant, who shamefully confesses he was defeated by the guardian of a magic fountain that unleashed a storm when he spilt its water on a hollow stone. What historians like Wace cannot find, writers of fiction are at liberty to invent.

The existence of marvels in Chrétien's Broceliande is put beyond doubt when Yvain, determined to avenge Calogrenant's shame, retraces his steps and finds everything exactly as the former described it. After unleashing the storm, Yvain fatally wounds the Knight of the Fountain, who flees to his castle, pursued by Yvain. The latter enters the gate just before the portcullis falls shut behind him, slicing off his spurs and bisecting his horse. The graphic scene etched itself into the memories of readers and listeners and can be found on several misericords in English churches.[23] Yvain is now imprisoned in the castle of the lord he has killed, and to make his life more difficult, he falls in love with the widow Laudine. Fortunately he is aided by her clever maiden Lunete, who lends him a ring that makes him invisible, and uses her shrewd insight into her lady to advance his suit. Chrétien delights in orchestrating 'impossible' situations (how can Laudine love the man who, as her husband's killer, she hates the most?) but, since his characters are endowed with some of his own inventiveness, they are quick to find solutions. Lunete points out that Laudine needs a protector and that Yvain must be a better one than her husband, whom he defeated. Although initially offended by these suggestions, Laudine needs him, and soon persuades herself by logical argument that she is justified in taking the position that her heart has already occupied: Yvain *must* become her husband.

Once the two are married, Chrétien returns to the conflict he explored in *Erec*, between love and honour, but with a twist. Yvain is warned about *recreantise* by Gawain, who persuades him to accompany him on a round of tournaments. Laudine agrees provided Yvain returns in a year's time. Once away from his wife, he lapses back into bachelor habits, and in the flush of chivalric success forgets his promise to return. As soon as he remembers, a messenger arrives to announce that Laudine has rejected him. Like Erec, then, Yvain is confronted with failure, and the crisis plunges him into madness. For a long time he lives as a wild man in the forest. The fantastical elements of the story only enhance Chrétien's powers of realistic observation. Yvain is healed when a damsel applies some magic ointment, but because he is naked (and attractive), she gets carried away and uses more ointment than required. With humour and delicacy, Chrétien observes the problems that arise for his characters – Yvain cannot be seen naked, the damsel cannot be seen to have seen him naked and cannot return to her lady with an empty pot of ointment – and their ingenious manoeuvres to avoid embarrassment.

When Yvain rescues a lion, the animal becomes his faithful companion. As the 'Knight with the Lion', Yvain gives succour to all and sundry and rescues Lunete, who at the end of the romance effects a reconciliation between him and his lady by trapping her in 'the game of Truth' (line 6624, Kibler, p. 378). Lunete makes Laudine swear that she will do all she can to restore the 'Knight with the Lion' to his lady's favour, and when the knight is revealed to be Yvain himself she is obliged to make up with him or commit perjury. Standing on her pride, she protests she is 'forced' to take Yvain back, but, as Chrétien concludes, everybody is happy (line 6799, p. 380).

Among Chrétien's other works, *The Knight of the Cart* and the *Story of the Grail* have left the richest legacy. (*Cligés* is not set in Arthurian Britain; the two heroes Alexander and Cligés, father and son, are Greek, and the romance is only Arthurian because both spend some probationary time at Arthur's court.) *The Knight of the Cart* is the first surviving story about Lancelot, the lover of Queen Guinevere. He rescues her from her abductor, the dastardly Meleagant, and like a latter-day Messiah liberates all those who are held captive in Gorre, the Land of No Return. In Chrétien's typically experimental handling of the story, the pursuit of Guinevere is seen through the eyes of Gawain, who sets out after the kidnapped queen only to discover he is on the trail of an unnamed knight who is ahead of him. When Gawain finally catches up with him, a passing dwarf who is driving a cart (used to transport criminals) tells them that the surest way of finding the queen is to get on the cart. Gawain sensibly decides to follow on horseback, so avoiding the ignominy of being regarded as a criminal, while Lancelot, after a moment's hesitation, throws caution to the wind and climbs in. His momentary dilemma is expressed as a conflict between Love and Reason, the demands of the former being entirely opposed to those of the latter. Lancelot's fault, in Guinevere's eyes, is not that he shamed himself by mounting the cart, but that he paused for a moment before so doing.

The opposition between love and reason also means that Chrétien's ethos is at odds with the modern billing of the romance, as 'telling of the adulterous relationship between Lancelot and King Arthur's wife' (thus the blurb on the back of Kibler's Penguin translation). It is only the villain Meleagant who conceives of their love as immoral. True lovers know that Love has its own laws and is itself a religion, so if Lancelot's actions are shameful and objectionable by all reasonable standards (Christian morality, chivalric honour), they are paradoxically necessary and meritorious in the cause of Love. The story, with its contrasting heroes, Gawain and Lancelot, explores the conflict between two competing value systems, but it also suggests that we cannot achieve truly heroic status by listening to both sides of the argument. Nothing less than blind obedience to love is demanded of Lancelot before he becomes the complete hero, and Chrétien demands the same from his readers if they are to share his vision that (in Matilda Bruckner's words) 'Lancelot is not the saviour of Arthur's queen and kingdom *in spite of* being an adulterous traitor; he redeems them *because* he's Guinevere's lover and best knight'.[24]

Chrétien's unfinished *Story of the Grail* is the darkest and most enigmatic of his romances. Significantly, the hero of the romance (Perceval) is an outsider to Arthur's court. Kept ignorant of his name and history, he is brought up in the Wild Forest by his mother, whom he abandons to become a knight. In the course of many adventures, the past gradually reassembles itself around the hero. On a few occasions he is brought into the ambit of Arthur's court, but the nature of his destiny seems to lie beyond it, as did his origin. Whilst staying at the Grail Castle, where he is welcomed by an invalid host, he witnesses a quasi-religious procession in which 'a grail' is carried, containing a single eucharistic wafer. The hero does not ask any questions, and for this he pays a heavy price. He is expelled from the castle, and learns from a lady holding a decapitated corpse (his cousin) that, *if* he had asked whom the Grail served, his host, the Fisher King, would have regained the use of his limbs. We last see Perceval crying for his sins in a hermitage, where his hermit uncle explains that he did not ask the question *because* he had wronged his mother, who died as soon as he left her. This explanation, like so many others in *The Story of the Grail*, invokes inscrutable principles of causality that raise more questions than they answer.

As if the adventures of Perceval were not long and complicated enough, Chrétien launches Gawain on a parallel quest. While Perceval vows to seek the Bleeding Lance, Gawain undertakes to raise the siege of Montesclere, but since various other challenges intervene, Gawain's list of missions-to-be-accomplished only ever gets longer. At the point where the romance finally breaks off (at line 9184), Gawain has fetched up in a mysterious otherworldly castle, making polite conversation with Arthurian characters (e.g. his grandmother Ygerna, Arthur's mother) who should long be dead. Four continuators of Chrétien's *Story of the Grail* took up the story that Chrétien left uncompleted (presumably because he died, as the second continuator says); in their attempt to finish it and tie up all the loose ends, they themselves used up another 60,000 lines.

One of the many questions Chrétien bequeathed to later writers is the nature and significance of the Grail. Chrétien used the word in its original sense, 'a serving dish', though he certainly elevates it beyond the ordinary by describing it in hyperboles and by giving it the sacred function of carrying the eucharist. Subsequent writers laid on the religious significance more thickly. Robert de Boron, author of the first cycle of Grail romances (*c.* 1200), tells us the Grail is the cup of the Last Supper, given by Pilate to Jesus' disciple Joseph of Arimathea. In the Vulgate Cycle *Quest of the Holy Grail*, the Grail becomes an emanation of the divine in the earthly world. In his incomparable *Parzival* (*c.* 1205), Wolfram von Eschenbach, who says he is illiterate, turns the grail into a stone named *lapsit exillis* (whatever that means). This stone was once the seat of the neutral angels and is now jealously guarded by the Grail family who live on the food it miraculously provides.[25] The story as developed by Wolfram finds its final consummation in Richard Wagner's last, sublime opera *Parsifal* (1882).

The format of the short Arthurian romance, exemplified by *Erec* and *Yvain*, was enthusiastically adopted by later writers. Renaut de Beaujeu's *Bel Inconnu* (*c.* 1190), adapted by Thomas Chestre into English as *Libeaus Desconus* (*c.* 1375), follows the adventures of a knight who like Perceval grows up in isolation and ignorance of his name. He eventually discovers he is Guinglain, Gawain's son, and finds love. Various motifs, including a beauty contest with a falcon as the prize, register Renaut's debt to Chrétien. Fergus, the hero of Guillaume le Clerc's *Fergus*, written in Scotland *c.* 1210, is an uncouth hero also modelled on Perceval – except that Fergus really is of peasant stock (see below, pp. 144–5). Two shorter burlesque Gawain romances, *La Mule sans frein* and *Le Chevalier à l'épée*, are so reminiscent of Chrétien that some believe he wrote them himself. As these examples suggest, Chrétien's imitators were especially fond of Gawain and his amorous indiscretions. In *La Vengeance Raguidel* by Raoul de Houdenc (*c.* 1210), Gawain sets off in earnest to avenge the death of Raguidel, but, as ever, it does not take him long to get into trouble with the ladies. Cleverly intertextual and full of exciting and comic incident, the later French verse romances offer excellent entertainment, but few can rival the suggestiveness achieved by Chrétien.

In *The Story of the Grail*, Chrétien himself moved beyond the format of the short romance – and again many writers followed in his footsteps. Chrétien's unanswered questions in the *Grail* were taken up in the Continuations of his unfinished poem, and in due course Arthurian matter encouraged further profuseness in the medium of prose. That, however, is a story for the next chapter.

NOTES

1 Muriel Whitaker, *The Legends of King Arthur in Art,* Arthurian Studies 22 (Cambridge: D. S. Brewer, 1995), pp. 86–8.

2 W. P. Gerritsen, 'Walewein's Welsh Antecedents', *Dutch Crossing,* 24 (2000), 147–57.

3 William of Malmesbury, *Gesta Regum Anglorum,* ed. and trans. R. A. B. Mynors, R. M. Thompson and M. Winterbottom, 2 vols. (Oxford University Press, 1998), I, pp. 520–1.

4 Marie de France, *Lais,* ed. Jean Rychner (Paris: Champion, 1977), trans. G. S. Burgess and K. Busby, *The Lais of Marie de France,* 2nd edn (Harmondsworth: Penguin, 1999).

5 The Anglo-Norman *Romance of Horn* (c. 1170) praises their skill; trans. Judith Weiss, in *The Birth of Romance,* Everyman Library (London: Dent, 1992), p. 66.

6 *The Mabinogion,* trans. Sioned Davies (Oxford University Press, 2007). Subsequent references to this work are in the text.

7 *The Celtic Sources for the Arthurian Legend,* ed. and trans. J. Coe and Simon Young (Llanerch: Llanerch Press, 1995).

8 My translation. This passage is not found in the text translated by Thorpe, and is cited only as a variant in Geoffrey of Monmouth, *The History of the Kings of Britain,* ed. Michael D. Reeve, trans. Neil Wright, Arthurian Studies 69 (Woodbridge: Boydell and Brewer, 2007), p. 143.

9 Unless otherwise indicated, *Vita Merlini* is cited from *The Life of Merlin: Geoffrey of Monmouth, Vita Merlini,* ed. and trans. Basil Clarke (Cardiff: University of Wales Press, 1973). This edition also contains extracts from earlier Welsh Merlin-related material. *The History of the Kings of Britain* is cited in the translation by Thorpe.

10 In Henry of Huntington's *Letter to Warinus* (1139), ed. Diana Greenway, *Henry, Archdeacon of Huntingdon* (Oxford: Clarendon Press, 1996), pp. 558–83, Arthur kills Mordred in a climactic showdown; in the French Vulgate *Mort Artu* (c. 1210) and in Malory, they kill each other.

11 Richard Barber, 'The *Vera Historia De Morte Arthuri* and its Place in Arthurian Tradition', *Arthurian Literature,* I (1981), 62–77 (p. 63).

12 Monmouth, *History,* ed. Reeve, p. 253.

13 *Wace's 'Roman de Brut': A History of the British,* ed. and trans. Judith Weiss, 2nd edn, Exeter Medieval English Texts and Studies (Exeter University Press, 2002). The information about the dedication to Eleanor is given by Wace's translator, Laȝamon; see *Laȝamon's Arthur: The Arthurian Section of Laȝamon's 'Brut',* ed. W. R. J. Barron and S. C. Weinberg (Harlow: Longman, 1989), line 22.

14 Possibly Chrétien is to be identified with a 'Christianus' who appears in local charters; see Ad Putter, 'Knights and Clerics at the Court of Champagne: Chrétien de Troyes's Romances in Context', in *Medieval Knighthood V,* ed.

Stephen Church and Ruth Harvey (Woodbridge: Boydell and Brewer, 1995), pp. 243–66.

15 Beate Schmolke-Hasselman, *The Evolution of Arthurian Romance*, trans. Margaret and Roger Middleton (Cambridge University Press, 1998), pp. 232–40.

16 Evelyn Birge Vitz, *Orality and Performance in Early French Romance* (Cambridge: D. S. Brewer, 1999), pp. 86–119.

17 Elisabeth Schulze-Bussacker provides examples in 'Proverbes anglo-normands', *Cahiers de civilisation médiévale*, 37 (1994), 347–64.

18 R. Bezzola, *Le Sens de l'aventure et de l'amour* (Paris: Jeune Parque, 1947), pp. 94–5.

19 This play of names is typical of Chrétien: Yvain loses his name to become the 'Knight of the Lion'; the identity of 'The Knight of the Cart' is unknown until Guinevere names him Lancelot; the hero of *The Story of the Grail* does not know his name, but 'guesses' it is Perceval. Neither Enide nor Laudine is named until the marriage. Since Chrétien's titles collude in this play, the modern title *Erec and Enide* is inept. Chrétien called it the 'story of Erec' (19).

20 Elspeth Kennedy, 'Failure in Arthurian Romance', *Medium Ævum*, 50 (1991), 16–32, repr. in *The Grail: A Casebook*, ed. Dhira B. Mahoney, Garland Reference Library of the Humanities (New York: Garland, 2000), pp. 279–300.

21 The obvious parallel is with the story of Griselda; this connection is made explicit in the fifteenth-century Burgundian prose adaptation of *Erec*.

22 *Roman de Rou*, ed. A. J. Holden (Paris: Picard, 1970–3), lines 6373–98 (my translation).

23 Whitaker, *Legends*, pp. 97–8.

24 Matilda Tomaryn Bruckner, 'An Interpreter's Dilemma: Why are there So Many Interpretations of Chrétien's *Chevalier de la Charrete*?', *Romance Philology*, 40 (1986), 159–80 (p. 178).

25 Friedrich Ranke, 'The Symbolism of the Grail in Wolfram von Eschenbach', in *The Grail*, ed. Mahoney, pp. 367–78.

3

JANE H. M. TAYLOR

The thirteenth-century Arthur

Twelfth-century France left two quite distinct legacies to the adept of romance. On the one hand, it provided what was confidently thought to be an historical Arthur, the Arthur whose life-story and political mission were celebrated by the unimpeachable Geoffrey of Monmouth and his authoritative verse-translator and adapter Wace. On the other, it bequeathed a sequence of wonderfully inventive verse romances which focused on individual heroes more or less loosely attached to Arthur and his Round Table: the romances principally of Chrétien de Troyes, of course, but also of the Tristan tradition. The writers of the previous century had elaborated much of the portfolio of structures and motifs and narrative patterns which were to characterise romance: the ethic of solitary and individual enterprise; the knight-errant hero and the quest; the search for chivalric identity; the court of Arthur as the point of departure and the benchmark for individual adventure; the tournament as the locus for chivalric competition; the exploration of sexuality and desire; the conflict and reconciliation of love and chivalry; the pleasures of deferral; the problematic and irresistible ultimate adventure, the Grail. Richly provided thus with material and inspiration, the writers of the thirteenth century respond with three distinct and distinctive strategies:

(1) In verse, celebrating more and yet more individual Arthurian heroes and their quests.
(2) In prose, and much more innovatively, synthesising history and romance in encyclopedic, over-arching cycles like the Vulgate Cycle and the Prose *Tristan*.
(3) In verse or sometimes in prose, embroidering, sometimes interminably, on Chrétien's temptingly unfinished masterpiece, the *Conte du Graal* (*Perceval*).

It is scarcely an exaggeration, in the thirteenth century, to talk of an Arthurian industry, with opportunist poets, prose-writers, copyists, translators, sedulously exploiting the new romances and their new conventions.

The outstanding example of the third strategy, the phenomenon that consists in embroidering on Chrétien's *Graal*, and one which is also, and incidentally, an excellent illustration of movement towards the second strategy I have just mentioned, the movement toward thesis and compilation, is provided by the four texts collectively known as the *Perceval* Continuations.[1] To these we should add two 'prequels' designed to explain the hero's antecedents and to warrant certain key events in Chrétien's romance: the first known as the *Elucidation*, the second, *Bliocadran*, both dating from the early thirteenth century. And because this opportunistic process of sequel and prequel is especially visible in the case of the Grail romances, I propose to begin this chapter by exploring the tangled history of the Continuations. Chrétien, as we saw in Chapter 2, abandoned his *Conte du Graal* unfinished: Perceval himself we last see as he seems to have achieved a degree of spiritual maturity, but the latter part of Chrétien's romance is devoted to a complex series of adventures centring on Gawain; we are left with our curiosity unsatisfied, in other words, as to the nature of the Grail, the fate of Perceval, and the role of the secondary hero, Gawain. Interestingly enough, the First Continuation, of which a first version dates from around 1200 but which was itself further extended, and extended again, in the very early thirteenth century, concentrates very much on Gawain: was it perhaps the case that the combination of elusive Grail, and a hero clearly much enjoyed by the public as evidenced by the number of thirteenth-century Gawain romances to which I return below, was irresistible? The First Continuation, in any event, offers a string of complicated, episodic, highly inventive, and often rather uncourtly adventures – a chastity test, a beheading test, seductions, children mislaid and found – which bring Gawain, ultimately but unsuccessfully, to the Grail Castle: unsuccessfully, of course, because he cannot become the Grail hero, but also, perhaps, precisely because of the pleasure of deferral to which I referred above. Elements of these adventures could seem to draw on motifs provided by Chrétien himself: thus the Grail dispenses food, and the Broken Sword and the Bleeding Lance that had featured rather briefly in the *Conte du Graal* make more extended appearances. But much of the First Continuation looks very much like an anthology of exuberant Arthuriana from sources quite independent of Chrétien, with individual episodes which easily lend themselves to a form of serialisation.

Crucially, however, the First Continuation itself is unfinished – indeed, it never returns to Perceval – and it is unsurprising that, soon after 1200, another poet (who may have been a certain Wauchier de Denain, otherwise known as an author of saints' lives) should have been tempted into composing a Second Continuation. This is distinctly more controlled than the First; above all, it returns to Perceval and thus to a Grail quest proper, although still not single-mindedly since Perceval is made to follow a complicated series of interlocking adventures, most of which have nothing to do with the Grail, and since Gawain remains what he was in Chrétien's *Conte du Graal*, a major player. Perceval, however, in this Second Continuation, does revisit the Grail Castle – and the unaware reader might imagine that he would ask the crucial questions. Alas: was Wauchier conscious of the opportunity he was leaving to a successor? Or did he too seek to exploit the pleasure of deferral? It turns out that Perceval has still not reached a sufficient level of spiritual and chivalric perfection, and the romance ending is postponed again: the way is left open for a Third Continuation, this one by a certain Manessier, written in Flanders between 1214 and 1227.

This third sequel takes many of its cues from Chrétien's *Perceval*, but Manessier seems to have read some of the other Grail texts to which we shall come later in this chapter, and notably the *Queste del Saint Graal*. Accordingly, although Gawain's adventures still figure quite large in Manessier's (Third) Continuation, the focus switches to Perceval and to the Grail itself: this time, Perceval is permitted by the writer to reach the Grail Castle, to ask the necessary questions, and to engineer the miraculous cure of the Fisher King; after a final visit to Arthur's court, he returns to the Grail Castle and accepts his destiny, the crown and lands of the Fisher King – and seven years later becomes a holy hermit, dies in an odour of sanctity and is taken up into Heaven with the Grail. Which, of course, makes 'continuation' in the strictest sense impossible, and seems to have inspired another rather ingenious continuator to pursue another strategy: not continuation, this time, but something we might call 'in-fill'. The so-called Fourth Continuation, by a certain Gerbert de Montreuil, also from the court of Flanders and writing in the 1230s, is an interpolation, to be fitted in chronologically between the Second and Third Continuations, and seems to be designed to fill out details from the latter; some attention is paid once again to Gawain, although the romance does centre on Perceval and indeed ultimately brings him to the Grail Castle. There is a proliferation, in this Fourth Continuation, of sermonising hermits, and Gerbert's tone is distinctly moralistic.

For completeness, I shall merely mention the two 'prequels', both also dating from the thirteenth century: the so-called *Elucidation*, which is found in just one surviving manuscript which also contains *Perceval*, and *Bliocadran*, found in two, are both designed as explanatory and as careful introductions to Chrétien's *Perceval*.[2] The former, which is a tissue of marvels and folklore elements, seems to make Gawain and Perceval equal partners in the quest for the Grail; the latter concentrates on Perceval's paternal ancestry, and on the tragic events which Perceval's mother had recounted in

Chrétien's *Conte du Graal*, and which had meant that the young man was brought up in perfect isolation from the world of chivalry.

I have spent so long on the tangled history of the Continuations because, in sum, they are such striking evidence of three phenomena in the development of thirteenth-century Arthurian romance. The first is the fascination of the Grail: no other individual motif has provoked such excitement or inspired such creativity – although astonishingly, and for no obvious reason, that fascination is not replicated in England until the fifteenth-century Grail narratives (Hardyng, Lovelich, Malory). The second – which I have emphasised repeatedly – is deferral: 'ending', which one would expect to be the first consideration of any continuator, is not, it seems, a preoccupation. The third, and it is something to which I shall return later in more detail, is the marked tendency towards cyclicity, that is, the attempt to build a cohesive, pseudo-historical narrative from disparate parts; it is interesting that patrons and copyists appear to have recognised and welcomed this in commissioning, and constructing, vast cyclical manuscripts like Bibliothèque nationale de France fr. 12576 and BnF n.a.f. 6614 (both copied in the second half of the thirteenth century, probably in the same workshop, and both containing the *Conte du Graal* and all four Continuations: a remarkable 75,000 lines-worth of Grail texts). In these last two respects, the Continuations, as we shall see, adumbrate narrative patterns and structures which will henceforward dominate the genre.

I shall return below to cyclical manuscripts and the development of narrative cycles, both of which are fundamental to the development of Arthurian romance in the thirteenth century. First, however, and as additional evidence of the lure of the Grail, we need to look at some of the discrete avatars also launched by Chrétien's *Conte du Graal*, some of which, indeed, seem to have been available to the writers of the Continuations. Of these, the most influential is Robert de Boron's *Estoire dou Graal*.[3] Robert wrote at the turn of the thirteenth century, in northern France. His knowledge not just of the Bible but of the Apocrypha is remarkable, and it is he who is responsible for the leap of imagination which transforms Chrétien's mysterious but nebulous Grail into the cup of the Last Supper and the vessel in which Joseph of Arimathea collected Christ's blood after the Crucifixion; it is also Robert who shows (rather incoherently, it must be said) how the Grail migrated from the Holy Land to Arthurian Britain, thus giving Britain, and Arthur, so privileged a place in Redemption history. To Robert are also attributed two other romances, one with relative security, the *Merlin*, and another in prose, more doubtfully (the textual history of this group is a tangled one, and the manuscripts do not name Robert): what is usually called the *Didot-Perceval*, which embroiders on Chrétien's *Conte du Graal* with additional episodes, then completes it with yet another, different, version of Perceval's achievement of the Grail and the end of Arthur's own kingdom; this romance draws on the Second Continuation and on Wace's *Brut*. The *Estoire*, the *Merlin*, and the *Didot-Perceval* form a trilogy; the first two were put into prose soon after 1200. This group of romances, sometimes known as the Little Grail or Robert de Boron Cycle, were remarkably influential, and in particular, as we shall see, on what is now thought of as the 'canonical' version of the Arthurian legends, the Vulgate Cycle. First, however, we should explore some other of the offspring of Chrétien's Grail romance, one in France, the other, more spectacularly, in Germany.[4]

The first of these, the French avatar, is the *Perlesvaus*, sometimes known as *The High Book of the Grail*, which dates from the first half of the thirteenth century.[5] This is a sizeable text based around Perceval (here called **Perd-les-vaus**, since his father had *lost* [*perdu*] some of his lands); it recounts his successful completion of his quest for the Grail, via a profusion of baroque adventures, some of them shockingly violent, which oppose the Old Law (the Jewish and other faiths) and the New Law, Christianity. Unusually, Arthur himself is a protagonist, rather than simply presiding over his court at Camelot: it is he who inaugurates the adventures when he ventures into the forests, and he also visits the Grail Castle where he has a vision of the Grail.

The second text that needs exploring here – the German text which I called 'spectacular' – is that by the most influential perhaps of all of Chrétien's epigones: Wolfram von Eschenbach's *Parzival*,[6] composed for the most part in the first decade of the thirteenth century, and, at nearly 25,000 lines, an adaptation and elaboration far more than a simple translation of Chrétien's *Conte du Graal*. It is in fact a radical reworking, largely Wolfram's own: it is possible that he may have known some of the Continuations, but he seems not to have known Robert de Boron's *Estoire*. In particular, he remakes the Grail, which in the German romance becomes not a dish (as Chrétien had painted it) nor a chalice (as it had been for Robert) but, uniquely, a stone with mysterious powers guarded in a Grail Castle called Munsalvæsche by an order of Grail Knights. Wolfram re-orients Chrétien's text by attributing far greater importance to the spiritual strand which the latter simply adumbrates; he also innovates by integrating the Gawain and Perceval stories, which Chrétien had kept almost entirely separate, into a sequence of adventures in which the two heroes act conjointly. Wolfram, of necessity, has to devise an ending for the unfinished text: he does so by having Parzival ask the Grail questions, as a result of which Anfortas, the existing Grail king, is cured and is succeeded by Parzival. I said that Wolfram's version was spectacular; it is marked by the author's powerful imagination and sense of cohesion, and by its own popularity: it is the best-transmitted of German courtly romances,[7] and it is, of course, the version of the Grail story adopted by Wagner and therefore among the best known.

Wolfram's *Parzival*, however, has taken us away from the mainstream of thirteenth-century Arthurian romance, which is indisputably centred in France. I referred earlier to the cyclical manuscripts which brought together Chrétien's *Conte du Graal* with one or more of its Continuations; an even more spectacular example of the second movement, towards compilation and towards overarching pseudo-historical cycles, is provided by a manuscript also in the Bibliothèque nationale de France, fr. 1450, copied in the second quarter of the thirteenth century. This highly ambitious manuscript proposes a world history, no less: the compiler starts with the romance-history of the Trojan War (Benoît de Sainte-Maure's *Roman de Troie*) and the romance-history of Rome (the *Roman d'Eneas*); he then transcribes the early section of Wace's romance-history *Roman de Brut* as far as Arthur's reign; within what Wace presents as the period during which Arthur created and fostered the Round Table, the compiler then sets all five of Chrétien's Arthurian romances, and a part of the text of the First Continuation, as testimony, it seems, to Arthur's peace-making and state-building. To give the impression of a seamless progression from text to text, the compiler has indulged in some light text-editing: he removes, for instance, the prologues to *Erec et Enide* and *Perceval*, and adds a few transitional verses to introduce Chrétien's texts. In a sense, what he has done is to introduce his own *conjointure*, his own re-articulation of Chrétien's discrete romances: they become incidents in a larger, trans-historical *summa* in which texts that blur the distinction between romance and chronicle give them an authority and a meaning well beyond the excitement of the individual chivalric adventure.

The phrase I have used here, *romance-history*, was designed to draw attention, with Wace and Benoît and the *Roman d'Eneas*, to the essential ambiguity between historiography and romance which I mentioned in my first paragraph and which will also characterise the major and most far-reaching innovation of thirteenth-century Arthurian romance in France: the development of the narrative cycle devoted to the king, and specifically in *prose*. I stress prose: virtually all those Arthurian romances to which I have alluded so far – Chrétien's own, the Continuations, indeed Wolfram's *Parzival* – have used verse, a medium, significantly, treated with some distrust, by clerics and in France, because thought to be inherently unreliable. The highly inventive composers of what was to become the canonical great Arthurian cycle, the *Lancelot-Grail*, or Vulgate Cycle, to which I turn now, chose, by contrast, prose, regarded as the vehicle for historical legitimacy: they also, as we shall see, sought diplomatically to align their own work with Wace's authoritative

Roman de Brut. I say 'canonical': this, ultimately, is the version of Arthurian romance on which Malory drew,[8] and it is therefore, indirectly, the version with which modern English readers are most familiar. The Vulgate Cycle consists of five parts.[9] Its core – the largest segment by far, and the first to be composed – is generally known as the *Lancelot en prose* (*Prose Lancelot*);[10] it develops Lancelot, to whom of course Chrétien had devoted his *Chevalier de la charrete* (*Knight of the Cart*), by offering an account of his ances-try, of his childhood with the Lady of the Lake, of his adolescent prowess, and of his passionate love-affair with Arthur's queen, Guinevere (along with a string of other chivalric quests and adventures, his and those of other Arthurian knights). This core text – composed, it seems, between 1215 and 1230 or so – has two sequels also written in much the same time-frame: the *Queste del Saint Graal* and *La Mort le roi Artu*.[11]

The first of these, heavily influenced by Cistercian doctrine, differs mark-edly in tone from the *Lancelot en prose*: it displaces the previous Grail hero, Perceval, in favour of a new hero, Galahad, who is often presented as the type of Christ, and although it allows Lancelot a vision of the Grail, he is disqualified from full success in the quest by his adulterous love for Guinevere. *La Mort le roi Artu*, by contrast, returns to the more worldly concerns of Arthur and his Round Table, and relates the deaths of Arthur and Lancelot, the end of chivalric endeavour, and the destruction of Arthur's kingdom. These three sections – the *Lancelot en prose*, *La Queste del Saint Graal* and *La Mort le roi Artu* – are usually thought to have been composed sequentially, between 1215 and 1230; critics generally consider that they have an overall architecture, to the extent that some at least believe – from patterns of narrative echo and cross-reference and contrast – that a single powerful imagination may have been responsible for all three. They would, however, agree that it was different authors who were responsible for the two 'prequels' that constitute the Vulgate Cycle in its most complete form.

The first of these prequels, *L'Estoire del Saint Graal*, is designed to show how the Grail travelled from the foot of the Cross to the Britain of Joseph of Arimathea, and how its advent christianised the kingdom. It draws exten-sively on Robert de Boron's *Estoire*, but expands it to mesh with the existing *Lancelot-Graal-Mort Artu* group by accounting for places and characters in the latter. A second writer was responsible for what is known as the Vulgate *Merlin*, which consists of two sections, the *Merlin* proper, and what is usually called the *Suite du Merlin*: this sequence, again partly based on Robert's *Merlin*, is designed to explain Arthur's conception and child-hood, his coronation after he pulls the sword from the stone, his early (and politically and militarily difficult) reign, the formation of the Round Table, his marriage with Guinevere, and his defeat of the enemies of Britain, the

Romans and the Saxons. These two texts – the *Estoire del Saint Graal* and the Vulgate *Merlin* – were undoubtedly the work of two writers different from those of the *Lancelot-Graal-Mort Artu* group; critics until now have always considered that they were composed somewhat later, but recent manuscript evidence might seem to suggest, rather disconcertingly in terms of conventional critical belief, that in fact a cyclical version of the romance including the *Estoire*, the *Merlin* proper, and at least part of the *Lancelot en prose* may have been in existence as early as 1220.[12]

More important for my purposes than debates as to the relative priority of the romances of the Vulgate Cycle, however, are the literary and structural techniques developed by the writers to 'manage' this astonishing mass of material and the vast, pseudo-historical time-frame that the Cycle purports to cover. I say pseudo-historical: the Cycle overall (and especially the Vulgate *Estoire* and *Merlin*, and *La Mort le roi Artu*) borrows from what, in my first paragraph, I called the unimpeachable Geoffrey of Monmouth and the authoritative Wace elements that contemporary readers would almost certainly have treated as pertaining to the historical Arthur, the Arthur who succeeded Uther Pendragon. The *Merlin* makes 'historically authenticated' Saxons invade Britain, while the *Mort Artu* has historical Roman legions fight battles with Knights of the Round Table, and has Arthur meet his end at the hands of the Mordred who is made to destroy Arthur's kingdom in Geoffrey's *Historia Regum Britanniae* (*History of the Kings of Britain*) and in Wace's *Brut*. True, the distinction between 'history' and 'romance' is less clear-cut in the thirteenth century than it seems to us today – but it is as if the Arthurian fictions, that in their verse form could be airily dismissed as *vain et plaisant*, 'fun but false', by the thirteenth-century poet Jehan Bodel,[13] needed, in their more plausible prose form, to be grounded in validating details. The Cycle claims, significantly if spuriously, to have been written by a cleric called Walter Map, who lived, quite historically (d. 1209/10), in England in the reign of Henry II, as if the readers might find it reassuring to have the corroboration of an authentic, and verifiable, voice from Anglo-Norman England.

Pseudo-history, however, provides no more than the barest framework for the narrative core of the Vulgate Cycle: the vast *Lancelot en prose*, composed somewhere between 1215 and 1220, and which occupies no fewer than three large folio volumes in the old Sommer edition (see note 9). Its core, in turn, is an abbreviated adaptation of Chrétien's *Charrete*, the verse romance which, as we saw in Chapter 2, epitomised, with its hero Lancelot and his love for Arthur's queen, Guinevere, the conflict and resolution of love and chivalry, duty and identity. In outline and in this small compass, the episode is identical, simply compressed: a knight shamed by using a cart rescues the queen with whom he is passionately in love. What differs, radically, is the writer's tone: where Chrétien, we remember, was witty, ironic, the writer of the *Lancelot en prose* is passionately committed to Lancelot's heroism and unbending devotion; his romance is to be an unambiguous paean of praise to Guinevere and Lancelot, but on a vast and panoramic scale. To this end, and in some ways rather like the writers of the Continuations that we discussed earlier, the writer takes mere hints present in Chrétien's romance and weaves whole complex, intricate narrative developments, and new ideologies, around them. Chrétien, for instance, in the *Charrete*, had hinted at Lancelot's connections with a fairy patroness (lines 2335–47); from that bare suggestion comes a long narrative development whereby Lancelot is spirited away at his birth by the Dame du Lac, who brings him up beneath the Lake and instructs him in the nature and exercise of chivalry. That pleasingly heroic upbringing, however, requires a further rationalisation: how did a human child come to such an upbringing? The answer, the fictional 'back-story', has to do with a new genealogy: Lancelot's father, King Ban of Benoyc, is unjustly deposed by a certain Claudas and dies beside the Lake – which makes the baby ripe for rescue. This process of retrospective rationalisation via amplification, which Matilda Tomaryn Bruckner calls 'centripetal intertextuality', is characteristic of the Vulgate Cycle as a whole:[14] the mere *fait divers* which is Chrétien's *Charrete* acquires depth and resonance as it is fully embedded, and exploited, in the larger, and far more ideologically complex, world of Arthur's court.

Larger and more complex: as this remark hints, and as I have already suggested, the Vulgate Cycle may have its roots in the story of the love of Lancelot and Guinevere, but it is also, and fundamentally, a component in the overarching pseudo-history of Logres (Arthur's realm, from the Welsh name for England) and Camelot, and above all, in the wake of that fascination with the Grail which we discussed earlier, in pseudo-Redemption history. And this, of course, is something which poses ideological questions, and questions of narrative cohesion. Ideological questions, first. Inescapably, the story of Lancelot's love for Guinevere is tainted by eroticism, and by what is, ultimately and inescapably, treason. As the achievement of the Grail comes to be defined as a badge of spiritual excellence, Lancelot, sullied by that history of adultery, can no longer predominate. The architect(s) or author(s) of the Vulgate Cycle are ingenious. Lancelot, it is said, is named after not one but two of his ancestors: Lancelot certainly, but also Galahad, son of Joseph of Arimathea. For the purposes of the *Queste del Saint Graal*, the authors disjoin the two names: Lancelot remains as the epitome of passionate love, and it is his son, Galahad, named for the ancestor whose connections link him directly to Christ, chaste and unsullied, engendered in mysterious and magical circumstances, who usurps his father's name and takes on the role of spiritual hero. He it is who finally achieves the Grail, presented as the ultimate adventure of Arthur's kingdom – and with that achievement, as the *Queste* reiterates, puts an end to the 'adventures' of Logres; with him, the Grail itself is translated to the 'otherworld' of Sarras from which it cannot return. And lest the Grail quest come to seem a mere parenthesis in the biography of Lancelot and the history of Arthur, it becomes their defining moment: in the wake of the disappearance of the Grail, in that branch of the Vulgate Cycle known as *La Mort le roi Artu*, the Knights of the Round Table lose the chivalric impetus that built the kingdom; Lancelot's and Guinevere's passion, and treachery, are betrayed to Arthur; and Arthur himself is made responsible for his own downfall when his incest with his sister is made to produce the Mordred who had been the motor of the end of the Arthurian world in Geoffrey's *Historia* and Wace's *Brut*.

I have been dismayingly brief here, especially considering the European importance of the Cycle – though oddly enough not in England: apart from *Sir Tristrem* (not strictly Arthurian), the only surviving thirteenth-century Middle English Arthurian romance is *Arthour and Merlin*, which is partly adapted from the Vulgate *Estoire de Merlin* and gives the early history of Arthur's kingdom.[15] Among the thirteenth-century translations and adaptations into Middle Dutch are three components of the so-called *Lancelot compilation*, including a *Queeste vanden Grale* in c. 1280, and three other Lancelot poems; one of them, *Lantsloot van der Haghedochte* ('Lancelot of the Cave'), survives only in fragments, but it must have been a monumental piece of work: some 100,000 lines! Germany, meanwhile, had seen the production of the *Prosa-Lancelot*, a translation of the Vulgate done over a number of years and by a succession of (more or less slavish) translators, and, early in the thirteenth century, a rather original take on the *Lancelot* theme with Ulrich von Zatzikhoven's *Lanzelet*, which seems to create its own Celticising otherworld, and to have developed a Lancelot independent of both Chrétien and the prose romances, a Lancelot who champions Guinevere but without, it seems, becoming her lover.

The complexities of the Vulgate Cycle defy summary, but what does emerge, I hope, is the very distinctive drive towards coherence, towards what is often called *cyclicity*, which marks the construction of this extraordinarily ambitious compilation. This is, of course, something that we noted earlier, with the *Perceval* Continuations and the Robert de Boron cycle – but it is elaborated and perfected in the Vulgate. By 'coherence', here, I mean not only narrative coherence – that is, the care taken to avoid internal contradictions and inconsistencies as between each new component – but also ideological coherence: the provision, to return to a term discussed in Chapter 2, of a *sens* and a *conjointure* to govern the fiction of Arthur's kingdom. As the core story of Lancelot's passion for Guinevere is grafted onto the larger history of Logres,[16] and that again onto the even larger history of the Grail and Redemption, so there emerges the image of an ideological continuity, an ordered vision of world history. It is not fate which destroys the Arthurian idyll, but, as we have seen, moral and spiritual forces generated by the characters themselves, and which are made to find their narrative roots often hundreds of pages previously. This is a vision of world history that is encapsulated in the dream of Fortune's Wheel which Arthur is vouchsafed before the final battle on Salisbury Plain,[17] and which epitomises an organic understanding of world history and the rise and fall of kingdoms and civilisations, subject, as is all creation, to the cycle of birth, maturity and death.

But it is important not to give the impression of a taut, uncompromisingly linear narrative. I spoke earlier of the complexity of this suite of romances; it is no exaggeration to say that the authors luxuriate in the multiplication of individual heroes and their adventures. As many as twenty knights, for instance, are on one occasion dispatched simultaneously in search of Lancelot – and the modern reader senses the writer's pleasure in the ways in which he has controlled different narrative threads and made them intersect in ways which suggest cross-readings.[18] He, or they, have developed a distinctive and original technique to 'manage' these sometimes almost unbearable complexities: a technique usually referred to as *interlace*, or *entrelacement*. By this, on the simplest level, is meant the interweaving, or alternating, of the adventures of a series of individual heroes. But interlace is in fact something rather more ambitious. It involves, for instance, a careful hierarchisation of adventures – so that, in the instance of the twenty knights, the writer explains, carefully, that he will concentrate on Gawain, because it was he who ultimately found Lancelot, and on Hector, because in a separate but interlocking series of adventures he found Gawain and became Gawain's companion in the successful quest for Lancelot. This is, in other words, a controlled narrative: the writer stresses his intention that the adventures of Lancelot and his companions, however multifarious, will remain coherent. Crucial to this sense of control is the pattern of narrative which alternates assembly with dispersal: the great religious festivals which bring the Round Table together at Arthur's court as both the locus for communal activity (feasts, celebrations, above all, tournaments) and the arena from which individual knights, often at the prompting of some great court event (challenges issued, news brought), are scattered to solitary adventure. Crucial also, and for individual heroes, is a pattern alternating chivalric activity with withdrawal: in Lancelot's case, for instance, periods of recovery from wounds, periods of imprisonment, or retirement to the Lake, which make a narrative switch from him to Gawain or Hector structurally plausible. The sense of control extends to the time-line of events within the cycle which, as Ferdinand Lot shows, is worked out with remarkable consistency;[19] it is difficult to avoid the conclusion that the writer(s) are intent on making their huge and ambitious romance cycle conform to a planned and prearranged structure of narrative coincidences and interdependencies.

These two techniques, the structural, cyclicity, and the organisational, interlace, were clearly highly admired: the evidence for this lies in the assiduity with which later writers borrowed them, and indeed refined them. In around 1250, for instance, two writers who call themselves Luce del Gast and Hélie de Boron undertook the composition of a huge prose cycle for the Tristan legend: what is now known as the Prose *Tristan*.[20] The bare bones of this vast romance, and its cast of characters, derive from the verse romances of the twelfth century – but the writers' project involves Tristan's definitive incorporation into the Arthurian universe as one of a trinity of pre-eminent heroes: Lancelot, Gawain and Tristan. In this huge compilation Tristan is only peripherally the tragic lover; much more importance is attached to the string of chivalric adventures, analogous to those of his friend and frequent companion Lancelot, that he undertakes than to his (unsuccessful) participation in the Grail quest; the Cornish element in his life history is minimised by the demonisation of King Mark (who becomes a cowardly poltroon finally responsible for Tristan's death by poisoning). Also remarkable is another case of re-compilation. Not long after the completion of the Vulgate Cycle, somewhere between 1235 and 1240, an unknown compiler (or possibly more than one: he/they call himself/themselves Robert de Boron) undertook a radical revision: what is now known as the Post-Vulgate *Roman du Graal*.[21] This latter remains fragmentary, known only from surviving sections and from translations largely into Spanish and Portuguese. What is astonishing about what must have been a huge and demanding exercise is its drive towards increased coherence, towards a comprehensive history of the Arthurian kingdom. To that end, the author(s) not only modify the Vulgate in order to interlace it with the *Tristan*, they also, and assiduously, incorporate elements of the Prose *Tristan*, so that Tristan, extraordinarily, is associated with Galahad. Contemporary readers, it is plain, appreciated what we think of as unwieldy romances, and demanded more: the Prose *Tristan* was subject to greater or lesser adaptation across the whole of the Middle Ages and into the sixteenth century; the Vulgate Cycle was rewritten or recast several times in the course of the later Middle Ages. In England authors including Malory drew heavily on both the Vulgate Cycle and various of its descendants, including the Post-Vulgate Cycle (now known as the *Roman du Graal*) and the Prose *Tristan*.

But although the importance of the great prose cycles in the elaboration of Arthurian romance cannot be overestimated, it is important to remember a flourishing parallel concern: this time with the adventures, couched in unapologetic verse, of individual Arthurian heroes, and notably Gawain. These romances, twenty-eight or so of them in France, tend to take Chrétien's own romances as models, and are hence often known as the epigonal romances. True, each romance individually seems to have had nothing like the impact of the great prose cycles: a surprising number of them, twenty or so, now exist only in single manuscripts, something which suggests a mode of consumption and reception which remained resolutely local – local enthusiasms presumably accounting for the fashion for large romance-collections (as with anthology manuscripts like Chantilly 472, or Bern, Burgerbibliothek, 354). A large proportion of these discrete verse-romances consists of romances about Gawain:[22] he is made the principal character, for instance, in shorter romances like *Le Chevalier à l'épée* or *La Mule sans frein* (both from the very late twelfth or very early thirteenth centuries). What characterises these early Gawain romances is their burlesque, faintly louche atmosphere: Gawain appears, consistently, as a flirt if not an outright seducer, offering enthusiastic kisses (but never love or marriage) to passing ladies, escaping irate husbands by a hair's breadth. Interestingly, however, rather later writers seem to have wanted to restore Gawain's heroic status, and he appears as a valiant figure in a few thirteenth-century tales: Gawain's adolescence, for instance, is the subject of the fragmentary *Enfances Gauvain*, which dates from the 1230s and seems to be the story of Gawain's rise to chivalric excellence. As the thirteenth century wears on, romances dedicated to Gawain proliferate – but these, it seems, are much influenced by the tentacular development of the prose romances: in *La Vengeance Raguidel*, for instance, or *L'Atre périlleux*, both dating from the mid- to later thirteenth century, Gawain undertakes a string of complicated, extravagant, interwoven adventures, still faintly ironic, or even, in the case of the *Vengeance*, faintly parodic, still leaving Gawain as a seducer sedulously avoiding matrimony.[23] The *Vengeance* in particular draws on many of the livelier motifs of romance: a challenge to Arthur's knights conveyed by a dead body, a decapitation machine, a cloak only to be worn by men whose wives are faithful (and which shows, of course, that the knights of Arthur's court are cuckolds to a man), intelligent greyhounds, a lady who has vowed to ride her horse backwards until she meets Gawain. The romance, in other words, is an exuberant meeting-ground for multitudinous narrative strands: studded with the standard tournaments and duels that test the prowess of its hero, punctuated with the conventional damsels in distress who are the motors of the action, and strongly charged with folklore motifs. As indeed are so many of the discrete romances of the thirteenth century which explore a hinterland of Arthurian romance untouched by the great cycles. There are, for instance, opportunistically, romances devoted to Gawain's sons (*Le Bel Inconnu* and Robert de Blois's *Beaudous*); romances devoted to Gawain's associates (*Gliglois* or Raoul de Houdenc's *Meraugis de Portlesguez*) – and romances in addition which, perhaps for an identifiable readership, invent their own heroes, like the twelfth-century *Fergus*, which seems to have been designed specifically for a Scottish audience, or *Floriant et Florete*, which is very much attached to its setting in Sicily, and which may, therefore, to some extent also reflect particular political and social environments. These discrete romances, in other words, may have been notably responsive to the desires of particular audiences, and it may be, as I suggested earlier, that this is reflected in the fact that most of them seem not to have circulated at all widely.

I stress the variety of romance types – cyclic and discrete – because thirteenth-century Arthurian romance, outside France, reflects just this variety, and just this affection for Gawain as hero. One of the best-known romances in Flemish, for instance, Penninc and Pieter Vostaert's *Walewein* (*c.* 1260), is a headily inventive Gawain story turning on a wonderfully complex quest, in which Gawain plays the leading (but positive) role:[24] accompanied by a talking fox, Gawain embarks on a highly complex series of interlocking quests through picaresque and supernatural adventures (fights with dragons and devils, encounters with the dead). In Germany, at roughly the same date, another verse romance, *Diu Crône*, by a certain Heinrich von dem Türlin, also focuses, with a decidedly satirical, not to say misogynist touch on Gawain:[25] it is, rather loosely, a Grail romance in which Gawain actually achieves the adventures of the Grail – but it is distinctly comic and irreverent, and Gawain, despite his success, is difficult to see as a worthy hero. Heinrich draws on a very wide range of sources, from Chrétien to the Continuations to (perhaps) the *Perlesvaus*, to construct a Grail world in which the hero is resolutely secular.

These last paragraphs may, I fear, have seemed very much like a catalogue – but it is only so that we can bring out the extraordinary richness of the thirteenth-century Arthur in France and beyond: the riotous proliferation of Gawain romances on the one hand, and, on the other, the variety of tones and motifs and geographical settings which characterise not just these, but also the other Arthurian verse-romances. The twelfth century, in France, is often thought of as the heyday of romance; in fact, the thirteenth century is richer by far, more inventive, more exuberant – and, it seems, more receptive to Arthurian literature of all sorts. It is the thirteenth century, in other words, that institutionalises the parameters of what the modern reader will think of as 'the Arthurian legend'; that makes Arthur,

author promises his audience 'a tale that trewe es and nobyll / Off the ryeall renkys of the Rownnde Table' (lines 16–17). Indeed the tale does purport to be both true and noble; but modern criticism has put in question, not only its truth, of course, but also its nobility, and especially the nobility of its hero. So far from seeing in the poem the glorification of a great national commander, many readers – including its most recent editor, Hamel – have understood it as an anti-war piece, prompted perhaps by reaction against the inconclusive campaigns of Edward III in France. Thus Hamel speaks of 'the poem's criticism of imperialistic war'.[6] Where fighting is concerned, the poet's narrative manner will naturally amplify violence and injury as well as courage and skill; but this cannot in itself be taken to imply any condemnation of the activity. The main critical issue lies elsewhere, in that part of the action, added by the poet, where Arthur passes from defending his own territory to conquering lands held by the Emperor of Rome, first in Lorraine and then in Italy. It is at this point that Arthur's war-plans, according to some, 'become openly imperialistic' (Hamel's note to lines 2399–405). But such judgements either overlook or dismiss Arthur's claim to the Empire as his rightful 'heritage' (lines 359, 643, 1309), a claim based on his descent from those British kings – Belinus, Brennius and Constantine – who formerly ruled Rome (lines 275–87, 520–1, 1310). To modern eyes, of course, this justification will seem neither good history nor good international law; but just such an argument, as noticed earlier, was used by English kings of the time, when they cited Geoffrey of Monmouth in support of their claims on Scotland.

Yet there is explicit criticism of Arthur at one point, in the course of the account of his dream about the Wheel of Fortune, added by the poet at lines 3227–455. This episode was probably suggested by one that occurs at a different point in the French *Mort Artu*, where Arthur, on the eve of his final battle, dreams of Fortune throwing him down from her wheel and teaching him that '"earthly pride is such that no one, however high he sits, can fail to fall from his worldly eminence"' (Lacy, Ch. 176, IV.150). This dream made an impression on other writers, too, inspiring Boccaccio to include a potted history of Arthur's reign in his *De Casibus Virorum Illustrium*, where Arthur's rise and fall are meant to illustrate the fickleness of Fortune's favour. The English poet, however, is unusual in combining the topic of Fortune with that of the Nine Worthies and so associating his hero with 'the nobileste namede in erthe' (line 3439), all of whom have suffered, or will suffer, the same fate – the six Classical and Old Testament heroes from the past, and the two Christians still to come, Charlemagne and Godfrey of Bouillon. Both these latter were to fight against the enemies of God (lines 2422–35), and Arthur can claim the same crusader justification for his conquests, since the Emperor of Rome, himself a heretic (line 1307), has an army largely composed of pagans and Saracens. Nevertheless, the 'philosopher' who interprets Arthur's dream for him, speaking like a Christian priest to a man newly faced by the imminence of death, does condemn his way of life and calls upon him to confess and repent:

> 'Thow has schedde myche blode, and schalkes distroyede,
> Sakeles, in cirquytrie, in sere kynges landis.
> Schryfe the of thy schame and schape for thyn ende.' (lines 3398–400)
> ['You have shed much blood and arrogantly killed innocent men in many
> kings' lands. Confess your shameful deeds and prepare for your end.']

The charges are serious, for sure, nor does Arthur attempt to deny them; but the philosopher's judgement has no apparent consequences for the rest of the poem, either for Arthur's own conduct or for the author's view of him. Arthur responds to the episode only with anger at the news about treachery back home; and the ensuing progress of his revenge on Mordred seems to leave any moral criticism quite behind. It is a just cause, justly pursued; and in his last battle against the forces of the usurper (including again many 'Saracens') Arthur figures simply as a brave and prayerful Christian leader who wins great glory in death.

Romance

The chronicle tradition stemming from Geoffrey's *Historia* had little time for the marvellous or for the individual adventures of Arthur's knights; but Wace went so far as to allow that such wonders and adventures did occur – in the twelve years of peace which followed the young Arthur's first conquests: 'In this time of great peace I speak of – I do not know if you have heard of it – the wondrous events [*merveilles*] appeared and the adventures were sought out which ... are so often told about Arthur that they have become the stuff of fiction: not all lies, not all truth, neither total folly nor total wisdom.'[7] Robert Manning followed Wace in assigning 'the many adventures that men read of in rhyme' to these same twelve years.[8] So it was open to fourteenth-century writers to give their romances of adventure some semblance of historical respectability by attributing them to that early, carefree period. The author of *Sir Gawain and the Green Knight* evidently had this in mind when, after his serious historical prologue tracing the succession of British kings down from the Trojan Brutus, he introduced Arthur and his followers as all 'in their first age' (*Sir Gawain*, line 54), living in expectation, not of war, but of adventures and marvels.

In France, Jean Froissart, the contemporary of Geoffrey Chaucer, better known for his *Chroniques*, follows this tradition in his *Meliador*, described as 'the last and the longest of the French Arthurian romances in verse'.[9] He begins his enormous poem by setting its action at a time when Arthur was reigning in his youth, going on to explain that this was nine or ten years (Froissart the chronicler!) before knights such as Lancelot and Gawain rose to their prominence. Yet that was already a time when 'many fine knightly feats [*chevaleries*] came to pass in Great Britain' (lines 38–9). In *Meliador* these feats are prompted by the vow of a Scottish princess, Hermondine, that she would marry only the knight acknowledged at Arthur's court as the most valiant and courteous of all. Many aspirants for her hand, including the hero, Meliador, undertake the quest; and he and his rivals perform many 'belles chevaleries' in single encounters and tournaments. The court of Arthur and his queen at Carlyon provides a central focus for this proliferation of adventures, but none of the knights undertaking them, with the single exception of Sagremor, has any earlier history in Arthurian writing. Froissart simply invents them, taking their knightly exploits out of stock. By the fourteenth century, the great days of French Arthurian romance had passed, and sophisticated poets such as Froissart, when they did occasionally use an Arthurian setting, paid little attention to the great original heroes and their too-well-known stories.

The same is generally true of other writers of the period. Much energy is spent, not on the writing of new Arthurian romances, but on taking stock of inherited material, and on organising it into coherent cycles. The early-fourteenth-century Middle Dutch *Lancelot Compilatie*, possibly compiled by Lodewijk van Velthem, is the product of such energies, as is the Italian *La Tavola Ritonda*, an eclectic amalgamation of French and native Italian Arthurian traditions. Thomas Malory's *Morte Darthur*, discussed in the next chapter, is an English example. Of course, there are exceptions. In France the vast *Perceforest* (mid-fourteenth century) tells the story of how chivalry was established in Britain under Arthur's forebears, while *Ysaïe le Triste* (c. 1400) follows the adventures of Tristan's son. Yet while these original productions are consciously Arthurian by association, their focus is clearly not on Arthur and the 'golden generation', but on the generations that preceded and followed them.[10] It is as if, like their English contemporary Chaucer, French writers considered that there was no further mileage to be had from the original heroes and their well-known stories – from 'Gawayn, with his olde curteisye', or from 'the book of Launcelot de Lake, / That wommen holde in ful greet reverence' (*Canterbury Tales* v.95, VII.3212–13).

Chaucer did write one story which he set in 'th'olde dayes of the Kyng Arthour, / Of which that Britons speken greet honour' (*Canterbury Tales*

III.857–8), assigning it to his Wife of Bath – evidently one of those women who held the romances of Arthur in great reverence. But in 'The Wife of Bath's Tale', as in *Meliador*, the court of Arthur plays little part in the action, and the male protagonist, being anonymous, has no Arthurian credentials. Yet other English poets of the time took more interest in knights of the Round Table than Chaucer did. Indeed, whereas in France, as in Germany, the main age of Arthurian writing lay well in the past, the fourteenth century saw a belated flowering in England, not only with *Sir Gawain and the Green Knight* but also with a number of poems that derive more directly from classic French forerunners.

Ywain and Gawain is a poem translated from the *Yvain* of Chrétien de Troyes. The rendering was made somewhere in the more northern parts of England, perhaps about the middle of the century. Nothing is known about the author or his circumstances; but his editors assert that 'the poem is clearly the work of a minstrel catering for the sober, realistic audience of a provincial baron's hall, an audience whose sensibilities and sympathies were not adjusted to Chrétien's elaborate and subtle representations of courtly love or to high-flown chivalric sentiment'.[11] The English poet certainly does cut down on the more elaborate and high-flown passages that he found in the French, manifesting some impatience with Chrétien's leisurely narrative and reducing it from 6,818 lines to 4,032; but it will not do to describe him as a minstrel – or not as that term is commonly understood. In reality *Ywain and Gawain* is the most writerly of all the English Arthurian metrical romances. The anonymous author has mastered an English version of the French octosyllabic couplet, saying what he has to say in verse that is generally strong and pointed, with very few of those fillers and tags commonly associated with minstrel rhyming.

While reducing the French by more than a third, the English sacrifices little in its telling of the story: Ywain's killing of the Knight of the Fountain, his marriage to that knight's widow, his departure to follow knightly adventure, his failure to return to his wife on the promised day, his resulting remorse and madness, and his subsequent feats of chivalry leading up to the climactic battle with his friend Gawain and the eventual reconciliation with his wife. Where Chrétien indulges in what must have seemed preciosity to his English translator, the latter does make some quite drastic cuts; but he is not blind to the more subtle points of the French. Thus, Chrétien expatiates on the curious conjunctions between Love and Hate in a story whose hero falls in love with a woman who has every reason to hate him as the killer of her husband, a hero who later, without knowing it, fights the friend that he loves. The reflections of Yvain on falling in love with Laudine occupy 150 lines in the French: Yvain 'aimme la rien qui plus le het' ['loves the being who hates him most', line 1361]. The translator shortens this passage drastically (lines 871–906), but renders the essential point well in his northern English:

Luf, that es so mekil of mayne,
Sare had wownded Sir Ywayne,
That whare so he sal ride or ga,
His hert sho has that es his fa. (lines 871–4)
['Love, whose strength is so great, has wounded Sir Ywain grievously,
    so that, wherever he goes, on horse or on foot, she who is his enemy
    has possession of his heart.']

Again, the hero's last battle with his friend Gawain, each of them unknown to the other, prompts Chrétien to an elaborate passage of reflection on Amors and Haine (lines 5998–6105). After 'proving' that the two knights may each be said truly both to love and hate each other at the same time, he goes on to explain how this can be, with an allegory of Love and Hate sharing the same lodgings. The English poet cuts the allegory, but makes Chrétien's point clearly enough. It is a great wonder, he says,

That trew luf and so grete envy
Als bitwix tham twa was than,
Might bath at anes be in a man. (lines 3522–4)
['that true love and such great hostility as was then between the two
    of them should both be in a man at the same time.']

There are signs, however, that the translator himself thought of the story in somewhat different terms. The opening scene of the French describes how, at Arthur's Pentecost feast, knights and ladies talk among themselves mostly about the joys and sorrows of love, and this prompts Chrétien to reflect on the decline of love in modern times (lines 13–32). In the English version, however, the knights and ladies speak about deeds of arms and hunting, not about love, and the poet goes on to lament the decline, not of love, but of *trowth*, 'truth' (lines 33–40). This word, a key item in fourteenth-century English moral vocabulary, denoted all kinds of fidelity – to a lord, a companion, or a lover, and also to one's own pledged word. The story of Ywain positively invited interpretation in these terms, since it turned on the hero's failure to rejoin his wife on the appointed day, thus both breaking his promise and showing himself no longer 'trew of love' (line 1539). In both versions, the wife's messenger accuses the hero of treachery, but the English strengthens this with an emphatic triple condemnation: Ywain is 'traytur untrew and trowthles' (line 1626). Such is the grave fault from which Ywain has to redeem himself, first by the madness and degradation that his realisation of it causes, and then by his faithful performance of knightly good deeds in the rest of the poem.

The romances of Chrétien de Troyes have one other Middle English derivative, *Sir Percyvell of Galles*, but this is very far from being a translation. Indeed, it differs so widely from Chrétien's Perceval story, the *Conte du Graal*, that it may well derive from some other, though certainly related, source.[12] Its manner is popular and quite unlike Chrétien's. Thus the English poet exploits much more broadly than the French all the potentialities for comedy in the ignorance of a young hero brought up by his widowed mother in the wilds: Percyvell is a 'fool' knowing nothing of chivalry and making grossly silly mistakes, as when he persists in referring to knights' chargers as 'mares'. *Sir Percyvell* employs a version of the tail-rhyme stanza that Chaucer imitated in 'Sir Thopas', and its style is rough-and-ready, with many loose and approximate forms of expression. Nothing is known about the circumstances of its composition, but the poem is a distinctly less writerly piece than *Ywain and Gawain*, as one can see from its opening words: 'Lef, lythes to me / Two wordes or thre' ['Friends, listen to me for just a couple of words']. Its version of the Perceval story may be compared with that in a contemporary Italian *cantare*, the *Carduino*. *Cantari* are said to have been recited by entertainers in the piazzas of Tuscan cities, on Arthurian subjects among many others. *Carduino* models the career of its eponymous hero quite closely on that of Chrétien's boy Perceval up to the time when he arrives at the court of Arthur: Carduino too is brought up in the wild by his widowed mother knowing nothing of chivalry.[13] Like *Sir Percyvell*, this poem represents medieval Arthurian narrative at its most popular, as entertainment for a listening audience. In both, the story is simplified and the style adapted for the ready understanding of listeners.

In 'Sir Thopas', his burlesque imitation of such facile verse, Chaucer makes an unmistakeable borrowing from *Sir Percyvell* (*Canterbury Tales* VII.915–16, very like *Percyvell* lines 5–7). He would probably have agreed with his Harry Bailey in condemning the poem as 'rym dogerel'; but it is far from suffering from that other defect which so exasperated the Host. Whereas the story in 'Sir Thopas' shows no sign of getting anywhere, *Percyvell* has a strong forward thrust directed towards its emphatic happy ending. Here as in *Carduino* – though in very different circumstances – the hero ends up married to his beloved and reunited with his old mother. The *Conte du Graal* (*Story of the Grail*) has no such ending, for Chrétien left the poem unfinished with many loose ends after more than 9,000 lines. The English follows the sequence of events in the *Conte* quite closely up to Percyvell's first victory when he killed the Red Knight; but thereafter it largely takes its own course, paying no attention to the parallel adventures of Chrétien's Gawain and even avoiding all mention of the Holy Grail. The result has the familiar shape of a traditional tale: a young and innocent protagonist overcomes all adversaries, revenges the death of his father, and wins a wife and a kingdom. Unlike Carduino, Percyvell does not quite live happily ever after, for the last stanza reports that he died fighting in the Holy Land, like some of the knights at the end of Malory's *Morte Darthur*; but that was in itself the best of all possible endings, since those who died on crusade were thought to go straight to heaven.

Three other English poems of the time also go back, directly or indirectly, to individual twelfth-century French sources: *Sir Landevale*, *Sir Launfal*, and *Lybeaus Desconus*. The first two of these both derive from one of the Breton lays of Marie de France, *Lanval*.[14] The earlier of them, *Sir Landevale*, is translated from Marie's text, closely at times and freely at others, in the same octosyllabic couplets as its original. In Marie's poem, as in 'The Wife of Bath's Tale', women command the plot. There is a mysterious mistress, who grants Lanval her love on the one condition that he never reveals it, and a wicked queen who, when he rejects her advances, accuses him of being gay and so provokes him into speaking out in praise of his secret mistress. *Landevale* cuts the allusion to homosexuality and much simplifies the legal processes that arise when the queen falsely accuses Landevale to King Arthur. The English poet generally makes the points of Marie's elegant narrative more explicit, with much more clarifying direct speech than in the French, as he does at the end of the story. In both poems, once the otherworld mistress has vindicated the hero by revealing herself to Arthur's court, she rides away, carrying Lanval off to the Isle of Avalon, never to be heard of again. But on what terms does the lady now come to accept back a lover who has broken her solemn prohibition (*geis*, in Irish)? Where Marie's swift and elegant conclusion offers no answer, *Landevale* explains with a new dialogue of apology and forgiveness between the two.

Later in the fourteenth century, *Landevale* was rewritten and considerably expanded in the tail-rhyme metre by a poet who, most unusually for such a writing in English, names himself: 'Thomas Chestre made thys tale.'[15] This version, *Sir Launfal*, is much more remote in both style and spirit from Marie's than *Landevale*. In particular, Chestre takes pains to establish the masculine credentials of a hero who, in the earlier versions, does little more than fall in love and suffer at the hands of women. In his version, the fairy Tryamour gives Launfal a steed and a squire, both of which he then employs, first in a tournament (lines 433–504) and then in single combat with a gigantic adversary (lines 505–612). Launfal's victories in these added episodes vindicate his masculine 'noblesse', helping to make him, so far as the story allowed, more of a conventional hero. At the end of the poem again, where both Marie and her English translator have Lanval jumping up to sit behind his mistress on her palfrey, Chestre saves his dignity by mounting him on his own warhorse; and even after he has ridden off with her 'into Fairy', Chestre's hero persists in his knightly vocation. For ever since, upon a certain day of the year, when his steed is heard to neigh, Launfal can be seen waiting to fight any challenger who wishes 'to keep his armour from rust'.

Thomas Chestre was a contemporary of Chaucer, whose tail-rhyme burlesque evidently owes some of its well-worn epithets and predictable rhymes to *Launfal*. 'Sir Thopas' also has a list of notable romances which includes 'Sir Lybeux', alluding to what is probably another of Chestre's writings, *Lybeaus Desconus*.[16] The hero of this poem, the Fair Unknown, comes to Arthur's court knowing neither his own name (Guinglain) nor that of his father (Gawain). His second-generation adventure takes a classic circular form: departure from the court on a quest followed by return there in triumph. His assignment is to rescue the lady of Synadowne from two evil enchanters, an adventure in which he succeeds only after proving his prowess in six testing encounters with a variety of knights and giants on the way. Unlike *Launfal*, of which only one copy is known, *Lybeaus Desconus* survives in six manuscripts, and these exhibit clear signs of textual transmission by memory. It may also be that Chestre himself relied on his memory for the story he tells, which corresponds to the first part of the much longer version given by Renaud de Beaujeu in his *Le Bel Inconnu*, written about 1200.[17] But the exact transmission of the material is obscure. A similarly abbreviated version appears in the second canto of the aforesaid Italian *Carduino*, where the hero, after his reception by King Arthur, is dispatched by him on the same Fair Unknown quest. If Chestre had indeed read Renaud's poem and was recalling it, then his memory has greatly simplified the story. Thus the hero's encounter on his way to Synadowne with the enchantress of the Ile d'Or takes a quite different form. In the French, the lady makes just a single visit to Guinglain's bedroom, causing him to fall seriously in love with her, with consequences for the rest of the story as Renaud tells it. In *Lybeaus*, the hero stays for more than a year with the enchantress – 'Alas he ne hadde ybe chast!' (line 1414) – yet nothing follows from this discreditable episode. In particular, it proves to have no bearing on his subsequent marriage to the lady whom he rescues at Synadowne. Chestre's poem, unlike Renaud's, is content to rely on its simple departure-and-return structure, offering the reader little more than a string of exciting episodes that can be enjoyed and then forgotten.

Much the most remarkable of Arthurian writings in Middle English is *Sir Gawain and the Green Knight*.[18] Its sole surviving manuscript copy was made about the year 1400 and the composition of poem itself, in all probability, dates from not long before that. Like *Morte Arthure*, *Sir Gawain* belongs to the so-called Alliterative Revival in fourteenth-century England, telling its story in the distinctively insular alliterative line (in which the same initial sound is repeated in at least three stressed syllables). Although the identity of the author is unknown, his dialect of English shows him to have been brought up in the north-west Midlands, somewhere near the borders of Cheshire and Staffordshire – the same provincial region that the poem's hero enters after crossing onto the Wirral in his journey to the Green Chapel. Yet *Sir Gawain* is very far from insular or provincial in character. The author has evidently read widely in courtly French romances, including those of Chrétien de Troyes and the various continuations of his *Conte du Graal*; and he takes for granted a familiarity with the conduct of affairs there, such as the conventional behaviours of a challenging knight, a welcoming host, or a tempting lady.[19] Thus he would not have expected his readers to be surprised, as many are today, by the explanation he offers for the chief marvel in the poem, a Green Knight who can survive decapitation. French prose romances like to rationalise such wonders by tracing them back to the book-learning of Merlin.[20] So when at the Green Chapel Bertilak attributes his transformation to the magic arts learned by Morgan le Faye – a traditional adversary of Arthur and Guinevere – as a result of her love affair with that notable clerk (lines 2446–61), he is to be understood as doing no more than supply what any reader of French romance might look for in the circumstances. The explanation is taken out of stock.

Despite this profound general debt, however, *Sir Gawain* has no single French original. Rather, its plot represents a fresh combination – what Chrétien called a *conjointure* – of elements drawn from several sources. Chief among these is the adventure now known as the Beheading Game, proposed by the Green Knight at Arthur's court and undertaken there by Sir Gawain. The terms of this strange 'Christmas game', as the Green Knight calls it, make two kinds of demand on the hero. To behead the challenger with a single stroke in the first place calls for strength and skill, and to present himself later and submit to a return blow requires him to keep both his nerve and his word. This story, which can be traced back to Irish sources, figures as an episode in four French romances, most notably in the *Livre de Caradoc*, part of one of the continuations of Chrétien's unfinished *Perceval* poem.[21] In all these other versions it is individual knights who are put to the test; but *Sir Gawain* presents the adventure as a challenge to the reputation of the whole Round Table (lines 309–15, 2456–8), and it is as a representative of his great order of chivalry that Sir Gawain engages upon it. In the event, he successfully fulfils the terms of the affair, turning up on time at the Green Chapel and submitting without resistance to the single return blow. So, when he returns to Camelot, he can be welcomed by his companions as a hero who has upheld 'the renoun of the Rounde Table' (line 2519) by achieving an adventure that had seemed to promise nothing but either shameful failure or certain death.

The logic of stories such as this predicts that a hero who faithfully keeps to his agreement will be spared by his adversary at the return match, as Caradoc is spared by his tester with praise for his courage and trustworthiness; and it promises to be simply so in *Sir Gawain* too, for when the Green Knight first welcomes Gawain for their final encounter at the Green Chapel, he congratulates him on keeping his appointment and on 'timing his travel as a true man should' (lines 2238, 2241). Yet in the scene that follows, the Green Knight seems much more concerned with Gawain's conduct, not in the Beheading Game, but in the so-called Exchange of Winnings episode. This turns out to have been a second, supervenient test of the hero's qualities as a 'true man', initiated when his host at Hautdesert proposed that over the last three days of his Christmas stay they should agree to exchange whatever they happened to acquire – he on the hunting field, his guest in the castle. The seductive visits of the host's wife on each of these three days present obvious sexual trials, as in *Lybeaus* and many other romances, but Gawain resists her advances, though not without some difficulty and much embarrassment, and he gets away with nothing more compromising than a series of kisses – and these he duly pays over to his host each evening as 'winnings'. It is in the aftermath of these temptations, indeed, after the lady has finally confessed defeat, that the crisis of these scenes occurs. In parting, the lady offers Gawain as a keepsake what she says is a belt of hers that has life-saving powers, and Gawain, faced with the prospect of death at the Green Chapel on the following day, accepts it and agrees to conceal the gift from her husband. By so doing, he commits himself to breaching the settled terms of the exchange agreement.

It is customary for a knight on quest to encounter a variety of challenges on the way to his main adventure, and these commonly, as in the English *Lybeaus*, do no more than severally confirm his chivalric credentials. The *Gawain*-poet, however, passes rapidly over such miscellaneous encounters, with dragons, giants and the like (lines 715–25), reserving his descriptive powers for the hero's Christmas stay at Hautdesert. The sheer length of this episode (1313 lines out of a total 2530) will alert a reader to its likely importance, but Gawain is not reading the poem. Indeed, where the Exchange of Winnings is concerned – a test not drawn from the Arthurian repertoire – he has every reason to be off his guard. It is proposed by his host simply as a Christmas game, intended to keep them both entertained over the three slack days that remain between the breaking up of the main holiday house-party and Gawain's departure on New Year's Day. Yet at Hautdesert, as at Camelot, he has plighted his troth, swearing three times to the Exchange in due form (lines 1108–12, 1403–9, 1668–9); and it is to this issue, in the event, that his adversary chiefly addresses himself at the Green Chapel, withholding two swings of his great axe in recognition of Gawain's good faith of the first two days and inflicting a flesh wound in return for his failure on the third. In his speech of explanation, the Green Knight judges him to have been lacking 'a little' in his 'lewté' or good faith on that occasion (lines 2366–8); yet he blames him the less, he says, since it was because 'he loved his life' that Gawain clung on to the belt – a politer way of referring to his fear of death, a natural passion which this poem acknowledges much more freely than most romances of adventure. Taking account of everything, the adversary – now at last revealed as Sir Bertilak de Hautdesert – passes a most favourable final judgement upon his fellow knight, and his parting words declare his high esteem for Gawain's 'grete trauthe' (line 2470). Yet Gawain on his part responds to these revelations with violent self-reproaches, accusing himself of cowardice in the face of death, and above all of 'trecherye and untrawthe' (lines 2378–86).

Despite his successful accomplishment of the beheading adventure, his return to Camelot brings no relief for Gawain. He persists in his deep mortification and accepts no comfort from the congratulations of the court. This makes for a most unusual ending. Heroes of romance not uncommonly commit faults, but by the end these will most often be either forgiven or forgotten, as in *Ywain*, *Launfal* or *Lybeaus Desconus*. *Sir Gawain*, though, ends on an unresolved discord, with the hero, his adversary and his companions quite failing to agree on the outcome of the affair. The continuing mortification of the hero itself has ample warrant. Earlier in the poem, when Gawain first set out from Camelot, the poet took advantage of the liberties allowed in Arthurian heraldry to invent for him a new coat of arms, a gold pentangle on a red field. The lengthy interpretation of this at lines 619–65 lists many qualities in which Gawain is known to excel, but the overall significance of the sign derives from its first establishment by no less than Solomon 'in bytoknyng of trawthe', as an emblem of 'truth', or integrity. So it cannot be a light matter for its bearer to return to Camelot, as he does, with his pentangle supplemented by a new 'token of untrawthe' (line 2509) – the lady's green belt, which he swears he will wear for the rest of his life as a reminder of his fault. Yet it does not follow that one can dismiss the much more favourable judgement of his adversary. Sir Bertilak has had inside knowledge of the whole affair, as both Green Knight and lord of Hautdesert, and his assessment of it seems eminently fair and balanced – the sort of balance that Gawain himself should not be expected to achieve, or not, certainly, in the immediate aftermath of his experience. More questionable are the responses of Gawain's companions at Camelot. Modern criticism, indeed, has been inclined to condemn them for frivolity. So one scholar sees the poem as aiming its representations of 'the immature young king and his coterie of young chamber knights' at the court of Richard II, commonly criticised at the time in just such terms.[22] Yet Camelot, I have suggested, had every good reason to congratulate its representative on upholding the renown of the Round Table, and living to tell the tale. All three parties, in fact, can justify their differing assessments by virtue of their very different standings in the affair. It makes for a challenging conclusion to this, the most artful of all Arthurian writings in English.

NOTES

1 See Juliet Vale, 'Arthur in English Society', in *AoE*, pp. 185–96, and James P. Carley, 'Arthur in English History', *ibid.*, pp. 47–67.

2 *The Brut or The Chronicles of England*, ed. F. W. D. Brie, EETS, o.s. 131, 136 (Oxford University Press, 1906, 1908), pp. 67–91. See Lister M. Matheson, *The Prose 'Brut': The Development of a Middle English Chronicle*, Medieval and Renaissance Texts and Studies 180 (Tempe, AZ: Medieval and Renaissance Texts and Studies, 1998). Discussion and references in *AoE*, pp. 32–8.

3 Robert Mannyng of Brunne, *The Chronicle*, ed. Idelle Sullens, Medieval and Renaissance Texts and Studies (Binghamton, NY: Centre for Medieval and Early Renaissance Studies, 1996). It is discussed along with other chronicles by Thorlac Turville-Petre, *England the Nation: Language, Literature, and National Identity, 1290–1340* (Oxford: Clarendon Press, 1996), Ch. 3.

4 *Morte Arthure: A Critical Edition*, ed. Mary Hamel, Garland Medieval Texts 9 (New York and London: Garland, 1984).

5 On the sources, see Hamel's edition, pp. 36–42.

6 Hamel's edition, p. 57, with reference to other discussions. An early statement of a similar view is by William Matthews, *The Tragedy of Arthur: A Study of the Alliterative 'Morte Arthure'* (Berkeley, CA: University of California Press, 1960).

7 Wace, *Roman de Brut*, ed. and trans. Judith Weiss, *Wace's 'Roman de Brut', a History of the British: Text and Translation*, 2nd edn, Exeter Medieval English Texts and Studies (University of Exeter Press, 2002), lines 9787–95. See Ad Putter, 'Finding Time for Romance: Mediaeval Arthurian Literary History', *Medium Ævum*, 63 (1994), 1–16.

8 Mannyng, *Chronicle*, lines 10391–400. Laȝamon expanded upon the same passage of Wace in his *Brut*, lines 11454–75.

9 I cite from the discussion of the poem by Alexandre Micha, in *ALMA*, pp. 391–2. *Meliador* extends to more than 30,000 lines in the edition by Auguste Longnon, 3 vols., SATF (Paris: Firmin Didot, 1895–9).

10 See Richard Trachsler, *Clôtures du cycle Arthurien: Etude et textes*, Publications romanes et françaises 215 (Geneva: Droz, 1996), especially pp. 258–9.

11 *Ywain and Gawain*, ed. Albert B. Friedman and Norman T. Harrington, EETS, o.s. 254 (Oxford University Press, 1964), p. xvii.

12 For a text of *Sir Percyvell*, see *Middle English Metrical Romances*, ed. W. H. French and C. B. Hale (New York: Prentice Hall, 1930, reissued in one vol., New York: Russell and Russell, 1964), pp. 529–603. Robert W. Ackerman supposes a lost source (*ALMA*, pp. 509–11); but see Ad Putter, 'Story Line and Story Shape in *Sir Percyvell of Galles* and Chrétien de Troyes's *Conte du Graal*', in *Pulp Fictions of Medieval England: Essays in Popular Romance*, ed. Nicola McDonald (Manchester University Press, 2004), pp. 171–96.

13 *Carduino*, ed. P. Rajna in his *I Cantari di Carduino giuntovi quello di Tristano e Lancielotto* (Bologna: Romagnoli, 1873; reissued Bologna: Forni, 1968).

14 The edition of *Sir Launfal* by A. J. Bliss (London and Edinburgh: Thomas Nelson, 1960) also includes texts of *Sir Landevale* and Marie's *Lanval*. On all three, see A. C. Spearing, 'Marie de France and her Middle English Adaptors', *Studies in the Age of Chaucer*, 12 (1990), 117–56; also Myra Stokes, 'Lanval to Sir Launfal: A Story Becomes Popular', in *The Spirit of Medieval English Popular Romance*, ed. Ad Putter and Jane Gilbert, Longman Medieval and Renaissance Library (Harlow: Longman, 2000), pp. 56–77, and *AoE*, pp. 130–5.

15 *Sir Launfal*, ed. Bliss, line 1039. Bliss, pp. 24–31, discusses other, minor sources, including the anonymous Breton lay *Graelent*.

16 *Lybeaus Desconus*, ed. M. Mills, EETS o.s. 261 (Oxford University Press, 1969), discussing Chestre's authorship on pp. 64–8. Echoes of *Launfal* and *Lybeaus* in 'Sir Thopas' are pointed out in the notes to the *Riverside Chaucer*.

17 *Le Bel Inconnu*, ed. and notes by M. Perret, trans. M. Perret and I. Weill, CFMA (Paris: Champion, 2003). Lines 1415–16 of *Lybeaus* suggest that Chestre may have known the later part of Renaud's story, where the hero returns to the Ile d'Or and suffers at the hands of its lady.

18 See generally *A Companion to the Gawain-Poet*, ed. Derek Brewer and Jonathan Gibson, Arthurian Studies 38 (Cambridge: D. S. Brewer, 1997); also *AoE*, pp. 164–83.

19 See Ad Putter, *'Sir Gawain and the Green Knight' and French Arthurian Romance* (Oxford: Clarendon Press, 1995).

20 See Elspeth M. Kennedy, 'The Role of the Supernatural in the First Part of the Old French Prose *Lancelot*', in *Studies in Medieval Literature and Languages in Memory of Frederick Whitehead*, ed. W. Rothwell and others (Manchester University Press, 1973), pp. 173–84.

21 On the sources, see Elisabeth Brewer's chapter in *Companion to the Gawain-Poet*, pp. 243–55. For *Caradoc* in particular, see Larry D. Benson, *Art and Tradition in Sir Gawain and the Green Knight* (New Brunswick, NJ: Rutgers University Press, 1965), pp. 16–36 and 249–57.

22 Christine Chism, *Alliterative Revivals* (Philadelphia, PA: University of Pennsylvania Press, 2002), p. 91.

5

BARRY WINDEATT

The fifteenth-century Arthur

From any modern perspective the dominating achievement of fifteenth-century English Arthurian literature is Sir Thomas Malory's *Le Morte Darthur*. But Malory's *Morte* was not composed until 1469–70 and not printed until 1485, and its compendious perspective filled a space previously occupied for English audiences by works focused on particular aspects and fragments of Arthurian history, supplemented for some by familiarity with continental traditions. In Caxton's preface to his *Morte* edition – which stresses the number of books about Arthur in other languages, yet only 'somme in Englysshe, but nowher nygh alle' – the material proofs of Arthur's historicity include books (Malory p. cxlv.20–2):[1] not only Arthur's tomb at Glastonbury but *Polychronicon*'s account of his body's rediscovery and reburial; not only 'at Wynchester the Rounde Table' but the accounts of Arthur's life in Geoffrey of Monmouth and Boccaccio's *De Casibus Virorum Illustrium* (or, in practice, Lydgate's influential English version in his *Fall of Princes* [1431–8]). Malory's *Morte* is the outcome of a discerning and knowledgeable ambition to create an 'Arthuriad' in English, a compendium that draws together sequentially the authoritative accounts (largely to be translated from French sources) of all significant aspects of King Arthur's life and reign and the history of the Round Table fellowship. Malory's Arthuriad belongs to a late-medieval Europe-wide fashion for compendious Arthurian compilations. In the fifteenth century, these include the scribe-compiler Micheau Gonnot's attempt (c. 1470) to select, condense and recombine his vast French prose romance sources into a coherent Arthuriad, entitled *Lancelot du Lac* (but including Tristan and Merlin material); and the Bavarian scribe Ulrich Fuetrer's compilation from German Arthurian sources in his *Buch der Abenteuer* (c. 1481–92). One aspect of Malory's immense subsequent influence lies in his perception that there might be a unity that made sense of Arthur's career and the Round Table world as a whole. In exploring the fifteenth-century Arthur this chapter will broadly follow the sequence in which Malory treats his Arthurian themes, while also relating *Morte Darthur* to contemporary witnesses.

Tales of King Arthur

Before Malory the prevalent fifteenth-century view of Arthur's career remained that of Geoffrey of Monmouth, as mediated through the vernacular prose chronicles or Bruts, in which Arthur was a charismatically energetic and effective king, supported by his loyal knight Gawain in conquering extensive dominions until brought down by his usurping nephew Mordred. Such is the view of *Arthur*, a 642-line English verse outline of Arthur's life, written in the late fourteenth or early fifteenth century.[2] This chronicle-based perspective on Arthur was supplemented by audiences' exposure to romances focused on exploits of Round Table knights, and by texts catering to the English interest in Merlin. The English fifteenth century not only saw unparalleled translation activity but also much recopying of earlier romances, as in the revision of the thirteenth-century *Arthour and Merlin* (derived from the French *Merlin*) into a briefer version extant in fifteenth-century copies, which concludes before Uther's coronation.[3] Remarkably, the Vulgate *Estoire de Merlin* was translated into English twice in the mid-fifteenth century: in the 27,852-line verse *Merlin* by the London skinner Henry Lovelich, and in the anonymous Prose *Merlin*, the most substantial English prose romance before Malory which spans the period from Merlin's conception to the birth of Lancelot.[4] Vast yet incomplete, these close translations of the *Estoire* witness to the English fascination with Merlin, as does a fifteenth-century commentary in English on Merlin's prophecies.[5] Legends of Merlin's early career fed into a curiosity about the early history of the island, but because Malory's focus is on Arthur he neglects these themes in his opening *Tale of King Arthur* and only picks up some way from the beginning of his source, the Post-Vulgate *Suite du Merlin*, with the stories of Arthur's begetting and birth, and how he draws forth the sword from the stone. From the *Suite* Malory derives the tales of Arthur's establishment of his rule, Balin and Balan, Arthur's wedding to Guinevere, Accolon, and Pelleas.

The focus on Arthur's early career alternates with other characters, episodes and themes from romance. In such accommodations Malory's work finds precedents in the eclectic compilations of chronicle writers, for whom boundaries between history and romance proved porous. Indeed, the origins of Arthur were synonymous with the definition of the country, for as one fifteenth-century chronicle explains, its very name was previously disputed, till Uther named England after his wife Ingerne.[6] By contrast, in Scots tradition, the illegitimate Arthur usurped the rightful heir Mordred, son of Uther's only legitimate child Anna and Lot of Lothian, so that Mordred's rebellion becomes his bid for his birthright.[7] Questions surrounding Arthur's legitimacy, and hence his right to rule, made this as significant as it was sensitive, as too was the romance-derived episode of Arthur's incestuous begetting of Mordred and his subsequent, Herod-like, massacre of infants. Abridging and simplifying his French model, Malory outlines his cast of characters in a designedly hurried sequence of episodes, navigating an objective course through incidents heavy with implication, in the shifting negotiation between history and historicised romance that will characterise *Morte Darthur*.

History gives way to romance in the last section of Malory's first tale, the adventures of Gawain, Ywain and Marhalt. Here Gawain is the faithless womaniser and shallow reprobate of French romance who, having sworn to help a knight hopelessly in love with a lady who hates him, tricks the lady into bed with himself – a far cry indeed from the heroic and virtuous Gawain who remained a particular hero of writing in English until the end of the Middle Ages.[8]

Gawain

Sir John Paston owned several Arthurian books, including 'þe Dethe off Arthur' and 'the Greene Knyght', the latter presumably a Gawain romance.[9] Along with his interests in chivalry and heraldry – and by the late Middle Ages a sophisticated heraldry had also been developed for the parallel universe of the Arthurian world – Sir John Paston's library inventory suggests how romances of Gawain formed part of Arthurian reading in fifteenth-century England. Malory's following of the French tradition of a morally flawed, even criminal Gawain finds few echoes in English apart from *The Jeaste of Sir Gawayne*, a late fifteenth-century anti-romance derived from several episodes in the First Continuation of Chrétien's *Perceval* that show Gawain in a dishonourable light: his seducing of the Damosele de Lis and his anti-climatically inconclusive combat with her brother. Gawain's unique prestige among readers of Arthurian legend in English is borne out by a cluster of distinctly popular, predominantly northern, late-medieval romances. Both *Sir Gawain and the Carl of Carlisle* (c. 1400) and *The Carl of Carlisle* (c. 1500) recount a similar adventure in which only Gawain courteously respects the authority of a giant 'Carl' in his own domain, where Kay, Baldwin and Gawain seek lodging. In both romances – as also in *The Turk and Gawain* (c. 1500) and *The Grene Knight* (c. 1500) – Gawain plays a central role characterised not only by his brave submission to tests, challenges and exchanges of blows but also by his avoidance of coercion and courteous respect for others' identity. More ambivalent is the presentation of Arthur, as contrasted with Gawain, in some other late romances. In an analogue of 'The Wife of Bath's Tale', *The*

Wedding of Sir Gawain and Dame Ragnell (*c.* 1450), Arthur, finding himself at the mercy of a knight whose lands Arthur has appropriated and bestowed upon Gawain, must save his life by promising to return in a year to answer the question what women most desire. A 'Loathly Lady', Dame Ragnell, promises the question's answer if she can marry Gawain. To save Arthur's life Gawain courteously agrees, and Ragnell's transformation into a beautiful bride rewards Gawain's courtesy and respect for others' autonomy in a tale where Arthur himself – not in control of events – is presented in a questionable and undignified light.

Even more ambivalent is the Arthur of *Golagros and Gawain*. Written in later fifteenth-century Scots, this ambitious alliterative poem is derived, but radically reconceived, from two episodes in the First Continuation of Chrétien's *Perceval*. The first episode focuses on Arthur's attempt to obtain provisions for his company from a castle he passes while on pilgrimage. Kay, sent first, helps himself boorishly and affronts the lord of the castle, who knocks him down. Sent second, Gawain courteously acknowledges the lord's autonomy over what is his, so the lord equally courteously places his people and possessions at Arthur's service. This forms a thematic prelude to the much longer second episode, which more elaborately explores how courtesy and respect for others can trigger a reciprocity that resolves conflict. Passing a castle and learning that its lord, Golagros, owes allegiance to no one, Arthur imperiously determines to compel its lord to pay homage to himself. Eventually Gawain fights Golagros. Defeated in front of his people and mindful of his forefathers' proud independence, Golagros prefers death at Gawain's hands to the shame of submission, but encouraged by the admiring and sympathetic Gawain, he devises a stratagem to preserve his own life and honour. If Gawain will pretend to be defeated, his kindness will be repaid and Golagros' honour safeguarded. One courteous submission triggers more: Golagros, with his people's assent, accompanies Gawain and duly offers his allegiance to Arthur. Although Arthur in return nobly releases Golagros, this may not altogether dispel the critique implicit in the comparison between Gawain's courteous respect for others in both episodes and Arthur's imperious impetus to compel submission and to appropriate – inevitably reminiscent of medieval English kings' claims to suzerainty over Scotland, based on the supposedly historical precedent of Arthur's rule over the whole island in one Arthurian empire.

'King Arthur that was Emperor'

For a vivid vernacular witness to the chronicle tradition of imperial Arthur's triumphant conquest of western Christendom and of Rome itself,

Malory turned, after his opening *Tale of King Arthur*, to the Alliterative *Morte Arthure*. In his prosification of earlier Arthurian sources in verse Malory may again be seen in a broader European context, for the Dukes of Burgundy commissioned new prose adaptations of old romances. To sharpen the focus on Arthur, Malory compresses and cuts the poem by about half, omitting the last third: the lavish alliterative descriptions of feasts, scenery, arms and apparel receive short shrift. Caxton's exceptionally interventive editing of this tale went even further and disguised how far Malory was content to rely on prosifying the alliterative poem's text, retaining much alliteration even as he revised the poem's implications. Malory drops most of the poem's implicit reservations about an Arthur whose reach of ambition is mapped on to the extent of his conquests. In place of the poem's aesthetic of ferocity and bombast, Malory chronicles a more chivalrously compassionate conqueror, while radically revising for his own design the role of Arthur's campaign against Rome. In Geoffrey of Monmouth's chronology there had been a nine-year peaceful lull between Arthur's European conquests and the campaign to overcome Rome itself, which is both his crowning achievement yet also (implicitly) a hubristic overstepping, promptly undermined by news of Mordred's treachery at home. By contrast, Malory locates the Roman war in his Arthuriad as an early triumph long before Arthur's death (as in the *Estoire de Merlin*). Arthur's betrayal and downfall after his Roman war are rewritten – perhaps influenced by Hardyng's *Chronicle* – into his coronation in Rome, now not simply emperor of Britain but also of Christendom, although the *Morte*'s later books are unconcerned with how Arthur actually governed such vast dominions. The historicity of Arthur's Roman war was already disputed by some fifteenth-century writers who noted that, since there was no such emperor, Arthur could not have defeated Lucius.[10] Henceforward the focus of the *Morte* will be on the deeds and adventures of the Round Table, and for that Malory has prepared not only by retaining the Alliterative *Morte*'s flawed figure of Gawain but also by placing his own emphasis on the knightly prowess and courage in the Roman wars of Sir Lancelot (usually ignored in chronicle versions of this campaign).

Lancelot

Although Lancelot is not the focus of any narrative in English before the fifteenth century, he was already familiar to English readers of French romance. Apart from Malory's, the only treatment in English of Lancelot's earlier career (which also ignores his childhood) is *Lancelot of the Laik*, a later fifteenth-century Scots adaptation into rhyming couplets of a portion of the Old French Prose *Lancelot* from the thirteenth-century Vulgate Cycle. The one surviving copy is incomplete at 3,484 lines, and the prologue indicates that this fragment represents at most two thirds of the whole, whether or not that was ever completed.[11] Lancelot's birth, nurture and early adventures are only mentioned in order to be dismissed in an eighty-line *occupatio* (declaration of what will not be included), which also pays scant attention to the beginnings of Lancelot's love for Guinevere. The Scots poet adds the prologue, including a dream vision in which the narrator, unlucky in love, is bidden either to reveal his love to his lady or to write a 'trety' of love or arms – something joyful, not sorrowful – which will enable his lady to discover his love-service. Selecting the story of Lancelot, and thereby aligning his love with Lancelot's for Guinevere, the poet highlights Arthur's wars with Galehaut, Lord of the Distant Isles, as the opportunity for Lancelot to display his valour, eventually to be rewarded by Guinevere's love. The prologue indicates that the poem when complete would include Lancelot's mediations for peace between Arthur and Galehaut and how Venus rewards Lancelot 'and makith hyme his ladice grace to have' (line 311). In the absence of these episodes, a lengthy section in the mirror-for-princes tradition, reproving and advising Arthur on good governance (and building on the Prose *Lancelot*'s concern with kingship), comprises a quarter of the surviving fragment, for the poet exploits the Lancelot story's thematic potential to explore avoidance of aggression and pursuit of reconciliation within the context of chivalric society. Not unlike Malory, the Scots poet fashions highly selective borrowings from the much longer Prose *Lancelot* into his own reading of Lancelot's knightly career, here uncoupled from responsibility for the Round Table's downfall far in the future, but also complemented by a traditional insular emphasis on the heroic accomplishments of a valiant Gawain deeply cherished by an Arthur whose qualities and flaws are both on display.

For his own *Tale of Sir Lancelot du Lake* Malory adapts and conjoins episodes from the Prose *Lancelot* in a highly selective way. Malory's other material derived from the Prose *Lancelot* (its version of the Knight of the Cart episode in which Lancelot sleeps with Guinevere) is only used much later in the *Morte*, for in this early tale Malory adds Lancelot's response to a damsel's leading question about his relationship with Guinevere: that both marriage and liaisons with paramours are incompatible with a life of knighthood (p. 270.28–p. 271.4 [VI.10]). Through Malory's recontextualisation his borrowed episodes gain new significance as successive provings of the greatest knight in this world and his devotion to Guinevere. Malory ignores the Prose *Lancelot*'s account of Lancelot's birth and nurturing, nor does he dramatise Lancelot's love for Guinevere, but allows it as an implication, mentioned by others (p. 257.26–8 [VI.3]; p. 281.14–15 [VI.15]). This crowns the tale's thematic focus on Lancelot's knightly service of ladies; where Lancelot's love for Guinevere in the Prose *Lancelot* represents something lustful and sinful, Malory's episodes chronicle only Lancelot's unshakeable loyalty to the queen in trials of devotion through which, implicitly, great love manifests itself in great chivalry, and Malory's Lancelot insistently affirms Guinevere's fidelity to Arthur (p. 258.5–6 [VI.3]). Closure is culminative as Lancelot's overcome opponents are despatched back to report to Guinevere.

Tristram

In his *Book of Sir Tristram* Malory provides the only extant fifteenth-century narrative treatment in English of the Tristan story. In drawing on some version, still unidentified, of the thirteenth-century French Prose *Tristan* Malory is abreast of contemporary fashion in furnishing an English account of an influential text (surviving in some eighty manuscripts and fragments, and translated into other European vernaculars). But whereas the earlier, now better-known, verse accounts focused on the obsessive and destructive passion of Tristan and Iseult – claustrophobic, antisocial, furtive and amoral – later medieval taste preferred the story as in the Prose *Tristan,* contextualised by the parallel adventures, inset stories and mirroring episodes of a cast of characters. Fundamentally, Malory's French source charted three phases: Tristan's progress towards inclusion as a Round Table knight; possession of his love, La Bele Isode; and the conversion of his Saracen rival, Sir Palomides. But if the book's underlying form is Tristram's biography as a knight, its profusely episodic and self-generating structure of adventures reflects how Tristram's chivalrous career is shaped by the patterns of chivalric society. So Tristram's own path towards incorporation into the Round Table fellowship is shadowed by the inset story of 'La Cote Male Tayle' (Kay's belittling epithet for a young unknown who must prove himself as a knight), while the tale of Tristram's winning Isode is paralleled by that of another nephew whom King Mark hates and persecutes, Alexander the Orphan, and his pursuit of love and vengeance. In the book's last phase Tristram's rivalry and eventual reconciliation with Palomides goes in parallel with the mutual admiration of Tristram and Lancelot, whom Tristram almost matches in chivalric endeavour, as in love's sufferings and madness, so that the tale of Lancelot and Elaine may be aptly inset into the *Tristram,* and with it the begetting of Galahad and the inception of the Grail quest. Interwoven too are darker threads: the murder of the good knight Lamorak by Gawain and his brothers, and Gaheris' beheading of their mother Morgause, Lamorak's mistress. Such crimes of unchivalrous feuding and clan vendetta point ahead beyond the Grail to division and disaster to come, when the treacheries that stain the *Tristram* will be recalled (during the roll-call of knights assembled at the Healing of Sir Urry). That Tristram's own treacherous murder by Mark is not recounted within Malory's *Book of Sir Tristram* but only recalled in retrospect much later is characteristic of Malory's 'noble and joyous book'. Writing in 1467 about a tournament at Eltham, Sir John Paston II bears witness to the revival of tournaments in the decade of the *Morte*'s composition: 'it was the goodliest sight that was sene in Inglande this forty yeares of so fewe men' (I, p. 396). Here is a world focused on tournaments as displays and trials of prowess, in which chivalrous competitiveness eventually cannot exclude something murderously rivalrous.

Yet if Malory's *Tristram* portrays a fantasy of chivalric society – floating free of concern for any historical moment or political responsibility – it defines its own realities. Here is a Tristan romance in which the supernatural, and even the love potion itself, are marginal, and in which love, although acknowledged as a condition, is little explored for itself and can be variously the object of wry dismissiveness as well as eloquently espoused. Sir Dinadan – whose dry wit voices a contrarian critique – remarks to Tristram: '"suche a folysshe knyght as ye ar ... I saw but late this day... And there he lay lyke a fole grennynge and wolde nat speke... And well I wote he was a lovear ..."' (p. 688.31–p. 689.2 [x.55]). Of his wife's infidelity the cuckolded Segwarides only remarks that he '"woll never hate a noble knyght for a lyght lady"' (p. 442.7–8 [VIII.38]), and when Sir Dinas' paramour not only elopes with a rival but takes with her two of Dinas' hunting dogs, 'than was he the more wrother for hys brachettis, more than for hys lady' (p. 550.24–5 [IX.40]). Yet while Dinadan commonsensically declares '"in all the worlde ar nat two such knyghtes that ar so wood as ys sir Lancelot and ye, sir Trystram!"' (p. 508.4–6 [IX.24]), this book also chronicles movingly the love at first sight of Alexander and Alys, and Elaine's hopeless affirmation of her devotion to Lancelot: '"I woll lyve and dye with you, only for youre sake; and yf my lyff might nat avayle you and my dethe myght avayle you, wyte you well I wolde dye for youre sake"' (p. 825.34–p. 826.2 [XII.5]). Through her story the very beginning of the Grail quest is enfolded into this book's celebration of the possibility of a chivalrous society. The *Tristram*'s sheer extent – despite being slimmed to a sixth of its French original it still constitutes a third of the *Morte* – points to the values Malory sees in it: it can stand for the extended summer of Arthurian chivalry at the heart of his Arthuriad, between Arthur's youthful conquests and the inception of the Grail quest.

The Holy Grail

As with the fascination exerted by the figure of Merlin, English interest in the early history of the Grail was part of an engagement with the earliest history of Britain, and this is reflected in Henry Lovelich's 23,794-line verse *History of the Holy Grail* (c. 1430), translating the Vulgate *Estoire del Saint Graal*.[12] Malory probably knew another fifteenth-century treatment of the Grail theme in the *Chronicle* of John Hardyng, who is exceptional among chroniclers in including two topics from romance tradition: Joseph of Arimathea's conversion of Britain and Galahad's Grail quest. In French Arthurian legend Joseph transports the Grail to Britain, but in fifteenth-century English tradition what Joseph brings to Glastonbury is, in Hardyng's words, two phials of bloody sweat collected during the burial of Christ's body: the theologically heterodox Grail undergoes transmutation into more orthodox relics. Paralleling the earlier invented tradition of Arthur's being buried at Glastonbury, a belief developed that Joseph was buried, with the phials, somewhere in the vicinity of Glastonbury, and a future rediscovery of his grave and the miraculous implications of this were the subject of prophecy. All this is part of a wider fifteenth-century emphasis on 'Joseph of Glastonbury' as the apostolic missionary to Britain and a new English national saint, and such affirmation of Britain's conversion within living memory of Christ's ministry had major diplomatic implications. At the Councils of Pisa (1409), Constance (1417), Siena (1424) and Basle (1434), the English delegations invoked England's conversion by Joseph in bolstering her claims to rank as a nation alongside France, Spain, Germany and Italy; the date of Joseph's arrival was moved progressively earlier in order to counter impertinent French claims for the primacy of their St Denis. A surviving letter from an abbot of Glastonbury is apparently a diplomatic response to a lost missive from Henry V pressing for the discovery of Joseph's grave, which, if it had been attempted, would have been a fifteenth-century fabrication to equal that of Arthur's tomb.[13]

Indeed, Joseph's tomb was already to be found at Glastonbury according to some accounts, including Hardyng's versions of Galahad's Grail quest.[14] Here Galahad is Lancelot's legitimate son by his marriage to Elaine, for Hardyng works in the chronicle tradition that ignores the romance theme of Lancelot's adultery with Guinevere and makes Gawain Arthur's worthy lieutenant; his chronicle sidelines the Vulgate Grail's narrative of their penitence and failure. Here the Grail is less eucharistic symbol than emblem of an order of chivalry with a rule similar to those of historical late-medieval orders and redolent of the oath to be sworn by Arthur's knights in Malory's *Morte* (p. 120.15–27[III.15]). Hardyng passes over the Grail vision in a few lines, and his Galahad dies later, at the close of a godly life passed in good works; Perceval does not die at Sarras, but takes Galahad's heart, encased in gold, back to Arthur's court and thence to be buried beside Joseph of Arimathea in the chapel of Our Lady at Glastonbury. Thus the Grail story has been developed into an adventure creditable to Arthur and his court, whose honour and standing are increased rather than interrogated after the Grail quest. In approach and method Hardyng is an exponent of a chivalric historiography that also characterises the contemporary Burgundian chronicler Jean de Wavrin's *Recueil des croniques et anchiennes istories de la Grant Bretaigne* (1471), commissioned by Edward IV, which refashions chronicle for knightly readers familiar with romance.[15] Hardyng's alignment of the Grail with orthodoxy, and his focus on Glastonbury and on the Grail quest as the antecedent of contemporary chivalry, help contextualise Malory's *Tale of the Sankgreal* within fifteenth-century English piety and historiography.

Malory's approach to the Vulgate *La Queste del Saint Graal*, compressing and condensing it, produces an English version little more than a third of the French original's length. The episodes of the *Queste*'s patterned narrative are retained, but Malory reduces or excises the commentary of explanation provided by the hermits who populate the Grail quest's landscape, ever prompt to interpret every adventure, dream or symbol. Yet even though the substance of what survives into the *Sankgreal* may correspond to equivalent material in the *Queste*, the outcome of Malory's editing (and his few but pointed additions) is a distinctively less pessimistic reading of the Grail quest's implications for Arthurian society. In the French *Queste* the familiar structures of knightly adventure in pursuit of the Grail prompt complex allegorical exposition, in which chivalry is inevitably found wanting. In his *Sankgreal* Malory prefers a different dynamic between knightly exploit and interpretation. His is still a symbolic narrative in which all actions are subject to spiritualising explanation. But his omission of so much of the retrospective commentary that controls the *Queste*'s narrative makes knightly adventure rather than religious exposition his text's central focus and no longer merely the pretext for disparagement from an otherworldly perspective. Instead of mystical or typological expositions Malory's hermits offer ethical judgements, while his removal of explanation more pervasively gives the sense of involvement in a mystery for both knights and readers.

Malory's *Sankgreal* represents a mature accommodation of the claims of the celestial and the this-worldly, the spiritual life and the bodily. The absolutist otherworldly impetus of the Grail quest as accomplished by the perfect knight, the virginal Galahad, must remain the *Sankgreal*'s determining measure of perfection. That all of Arthur's knights except Galahad, Perceval and

Bors fail in their Grail quest must also remain an indictment of the Round Table's collective failure to maintain the integration of chivalric and spiritual goals. But Galahad and Perceval are born only to fulfil their otherworldly destiny and, having achieved the Grail, never return to this world, while the abjection of Gawain's failure falls absurdly short of what knighthood could attain. Might there be a middle way? In his Lancelot, as in his Bors, Malory works out empirically his own accommodation between the demands of this world and the next. In the *Queste* Lancelot the sinner already played an important role as a foil to his perfect son Galahad, but Malory transforms this so that the ignominy of Lancelot's failure in the French becomes in the *Sankgreal* the honour of having come so very near to success. The pure virginal Galahad may attain a prize that is barely open to most men, but for Malory Lancelot can still be the best knight, albeit the best knight in the world. This is suggested by Malory's revisions of his source, in which hermits encourage and praise Lancelot even as they dispense otherworldly counsel, and a hermit gives to Gawain an accurate prophecy of Lancelot's holy death. Whereas in the *Queste* a hermit exacts an unequivocal undertaking from Lancelot to shun adultery, this becomes in the *Sankgreal* a much less exacting demand, to stay away from the queen 'as much as ye may forbere' (p. 897.25–6 [XIII.20]), and this undertaking Lancelot may sincerely claim to have honoured. Throughout his quest Lancelot's impulses remain those of a chivalrous knight who instinctively falls back on his knightly prowess: he makes mistaken choices, misjudging outward appearances. When he trespasses into the vicinity of the Grail to proffer assistance to an elderly priest, his generosity of spirit is insufficient to bring him nearer the Grail or prevent his punishment, yet manifests his chivalrous greatness of heart. This is his best, and seen in the light of the Grail it is ultimately not enough – but in this failure there is nonetheless both a pathos and an accomplishment of honour that are worlds away from Malory's source.

It was twentieth-century fashion to believe that in ostensibly fudging the Grail quest's otherworldly point, Malory in his own way also failed to see the Grail, and could only fumble with the numinous. In truth, for Malory the Grail, stripped of its unorthodox associations, is the vessel of Christ's blood brought to Britain by Joseph of Arimathea and so acts as a focus of eucharistic devotion, and yet Malory adds his own vision of the Grail's transformative power, that enables knights to see each other apparently 'fayrer than ever they were before' (p. 865.22–23 [XIII.7]). Indeed, Malory's accommodation through Lancelot of earthly and spiritual loyalties attempts something that reflects the developing lay spirituality of his own century, with its opportunity to pursue a mixed life of action and contemplation in this world. When, after the *Sankgreal*, a wounded Lancelot is healed by a knight-turned-hermit, Sir Baldwin, Malory invents for the Arthurian past a progression and interaction between knighthood and spiritual life that the nostalgic tone suggests would have been his contemporary ideal (p. 1076.14–17 [XVIII.13]). Moreover, in adding a final scene to the *Sankgreal*, so that Bors delivers verbatim a pointed message to Lancelot from his departed son to remember '"thys unsyker [uncertain] worlde"' (p. 1036.28 [XVII.23]), Malory makes his book both open and close with Lancelot, as if to confirm that it is the mixed life of Lancelot in this world that is his theme.

'The Most Piteous Tale'

Afftir the bataile Arthour for a while
To staunche his woundis and hurtis to recure,
Born in a liteer cam into an Ile
Callid Avaloun; and ther of aventure,
As seid Gaufrid recordeth be scripture,
How kyng Arthour, flour of chevalrie,
Rit with his knihtis and lyveth in Fairye.

Thus of Breteyne translatid was the sunne
Up to the riche sterri briht dongoun –
Astronomeeres weel reherse kunne –
Callid Arthuris constellacioun ...

This errour yit abit among Bretouns,
Which foundid is upon the prophecie
Of olde Merlyn, lik ther oppynyouns:
He as a kyng is crownid in Fairie,
With sceptre and suerd, and with his regalie
Shal resorte as lord and sovereyne
Out of Fairye and regne in Breteyne ...

The Parchas sustren sponne so his fate;
His epitaphie recordeth so certeyn:
Heer lith kyng Arthour, which shal regne ageyn.
(John Lydgate, *Fall of Princes*, 8.3095–3122)

Lydgate's response to Arthur's end is much elaborated from his source, Laurent de Premierfait's French version of Boccaccio's *De Casibus*. Having reported that Arthur 'to the deth was wounded', Lydgate cites Geoffrey of Monmouth's account of Arthur undead in Avalon before following this with his alternative account of Arthur's Troilus-like apotheosis and transformation into a constellation.[16] To this is then juxtaposed the 'British Hope' of

Arthur's return from Avalon, where Lydgate's very rejection of such delusion registers all its allure – only to be followed in turn by a report of Arthur's epitaph which at once confirms that he is entombed, yet thereby rehearses the hope of his reigning again. After an envoy to the story proper, Lydgate adds his own final criticism of unnatural kin, plangently condemning the national division and desolation wrought by Mordred's treachery. This brief biography of Arthur was sufficiently popular to circulate separately excerpted in manuscript selections and anthologies, and Lydgate's account of Arthur's end presents a montage of swiftly juxtaposed alternatives that both reflects and influenced the range of fifteenth-century readings of Arthur that Malory draws together. Despite Arthur's celebrated tomb at Glastonbury, wistful allusions continue to be made to the king's survival and future return. The Latin inscription that Lydgate's epitaph translates ('Hic iacet Arthurus rex quondam rexque futurus': here lies Arthur the once and future king) is widely declared to be that inscribed on Arthur's tomb, even though eyewitness accounts of that Glastonbury tomb until the Reformation record a quite different inscription. By the fifteenth century, interpenetration of chronicle and romance traditions ensured an intertextuality in which there was always more than one truth about Arthur, not least in the way Arthur's end is only one, and not the last, of the endings through which the legend concludes.

To complete his Arthuriad Malory presents two further tales after the Grail quest, the *Book of Sir Lancelot and Queen Guenevere* and the *Tale of the Morte Arthur*, for which he could find the corresponding material in the thirteenth-century Vulgate *Mort Artu*. However, a remarkable Arthurian poem in English had preceded Malory in drawing upon and 'reducing' the *Mort Artu*, so presenting the first account in English of the romance tradition version of the Round Table's downfall, and with that the first mention in English of the illicit passion of Lancelot and Guinevere. This was the Stanzaic *Morte Arthur*, now surviving in only one manuscript of *c.* 1460–80, although perhaps written *c.* 1400, or indeed earlier.[17] Malory knows and draws on the Stanzaic *Morte* as well as the *Mort Artu*, as is confirmed by his closeness in places to the Stanzaic *Morte*'s phrasing, and his use of some details not in *Mort Artu*. For his penultimate tale Malory follows the Stanzaic *Morte* in recounting 'The Poisoned Apple' and 'Fair Maid of Astolat' episodes as the opening two of his five sections, but then introduces his invented episode of 'The Great Tournament', follows that by reverting to the Prose *Lancelot* for 'The Knight of the Cart' (not in the Stanzaic *Morte* or *Mort Artu*), and concludes with another episode apparently of his own invention, 'The Healing of Sir Urry'. Yet while in these latter three sections Malory departs from the narrative in his sources, his inclusion of 'The Knight of the Cart' parallels the Stanzaic *Morte*'s focus on passionate feeling and sentiment, just as the supreme courtly pageants of tournament and solemn assemblage of the fellowship in the other episodes are at one with an affinity with ceremonious courtly observance in the Stanzaic *Morte* as in contemporary life. (The prize of a diamond in Malory (p.1098.15–16 [XVIII.21] and p.1153.15–16 [XIX.13]) was apparently an English court tradition, mentioned in a treatise on tournaments amongst Sir John Paston's books.)[18] With its elegiac retrospect on the chivalric idyll, its empathy with the lovers, and its ballad-like stylisation of key moments and reactions, the Stanzaic *Morte* presents a lyrical and popular distillation of *Mort Artu*'s more analytical and dispassionate account. Malory absorbs the lessons of both models, rewriting *Mort Artu* in mind of the Stanzaic *Morte*'s passionate intensification of focus, tempo and style, albeit always with his own sense of structure and implication.

Most significant of Malory's structural changes is his interpolation of the 'Knight of the Cart' between 'The Poisoned Apple' and Lancelot's rescue of Guinevere from the stake; he thus creates a threefold sequence of occasions on which Lancelot deploys his knightly prowess to defend Guinevere's reputation in ever-more questionable contexts. Guinevere is innocent of the poisoning accusation and Lancelot may fight justly to exonerate her. On the second occasion the lovers escape disgrace by a technicality: Lancelot can fight justly to exonerate the queen only because Mellyagaunce has mistakenly accused her of sleeping with her wounded knights rather than with Lancelot. On the third occasion Lancelot has been ambushed in Guinevere's bedchamber, but such is his supreme prowess that he can rescue her from consequently being burned at the stake as an adulteress, although in this fatal mêlée Lancelot accidentally kills Gawain's beloved brother Gareth, so triggering the unending strife in which the Round Table implodes.

In the *Mort Artu* Malory knew an interpretation of the Round Table's fall that, coolly disapproving of what it narrates, could be unambiguous. This Arthur – obstinately proud, wilful, vengeful – ignores all warnings and precipitates his kingdom's downfall, to which the longterm adultery of Lancelot with Guinevere contributes. By contrast, in the Stanzaic *Morte*, Malory knew a more respectful understanding of Arthur and a sympathetic identification with the love of Lancelot and Guinevere, even if its destructiveness is acknowledged. In the concluding movement of his own *Morte* Malory contends critically with almost every aspect of the Arthurian legend, revising it in line with a distinctive interpretation of chivalric values and Arthurian society, and of its principal characters, not least Arthur himself. Malory's Arthur is altogether more kingly than in the French. Malory leaves imprecise how much his Arthur guesses about the adultery, and this uncertainty and Arthur's magnanimous readiness to think well of Lancelot give the king greater dignity than in *Mort Artu*, where Arthur receives explicit evidence of the love-affair, yet remains ineffectual. Malory adds the speech in which Arthur values the corporate ideal of the Round Table not only more highly than his wife ('"for quenys I myght have inow"') but also more than any personal interest or injury (p. 1184.1–11 [xx.9]). Malory's Arthur will take back Guinevere willingly, heeds warnings from Gawain's ghost and tries to avoid what he foresees will be a disastrous conflict with Mordred. Arthur's dream of his fall from Fortune's wheel – and with it the implied deserts of a proud, sinful man – receives less emphasis than in other accounts of his downfall (such as the Alliterative *Morte*). Malory's account of Arthur's passing is sublimely ambivalent, but in a way that is more positively open-ended than other versions. On the one hand Malory adds to the Stanzaic *Morte*'s account his Arthur's chillingly cheerless parting words to Bedivere: '"Comforte thyselff," seyde the kynge, "and do as well as thou mayste, for in me ys no truste for to truste in …"' (p. 1240.31–2 [xxi.5]). Yet if this seemingly commends a relinquishing of Arthur, Malory's invocation of the 'British Hope' – that by God's will Arthur has gone to another place, but will return (p. 1242.22–5 [xxi.7]) – makes bold to associate the divine will with this inextinguishably renewing idea of Arthur. Here the *Morte*'s equivocation is both individual and part of a broader tradition seen in Lydgate's curious montage of successive endings to his life of Arthur.

Even Malory's Gawain – throughout the *Morte* a disappointment to knighthood – is rehabilitated by his repentant ending, acknowledging his responsibility. Above all, in his ambivalent presentation of the love of Lancelot and Guinevere Malory achieves a precarious equipoise that enables the *Morte* to balance and hold together the crucial values of chivalric society. As ever, Malory's narrative is unconcerned to dwell on the experience of love for its own sake and only acknowledges any sexual intercourse between Lancelot and Guinevere when the plot demands, focusing rather on episodes that try the lovers' constancy. Indeed, the shrewishly capricious personality of Malory's Guinevere, who so takes her lover for granted, catches something of the unromantic reality of a long-established relationship as Lancelot experiences it. Yet Malory's Guinevere has immortal longings in her, and comes to an end that both transcends her life and character, yet proves a development of her earlier constancy. In *Mort Artu* Guinevere's withdrawal to a nunnery is motivated less by repentance than by fear of both Mordred and Arthur. It is from the Stanzaic *Morte* that Malory develops the renunciation scene, worthy of grand opera, in which

Lancelot visits a repentant Guinevere in the nunnery (a different version of this episode also appears in one *Mort Artu* manuscript).[19] She publicly confesses their sinful love, laments the ruination this has wrought, and dismisses Lancelot for ever, refusing him even one last kiss. But whereas in the Stanzaic *Morte* Guinevere's death is reported after Lancelot's, Malory reverses the sequence so that Guinevere dies first, knowing that Lancelot is on his way to her yet praying that she may die before seeing him. In so implying Guinevere's need still to deny and avoid her love, Malory suggests the hold it retains, yet through her penitence and renunciation the queen gains salvation: 'whyle she lyved she was a trew lover, and therefor she had a good ende' (p. 1120.12–13 [XVIII.25]).

Like his Guinevere – indeed, because of her – Malory's Lancelot comes to a good end, and his end is a token of his loyalty as a knight and lover, even though his love has involved sin. For Malory, writing amidst the disorder and uncertainty that was the later fifteenth century, stability and loyalty are supreme values, which he idealises in the Round Table fellowship as a society and in personal conduct, to the detriment of the present day ('Thys ys no stabylyté. But the olde love was nat so', p. 1120.2–3 [XVIII.25]). In its development Malory's *Morte* implies that Lancelot's constancy to Arthur and Guinevere as knight and as lover far outweighs the sinfulness of his adulterous love, and so there is no contradiction between his loyalty and love. Such is the emotional logic of the *Morte*'s yearning identification with Lancelot's sheer chivalry (as in his noble speeches when returning Guinevere to Arthur, or when besieged at Benwick by Arthur and Gawain) that the incommensurate cost of exposing his adultery – the ruin of a whole society, set in train more by malice than concern for truth – comes to seem much the greater evil than the accommodations by which the Round Table has come to function in the post-Grail world.

This *Most Piteous Tale of the Morte Arthur Saunz Guerdon* is designedly one of intense pathos. Even after Lancelot has loyally emulated Guinevere in retreating to a hermitage Malory shows his hero attempting to bridge and reconcile his loyalties in the *Morte*'s invented sequence where Lancelot, warned by a vision, learns of Guinevere's end and oversees her burial beside Arthur at Glastonbury. Malory's account is charged with the pathos of a great love renounced, and at the moment of Guinevere's interment Lancelot swoons. Reproached by a hermit, Lancelot responds that his grief was not 'for ony rejoysyng of synne' but because 'my sorowe may never have ende' at his sense of responsibility (p. 1256.27–38 [XXI.11]). Malory has his Lancelot pine away, refusing food – 'Ever he was lyeng grovelyng on the tombe of kyng Arthure and quene Guenever' – but for

Malory Lancelot is to be commemorated as a knight even if he died as a hermit. Although Ector's happening on Lancelot's funeral is Malory's borrowing from the Stanzaic *Morte*, it is Malory who has Ector utter his eloquent eulogy of Lancelot's knighthood, just as it is Malory who rewrites his sources so as not to leave the surviving Arthurian knights as hermits, but rather to send them forth on crusade to the Holy Land, ever seeking to fuse the mixed life of chivalrous practice with spiritual calling ('And there they dyed upon a Good Fryday for Goddes sake', p. 1260.14–15 [XXI.13]).

Throughout the English fifteenth century, to read about Arthur and the Round Table was to encounter an ideal, and the court of King Arthur provided an imagined model for courtly life and conduct. On Christmas Day 1400 the eight-year-old Princess Blanche presided over a tournament at Westminster for which survive the fictitious letters of challenge, playfully alluding to such Arthurian figures as 'Palamides' and a spoof 'Lancelot de Libie', while Blanche's father, the usurper Henry IV, is Arthur's successor.[20] Writing to his mother in 1468 from Bruges, where Edward IV's sister had married the Duke of Burgundy, Sir John Paston III reaches for an Arthurian comparison: 'And as for the Dwkys coort ... I herd neuer of non lyek to it, saue Kyng Artourys cort' (I, p. 539). Hardly surprising, for the Duke, Charles the Bold, enjoyed having Arthurian romances read to him; his wedding to Margaret of York was celebrated with Arthurian-themed tournaments, and his homes were decorated with tapestries with Arthurian motifs.[21] Arthurian precedents informed Edward IV's renewal of the Order of the Garter, still being invoked in 1493 by Henry VII,[22] who at his Richmond Palace had wall-paintings depicting Arthur along with Brutus, Hengest and later valiant English kings,[23] and who gave the name Arthur to his eldest son, born by design at Winchester in 1486. At some jousts in 1508 James IV of Scotland apparently aimed at playing some latterday Sir Perceval: 'he wald be called a knycht of King Arthuris brocht vp in the wodis'.[24] Since kings such as Edward IV traced their lineage back to Arthur, and Henry VII's coat of arms showed the legendary British kings Brutus and Belinus with Arthur in one quarter, it was conventional to compare sovereigns flatteringly to Arthur.[25] Especially in his pan-European role as one of the Nine Worthies, Arthur is part of decorative schemes and civic ceremonial and pageant;[26] he welcomes Margaret of Anjou to Coventry in 1456, and his namesake Prince Arthur in 1498.[27] In 1501 the pageants welcoming Prince Arthur's bride, Katharine of Aragon, make allusion to King Arthur – not as in Avalon, but by now residing in the star Arcturus.[28]

NOTES

1 Primary texts frequently mentioned in this volume are referenced in abbreviated form (for Malory, page and line number, plus Caxton's book and chapter references); for full bibliographical details see pp. xii–xiv.

2 *Arthur*, ed. F. J. Furnivall, EETS, o.s. 2 (London: Trübner, 1864).

3 *Of Arthour and of Merlin*, ed. O. D. Macrae-Gibson, 2 vols., EETS, o.s 268, 279, (London: 1973, 1979); see II, 40–4. From this shorter version Wynkyn de Worde printed *A Lytel Treatyse of the Byrth and Prophecye of Marlyn* (*c.* 1500).

4 Henry Lovelich, *Merlin*, ed. E. A. Kock, 2 vols., EETS, e.s. 93, 112 (Oxford University Press, 1904, 1913); *Merlin*, ed. H. B. Wheatley, 4 vols., EETS, o.s. 10, 21, 36, 112 (London: Paul, Trench, Trübner, 1865, 1866, 1869, 1898).

5 *The 'Prophetia Merlini' of Geoffrey of Monmouth: A Fifteenth-Century English Commentary*, ed. Caroline D. Eckhardt (Cambridge, MA: Medieval Academy of America, 1982).

6 'A Short English Chronicle', ed. J. A. Gairdner, in *Three Fifteenth-Century English Chronicles*, Camden Society, n.s. 28 (London: Camden Society, 1880), p. 10.

7 *Cronycle of Scotland in a Part*, ed. T. Tompson, in *The Bannatyne Club Miscellany*, 3 vols. (Edinburgh: Bannatyne Club, 1827–55), III, pp. 35–43 (p. 39).

8 Gawain's popularity is also attested by the five surviving fifteenth-century manuscripts of the fourteenth-century *Lybeaus Desconus*, the story of Gawain's illegitimate son, discussed by Burrow, p. 78.

9 *Paston Letters and Papers of the Fifteenth Century*, ed. Norman Davis, 3 vols. (Oxford: Clarendon Press, 1976), I, pp. 517–18. All reference to the Gawain texts discussed in this section is to Thomas Hahn (ed.), *Sir Gawain: Eleven Romances and Tales*, TEAMS (Kalamazoo, MI: Medieval Institute Publications, Western Michigan University, 1995).

10 Antonia Gransden, *Historical Writing in England, c. 1307 to the Early Sixteenth Century*, 2 vols. (London: Routledge, 1974–82), II, p. 398.

11 *Lancelot of the Laik*, ed. M. M. Gray, Scottish Text Society 2 (Edinburgh: Blackwood, 1912); see also *Lancelot of the Laik and Sir Tristrem*, ed. Alan Lupack, TEAMS (Kalamazoo, MI: Medieval Institute Publications, Western Michigan University, 1994). The French source *Lancelot* is discussed above by Taylor, p. 59.

12 Henry Lovelich, *History of the Holy Grail*, ed. F. J. Furnivall, Parts I–IV, 4 vols., EETS, e.s. 20, 24, 28, 30 (London: Trübner, 1874–8); ed. D. Kempe, Part V, EETS, e.s. 95 (London: Trübner, 1905).

13 James P. Carley, 'A Grave Event: Henry V, Glastonbury Abbey, and Joseph of Arimathea's Bones', in James P. Carley (ed.), *Glastonbury Abbey and the Arthurian Tradition* (Cambridge: D.S. Brewer, 2002), pp. 285–302.

14 *A Glastonbury Miscellany of the Fifteenth Century: A Descriptive Index of Trinity College, Cambridge, MS. O.9.38*, ed. A. G. Rigg (Oxford University Press, 1968) includes a Latin epitaph for Joseph (p. 117).

15 Jean de Wavrin, *Recueil des chroniques*, ed. W. Hardy and E. L. C. P. Hardy, 5 vols. Rolls Series 39 (London: Longman, 1864–91).

16 *Fall of Princes*, VIII.3102–22, ed. H. Bergen, EETS, e.s. 121–4 (Oxford University Press, 1924–7). Premierfait remains unedited; the Arthurian section is included by Bergen (IV.327–36).

17 Edited by L. D. Benson in *King Arthur's Death: The Middle English Stanzaic Morte Arthur and Alliterative Morte Arthure* (Indianapolis, IN: Bobbs-Merrill, 1974; repr. Exeter University Press, 1986).

18 Viscount Dillon, 'On a MS. Collection of Ordinances of Chivalry of the Fifteenth Century, Belonging to Lord Hastings', *Archaeologia*, 57 (1900), 27–70 (p. 40).

19 The variant text is included in *Mort Artu*, pp. 264–6 (Lacy, IV. 158fn2).

20 Heiner Gillmeister, 'Challenge Letters from a Medieval Tournament and the Ball-Game of Gotland', *Stadion*, 16–17 (1990–1), 184–221.

21 As recollected in *Memoires d'Olivier de la Marche, maître d'hôtel et capitaine des gardes de Charles le Téméraire*, ed. H. Beaune and J. d'Arbaumont, Société de l'histoire de France, 4 vols. (Paris: Librairie Renouard, H. Loones, successeur, 1883–8), II. 217, 11–122. On tapestries, see R. Vaughan, *Valois Burgundy* (London: Allen Lane, 1975), p. 163. For Arthurian books in French ducal and royal collections, see Roger Middleton, 'The Manuscripts', in *AoF*, pp. 8–92 (pp. 60–71).

22 *Calendar of State Papers, Venetian*, ed. Rawdon Brown, 38 vols. (London: Longman and HMSO, 1864–1947), I (1202–1509), no. 790.

23 See *The Receyt of the Ladie Kateryne*, ed. Gordon Kipling, EETS, o.s. 296 (Oxford University Press, 1990), IV.805–21.

24 J. Leslie, *Historie of Scotland*, trans. J. Dalrymple, ed. E. G. Cody and W. Murison, 2 vols., STS, 19, 34 (Edinburgh and London: Blackwood, 1889–95), II, p. 128.

25 'Ballade to King Henry VI', in *The Minor Poems of John Lydgate: Part II, Secular Poems*, ed. Henry Noble MacCracken, EETS, o.s. 192 (Oxford University Press, 1934), pp. 624–30.

26 A French example from 1487 is included in Richard Trachsler, *Clôtures du Cycle Arthurien: Etude et textes* (Geneva: Droz, 1996), pp. 465–500.

27 *The Coventry Leet Book*, in *Two Coventry Corpus Christi Plays*, ed. Hardin Craig, EETS, e.s. 87 (Oxford University Press, 1957), p. 113.

28 *Receyt of the Ladie Kateryne*, II.407–8, pp. 439–40. Recounting Jason's voyage to Colchis, Lydgate notes how experienced mariners navigate by 'Arthouris Plowe', i.e. Charles's Wain in Ursa Major: *Troy Book*, ed. H. Bergen, EETS, e.s. 97 (London: Kegan Paul, 1906), I.682.

6

ROB GOSSEDGE AND STEPHEN KNIGHT

The Arthur of the sixteenth
to nineteenth centuries

The disappearing king

Great writers tend to impress and also debilitate their successors. Malory exemplifies this, with six separate editions of *Le Morte Darthur* by 1634 and no innovative treatment of Arthur and his world in the same period. In his case – as probably also with others like Chaucer, Shakespeare and Scott – there were more reasons for the diminuendo than mere anxiety of influence. One was focused on history. British scholars, notably the Scots, were increasingly doubtful of Geoffrey of Monmouth's account of Arthur: after Polydore Vergil's clear-headed dismissal of any historical standing in 1534, only committed Arthur loyalists like John Leland, writing in Latin in 1544 (translated into English in 1582), accepted the full story, and their numbers steadily reduced, though the position survived into the eighteenth century. Another source of Arthurian doubt was the increasing value given to classical learning over medieval tradition: Aeneas had become a more credible nation-builder than Arthur. At the same time the new style of Tudor administrative organisation (like Caxton's *Le Morte Darthur* stemming from 1485), with a standing army, ministers of state and the development of something like a civil service, made the idea of a king ruling through his great warriors with advice from a magical grand vizier seem both improbable and irrelevant. Protestantism itself recoiled from Arthur's Catholic ambience, especially the Grail story, and Puritan moralism found the cheerful violence and sexual awareness of romance unappealing – Roger Ascham famously summed Malory up in 1570 as 'open mans slaughter and bold bawdrye'.[1]

Such attitudes did not mean the medieval riches of the Arthur myth were not still enjoyed. John Bale, also writing in Latin, said in 1548, 'In our times, Malory enjoys an illustrious reputation',[2] and as well as the *Morte Darthur* reprints three somewhat abbreviated prints of *Arthur and Merlin* appear between 1499 and 1529, as do a few manuscript versions of popular texts, like the late Gawain romances and the ballads drawn from Malory in the 1640s Percy manuscript. R. S. Crane and Helen Cooper have shown how medieval romances fared under Renaissance taste:[3] typically Lord Berners's *Arthur of Little Britain*, written by 1520, is about a later gentleman-knight, Arthur of Brittany, while Sir Philip Sidney deployed chivalric events and romance plots in a highly Italianate form in his *Arcadia*, especially the *New Arcadia* published posthumously in 1590, and Thomas Hughes squeezed Arthur into the Procrustean bed of Senecan tragedy in *The Misfortunes of Arthur*, performed at the Inner Temple in 1587.

Another sublimation of the medieval Arthur story was his deployment as an icon to validate the seizure and maintenance of royal power, and a more general use of Arthurian display to euphemise military power from Edward I to Henry VIII.[4] Malory's impact generated splendid artificial knightly tournaments like Henry VIII's prestige-creating Field of the Cloth of Gold, not specific memories of Arthur. The king's treatment grew increasingly unmedieval: although Henry VII's elder son was named Arthur for dynasty-strengthening reasons, at the celebrations of his adulthood in 1501 he was represented as Arcturus – the classically oriented name of a star.[5] The clearest sign that Arthur had value primarily as a generalised symbol of power is in Spenser's *Faerie Queene* (published 1590–6), where, drawing on the spirit of Ariosto's Renaissance reshaping of the medieval Roland story, *Orlando Furioso*, Arthur is not a major participant: though he does right some wrongs, he centrally symbolises the 'Magnanimous Man', a Platonic concept combining the separate virtues represented by separate knights. Being an ideal, he is written out of history. For Spenser the son of Gorlois is called Artegall – Arthur's equal, and he is also only a prince: however symbolically valuable, he is always junior to Queen Elizabeth.

National history still had some room for Arthur as a character in the ancient drama of founding Britain: whether writing in prose like John Speed or verse like William Warner, chroniclers who largely ignored Geoffrey's fabulous history retained the idea of Arthur defeating the Saxons in a way both historically obscure but also – to this day – ideologically attractive. Michael Drayton, with his interest in earlier myth and local traditions, goes somewhat further, writing in *Poly-Olbion* of Arthur's death in Cornwall (Song 1: Arthur's birth is only discussed in the notes) and his grave at Glastonbury (Song 3); then in the voice of British bards in Song 4 he recapitulates Arthur's deeds from Geoffrey of Monmouth and expresses regret that there is no true Arthurian epic, which might have surpassed even Homer.[6]

The arrival of the new Stuart dynasty in 1603 refocused Arthur as royal propaganda, with the prophecies of Merlin justifying James VI of Scotland's claim to Elizabeth's throne, and a popular anagram of Charles Iames Stuart was 'Claimes Arthur's Seat' – Arthur's Seat is a hill in Edinburgh, making it seem the more credible. Some writers were involved: Robert Chester's 1601 poem sequence *Loves Martyr* celebrates Arthur as a royal model, but in 1611, apparently to honour the Stuarts, this segment is foregrounded and the work is retitled *The Annals of Great Britaine*. Ben Jonson, never an enthusiastic medievalist (though he, like many, toyed with the idea of a British epic), wrote a finely worded text for Inigo Jones's equally fine – but classical – designs in *Prince Henry's Barriers*, celebrating in early 1612 the adulthood of the first son of James I, though it was Merlin rather than Arthur who made possible the antique validation of the prince.

Royal propaganda was a narrow genre, and popular culture was at least as fruitful for Arthur. As his noble story drifted away from the interests of high culture, it did not fade from human memory. Just as Gothic architecture survived in the humble hands of local craftsmen, able to recut an ogival arch and patch a perpendicular window, so Arthur as the image of honour and the overseer of a fair and peaceful civilisation was not forgotten. For some two centuries he appeared only in the lower worlds of popular culture and political propaganda, but like many heroes before him he passed unscathed through the depths, and he was able to resume his power to command and inspire artistic attention when his central image of earnest but troubled authority was, at least two centuries later, to become of compelling interest to major authors.

Arthur in the underworld

The reflex to the stilted intellectualism of Hughes's *The Misfortunes of Arthur* is another Temple play, recently discovered, *Tom a Lincoln* of about 1611. This is the people's Arthur: the king's illegitimate son Tom arrives at court and does well, like Lancelot or Gareth before him. More popular still was Richard Johnson's *The Historye of Tom Thumb* (1621): the tiny hero comes to Arthur's court and also gains great honour. A more elevated Arthur was now strictly political: Thomas Heywood's *The Life of Merlin* (1641) follows Geoffrey of Monmouth to suggest Arthur as a model of true British kingship like Charles I himself, and the simple prose *Life of King Arthur* (attributed to the balladeer Martin Parker, though he died three years before it appeared) re-validates royalty in the year of the restoration, 1660. Such mixtures of comedy and royalism would not have encouraged Milton to pursue his ideas of an Arthurian national epic, even if his scholarly researches, as realised in his *History of Britain* (published 1670, though written between 1649 and 1655), had not persuaded him that this was an inauthentic story. Dryden was the third great seventeenth-century writer to muse on an Arthurian epic, but like Jonson and Milton he set aside the idea and just planned a propagandist opera for Charles II, then James II. History moved faster than the writer and he found himself reworking his material after 1688 to please the Protestant incomer, William of Orange. The printed version has a preface noting the author's problems, but at least a great poet, with the help of Henry Purcell's superb music, could make something of such an awkward situation.

In *King Arthur: The British Worthy* (1691) Dryden ignores Malory's medieval adventures and develops a martial romance where Arthur loves the fair blind Emmeline and his rival is the Saxon prince Oswald: both are represented by their magicians, the splendid but only semi-effectual Merlin, helped by the classical-style spirit Philidel, versus the evil Saxon enchanter Osmond with his dark familiar Grimbold. The battles go rather easily the British way, but the music and magic provide erotic tension: under-dressed Sirens, including a fake and very tempting Emmeline, entice Arthur until 'A Lazie Pleasure trickles through my veins' and in the brilliant 'shivering' scene the music slowly brings to life the frost demon as the chorus sing with incremental excitement, ''Tis love, love, love that has warm'd us'.[7] The text asserts that Arthur's courage, Christian magic and the blessings of God unite a once-divided kingdom: so idealised a message is easily transferred from Charles and James to William. The energy of peasants and artisans, supervised at a distance by the military gentry, drives the country forward, as in their robust harvest song ending 'And Hoigh for the Honour of Old England', and finally these unproblematised natural riches and new social unities are absorbed in divinely-favoured nationalism in the climactic song 'Fairest Isle, all isles excelling'.

Dryden's only negative impact was to inspire imitation by the much less skilful Sir Richard Blackmore, doctor and ideologue to the new monarchy. In *Prince Arthur* (1695) he offered a national epic, 'an heroick poem in ten books' directly praising the new king and his party. Uther (replacing Merlin in this role: kings have the knowledge now) gives a lengthy historical prophecy entirely omitting the Stuarts and predicting 'a brave Nassovian' as 'the great Deliverer to come' (William of Orange's family was also linked to Nassau, a duchy in central West Germany).[8] The evil Saxon Octa is evidently James II and the Saxons are clearly Catholics: the weakened, semi-diabolic and side-changing Merlin appears to represent Dryden himself. The epic did well, presumably because of its political partiality, and in 1697 Blackmore produced a sequel, *King Arthur*, in full Virgilian style with twelve books. In the preface, as well as pompously dismissing his critics, Blackmore claims Geoffrey of Monmouth as his source, but merely focuses on wars with France where, to contemporary satisfaction, 'The valiant king the haughty

French subdued'.[9] The Tories ridiculed Blackmore's appropriation of ancient kingship for mere Whiggery. John Dennis assembled a fairly serious book in response, Dryden merely called Blackmore 'a Pedant, Canting Preacher and a Quack', and later, in *The Dunciad*, Alexander Pope elegantly stigmatised him as 'the everlasting Blackmore'.[10]

Arthur himself soon felt the thrust of Tory ridicule when Henry Fielding deployed the popular tradition to parody forms of theatrical pomposity he associated with the Whigs under Sir Robert Walpole. *Tom Thumb: A Tragedy* appeared in 1730 and was rapidly worked up as *The Tragedy of Tragedies: The Life and Death of Tom Thumb* with (in the printed version) many mock heroic notes identifying Fielding's targets, frequently including Dryden. The jokes start with the *dramatis personae*: Arthur's queen is 'Dollalolla: a woman entirely faultless saving that she is a little given to Drink; a little too much a Virago towards her Husband. And in love with Tom Thumb'.[11] Tom becomes a military hero (mocking Blackmore's Arthur redefined as 'the bold Nassovian') but, tragically, is consumed by an inattentive cow. The other characters are distraught and the play ends in ludicrous parody of dire classical tragedy: everybody dies at each other's hands and Arthur, the last left alive, stabs himself, crying 'And take thou this'.[12] Hugely popular in its time, *Tom Thumb* reappeared well into the nineteenth century, and had two almost equally popular variant forms, the musical *The Opera of Operas* (1733), created by Eliza Haywood, the actress and novelist, with her partner William Hatchett, and a further cut-down, *Tom Thumb: A Burletta* (1780), by Kane O'Hara. Fielding's text, often shorn of its direct anti-Whig satire, lived on as part of the popular riches of the Arthur tradition.

However, the idea of a monarch both historical and mythical was never entirely forgotten: in 1718 Aaron Thompson published the first translation of Geoffrey of Monmouth into English prose and the introduction argues strongly, if not very credibly, for Arthur's historical and patriotic value. Through this work, and perhaps some surviving knowledge of Malory and medieval romance, Arthur was available as a token of British national authority, though few took this up and to little effect. Horace Walpole, early Gothic author and son of Sir Robert, wrote a poem, sadly lost, using Arthur as a figure of British heroism at the battle of Quiberon Bay in 1759; almost as fugitive is the play by William Hilton, *Arthur, Monarch of the Britons*, published in 1775, which links Arthur to the Seven Years War against France.

Two major figures of the period were familiar with the early material, but in different ways found only limited value in Arthur. Thomas Percy's influential *Reliques of Early English Poetry* (1765) presents the king as a figure of popular entertainment: his famous 1640s manuscript contains three simple versifications from Malory, a very brief summary of Geoffrey of Monmouth (with Arthur, unusually, speaking in the first person) and two comic poems 'The Marriage of Sir Gawain' and 'The Boy and the Mantle'. In the same period Thomas Warton wrote with great knowledge of medieval romance, in French as well as English; though he valued Spenser greatly, he felt Arthur should have been made a central active hero, not just a symbol of greatness.[13] But if Warton senses a mythic image, he also contains Arthur in history. In his poem 'On the Grave of Arthur' a Welsh bard tells Henry II about the king's mysterious end, but then another bard contradicts the idea of 'Merlin's potent spell' and says Arthur is buried at Glastonbury: King Henry has the place excavated and the grave is found.

The Romantic poets had no significant interest in the Arthurian myth. While Gray's image of 'The Bard' inspired a poet-visionary Merlin with a long beard, that only led to casual references or even negative treatments, as in Wordsworth's 'The Egyptian Maid'. Merlin is basically a villain who drowns the maid, but the Lady of the Lake supervises her healing by Galahad, who then marries her. There is little of Malory in this sentimental and somewhat orientalist fable beyond a memory of Elaine of Ascolat and the Healing of Sir Urré. The Lady's link with the Lake seems to have brought her at least some popularity with the Romantics, but they found Arthur without value as a figure of human morality and sincere sentiments. Coleridge was to say in 1833: 'As to Arthur, you could not by any means make a poem on him national to Englishmen. What have we to do with him?'[14]

There were some uses for Arthur in this period that develop either his comic or propagandist roles. John Thelwall, a Jacobin, atheist and radical speech-maker, who was imprisoned for sedition in 1794, published in 1801 'The Fairy of the Lake', a verse drama that like Dryden, Blackmore and Hilton focused on war with the Saxons. But the main action is between the Saxon enchantress Rowena and the loyal Lady of the Lake: Rowena captures Arthur and his knights, the Lady rescues them, and after Tristram and Guinevere are killed she restores them to life as Arthur takes the throne of Britain in Geoffrey's Caerleon. There is much that is entertaining, even bawdy, about the play: Merriman calls it 'a tasteless concoction of freely manipulated romance elements, scrambled pseudo-history, "Cambrian" tradition, Northern mythology, and plain nonsense'.[15] But this mix is deliberate: Thelwall is challenging the conservative classicising of Arthur he saw in Dryden and Blackmore, and he questions the sanctity of both masculinity and royalty, as well as theatrical and narrative decorum.

A less searching satire is John Hookham Frere's *The Monks and the Giants*, an incomplete but quite widely read text published first in 1816, which is more a satire on bourgeois values, both behavioural and political, than an Arthurian statement. The work is presented as by the brothers

'William and Robert Whistlecraft, of Stow Market, in Suffolk, Harness and Collar Makers', and the primary title is 'Prospectus and Specimen of an Intended National Work'. Frere, a conservative, is, like Coleridge, denying the possibility of an Arthurian national epic – except perhaps in the minds of the vulgar.

Arthurian satire also appears in John Moultrie's 'La Belle Tryamour', published in 1837, a Byronic version of the tail-rhyme romance Sir Launfal, where Merlin cures Arthur of 'the blue devils' (i.e. depression) by giving him a magic glass, as in Spenser. The same spirit of educated fun is behind Thomas Love Peacock's early brushes with Arthuriana: 'Sir Hornbook' (1818) is a lively allegorical instruction in grammar, 'The Round Table' (1817) is an amusing but historically educational poem, and in Calidore (1816), larger in ambition but not much more than a sketch, a Spenserian knight arrives in the present, to be baffled by paper money and other modern elaborations. Peacock's major Arthurian work is The Misfortunes of Elphin, a short novel published in 1829, but this relates to a quite different kind of Arthurian identity of the period, and to understand it another context needs to be explored.

Though Stephanie Barczewski has argued that both King Arthur and Robin Hood were recruited for a centralising British ideology by the turn of eighteenth century, there is little sign that this is the case.[16] She reads Frere's complex parody as positive nationalism, ignores the radical dissent basic to Thelwall and places great stress on a very minor loyalist poet published in Columbo in 1822, Ambrose Harding Giffard. Setting aside her simplification of the always in some way radical Robin Hood tradition (Scott, Keats, Leigh Hunt and Peacock in fact give him a stoutly non-establishment nineteenth-century initiation), she misses the fact that English poetry in this period has only an ironic or referential interest in Arthur. English scholars had assembled Arthurian materials by the early nineteenth century: George Ellis, Robert Southey and John Dunlop made widely available lists and synopses of Arthurian stories, Le Morte Darthur was republished three times in 1816–17 and Joseph Ritson had gathered the historical material in his Life of King Arthur, published posthumously in 1825.[17] But the English creative artists did not yet respond seriously to the myth. The authors who have a sense of Arthur's specific importance as an image of national identity are in fact Celtic. Scots, Welsh and Cornish scholars and authors around 1800 and after excavated and reworked Arthurian stories for their own self-consciously national political purposes.

Among his many medieval interests, Sir Walter Scott included the Arthur myth. He thought of editing Malory, but left him to Southey, and that may have been more than courtesy, as Scott's own Arthurian material is strongly Scottish in interest and he persuaded Ellis to let him edit *Sir Tristrem* (1804) so it could appear in Edinburgh, not London, claiming as its author the Scottish bard, popular prophet and Merlin equivalent Thomas of Erceldoune, and arguing that the poem showed the ancient 'Inglis' language of southern Scotland. In the same localising spirit his extremely popular poem 'The Lady of the Lake' (1810) borrowed for northern magic the most currently seductive title, and figure, of the Arthurian tradition. Appropriation also provides the basis of *The Bridal of Triermain* (1813). Arthur is the adulterous lover of, again, the Lady of the Lake, and when their daughter Gyneth appears at court she stimulates a violent tournament to select a husband, where Merlin's son (another diminishing invention) is killed; in anger Merlin sends her to sleep. But this Arthurian material is only the distant context for a present in which a sturdy Scots yeoman awakes the sleeping princess and marries her – evidently a figure of Scott's own relationship with this material. Anne Bannerman, a Scottish Border poet whom Scott much admired, rehandled in a parallel way the Arthur material in 'The Prophecy of Merlin' (1802). Arthur is defeated at Camlan, but here the king is entombed by 'the Queen of Beauty' beside the sea and there he will, like Merlin, 'slumber in the cave' before his return.[18] So Arthur is fallible, but undefeated – a symbol of Scotland and the Scottish imagination.

The Welsh were equally active. Scott drew his knowledge of the Tristan legend from William Owen Pughe's *Cambrian Biography* (1803), which, with the contemporary three-volume *Myvyrian Archaiology of Wales* (1801–7), transmitted early Arthurian poetry, Geoffrey of Monmouth and the 'Triads of the Island of Britain', three-line summaries of tradition which contained many Arthurian references. As in Scotland, local writers produced Arthurian material, such as Richard Llwyd: his 'The Bard of Snowdon, to his Countrymen' (1804) celebrated Arthur's victories and his quest for freedom, including Welsh freedom, as did David Lloyd's proto-nationalist 'British Valour, on St David's Day' (1812). A well-known poem was 'Taliesin's Prophecy' by Felicia Hemans, Liverpool-born but living in north Wales: it celebrates the grandeur of the Cymric past and the loss of Welsh independence, as Taliesin speaks of Welsh heroes, focusing on Arthur. The Welsh writers in English did not at this time include early prose narratives, no doubt because the major medieval texts *Culhwch and Olwen* and *The Dream of Rhonabwy* were largely unknown until Charlotte Guest's *Mabinogion* translation (1838–46), but they did create the idea of a Welsh, rather than British myth, an element in the Arthur tradition that still reverberates, and they and the Welsh archivists directly inspired Peacock's *The Misfortunes of Elphin*.

Both a gifted linguist and married in 1817 to a native Welsh speaker, Jane Gruffydh, Peacock was immersed in Welsh literary culture, rather than Arthurian legend.[19] At first the novel deals with the mythic inundation of Cardigan Bay – the dykes were ill-tended by the drunken Seithenyn – and then the birth and education of Taliesin. In the third section Taliesin rescues Guinevere and positions the British to fight the Saxons: the context is Arthurian, but the rescue is not based on the medieval 'Knight of the Cart' story, but the Latin life of the Welsh St Gildas, where Melwas abducts the queen. The novel is also, as usual with Peacock, firmly satirical: the inundation suggests the contemporary pressure for reform, and Seithenyn, who ignores it all, represents George Canning, the inactive Tory leader of the time.

The Cornish energetically developed a regional Arthurian identity. Thomas Hogg's poem *The Fabulous History of Cornwall* (1827) included an account of Arthur's reign drawn from local traditions, as does George Woodley's *Cornubia* (1819). A similar position is taken in John Magor Boyle's *Gorlaye* where the role of Merlin and Uther in the effective rape of Igraine is firmly reprehended – a local opinion heard before in William Hals's *The Complete History of Cornwall* (1736). More influential, at least in England, was R. S. Hawker, parson, scholar and poet who would advise Tennyson on Arthurian themes and locations, and would later link his vigorous verse 'The Quest of the Sangrail' (1865) very strongly with Cornwall, Cornish Christian values, and the authentically spelt Dundagel – not Tintagel.

To see the Arthur material as providing local identification for Scots, Welsh and Cornish may help explain as English ideology one curious feature of Arthurian texts through this period, namely the recurrent idea that Arthur dominates the regions to the north, Scandinavia and even further afield. A focal text is Richard Hole's verse epic, *Arthur or The Northern Enchantment* (1789). This starts with a naval disaster – but Arthur survives somewhere in northern Scotland. He goes on to beat Hengist, and rules a unified and broadly liberal Britain, but much of the fighting is in Scandinavia, even Lapland. Blackmore had set much of his action in the north, as does Thelwall, and Henry Milman's *Samor* (1818), a partly-Arthurian medieval epic, also often goes beyond the confines of Britain towards the pole. Perhaps even the shivering scene in Dryden's *King Arthur* has an arctic ideological thrust.

Geoffrey of Monmouth's Arthur fought in Scandinavia, presumably because Geoffrey was shaping him as a Norman-style king with a Viking heritage, and this was remembered. When the mage John Dee, of Welsh descent, prepared a validation for Elizabethan imperialism (itself recently discovered), including seeking the North-West Passage, he emphasised 'your Highness iust Arthurian claym' to Northern Europe and America, right up to the North Pole.[20] An ideological northernism lies behind Thomas Percy's surprising insistence that romance is a northern – he means German and Scandinavian – form, not the product of the Latin peoples. Even Warton, with his massive learning, was north-oriented enough to see Charlemagne as the homologue of Arthur.[21] It seems that a range of English writers found it compelling to imagine the conquest of the cold, bracing regions to the north as a kind of ideological, even political, response to the luxurious antiquity and power of the south.

The northern Arthur is one of the few interesting elements to be found in Bulwer Lytton's *King Arthur* of 1848, which looks backwards in being a verse epic in twelve books, in rejecting entirely Malory's story, and in attempting to construct a patriotic, though now imperial, vision of Arthur. It has several modern features, however: the Lancelot–Guinevere adultery is banished as an ancient mistake – Lancelot is in fact faithfully married to a woman named Genevra. Merlin is a romantic Druid (with some resemblance to T. H. White's version), and even Byron's influence appears in a long would-be comic sequence about Gawain. The ultimate message is as clumsily up-to-date as Blackmore's was in his time: this is a world of a unified Britain where 'Celt and Saxon rear their common throne', and yet as empire widens 'new born nations speak the Teuton's speech'.[22]

King of morality

Reginald Heber pointed a way forward for the Arthur myth. A gifted man who in 1826 died young as Bishop of Calcutta, he produced in 1816 'The Masque of Gwendolen', a powerful version of 'The Marriage of Gawain', with a dark Merlin who makes the heroine a loathly lady when she rejects him. But Heber's main Arthurian project was to versify Malory in the first true revival of *Le Morte Darthur*, started in 1810, before the three reprints of 1816–17. Though Taylor and Brewer feel he was 'missing the potential symbolic richness' of the myth,[23] the few completed sequences show him moralising Malory in often powerful stanzas. Morgue, Arthur's sister, is a major villain, avenging the mistreatment at court of Mordred her son, but Arthur is not the father: Heber censors this and much of Malory's violence. He also relegates the Holy Grail to little more than an ornament in Arthur's chapel, a view probably representing the dominantly 'Low' Anglicanism of this period.

Tennyson's wide reading surely included Heber, and he certainly knew both Malory and Southey's long preface to the 1817 edition, but he did not connect immediately with the great medieval version. When in 1832 he produced 'The Lady of Shalott', his source was an Italian novelette published in 1804,[24] providing much of the exotic and passionate element in the poem. He toned that down in the better-known 1842 version, a move possibly prompted by the much more positive account of Elaine, stressing the falsity of men, given also in 1832 in Letitia Elizabeth Landon's popular 'A Legend of Tintagel Castle'. By the early 1830s Tennyson was already thinking about a major Arthurian work. In his first ideas there were clear links to recent reworkings – Merlin Emrys was to be a foolish figure, though his name is authentically Welsh. Then by 1833 he had planned a basically symbolic version where Mordred represents 'the sceptical understanding' and Merlin is no more than 'worldly prudence'.[25] Malory soon came to be important to Tennyson: his early short poems on 'Sir Galahad' and 'Sir Launcelot and Queen Guinevere' sketch Malorian moments, and 'The Epic' (1837–8) suggests a twelve-book story on epic lines ending as Malory does, with the repentance of Lancelot and Guinevere. This was planned as a frame for his *Morte d'Arthur*, his tribute to his great friend Arthur Hallam, who died in 1833. This effectively recentred Malory in English literature and would provide the end of the *Idylls of the King*.

But nobility alone was not enough. When Tennyson's friend John Sterling reviewed the *Morte d'Arthur* in the *Quarterly Review* he felt it lacked 'passionate imagery' and also 'any stronger human interest',[26] and when the initially disheartened Tennyson returned to Arthur in the early 1850s (with Hawker's stimulus) he focused with some passion on what he saw as the very human problem of the role and power of women, recently dealt with – negatively – in *Maud* and *The Princess*.[27] The first two Idylls written were 'Nimue' (later 'Merlin and Vivien') and 'Enid' (later divided into 'Geraint and Enid' and 'The Marriage of Geraint'), and they appeared in a trial edition under the title *The True and the False*. Here in both title and text woman is stereotyped for ill and good. Vivien's overt and manipulative sexuality overcomes the gifted but ultimately morally weak Merlin, while Enid's purity and endurance save the rash and honour-obsessed Geraint. Arthur is 'the blameless king', untouchable by Vivien's scheming (who seems to owe something to Heber's Morgue) and above the misbehaviour of the court, including, it is already hinted, that of Lancelot and Guinevere ('Merlin and Vivien', line 1621). They are only passingly mentioned because these first idylls have almost nothing to do with Malory. The Merlin and Vivien story is based on the Vulgate *Merlin*'s extended encounter between Merlin and Vivien (summarised in Southey's 1817 preface), though the harshness of tone could derive from Malory's use of the more austere Post-Vulgate version. The story of Enid was drawn from Guest's *Mabinogion*, where it is one of the Welsh romances, itself bearing some still unclear relation to the *Erec et Enide* of Chrétien de Troyes.

The next two idylls turned directly to Malory to make clear the gendered moralism of the emerging Arthuriad: 'Elaine', closely retelling Malory's story of 'The Fair Maid of Astolat' – the same figure as 'The Lady of Shalott' but with her passions under closer English control – and 'Guinevere', an almost entirely imagined and highly censorious account of the adulterous but repentant queen. These made up the four 1859 *Idylls of the King* and this immensely successful publication made morality, in particular the avoidance of sexual misconduct, central to the myth of Arthur as a guide to the good maintenance of both the kingdom and the home. This domesticated version of the Arthurian legend would remain archetypal at least until the First World War.

As he moved on, Tennyson made the meaning of Arthur's values and the problems he faced extend beyond gender anxiety. In 'The Coming of Arthur' he saw him both as a leader who civilised a savage people and also a monarch with divine blessing. King Leodogran's doubts about Arthur's identity and royalty are resolved in a Christian visionary dream that showed 'the king stood out in heaven, / Crowned' ('The Coming of Arthur', lines 442–3). To close the idylls, Tennyson developed 'The Passing of Arthur' from his own *Morte*, with an extended Malorian introduction and new emphasis on the Christian, if uncompleted, nature of Arthur's mission. Elsewhere Tennyson added moral, even personally focused emphasis. 'The Holy Grail' represented Galahad as like John Newman of the Oxford Movement, a saintly person with a distracting, even delusionary, impact on normal Christians. In 'The Last Tournament' the adulterer Lancelot is listless, even depressive, while Tristram is erotically cheerful – and murdered by King Mark. In the crisis of both idylls Arthur is absent, righting wrongs: he and Tennyson do not share the medieval enthusiasm for love, religious or sensual. But Arthur's good work is not without its own ideal, even religious status. At the end of the Grail quest, Arthur's final words foresee the power of an ordinary person to imitate Christ:

> In moments when he feels he cannot die,
> And knows himself no vision to himself,
> Nor the high God a vision, nor that One
> Who rose again: ye have seen what ye have seen.
> ('The Holy Grail', lines 912–15)

But in 'The Last Tournament' Arthur's young knights lose control of themselves and the ensuing police riot shows the dream of moral order is, now at least, fated for failure. Powerful, moral and tragic, Tennyson's Arthurian project gained massive contemporary consent, and its central and dominating importance makes it in retrospect seem obvious, inevitable, as the voice of Victorianism. But in fact it was only Tennyson's great powers of concentration and endurance that rescued Arthur from the comic and political underworld and re-established him as a central figure of English literary value, to be deployed as such by many creative artists.

Some of the most imaginative and forceful re-creations of Arthurian material in the mid- and late nineteenth century were visual.[28] Tennyson's impact was considerable: as early as 1855 Moxon republished his 1842 *Poems* with wood-engravings, some Arthurian, based on work by painters as distinguished as Daniel Maclise and Dante Gabriel Rossetti, and in 1866–7 he produced new separate editions of the four 1859 *Idylls* with Gustave Doré's detailed and dramatic steel engravings. Equally ground-breaking were the moody photographs provided by the pioneer Julia Margaret Cameron for an 1875 edition of the *Idylls*. Many painters used 'The Lady of Shalott' as a theme, notably J.W. Waterhouse (1860) and, in a series leading to a great painting, W. Holman Hunt (1886–1905),[29] while Vivien was also popular – Frederick Sandys made her a brilliantly edgy *femme fatale* (1863), while Rossetti treated Nimue on several occasions. Edward Burne-Jones's massive 'The Sleep of Arthur in Avalon' (1881–98, reproduced on the cover and frontispiece of this volume), like James Archer's multi-episodic *La Mort D'Arthur* (1860), refers to Tennyson at some distance, as do most of the many Galahads, notably the lengthy sequence by G.F. Watts from 1856 on. But some major Arthurian paintings draw on Malory, such as William Morris's sole surviving oil, the masterly 'La Belle Iseult' (1858 – it is sometimes called 'Queen Guinevere' but though he was soon to write his 'Defence' of her, the pet dog on the bed suggests otherwise) and Rossetti's stark 'Lancelot and Guinevere at the Tomb of Arthur' (1855); and while Burne-Jones's masterpiece 'The Beguiling of Merlin' (1874) looks as if it could relate to Tennyson, it draws more directly on the French *Merlin*, via Southey.

Not only paintings were Arthurian. The Pre-Raphaelite Brotherhood as a body undertook in 1857 to decorate the Oxford Union with Arthurian scenes. The frescoes were of varied quality, and have now drastically faded through their creators' technical inexperience, but some of the work is worthy of its creators' great talents – notably Burne-Jones's 'Merlin and Nimue', Morris's 'Palomides' Jealousy of Tristram', and Rossetti's 'Lancelot at the Grail Chapel'. To make a location of such prestige and coded power centrally Arthurian matched the decision of 1847 – interestingly before Tennyson was a major force – to commission William Dyce to create Arthurian murals of a classical-Christian allegorical character (Whitaker calls them 'episodic and hortatory'),[30] but basically derived from Malory, for the rebuilt Houses of Parliament. In 1867 they were supplemented with melodramatic bas-reliefs in wood and stone by H. H. Armstead and together they shift the authority of the king to the people's representatives, a move parallel to Tennyson's general moralisation of Arthur's meaning.

In poetry the power of the *Idylls* attracted many imitators, such as General Edward Hamley's 'Sir Tray: an Arthurian idyll' (1873), Elinor Sweetman's 'Pastoral of Galahad' and 'Pastoral of Lancelot' (1889), and Alfred Austin's 'The Passing of Merlin' (1898). Tennyson's moral centring of Arthur, masculinity and royalty were grounds for dissent to some. Swinburne made some memorable jokes, calling the poem 'the Morte d'Albert' and saying that Vivien was a figure for a police court.[31] But his own major Arthurian work 'Tristram of Lyonesse', while certainly valuing sensual and passionate love more highly than the *Idylls*, actually presents it with just the same verbal richness and sonorous phrasing that Tennyson had made a voice for serious poetry. William Morris dissented more fully in his 'The Defence of Guenevere' which appeared in 1858 just as Tennyson was writing his 'Guinevere'. Morris makes her speak her own defence: but it is no defence at all, just defiance. She denies the charges, says she has made her choice, that she enjoys and invites onlookers to enjoy her own sensual athleticism, and waits for Lancelot's rescue, which comes very dramatically at the very end. Bryden comments on the 'psychological dimension' of the treatment of the myth by the Pre-Raphaelites.[32]

There were less polite critiques like 'The Coming K– : a set of idyll lays' (1873), a lurid satire directed at the Prince of Wales by S. O. Beeton, A. A. Dowty and S. R. Emerson, and the ironic reversing of Tennyson's story *The New King Arthur: An Opera without Music* (1885) by the American Edgar Fawcett. Americans tended to see the tradition differently: J. R. Lowell had in 1848 produced 'The Vision of Sir Launfal', which uses the simple fourteenth-century tail-rhyme romance and its hero's failure at Camelot as a way of criticising aristocratic certainties: Launfal's saving by the fairy mistress seems to some degree an American republican fantasy. A much more substantial critique was Mark Twain's 1889 *The Adventures of a Connecticut Yankee at the Court of King Arthur*, which identified stupidity and brutality in the sixth-century world of Arthur, though it is also a fully medieval world, drawing with some humour, but also some affection, on Malory. The hero, Hank Morgan, is the Yankee, a man of business, technology, egalitarianism, even vulgarity, and his opponent is the old Tory wizard Merlin, whom Twain's illustrator Dan Beard represents as an easily identifiable version of Tennyson.

Yet Twain, like Lowell, had more to say than making fun, and he trenchantly criticised old-world practices, including serfdom and Versailles-style licence. But he also found value in the past: Arthur, through his engagement with slavery and disease, and those who suffered from both, is a man of real courage, and the courtly lady Hank marries is his real love. The medieval world itself was beautiful, yet Twain links its beauty to his own remembered south, and slavery: he also shows how the modern democratic north generates its own negative forms in the inhumanity of mercantilism and, worst of all, the fearful weaponry by which the Yankee and his few friends eventually annihilate the whole knighthood of England. But it is Merlin, almost forgotten, who finally wins, and sends Hank back to his present, where he mourns, as the subtitle of the novel has it, 'The Lost Land'. So Twain invites our complex reaction to his brilliantly interrogative Arthuriad, that both opposes Tennyson and confirms his centring of Arthur as a focus of value and tragedy. Arthur was a focus for evaluating the period itself, as Bryden shows.[33]

That Arthur was regenerated as a central figure of cultural and social myth in this way can be in some part attributed to the scholarly archivists at work around 1800 and to the political energies that Arthur released in the Celtic world. But that was just the context for the redevelopment. While other Victorian artists did take the medieval world seriously, their work, like Matthew Arnold's *Tristan and Isolde* or William Morris's imitation of Norse saga, had little lasting impact; the scholarly, visionary and intensely poetic powers of Tennyson were the main force that set Arthur back at the centre of imaginative writing and evaluative thinking. In the four centuries after Caxton published Malory's great work, there had been many Arthurs – allegorical and farcical, patriotic and propagandist, iconic and ironic, defeatist and triumphalist, cowardly and imperialist, pathetic and empathetic. Through Tennyson and Twain he had ended up a Christian humanist, a moral figure of self-consideration and self-evaluation, always with a troublesome voice close to his ear, whether Vivien, Merlin, Hank or – as the twentieth century would show – the chaotic and tragic practices of human beings in the modern world. Arthur had returned from his long journey through the nether cultural regions of mockery and manipulation, and just as the figure had lent a stabilising evaluative focus to the tribulations of the Middle Ages, so he, with the increasingly authoritative Merlin beside him, would be a source of consolation and aspiration through the savagery of the twentieth century.

NOTES

1 *The English Works of Roger Ascham*, ed. William Aldis Wright (Cambridge University Press, 1904), p. 231. Not all works referred to in this essay have been cited in full. See *The Arthurian Annals: The Tradition in English from 1250 to 2000*, ed. Daniel P. Nastali and Phillip C. Boardman, 2 vols. (Oxford University Press, 2004), for full bibliographical details.

2 From *Scriptorium Illustrium Maioris Britanniae*, 2nd edn (1557), trans. Frank Kearney, in *Sir Thomas Malory: The Critical Heritage*, ed. Marylyn Parins (London: Routledge, 1988), p. 55.

3 R. S. Crane, *The Vogue of Medieval Chivalric Romance During the English Renaissance* (Menasha, WI: Collegiate Press, 1919), pp. 1–11, and the Appendix, 'Medieval Romance in England after 1500', in Helen Cooper, *The English Romance in Time* (Oxford University Press, 2004), pp. 409–29.

4 Juliet Vale, 'Arthur in English Society', in *AoE*, pp. 185–96.

5 Sidney Anglo, 'The *British History* in Early Tudor Propaganda', *Bulletin of the John Rylands Library*, 44 (1961), 17–48 (p. 32).

6 Michael Drayton, *Poly-Olbion*, Song 4, ed. J. William Hebel (Oxford: Blackwell, 1961), p. 58.

7 John Dryden, *King Arthur: The British Worthy: A Dramatick Opera* (London: Tronson, 1691), IV.ii.47 and III.ii.314.

8 Richard Blackmore, *Prince Arthur: An Heroick Poem in Ten Books* (London: Awnsham & Churchil, 1695), IV, p. 122.

9 Blackmore, *King Arthur: An Heroick Poem in Twelve Books* (London: Awnsham, Churchill & Tonson, 1697), XII, p. 347.

10 John Dennis, *Remarks on a Book Entituled Prince Arthur, an Heroick Poem* (London: Heyrick & Sare, 1696); Dryden, 'Prologue' to John Fletcher's *The Pilgrim*, *The Poems of John Dryden*, ed. James Kinsley, 4 vols. (Oxford: Clarendon Press, 1952), IV.1759, line 49; *The Poems of Alexander Pope*, Vol. 5: *The Dunciad*, ed. James Sutherland (London: Methuen, 1943), II.290, p. 137.

11 Henry Fielding, *The Tragedy of Tragedies: The Life and Death of Tom Thumb the Great* (London: Roberts, 1731), p. 1.

12 Fielding, *Tom Thumb*, p. 56.

13 Thomas Warton, *Observations on the Fairy Queen of Edmund Spenser* [1758], facsimile of the 2nd edn, 2 vols. (New York: Greenwood Press, 1968), pp. 6–7.

14 Samuel Taylor Coleridge, *Table Talk*, ed. Carl Woodring, in *The Collected Works of Samuel Taylor Coleridge*, ed. Kathleen Coburn, 16 vols. (London: Routledge, 1976), XIV, p. 441.

15 James Douglas Merriman, *The Flower of Kings: A Study of the Arthurian Legend in England and Wales between 1485 and 1835* (Lawrence, KA: University Press of Kansas, 1973), pp. 137–8.

16 Stephanie L. Barczewski, *Myth and National Identity in Nineteenth-Century Britain: The Myths of King Arthur and Robin Hood* (Oxford University Press, 2000).

17 George Ellis, *Specimens of Early English Metrical Romance*, 3 vols. (London: Longman, 1805); Robert Southey, 'Preface' to Sir Thomas Malory, *The Byrth, Lyf and Actes of Kyng Arthur* (London: Longman et al., 1817); John Dunlop, *The History of Fiction*, 2 vols. (London: Longman et al., 1814); Joseph Ritson, *The Life of King Arthur* (London: Payne & Foss, 1825).

18 Anne Bannerman, 'The Prophecy of Merlin', in *Tales of Superstition and Chivalry* (London: Vernor & Hood, 1802), p. 126.

19 For a recent discussion of the novel and its context see Rob Gossedge, 'Thomas Love Peacock's *The Misfortunes of Elphin* and the Romantic Arthur', in *Arthurian Literature*, 23 (2006), 157–76.

20 John Dee, *The Limits of the British Empire*, ed. Ken MacMillan with Jennifer Abeles, Studies in Military History and International Affairs (Westport, CT: Praeger, 2004), pp. 52–61 and 83.

21 Thomas Percy, Appendix II, 'On the Ancient Metrical Romances, etc', *Reliques of Early English Poetry*, 3 vols. (London: Dodsley, 1765), III, pp. 341–50; Thomas Warton discusses Charlemagne and Arthur in his 'Dissertation', 'Of the Origin of Romantic Fictions of Europe', in his *History of English Poetry* (London: Dodsley, Walter & Becket, 1774–81), I [unpaginated].

22 Edward Bulwer Lytton, *King Arthur* (London: Colburn, 1848), XII, pp. 190–1.

23 Beverly Taylor and Elisabeth Brewer, *The Return of King Arthur: British and American Literature since 1800*, Arthurian Studies 9 (Cambridge: D. S. Brewer, 1983), p. 63.

24 The anonymous story was *Qui conta come la Damigella di Scalot mori per amore di Lancialotto de Lac* ('Which tells how the Maiden of Scalot died for love of Lancialotto de Lac'), ed. Giulia Ferraro (Milan: Società Tipigraphica dei Classici Italiani, 1804).

25 See the Introduction to the *Idylls of the King* in *The Poems of Tennyson*, ed. Christopher Ricks (London: Longman, 1969), pp. 1460–1. For a discussion of these plans see Roger Simpson, *Camelot Regained: The Arthurian Revival and Tennyson, 1800–1849*, Arthurian Studies 21 (Cambridge: D. S. Brewer, 1990), pp. 201–2.

26 Repr. in *Tennyson: The Critical Heritage*, ed. John D. Jump (London: Routledge, 1967), p. 119.

27 For a discussion of ideology in the *Idylls of the King*, see Stephen Knight, 'The Phantom King: Tennyson's *Idylls of the King*', in *Arthurian Literature and Society* (London: Macmillan, 1983), Ch.5.

28 The following material draws on Muriel Whitaker, Ch. 8, 'The Art of Moral Buildings' and Ch. 9, 'Tennyson and the Artists', in *The Legends of King Arthur in Art*, Arthurian Studies 22 (Cambridge: D. S. Brewer, 1990).

29 Whitaker, *King Arthur in Art*, p. 213.

30 *Ibid.*, p. 183.

31 Quoted in *Tennyson*, ed. Jump, p. 321.

32 Inga Bryden, *Reinventing King Arthur: The Arthurian Legend in Victorian Culture* (Aldershot: Ashgate, 2005), pp. 104–8.

33 Bryden, *Reinventing King Arthur*, pp. 104–5.

7

NORRIS J. LACY

The Arthur of the twentieth and twenty-first centuries

The Arthurian legend of the twentieth and twenty-first centuries is a remarkably malleable body of material, capable of being expanded, contracted, or radically changed in form to fit the design of an author or the tastes of the public. Since 1900, and far more so since 1950, the legend has been shaped into social and political satire, comedy, science fiction and fantasy, feminist fiction, mysteries and thrillers, comic books, and more than a few examples of pure silliness, both on the printed page and on the screen and stage. In addition, we have a good many basic retellings of the traditional story, most inspired by Malory and recast either for adults or, more often, for young readers. Such adaptations are accomplished with varying degrees of fidelity either to the source or to the presumed spirit of the 'Arthurian period', whether that period is assumed to be the sub-Roman 'Dark Ages' or, more often, the high Middle Ages.

It is perhaps not entirely surprising that Arthur, in his modern incarnations, is most popular in literature written in English. He was known as King of the Britons, and in addition Middle English Arthurian literature includes the most influential late-medieval text, the works of Sir Thomas Malory. However, these two facts are not sufficient to explain Arthur's greater hold on the imagination of anglophone authors and readers. After all, the great flowering of Arthuriana occurred on the Continent, with France in the lead and other languages and lands close behind. In addition, just as Britain had its Malory, so did France have its Chrétien de Troyes (and the *Lancelot-Grail* Cycle and the Prose *Tristan*), and the German-speaking lands had equally great models in Wolfram von Eschenbach's *Parzival* and in Gottfried von Strassburg's *Tristan* as well, though in the strictest sense Gottfried is not an Arthurian author. (Arthur appears in many medieval Tristan texts but not in Gottfried's. Nonetheless, in the modern tradition the two legends have been fused.)

In fact, we ought perhaps to trace modern interest in Arthur not entirely to the Middle Ages but rather to the nineteenth century, when Malory's work was re-edited and thus rediscovered, and when Tennyson and the Pre-Raphaelites interpreted the legend in ways that proved popular and extraordinarily influential. This Arthurian Revival became an Arthurian 'explosion' during the twentieth century. Indeed, the encyclopaedic *Arthurian Annals* documents everything Arthurian (except academic scholarship) produced in English between 1250 and 2000.[1] The number of items runs to some 11,300. Moreover, the *Annals* demonstrate that just over 80 per cent of all Arthurian works in English date from the twentieth century, and more than half of that number – over 4,500 – were published in the last two decades of that century. We are therefore left with two questions that can be answered only partially: why is Arthur far more popular now than ever before? And why so much more so in the English-speaking world than elsewhere?

A partial explanation may be related to the 'post-modern' scepticism of modern anglophone and particularly North American audiences in regard to the very notion of an authoritative and 'correct' version of the legend. Fidelity to the conventional sources of authority, including not only Malory but also a long chronicle tradition and our knowledge of sub-Roman Britain, means a great deal to some authors (such as Mary Stewart or Rosemary Sutcliff) and to their readers, but little or nothing to many others, for whom the legend is no longer anchored in authoritative sources. In addition, and particularly in North America, Mark Twain must be singled out for his extraordinarily successful contribution to irreverent views of the Arthurian legend. He may well have done more than anyone else to establish Arthur as a central figure in anglophone popular culture, reinforcing the notion that the king and the legend are, or can be, whatever we want them to be.

The early twentieth century

Arthurian works of the very early twentieth century were largely a continuation of the Arthurian Revival of the nineteenth. The influence of Tennyson and of the Pre-Raphaelites remained strong. Poetry was the principal vehicle for the expression of Arthurian themes in the early decades of the century, although the novel, complemented eventually by film, would later become the dominant form. Dramas would continue to be written, but since Richard Hovey's major cycle of plays at the very end of the nineteenth century, only a small number of dramatic creations have been noteworthy. Meriting mention, however, is Thomas Hardy's *The Famous Tragedy of the Queen of Cornwall* (1923), concluding with Tristan killed by Mark, after which Iseult commits suicide. Also of note are dramas by Christopher Fry (*Thor, with Angels*, 1948), set in the sixth century, with Merlin as the prophet of Christianity; and by John Arden and Margaretta D'Arcy (*The Island of the Mighty*, 1974), in which violence and madness metaphorically represent social disorder in modern Britain. There are a good many others that deserve mention, but generally speaking, drama is not a prevalent Arthurian vehicle in the twentieth century.

A number of important Arthurian poems or poetic cycles appeared between the First World War and mid-century. Four poets stand out in particular. Edwin Arlington Robinson composed three fine poems on the subject of ill-fated love: *Merlin* (1917), *Lancelot* (1920), and *Tristram* (1927). His work, though appealing and well crafted, is now overshadowed as Arthurian poetry by T. S. Eliot's *The Waste Land* (1922), one of the seminal poems of the twentieth century. Drawing his inspiration less from original texts than from Jessie Weston's *From Ritual to Romance* (1920), Eliot appropriates the Arthurian theme of the waste land and its maimed king as a metaphor for the decay represented by the modern city. The poem is complex and difficult (though glossed by Eliot himself in notes), and its bitter pessimism is only slightly attenuated by its final line 'Shantih shantih shantih', which, Eliot points out, is the equivalent of 'The Peace which passeth understanding.'

Nearer to mid-century, Charles Williams published two collections of poems: *Taliessin Through Logres* (1938) and *The Region of the Summer Stars* (1944). Williams treats the rise and fall of Camelot and emphasises the mythic value of the Grail and quest. Finally, Welsh poet David Jones composed two difficult but important Arthurian works: *In Parenthesis* (1937) drew a parallel between the battlefields of the war and the Arthurian wasteland, and *The Anathémata* (1952) is also replete with Arthurian imagery, including reference to Christ's appearance to Galahad.

As illustrated by the preceding examples, the Arthurian legend provides a complex set of symbols, motifs and points of reference that can be appropriated by poets, novelists, filmmakers and others, with reasonable confidence that the reference will not be lost on the audience. Among those easily recognisable features of the legend are the Holy Grail and the quest, Merlin, the sword in the stone, the love of Lancelot and Guinevere, and the possible return of the 'once and future' king. The twentieth century saw these features recast in numerous forms and permutations, and later in the century a good many authors would increasingly liberate themselves from the traditionally authoritative sources, leading to some original and appealing creations but also to a good many eccentric works that appear to have no anchor at all in traditional models.

For convenience, I shall discuss Arthurian works within four admittedly imprecise and oversimplified categories: retellings, updated narratives, the use of Arthurian themes as metaphor or structure, and 'revisionist' views that reinterpret the Arthurian story irreverently or even cynically. These categories most often intersect and overlap, and of course any number of works fit uneasily or not at all into any of them.

Retellings

Most readers first become acquainted with the Arthurian legend through Malory's version as retold by modern authors, usually for younger readers and thus often simplified or bowdlerised. In general the Arthur presented in these retellings is an idealised figure, a noble and nearly flawless ruler betrayed by a Mordred who is generally presented as Arthur's nephew rather than his bastard son. That idealisation of the king often extends to other characters and situations, and not surprisingly a good many authors of retellings for children deal as delicately as possible with the relationship of Lancelot and Guinevere. The hesitation to dramatise Arthur's failings as well as his strengths and to acknowledge the flaws of characters other than Mordred surely accounts for the notion, held even by many adult readers, of an Arthurian Golden Age, 'one brief shining moment' of heroism and glory. Among the most popular and best retellings for young readers during the twentieth century are those of Howard Pyle, Rosemary Sutcliff, Penelope Lively, Susan Cooper, and, in the early parts of his Arthurian cycle, T. H. White.

Pyle published four Arthurian volumes, inspired primarily by Malory, between 1903 and 1910. His books praised the courage and moral rectitude of Arthurian characters and held them up as models to be emulated by modern readers. Sutcliff, one of the best of modern Arthurian authors, published four retellings for younger readers, as well as two novels for adults. Among the former are *Tristan and Iseult* (1971) and *The Sword and the Circle* (1981), the latter of which draws on Malory and a number of other sources. For adults, her *Sword at Sunset* (1963) is a complex and intriguing novel in which Arthur tells his story in the first person. (In her effort to be 'true' to a variety of sources, including the earliest legends, Sutcliff, like Mary Stewart and a few others, makes Bedwyr, not Lancelot, the queen's lover.) *The Whispering Knights* (1971) by Penelope Lively follows the adventures of three young people who, in re-enacting the witches' scene from *Macbeth*, happen to conjure up Morgan le Fay, whose evil designs are ultimately thwarted by the knights of the title, who are in fact prehistoric standing stones.

Susan Cooper is the author of a five-volume series intended for young readers and set in the present. Known collectively as The Dark is Rising, the series begins with *Over Sea, Under Stone* (1965) and *The Dark is Rising* (1973) and concludes with *Silver on the Tree* in 1977. 'The Dark' is an evil force opposed by a group of young people; though aided by Merriman (Merlin), they rely upon their own courage and ingenuity and eventually find the Grail and other symbols of power and compassion. T. H. White's *The Once and Future King*, a cycle of four novels published under that title in 1958, defies easy categorisation. It is a cycle that begins with a children's book, *The Sword in the Stone* (from 1938), but the nature of his work changes as his characters, especially Arthur, age and evolve. Passing, in the course of the four books, from juvenile fiction through romance to tragedy, White's cycle was to conclude with a fifth novel, *The Book of Merlyn*, but this last work was omitted and was published only in 1988. The evolution of the published tetralogy, however, is remarkable, as an amusing tale for children evolves into a strong and sometimes bitter antiwar document, replete with anachronistic but powerful allusions, for example, to an Austrian tyrant and his storm troopers.

White's work has been enormously influential and popular. Despite his misanthropy and his transformation of the cycle into an antiwar manifesto, its admirers retain in particular the evocation of Arthurian glory that lasted for 'one brief and shining moment' – a view that is reinforced not only by the fact that most readers doubtless know best the early part of the cycle, but also by the celebration of that Arthurian 'moment' by *Camelot*, the 1960 Lerner and Loewe musical based on *The Once and Future King* (and the 1967 film version of it, dir. Joshua Logan), by the Disney film of *The Sword in the Stone* (1963), and by the appropriation of the Camelot motif, immediately after the assassination of US President John F. Kennedy, as a metaphor for his brief tenure in the White House.

Among retellings for adults, I have already mentioned Rosemary Sutcliff. Other important efforts include those of Mary Stewart, John Steinbeck, Thomas Berger and Marion Zimmer Bradley. Stewart's Merlin novels – a trilogy to which a fourth novel concerning Mordred was added – are among the most popular and likely most enduring of twentieth-century Arthurian fiction. *The Crystal Cave* (1973), *The Hollow Hills* (1973) and *The Last Enchantment* (1979) present Merlin's story from his beginnings through his role in Arthur's education and coronation and finally to the enchanter's disappearance. Stewart innovates freely while still remaining relatively faithful to medieval sources, primarily but by no means exclusively Malory. John Steinbeck was drawn to Arthurian themes, especially through Malory. He used those themes to structure his *Tortilla Flat* (1935), and some critics have perceived Arthurian echoes in several of his other novels. However, he is also the author of an explicit retelling – or attempted retelling – of the legend as it is given in the Winchester manuscript of Malory. The result is the unfinished *The Acts of King Arthur and his Noble Knights* (1958–9, but published only in 1976). Steinbeck began the work as a straightforward retelling but soon began to innovate more and more freely. His vision also became increasingly pessimistic, and he began to emphasise the ultimate futility of chivalry: failures are frequent whereas victories are fleeting and often inconsequential. Steinbeck's correspondence at the time documents his growing difficulty in grappling with the legend, and eventually he cut it off abruptly without a conclusion.

Novels that focus on female characters or that tell their story from a woman's point of view were once, but are no longer, very scarce. The publication of novels and short stories that feature women is one of the major developments in Arthurian fiction of the second half of the century. The best-known representative of this trend is surely Marion Zimmer Bradley, who authored *The Mists of Avalon* in 1982. (It was made into a less than successful movie in 2001.) The novel, which has most often been characterised as feminist fiction, offers a nuanced view of the female characters, complex women not all of whom are virtuous and admirable. Apart from the female perspective, the most fascinating feature of the novel is the conjunction or conflict of the traditional pagan culture and the new Christian faith. In addition to Bradley's novel, we have trilogies focusing on female characters by Sharan Newman (*Guinevere*, 1981; *The Chessboard Queen*, 1984; *Guinevere Evermore*, 1985) and by Persia Woolley (*Child of the Northern Spring*, 1987; *Queen of the Summer Stars*, 1990; *Guinevere: The Legend in Autumn*, 1991). Other novels and stories focus on Guinevere, on Morgan, on Ninian (Vivian, Nimue), or, as Vera Chapman's title indicates, on *King Arthur's Daughter*, published in 1976.

Thomas Berger, in *Arthur Rex* (1978), offers a retelling that is also a revisionist view of the legend. It is a retelling unlike any other. With keen wit, irony and a mock-archaic style, Berger presents Uther as a hairy and smelly brute, Arthur as a pompous young king, and the Grail quest as (in Arthur's view) blasphemy, given that only the sinless can accomplish the quest and that only Christ was free of sin. The result is at the same time a fresh and engaging narrative and a comic masterpiece that capitalises on the flaws within Arthurian characters. The flaws had always been there, from Tennyson's 'The old order changeth' to White's 'one brief shining moment' (both of them anticipating the fall of Camelot even as they emphasise its initial glory), but it was only in the second half of the century that a realistic – some would say cynical – and revisionist interpretation of the legend would become almost routine. This observation, though largely accurate, is a generalisation that ignores earlier works such as Mark Twain's *Connecticut Yankee in King Arthur's Court* (1889). Many readers consider Twain's satirical presentation to be a diminution of Arthur, though ultimately the novel demonstrates that the notion of modern progress is illusory. If Camelot is silly, corrupt and even brutish, Twain implies, the modern world has simply discovered more efficiently brutish methods and machines of war.

Updating Arthur

Updating refers to the composition of works in which authors have one or more Arthurian characters, or sometimes the entire Arthurian cast, reappear in a contemporary context. Such an approach is invited by the 'cave legend' and the belief that Arthur will return in the time of Britain's greatest need, as well as by the related notion, despite the lack of medieval authority for it, of Merlin's immortality. C. S. Lewis, in *That Hideous Strength* (1945), updates the legend to the present, having Merlin awakened from his long sleep to oppose a group known as NICE (National Institute of Coordinated Experiments), whose purpose is to impose a new world order. The novel incorporates not only Merlin, but extensive Arthurian imagery including a Fisher King figure with a painful and incurable injury. Susan Cooper's The Dark is Rising series, discussed above, also falls into this category, as the three young protagonists have the aid of a reincarnated Merlin and of Bran, who here is the son of Arthur and Guinevere. Similarly, Roger Zelazny's story 'The Last Defender of Camelot' (1980; televised as an episode of *Twilight Zone* in 1985) has Merlin awakened in the twentieth century by contemporary embodiments of Lancelot and Morgan.

The category of updatings includes Peter David's often clever – and not infrequently tedious – trilogy: *Knight Life* (1987, revised 2002), *One Knight Only* (2003) and *Fall of Knight* (2006). Several Arthurian characters reappear in the modern world, and Arthur becomes mayor of New York and then president of the United States, after which he enters into a commercial venture to sell bottled water that has first been poured into the Holy Grail and thus endowed with healing powers. In Donald Barthelme's post-modern novel *The King* (1990), Arthur does not reappear, simply because he never disappeared. Having lived on 'a few centuries beyond the normal [life] span', he finds himself in England during the blitz. Enormously amusing and yet very serious, the novel equates the Grail with the ultimate bomb, which, in his most heroic act, Arthur chooses not to use. Less memorable is Dennis Lee Anderson's *Arthur, King* (1995), in which Arthur and the villain Mordred reappear during the blitz and do battle with each other.

Instead of reincarnating Arthur and others in the present, a good many novels feature modern characters who, often as a result of their fascination or extended contact with the legend, assume the personalities and identities of Arthurian figures. In general, this absorption of Arthurian identities and roles is a phenomenon of the later part of the century, but an earlier example is John Cowper Powys's powerful novel *A Glastonbury Romance* (1932). Not only do the protagonists exhibit the characteristics of Arthurian figures, but in this instance they are in part drawn into those roles by the attraction of the Glastonbury setting.

In addition to novels that update the legend to the twentieth century, a number go farther and set their stories in the future. They may allow access to an 'alternate universe' (Andre Norton's *Witch World*, 1963) or deal with time travel from the sixth century to the twenty-first and back (Fred Saberhagen's *Merlin's Bones*, 1995). An outstanding example of Arthurian science fiction is C. J. Cherryh's *Port Eternity* (1982), in which cloned beings are marooned in a space craft. Cherryh's novel is also representative of the class of works in which characters absorb Arthurian identities: when they were created, the cloned beings had been given Arthurian names, and once stranded, they gradually begin to act out the corresponding personas.

The legend as structure

As noted above, some of the most productive modern approaches to Arthurian composition involve the appropriation of an element – a motif or an episode – of the legend and its use to structure a text that may not be explicitly Arthurian at all. The quest (whether for the Grail or another goal) and the waste-land theme are no doubt the most prevalent choices. Eliot's *The Waste Land*, discussed above, is the most familiar and doubtless the most important representative of this approach. Also prevalent are parallels, either explicit or implicit, to the pattern of the medieval Tristan legend. The parallel may be to fated love, to the complications of a love triangle, or both. Among the prominent novelists drawn to this approach are James Joyce in *Finnegans Wake* (1939), Sir Arthur Quiller-Couch in *Castle Dor* (1961; completed by Daphne du Maurier long after Quiller-Couch's death in 1944), A. S. Byatt in *Possession* (1990), John Updike in *Brazil* (1994), and Joyce Carol Oates, writing under the pseudonym Rosamond Smith, in *You Can't Catch Me* (1995).

In roughly the last quarter of the twentieth century, authors and filmmakers tended more and more to use elements of the Arthurian legend to symbolise despair and futility rather than nobility and idealism. The American novelist Walker Percy is the author of the 1978 novel *Lancelot*, in which the title character is a bitter alcoholic whose actress wife sleeps with her director. Lancelot's jealousy and his effort to prove his wife's infidelity (by filming it) eventually lead him to murder and to incarceration in a mental hospital. Lancelot, true to his medieval namesake, fails to find the Grail, but he concludes that 'there is no unholy grail just as there was no Holy Grail'. Similarly, the film *The Fisher King* (1991, dir. Terry Gilliam) emphasises the violence of contemporary American society, dramatising a catastrophe that disrupted and ended lives: a radio disk jockey's words provoked the murder of a professor's wife, and the two men, one insane, the other burdened by guilt, are thrown together in what eventually becomes a story of mutual redemption. The Fisher King motif of the wound that requires a ritual cure is here applicable to both protagonists.

One of the most engaging Arthurian novels set in the present is David Lodge's *Small World* (1984). This is an academic novel in which characters frequently discuss Arthurian matters and especially the theories of Jessie Weston (see above), but it is also a text that is itself Arthurian, involving Persse (a Perceval figure), Arthur Kingfisher, and other characters whose names or behaviour mark them as projections of figures from traditional Arthurian legend. Authors may conceive of chivalry as medieval sport (though often a deadly sport), and some have updated the sports metaphor. Two of them are Babs Deal's *The Grail: A Novel* (1963), a story of American football in which the 'grail' being sought is a season without a loss, and Bernard Malamud's *The Natural* (1952), featuring a Perceval figure (though named Roy) who plays for the New York Knights, a baseball team managed by 'Pop Fisher'.

There are a great many other novels, dating from the last two or three decades of the twentieth century, in which Arthurian themes and motifs are played out in modern guise. Examples of the legend as metaphor include, in addition to Walker Percy's *Lancelot* (discussed above), Anthony Powell's *The Fisher King* (1986), Paul Griffith's *The Lay of Sir Tristram* (1991), Iris Murdoch's *The Green Knight* (1993), and Bobbie Ann Mason's *In Country* (1985). The last of these is an account of the lingering psychic damage, reminiscent of the Fisher King's wound, done to a Vietnam veteran and of the quest of his niece for knowledge of her father. The fact that Arthurian material continues to attract the attention of major authors who are not primarily Arthurian enthusiasts is one dramatic indication of the power and appeal of the legend. In addition, the fact that this legend has achieved, at least in English-speaking countries, something akin to a mythic status adds depth and resonance to texts that are not explicitly treatments of the Arthurian story.

Approaching a new century

As implied above, developments during the last two or three decades of the twentieth century have made it increasingly difficult to assign Arthurian works to neat and unambiguous categories. To the extent that this is true of traditional and main-stream media – commercial publishing, studio films, etc. – the new Arthurian directions must be an effect of powerful social and cultural transformations. Whether it is cultural instability, moral relativism, nostalgia for a real or imagined clarity in the past, rebellion against tradition, or simply the need to speak and write in ways unlike those of the past, the period often identified as post-modern has exploded the Arthurian legend. No longer content to retell the Arthurian story, many authors, filmmakers and others have interpreted it in new ways, have adopted new points of view, have used the legend for new purposes, and have in some cases stretched aspects of it nearly to the breaking point if not beyond.

Apart from the mainstream, the late twentieth century and the first years of the twenty-first have contributed not only new kinds of works but also new media by which the legend can be disseminated. Cartoons and comics and graphic novels, computer games and board games, role-playing games and game books, puzzles and colouring books and calendars and stamps – all have left their mark on the legend. Moreover, the proliferation of 'print-on-demand' books, self-produced films, and personal websites and electronic texts means that, for better or for worse, just about anyone can be an Arthurian writer. The result is literary chaos. This activity is an additional measure of the popularity and appeal of the Arthurian legend, but it occasionally leaves observers wondering how much weight that legend can bear. The Arthurian story has from the beginning accommodated variants and innovations; they were essential to its formation and to its dissemination, indeed to its survival. Large numbers of new characters were invented throughout the Middle Ages, and stories such as that of Tristan and Isolt, which had originally been independent narratives, were drawn into the Arthurian sphere. Adventures multiplied and might be assigned to different characters from one text to another. Moreover, authors could emphasise either the noble intent of Arthur's reign or the tragic end of Camelot – or attenuate that tragedy with the expectation of the king's eventual return.

Yet, despite the variants, innovations and reinterpretations, the traditional legend was 'anchored' by the authority of some of the great texts, from those of Geoffrey of Monmouth and Chrétien to Wolfram and Gottfried, from the Vulgate Cycle and Prose *Tristan* to Malory and Tennyson. Observers can only wonder what if anything is anchoring many of the recent and present manifestations of the Arthurian legend, and we can only venture, at best, informed guesses about the shape of future contributions. Can the legend accommodate a tryst in Death Valley between Lancelot and Madame Bovary (Christine Brooke-Rose, *Textermination*, 1991), Arthur as a vampire (S. N. Dyer, 'Knight Squadron', 1996), Princess Diana as the reborn King

Arthur (Elizabeth Ann Scarborough, 'Debriefing the Warrior Princess', 1998), or Arthur as the homosexual protagonist of a pornographic novel (Larry Howard, *The Song of Sir Rod the Long: A Gay Romance of the Round Table*, 2000)? Perhaps, in fact almost surely, the legend can survive all of that, but it has obviously become a pot-pourri from which one can take anything – or into which one can in effect dump almost anything. Although the novel remains the dominant form, no doubt because of its greater visibility and availability, there have been hundreds of recent poems (a great many of them from five to thirty lines long) and a very large number of short stories, many of which appeared in large collections. Another significant phenomenon, less frequent but still notable, is the republication of Arthurian material either in omnibus volumes or reissued, in revised form, under another title.

In terms of the approaches to Arthurian subjects, we observe toward the end of the last century an increasing use of humour and satire and an irreverent spirit that can reinterpret the legend in innovative fashion or pervert it and sap its vitality. Obviously, it is impossible to assign even an approximate date to such developments. Arthurian satire, for example, has been with us at least since Cervantes's *Don Quixote*, though the most familiar modern example may be Mark Twain's 1889 *A Connecticut Yankee in King Arthur's Court* (and the numerous and most often mediocre film and television dramatisations of his novel). But in general, science fiction, fantasy, parody and simple Arthurian silliness have multiplied greatly in the last quarter of the century, and a convenient, if greatly oversimplified, dividing point might well be 1975, which happens to be the year of *Monty Python and the Holy Grail* (dir. Terry Gilliam and Terry Jones). There exist well over 100 Arthurian films, but a good many professional Arthurian scholars readily acknowledge that, in their view, *Monty Python and the Holy Grail* is the best of them. It is an inspired spoof of the legend, and it is played in a register that creates humour in the name of, but not necessarily at the expense of, the story of Arthur and the Grail quest.

Many other films make the mistake either of taking themselves too seriously or of trying too ambitiously to tell the entire story. John Boorman's 1981 *Excalibur* suffers from the latter failing, beginning well but becoming muddled when the focus turns to the Grail. Nonetheless, Boorman's effort was at least a serious one, whereas films such as *First Knight* (1995, dir. Jerry Zucker) are lightweight attempts to capitalise on the popularity of the legend, and Stephen Weeks's two efforts to bring *Gawain and the Green Knight* to the screen (*Gawain and the Green Knight*, 1972, and *Sword of the Valiant*, 1982) proved inept. The 1989 *Indiana Jones and the Last Crusade* (dir. Stephen Spielberg) is an entertaining swashbuckler based on a modern Grail quest. *King Arthur* (2004, dir. Antoine Fuqua) made a less than successful effort to tell the (historically) 'true' story of Arthur as elaborated in what is called the Sarmatian connection (a theory according to which the Arthur story came to Britain with Sarmatian mercenaries). There are, as noted, numerous other Arthurian films, though the number of outstanding ones in English is small indeed. Viewers' favourites appear to be *Camelot* (1967, dir. Joshua Logan), Boorman's *Excalibur*, or, as noted, *Monty Python and the Holy Grail*.

2000 and beyond

Just at the turn of the century, critic and novelist Umberto Eco published *Baudolino* (2000), a sprawling and fascinating novel dealing with a counterfeit 'Grail' and with the quest, which, as one of Eco's characters comments, is far more important than the object being sought. That is a sentiment that had been expressed many times before and implied even in medieval texts. It had also been noted by Mark Twain and again by Nicholas Seare in *Rude Tales and Glorious* (1982), both of whom point out that the knights went out 'grailing' (as Twain put it) without knowing what a grail actually was. No matter: the search continues because it should and must.

The Arthurian deluge continues unabated, but the first years of the twenty-first century have given us few Arthurian creations that appear likely to endure. One that may have lasting power is *The King in the Tree* (2003) by Steven Millhauser. This is a Tristan story, drawn out of the medieval versions. The king in question is Mark, and the novel focuses on his jealousy and his betrayal by the legendary lovers Tristan and Isolt. Beyond that, we must note the phenomenal commercial success of Dan Brown's *The Da Vinci Code* (2003) and the 2006 film made from that novel. The book was a major best-seller with a multitude of admirers and also a good many detractors. The latter, for the most part, objected that the notion of the Templar conspiracy and the idea that the Grail is the bloodline of Christ – an idea taken from *Holy Blood, Holy Grail* by Michael Baigent, Richard Leigh and Henry Lincoln (1982) – are fanciful and without foundation. It seems unlikely that the novel will be widely read in the future. Far less known, though better, than Brown's novel is Kate Mosse's *Labyrinth* (2005), which juxtaposes the adventures of a twentieth-century woman, Alice, to those of her distant (thirteenth-century) relative named Alaïs. Set in the south of France (around Carcassonne and Toulouse), the novel takes as its subject the persistent notion of a Catharist Grail, which here is an elixir capable of prolonging life dramatically. For something completely different, we should take note of *Spamalot* (2005, by Eric Idle and John Du Prez), a Broadway send-up of the Arthurian and Grail stories. Inspired by the wonderful silliness of *Monty Python and the Holy Grail*, *Spamalot* quickly acquired a kind of cult status. Its popularity may prove to have a limited lifespan, but it illustrates in delightful fashion the versatility, the extraordinary 'elasticity', of the Arthurian legend.

Without the benefit of time and distance, literary judgements are extraordinarily difficult to make. Other twenty-first century works may stand the test of time and eventually become an important component of an expanded Arthurian canon, but at present none but Eco's and perhaps Millhauser's stand out clearly. Besides the rapid proliferation of Arthurian novels, poems and other forms (and the indifferent quality of many of these), we observe in the past two or three decades a striking dichotomy. At one pole there is a New-Age and almost mystical devotion to Arthur and to Arthurian places (especially Glastonbury). At the other pole is a steadfast refusal to take the legend seriously. What may come out of this dichotomy – or another one, pitting those who believe devoutly in Arthur's historicity against those who reject it – remains to be seen, and we may not know the answer for some decades.

Literatures other than English

As noted, twentieth-century Arthurian works in English drastically outnumber those in any other language. However, French, German, and other literatures have made substantial contributions to the development of the legend. Although the French, content to contribute Lancelot as a central figure in the legend, never claimed Arthur as their own, we might still expect modern French authors to take inspiration from the work of Chrétien de Troyes, from the *Lancelot-Grail* Cycle, or from the Prose *Tristan*. That has happened to an extent, but those works have influenced modern French Arthuriana far less than Malory has done in English. Compared with English texts, French Arthurian works are few and scattered.

Joseph Bédier's *Le Roman de Tristan et Iseut* ('The Romance of Tristan and Iseut', 1900) was a huge best-seller in France and elsewhere. This retelling of the Tristan story has gone through hundreds of editions and has been translated into numerous languages. In France alone, its influence was sufficient to move a good many others to retell the story or to compose new versions of it. Three well-known French authors have composed Arthurian texts, and these works, in contrast to Bédier's, demonstrate the French penchant for experimental and sometimes eccentric uses of the Arthurian legend. Guillaume Apollinaire, at the beginning of his career, published *L'Enchanteur pourrissant* ('The Putrescent Magician', 1904), which presents Merlin as an antichrist. The work begins after Merlin is dead, and other characters gathered around his grave express their sentiments about him and about other subjects. Paul Claudel was the author of *Partage de midi* ('Division of Noon', 1905; definitive version 1948). This is a Tristan story updated to the present and set on a ship. Here the inspiration is more Wagner – a major influence for a great many French authors – than Bédier or the medieval versions of the story.

Jean Cocteau published a drama, *Les Chevaliers de la Table Ronde* ('The Knights of the Round Table', 1937), contrasting the intoxicating effect of Merlin's spell with the liberating function of Galahad. Cocteau also wrote the screenplay for the film *L'Eternel Retour* ('The Eternal Return', 1943, dir. Jean Delannoy), an excellent updating of the Tristan story to the (then) present day. Elements of the Parsifal legend, influenced by Wagner and by Wolfram von Eschenbach, were treated twice by Julien Gracq, in the novel *Le Château d'Argol* ('The Castle of Argol', 1939) and the play *Le Roi Pêcheur* ('The Fisher King', 1945). Later in the century, especially during the 1970s and 1980s, novels and other works dealing with Merlin became more popular. Particularly successful was René Barjavel's *L'Enchanter* ('The Magician', 1984), narrating elements of Merlin's life and, in particular, his relationship to Viviane. Barjavel's novel also focuses on the Grail, noting that it was originally a vessel fashioned by Eve to contain the blood flowing from Adam's side.

Among several dozen other modern works that deserve mention, I shall conclude with two novelists/dramatists and one filmmaker. In Robert Pinget's novel *Graal Flibuste* (1955), an untranslatable title that refers to the Grail and to piracy, the narrator undertakes a quest to a waste land, but it is unclear why there is a quest or what its objective is; in any event, he neither achieves nor sees a Grail. Pinget makes ample use of Arthurian and Grail imagery and structures, but they are set into unfamiliar contexts and almost divorced from their original function. One of the most productive Arthurian authors in modern France is Jacques Roubaud, who has published a retelling of the Arthurian legend, in addition to a 'corrected' version of the medieval French romance *Silence* and, with Florence Delay, a cycle – as yet unfinished – of Arthurian dramas, *Graal-Théâtre* (1977–). Roubaud's work is experimental and 'post-modern', but it is also firmly rooted in a solid knowledge of its medieval sources. Of French Arthurian films, the best known are doubtless *Lancelot du Lac* (1974, dir. Robert Bresson) and *Perceval le Gallois* (1978, dir. Eric Rohmer). Bresson sets his film in the period following the Grail quest and traces the consequences of Lancelot's unsuccessful struggle to abandon his affair with the queen. Rohmer follows Chrétien de Troyes's account of Perceval literally (even using a modernised version of

Chrétien's text) but concludes the film with a dramatised Passion play. Using then-unknown actors, highly stylised sets, and a vocal chorus to present some of the narration, Rohmer intentionally gives his film a 'medieval' look and establishes obvious psychological distance between us and the story. The result is a visually beautiful film that some viewers admire greatly whereas others consider it dull and unengaging.

As with French (and even English) Arthuriana, German material and that in other languages must receive very short shrift here. The great medieval German authors Wolfram von Eschenbach and Gottfried von Strassburg, along with Wagner, are the foremost influences on modern Arthurian literature and film in German. Results include Richard von Kralik's play *Der heilige Gral* ('The Holy Grail', 1912), Albrecht Schaeffer's 1922 epic poem *Parzival*, and Adolf Muschg's novel *Der rote Ritter* ('The Red Knight', 1993). Hans Jürgen Syberberg's *Parsifal* is a filmed version of Wagner's opera; a highly innovative (and controversial) setting of the opera, it uses two actors – one male, one female – in the Parsifal role, and portions of it are played against a backdrop that is a gigantic copy of Wagner's death mask. The Tristan story has also attracted a great many modern authors writing in German. Drama has been a particular popular medium in the early twentieth century (continuing a trend from the previous century). Eduard Stucken, between 1902 and 1924, composed a cycle of eight dramas including plays devoted to Merlin, Tristan, and others, but emphasising the centrality of the Grail quest. Albert Geiger (1906), Ernst Hardt (1907), Emil Ludwig (1909) and Maja Loehr (1919) are among others who have reinterpreted the Tristan legend for the stage.

Interest in things Arthurian waned between the 1930s and the 1960s, after which authors returned to the traditional subjects – especially Parsifal/ Parzival, Tristan and Merlin. One of the most notable products of this renewed interest was Tankred Dorst's epic *Merlin oder das Wüste Land* ('Merlin or the Waste land', 1981), presenting the entire story of Arthur and the Grail. It should be noted that the interests of, and influences on, authors treating Arthurian themes in German have in recent decades been broadened well beyond the powerful triumvirate of Wolfram, Gottfried, and Wagner. Malory is among the early authors who have contributed to a renewal of Arthuriana in German, and a number of modern English and American novels have had German translations.

Other countries and other languages have contributed in important ways, though less frequently, to the elaboration of the Arthurian legend. A very small sampling would include Italian (Italo Calvino, *Il cavaliere inesistente*, 'The Nonexistent Knight', 1959), Polish (Maria Kuncewicz, *Tristan*, 1974), Breton (Pierre-Jakez Hélias, *An Isild A-Heul*, 'The Second Iseult', 1965), Japanese

(Nasume Sōseki, *Kairo-kō: A Dirge*, 1905), Spanish (Alvaro Cunqueiro, *Merlín y familia*, 1955, 1957) – and I have omitted a number of languages and many dozens, doubtless many hundreds, of titles.

Conclusion

A complete account of modern Arthuriana is impossible: the subject is too vast, and the number of items almost innumerable. Furthermore, even a highly selective account, as this one is, is destined to be outdated before publication. The flood of Arthurian books, songs, art, games and ephemera is not only continuing but increasing dramatically. What the Arthurian legend will look like in a decade or a century, and what will be thought of it then, can only be matters for speculation, even by those who are most informed. What appears obvious, however, is that, especially in English, aspects of the Arthurian legend will continue to appeal to large numbers of authors, filmmakers, readers and viewers. Nearly as obvious is the fact that we are witnessing a broad and free – some would say 'undisciplined' – adaptation of the legend reflecting the needs and tastes of the twentieth- and twenty-first-century publics. That is of course an inevitable phenomenon, and not necessarily an unfortunate one: every period and every society chooses its Arthur. We must wonder though whether the anchor of authoritative texts will hold or whether the legend will henceforth drift in any or all directions. And if the latter occurs, will Arthur still be Arthur? What is certain is that when Malory and some other authors, mostly modern, spoke of the 'once and future king', they could not have imagined the popularity and the nature of that Arthurian future, especially during the late twentieth century and beyond.

NOTES

1 *The Arthurian Annals: The Tradition in English from 1250 to 2000*, ed. Daniel P. Nastali and Phillip C. Boardman, 2 vols. (Oxford University Press, 2004); see this publication for further information about the English-language books discussed in this chapter, and also *AoF*, *AoE* and *AoG*. I wish to thank Raymond Thompson, Daniel Nastali, and Phillip Boardman for offering me information and advice during the composition of this chapter.

PART II

Themes

8

ELIZABETH ARCHIBALD

Questioning Arthurian ideals

'Romance purges life of impurities and presents chivalry in heightened and idealised form', according to Derek Pearsall.[1] This idealisation may have had significant social and historical functions. Pearsall cites the argument of Georges Duby that romance could soothe tensions between different social groups within the aristocracy by offering an idealised version of unity in the form of the Round Table; he also suggests that in twelfth-century France, 'The glamorizing of a royal court at which barons would attend for long periods, and so be prevented from building up a power-base in their own provincial lands, was very much in the interests of the monarchy'.[2] But the first twelfth-century French Arthurian romances were written not for the king but for powerful nobles. This may be one reason why the Arthurian court is not always presented as glamorised or united, nor is Arthur always a dynamic, astute or effective monarch. From its beginnings, Arthurian romance shows itself to be far from monolithic, far from uncritical. Oliver Padel suggests that in Welsh tradition Arthur was 'often an intrinsically comic character, and that Arthurian tales ... occupied a humorous role, perhaps approximately comparable with comic-strip literature today'.[3] Arthur's court is frequently extolled as the acme of chivalry, a tradition going back to Geoffrey of Monmouth, who described in his seminal *History of the Kings of Britain (Historia Regum Britanniae)* (1130s) how knights from all over the world flocked there, and how they fought in tournaments to impress their ladies (Thorpe, ix.11, p. 222). The romance genre emphasised this world of idealistic, individual chivalry, as opposed to *Realpolitik* and war. Yet from the twelfth century on, the idealisation of the Arthurian world was questioned in both Latin and vernacular texts; and this questioning has continued up to the present day. It is hardly surprising that historians have been doubtful about Arthur's existence and supposed achievements. More remarkable is the way in which both medieval and modern writers of fiction celebrate Arthurian ideals but simultaneously challenge them by means of comedy, irony, parody, satire, and sometimes outright criticism; it is on such fiction that I shall concentrate, looking at a range of narratives from the twelfth century to the present day.

These challenges are evident early on in a range of subtle and tantalising twelfth- and early thirteenth-century Arthurian narratives. Eugène Vinaver has described medieval romance as 'a questioning mode', and D. H. Green has argued for 'the presence of irony in this genre from the beginning, to an extent and with a sophistication not true of all narrative literature'.[4] It is certainly present in the pioneering work of the late twelfth-century poet Chrétien de Troyes, often described as the father of Arthurian romance. Arthur dominated Geoffrey's account, active in every campaign until brought low by treachery, but in Chrétien's five Arthurian romances the king is effectively marginalised in favour of the adventures of individual knights, some long-established members of his court, some newcomers, who occupy themselves during a period of peace in a series of challenging adventures. Unlike Geoffrey's heroic Arthur, Chrétien's king is passive, rarely leaves the court, and is never the protagonist of a major quest. In the *Chevalier de la charrete* (*The Knight of the Cart*) it is left to the initially anonymous Lancelot to rescue Guinevere when she is abducted by Meleagant – and indeed Gawain rebukes Arthur for his folly in allowing Kay to escort her in response to Meleagant's challenge (lines 226–7, Kibler, p. 188). In earlier versions of the abduction story it is Arthur himself who rescues her; does the fact that Chrétien's Arthur behaves so foolishly, and passively, constitute evidence of a critical attitude towards the legend?

Some of Chrétien's protagonists star in only one romance, and retire to happy domesticity at the end (Erec, Cligés, Yvain); but Lancelot, who makes his début in Chrétien's *Chevalier de la charrete*, cannot live happily ever after once he has rescued his beloved, since Guinevere is already married. Chrétien glorifies this love by showing Lancelot's single-minded commitment to rescuing the abducted queen, his ecstasy when she is kind to him, and his agony when she is not. But the text seems to become comic, even perhaps parodic, at times. When Lancelot is riding in pursuit of the abducted queen, he is so deep in dreams of her that he fails to hear the challenges of a knight guarding a ford, and is knocked off his horse (lines 744–7, pp. 216–17). When he finds her comb with some hairs left in it, he almost faints with emotion, and treats the hairs like religious relics:

> Never will the eye of man see anything receive such reverence; for he began
> to adore the hair, touching it a hundred thousand times to his eye, his mouth,
> his forehead and his cheeks. He expressed his joy in every way imaginable …
> nor did he fear that ulcers or any other disease could afflict him; he had no use
> for magic potions mixed with pearls, nor for drugs against pleurisy, nor for

theriaca, nor even for prayers to Saint Martin and Saint James. He placed so much faith in these strands of hairs that he felt no need for any other aid.

(lines 1460–78, p. 225)

Is this an admirable example of the extreme passion of 'courtly love', or is the poet slyly suggesting that such love can be taken too seriously? Chrétien did not finish this romance, but passed it on to another clerk, Godefroi de Leigni. Was this because he was unhappy with the subject matter imposed on him by his patron, the Countess of Champagne, or because he found it difficult to create a satisfactory closure for a story of forbidden love, which would come to an end only with the fall of Camelot?

Chrétien could have focused on Gawain, already established in the legend as Arthur's nephew and right-hand man, who is characterised as impulsive but heroic in Geoffrey's *History*. Gawain appears frequently in Chrétien's romances, sometimes with a major role but never as the protagonist; he is more often a foil to the hero, and is sometimes engaged in a parallel series of adventures. Peter Haidu goes so far as to call him 'a cardboard figure ... the somewhat ridiculous other of all knightly adventure'.[5] But he is the protagonist in a Latin romance, the *De Ortu Waluuanii* (*Rise of Gawain*), which may have been composed as early as the mid-twelfth century.[6] This Fair Unknown story draws on Geoffrey of Monmouth (in the account of Gawain's rearing in Rome), but the representation of Arthur is not at all Galfridian. After many adventures Gawain, who does not know his own identity, arrives in Britain. He knocks Arthur and Kay off their horses at a ford one night. Arthur returns to bed ashamed and soaking wet, and lies about what has happened to his queen, who is here a sorceress who has already foreseen these events. Gawain is told that he cannot serve the king unless he can prove himself, and at once a suitable adventure presents itself: rescuing the lady of the Castle of Maidens from a besieging pagan king. Arthur sets out with his troops, but feels afraid, since the pagan king has frequently defeated him. The battle goes badly and Arthur flees, mocked by Gawain, who then defeats the enemy single-handed. Arthur acknowledges Gawain as his nephew, and welcomes him to the court, where he discovers his true identity and meets his parents. That is the happy ending of the Fair Unknown plot – but if *De Ortu* was written only a decade or two after the appearance of Geoffrey's *History*, we may be astonished how the mighty are fallen: Arthur is presented as a coward, and his queen as a sorceress. Perhaps it is significant that this is a Latin Arthurian romance, a relatively rare species. The writer (possibly Robert of Torigni, Abbot of St Michel) may be deliberately mixing exciting adventure with criticism of Arthur-worship, to please an audience of clerics.

The same sort of problem is posed by the Arthurian adventure in Andreas Capellanus' much-discussed Latin treatise on love, probably written in the

1180s (or possibly in the 1230s).⁷ The final chapter in Book II, entitled 'De regulis amoris [The rules for love]', describes the quest of an unnamed British knight who is told that he cannot win his beloved unless he brings her the sparrowhawk which sits on a golden perch in Arthur's court (pp. 270–85). After various adventures the knight finds the palace, which is made of precious stones, and the king sitting on a golden throne, surrounded by ladies and knights. After defeating a knight in combat, the protagonist takes the sparrowhawk, and also a scroll attached to the perch containing 'the rules of love', announced by the king of love himself. The thirty-one rules take a rather extreme view of the demands of 'courtly love', such as 'Marriage does not constitute a proper excuse for not loving' (no. 1), and 'True jealousy makes the feeling of love grow' (no. 21). The British knight presents these rules with the sparrowhawk to his lady, who urges all her court to observe them.

Andreas clearly knows some of Chrétien's romances, but there are also Celtic aspects: Siân Echard points out that Arthur is part of a silent tableau, surrounded by knights and maidens in his fantastic palace made of precious stones, as if in a Celtic otherworld.⁸ Futhermore, the status of Arthur's kingdom as the source of guidance on love is ironic given that the rules seem to encourage adultery. Another problem is the placing of this Arthurian episode at the end of Book II. This is the culmination of the lengthy discussions of love, including definitions, debates, dialogues between potential lovers, and adjudications on hypothetical love scenarios. The sparrowhawk quest moves us from the possibly historical context of courts of love in Champagne to the fantastic world of Arthurian romance; the list of rules at the end might be regarded as the *reductio ad absurdum* of courtly love. Book III consists of a vitriolic condemnation of all erotic passion; here the king of love is Jesus the Bridegroom, and the rules are very different. Love and jealousy are now destructive and paralysing: love destroys the reputations of both men and women (contrary to the romance topos that love enhances a knight's valour and reputation), and leads to eternal damnation, so it must be avoided at all costs (pp. 320–3). Whether one takes the view that everything in Andreas is intended tongue in cheek, or that it is a balanced debate giving extreme examples of antithetical positions, or that Book III cancels out everything that has gone before, the significance of the Arthurian episode is certainly problematic, and it may be intended to be parodic.

The Arthurian court is presented as a place of meanness and injustice in *Lanval*, one of the twelve brief Old French lays (mini-romances) attributed to the mysterious Marie de France, which may have been written in England in the 1170s or 1180s (only *Lanval* has an explicitly Arthurian setting).⁹

The eponymous hero is unaccountably omitted from Arthur's distribution of gifts, but acquires a beautiful fairy mistress who showers him with money and favours. The queen propositions Lanval; on being rejected, she falsely accuses him of rape, like Phaedra or Potiphar's wife. Arthur is furious and demands the death penalty, but Gawain stands up for Lanval, and the court of barons modifies the sentence: if Lanval cannot produce the fairy mistress he claims is more beautiful than the queen, he must be exiled. The fairy appears and eclipses Guinevere; as she leaves, Lanval leaps up behind her and rides away to Avalon, never to return. Marie gives no moral at the end, but *Lanval* invites interpretation as an attack on the corrupt courtly world, where Avalon is preferable to Camelot for an active and attractive young knight. If the author was indeed a woman, *Lanval* could also be an attack on patriarchal feudalism, though the overt hostility to Guinevere might seem more characteristic of clerical misogyny.

Marie says that she is retelling traditional Breton lays; we do not know whether her source was already Arthurian, or whether she took an existing non-Arthurian story and rewrote it as Arthurian, as Chaucer apparently did with 'The Wife of Bath's Tale'. She or her source may have been prompted by the fact that in almost all versions of the legend Guinevere betrays Arthur with a man close to him (Mordred or Lancelot), and this leads directly or indirectly to the destruction of Camelot and the death of Arthur. In *Lanval* her attempted seduction of Lanval hints at that ending, and suggests a misogynistic view of her (and perhaps of queens more generally) as fundamentally untrustworthy. *Lanval* was one of the most popular of Marie's lays, to judge from the number of texts and variations that survive. In a fourteenth-century Middle English version, Chestre's *Sir Launfal*, Guinevere has a reputation for promiscuity. She announces that her eyes should be put out if Launfal's lover proves more beautiful, and at the end she is duly blinded by the breath of the departing fairy. This makes the negative characterisation more explicit than in Marie's version.[10]

In two French lays written only a few years after *Lanval*, the whole court is humiliated by a sexual scandal. In Robert Biket's *Lai du cor* and the anonymous *Lai du mantel*, both probably written about 1200, a gift sent to Arthur turns out to be a chastity test.[11] In the *Lai du cor*, King Mangoun of Scotland sends a magic drinking-horn to Arthur: if a husband is unfaithful or a wife jealous, the horn spills when the husband drinks. This happens to Arthur, but his rage is somewhat mollified when it also happens to all the other knights except Caradoc. In the *Lai du mantel* unchaste women find that the magic mantle shrinks on them, but it fits the only chaste woman at court, Caradoc's lady. It is noteworthy that so early in the development of the romance tradition writers chose to mock the Arthurian court in this way. Is this another clerical comment on the dangers of courtly love, and/or on the disturbing popularity of frivolous Arthurian stories of love and adventure? These *fabliau*-like tales are the antithesis of texts which emphasise the 'splendeurs et misères' of courtly love. They are misogynistic, but they also take delight in the dishonouring of Arthur and almost all his knights. Might this be connected to the fact that they are in French (though they were retold in various languages)? Lancelot is much less prominent in Middle English literature than in French, perhaps in part at least because he is a Frenchman who cuckolds the great English king. National politics and prejudices can have a bearing on attitudes to the Arthurian story, as can the desire of clerical authors to educate the aggressive nobility of the twelfth and thirteenth centuries into more courtly behaviour.

In another late twelfth-century or early thirteenth-century French Arthurian narrative, the criticism is less overt, but parody and comedy are to the fore. Guillaume le Clerc's *Fergus* is an Arthurian verse romance set in Scotland, and possibly written there too; it is a blatant mélange of episodes taken from the romances of Chrétien de Troyes, some quite comic, some a little darker.[12] Like Chrétien's *Perceval*, Fergus arrives at court as a naïve and untried youth – this in itself is a sort of critique of chivalry, in that the newcomer who breaks all the courtly rules does succeed and prosper, though of course he learns courtly behaviour in the course of the romance. A number of details suggest that Guillaume le Clerc is interested in drawing attention to romance conventions, early though it is in the history of medieval romance, and in gently subverting them. Fergus is the son of a rich peasant and a noble mother; when Fergus' father complains about the boy's desire to abandon farming for knightly pursuits, and accuses his wife of adultery, she replies briskly that Fergus is clearly taking after her side of the family (lines 478ff., trans. Owen, pp. 8–9). The status of Fergus' parents, and their conversation about his future, are reversals of medieval romance conventions: apparently lowborn heroes always turn out to be aristocratic in the end (or at least to have noble fathers). There may be an element of historical reality here: in the late twelfth century rich peasants were indeed being admitted to the knightly class. But elsewhere Guillaume definitely parodies and laughs at romance conventions, for instance when Fergus wears armour that is red with rust, or when the love-struck heroine Galiene tosses and turns in bed so violently that she tips the bed over.

Another area of possible satire or subversion concerns friendship between knights. In the opening of *Fergus*, Gawain and Ywain are presented as preferring each other's company to that of the rest of the feasting court. At the end, when Fergus returns to court, Gawain's welcome seems unnecessarily ardent, and Galiene, Fergus' beloved, is sidelined:

You could have walked slowly for a good four bowshots before they tired of their kissing: those noble knights made as great a fuss of each other as if they were full brothers.

The king and all the nobles at court run up at the sight of such rejoicing. Galiene came too, having witnessed the joyful scene. The two men take each other by the fingers and, hand in hand and most joyfully, go to meet the king.

(lines 6809–27, p. 110)

Homosocial bonding, especially among Round Table knights, is a staple of Arthurian romance, but in this case such intense friendship seems to be taken to ironic extremes. The tension between love and chivalry is often an issue in romance. Here the conventional happy ending of the marriage is framed by Gawain's welcome to Fergus, and by his final request that Fergus should not give up chivalric activity; this is an ominous echo of Chrétien's *Yvain*, where similar advice from Gawain has disastrous consequences for Yvain's marriage.

On his first quest Fergus has to fight the Black Knight, who is deeply displeased by the low status of his adversary:

'Are you one of the knights of that very wicked, abject King Arthur? His arrogance has been truly deflated. He's not worthy to be a king, because he daren't even put his trust in his own courage to enter this land in quest of the horn and the wimple. Instead he sends his menials who have come from other countries to serve at court as hirelings, when he's not prepared to take them permanently into his company. What's the reason for Gawain, Lancelot, Erec and Yvain not coming? Or Sagremor the Impetuous, or that ninny Perceval? Or else let that disreputable, cowardly king bring with him twenty knights, or his whole army should he want to. He's very craven to be so afraid of me.'

(lines 2303–22, p. 38)

Fergus is deeply shocked by this outburst; of course, he defeats the Black Knight and sends him to Arthur's court, as we expect. But it might be argued that the speech contains some home truths. Why does Arthur so rarely go on quests himself? And did late twelfth-century readers of Chrétien really think Perceval was a ninny? Owen comments: 'If Guillaume composed for a public as retentive and alert as himself, one must suppose that he devised his subversive ironies for general delight, not mere private satisfaction.'[13]

The early Arthurian texts I have discussed here testify to the fact that the legend was used for debate about contemporary issues as well as literary ones. In the late twelfth and early thirteenth centuries, Latin and vernacular writers played with Arthurian characters and themes to create comedy, pastiche, parody and satire, evidently assuming a well-read audience who would notice and appreciate the jokes and/or the criticism. These texts raise many questions about audience and intention, and indeed about genre: can we talk about romance and anti-romance, or transgressions of romance values and conventions, when Chrétien's foundational romances describing the chivalric values and practices of Arthur's court present such a tantalising mixture of seriousness and idealism with humour and irony? It is characteristic of Chrétien to present in his romances problems for debate both by the characters and by the audience (debate was a standard way of teaching in the Middle Ages, and debate poetry is common in Western European literature of the time). Chrétien explores the tensions between chivalry and marriage in *Yvain* and *Erec*, and between chivalry and religion in the unfinished *Perceval/Conte du Graal*. Though chivalry (often inspired by love) could be said to be the *raison d'être* of medieval Arthurian romance, questions are raised about it by Chrétien and many later writers (see also Gilbert, Chapter 9).

In the early thirteenth century, the Grail so enigmatically described by Chrétien takes on much greater importance, as do spiritual values. In the very influential French prose Vulgate Cycle, the quest for the Grail divides the sheep from the goats, and almost all the Round Table knights turn out to be goats. It is noteworthy that Arthur never considers going on the quest, and that he regards it as a disaster for his chivalric community, foreseeing that many knights will not return. In the French Vulgate *Queste* Lancelot reproves him sharply for his pessimism: '"In God's name, what makes you say that, my lord? A man of your position shouldn't have fear in his heart, but justice, hope and courage".'[14] Critics have debated the reasons why the Grail quest was inserted into the Arthurian legend. Is it a unique opportunity to show the qualities of the Round Table knights, and a compliment to Arthur that his men eventually succeed in the quest; or is it a test which shows up the worldly, selfish values of Camelot's earthly chivalry, where the paramount value is what Malory calls *worship*, reputation and honour, and where knights fight for their ladies rather than for God?

The Grail introduces the notion of sin into Arthurian romance. In this new context, in which the choice of black or white armour carries moral significance, and beautiful damsels in distress may turn out to be devils in disguise, the two greatest Arthurian heroes, Lancelot and Gawain, both encounter previously unknown difficulties. Adventures elude Gawain, who is unwilling to stop and learn from the many hermits who now populate the landscape. Love is no longer an acceptable spur to chivalric prowess and success: Lancelot cannot see the Grail fully because of his long affair with Guinevere, even though he confesses to a hermit that he should have been fighting for God rather than for the queen, and promises to change his behaviour. The only successful Grail knights are Galahad and Percival (both virgins), and Bors (who has only slipped up once); everyone else fails. This seems to create parallel universes: the Grail world is superior in spiritual terms, and may subvert the course of earthly chivalry – but it soon disappears from sight, whereas life at Camelot continues unchanged till Mordred's treacherous ambition and jealousy of Lancelot trigger the final civil war. Laura Ashe has recently argued that 'The Grail Quest, for all its immense popularity, wrought irreparable damage upon the secular, chivalric hero and the Arthurian court'.[15] But the didactic, and perhaps subversive, intentions of the writer(s) of the Vulgate Cycle are limited, it seems: though Lancelot fails in the Grail quest, he continues to be Top Knight till the very end of the Cycle, and is still allowed to die in the odour of sanctity (Malory ends in the same way).

Gawain's failure on the Grail quest is paralleled in non-Grail French romances by less admiring treatment. In thirteenth-century Germany, Heinrich von dem Türlin made Gawain the hero of a considerably secularised Grail adventure, *Diu Crône* (surprisingly, Kay is one of the Grail knights here); but Türlin's work does not suggest a high regard for chivalric ideals, and is sometimes subversive in tone. In Britain, however, Gawain (the local boy, as a Scot) was very popular, much more so than Lancelot the Frenchman. *Ywain and Gawain* is the only extant close reworking of Chrétien in Middle English, and Gawain's prominence is emphasised by the joint billing of the title. *Sir Gawain and the Green Knight* plays on his reputation as the epitome of courtesy and 'luf-talkyng', a reputation that precedes him even to the wilds of the Wirral (lines 901–27). His courage in the alarming Beheading Game cannot be questioned, but his moral integrity is challenged in the Exchange of Winnings contest, when he accepts and keeps secret the green girdle. He returns to Camelot burning with shame to tell his sad story and show the scar on his neck, 'þe token of untrawþe' (line 2509: perfidy, lack of integrity), but the court laugh and adopt the green girdle as a badge of honour. Critics cannot agree on the moral of this brilliantly enigmatic poem. Is it a celebration of chivalry and romance conventions, or an attack on them? Has Morgan, the instigator of Gawain's test, outwitted the Round Table, even though she has failed in her aim of frightening Guinevere to death, or has Gawain proved himself the best knight in an imperfect world where, as he says himself, '"Of destinés derf and dere / What may mon do bot fonde?"' (lines 564–5: as for destinies painful and harsh / What can man do but try?) Is the poem not just entertainment but a moral lesson, part of a strategy by clerical writers to tell Arthurian tales for exemplary purposes, and civilise thuggish knights?

Gawain and his Round Table companions were not universally admired in late-fourteenth-century England, however. Chaucer, the *Gawain*-poet's contemporary, seems to be fairly hostile to the Arthurian world; he mentions it very seldom, and when he does he tends to damn it with faint praise. In 'The Squire's Tale', he stresses that both Gawain and Lancelot are far removed from the contemporary world, Gawain in fairyland and Lancelot dead (v.95–7 and 283–7). He refers to Gawain as famous for his courtesy, but his praise of Lancelot for expertise in amorous behaviour seems more dubious and more appropriate to a clandestine affair, since it includes 'subtil lookyng and dissymulynges / For drede of jalouse mennes aperceyvynges'. In 'The Nun's Priest's Tale' about Chaunteclere the cock and his favourite hen, the narrator claims 'This storie is also trewe, I undertake, / As is the book of Launcelot de Lake, / That wommen holde in ful gret reverence' (vii.3211–13). This again could be read as criticism rather than praise: it implies that the story of Lancelot and his adulterous affair is a fiction that appealed in particular to impressionable and undiscriminating female readers. The Wife of Bath's Tale about what women want most (sovereignty) was probably quite well known in Chaucer's time. In some analogues, the knight searching for the answer to the question about women is Gawain, but in Chaucer the protagonist is an anonymous Arthurian knight, and the quest is punishment for a rape he has committed. Arthur is keen to execute the culprit; but the fact that one of his knights is a condemned rapist seems to constitute a criticism of old-fashioned Arthurian chivalry, as does the rudeness of the knight to the old woman who insists on marrying him as her reward for providing the answer to the question. Chaucer knew the romance tradition well, but often subverts it. He seems to show little interest in male heroism: his men are generally less interesting and complex than his women, and it is literary stereotypes of women, and examples of women's courage and endurance, that he repeatedly invites us to consider. Perhaps this is one reason why he avoids the Arthurian legend, and implicitly belittles Lancelot and Gawain on the rare occasions when he mentions them.

Dinadan might have been more to Chaucer's taste. He first appears in the French Prose *Tristan* (mid-thirteenth century) as Tristan's faithful companion, and also features in Malory, constantly questioning the conventions and values of chivalry. Malory's Dinadan complains that Tristan and Lancelot are both mad to fight against heavy odds, telling Tristan: ' "For onys I felle in the felyshyp of sir Launcelot as I have done now with you, and he sette me so a worke that a quarter of a yere I kept my bedde" ' (p. 508.6–8 [IX.24]). Dinadan also mocks the devotion of knights in love, telling Isolde: ' "Madame, I mervayle at sir Trystram and mo other suche lovers. What aylyth them to be so madde and so asoted uppon [besotted with] women?" ' (p. 693.27–8 [X.56]). When she replies reprovingly that a good knight must be inspired by love, he explains: ' "God deffende me!" seyde sir Dinadan, "for the joye of love is to shorte, and the sorow thereof and what cometh thereof is duras [affliction] over longe".' Dinadan has licence to jest – he even refers disparagingly to Sir Lancelot as '"the olde shrew [villain]'" (p. 665.23–4 [x.47]) – but he is no Thersites, contemptuously condemning the reckless and destructive pursuit of war and lechery. In spite of his barbed comments he is much appreciated by the court, who find his jokes hilarious (though Mark Twain's Connecticut Yankee took a very dim view of them), and modern critics argue that he is an upright character whose view of chivalry is honest but not destructive.

Dinadan's comments foreground the issue of heroism, as do so many Arthurian romances. It is not just a question of 'might is right'; *trouthe* – promise-keeping and moral integrity – is immensely important too. Sin and failure are particularly emphasised in Grail narratives, but they are also increasingly visible in later medieval Arthurian narratives (and in non-Arthurian romances too). Elspeth Kennedy stresses the importance of aspiration in relation to failure, and considers whether sometimes 'a questioning or testing of established conventions of romance is to some degree involved in the failure of the main hero'.[16] Although stories of failure may sometimes have been intended to be critical or subversive, and to undercut the appeal of Arthurian chivalry, they also invite the reader to consider sympathetically human imperfection and tendency to fail for very understandable reasons. The superman hero is not always credible or sympathetic: Galahad is a good example of this principle. Unsuccessful aspiration can be very appealing, and also useful in cautionary tales: the presentation of both Lancelot (in the Vulgate Cycle and Malory) and Gawain (in *Sir Gawain and the Green Knight*) seems to be guided by the principle immortalised in a frequently quoted poem about American football:

> For when the one Great Scorer comes
> To write against your name,
> He marks – not how you won or lost –
> But how you played the game.[17]

Even if a sense of sin and conscience is not so visible in the earlier Arthurian romances, in the later Middle Ages there seems to be a shift in Arthurian texts to stories about mistakes and failures. Indeed, failure is built into the Arthurian legend seen as a whole. Arthur and his Round Table knights do tame the wilderness and introduce civilisation – but it cannot last. Readers know the ending, which cannot be a happy one. In non-Arthurian romance, the hero tends to get the girl, regain his throne, produce heirs, and live happily ever after. Arthur, however, is betrayed by treachery from within his own family, disappearing (?dying) without a direct heir, and almost all the Round Table knights die too when the ideal world of Camelot collapses;

those who survive become hermits or crusaders. The flawed and doomed idealism and heroism of the Arthurian world are surely responsible to a considerable extent for the enduring appeal of the legend. Arthur's dream of gracious living and civilised ruling cannot last. It is wonderfully apt and ironic that the Kennedy administration, with its high ideals and violent disintegration, was nicknamed Camelot.

Post-medieval versions of the legend often deal in complex ways with notions of success and failure, conservatism and innovation, and with the sorts of playfulness and subversiveness that are present in medieval versions from very early on. Mark Twain, for instance, represents Camelot as a civilisation which urgently needs radical modernising, and the Grail quest as a completely futile exercise, the equivalent of the search for the North-West Passage (p. 97). Like one of the Round Table knights stamping out evil customs in Logres, Hank Morgan institutes all sorts of changes which are supposed to represent progress, both practical and moral. And yet in the end he deserves the soubriquet Sauns Pité, killing 25,000 knights in a day with his modern technology in an echo of the devastation caused by the American Civil War, and an unwitting prophecy of the First World War, and thus destroying the modernised England of which he had become so proud. What started out as a critique of fuddy-duddy chivalric ideals and feudal practices turns into a chilling picture of the negative effects of the industrial revolution and modern capitalism, and of the shift from a genuine desire for democracy to the selfish and ruthless tyranny of The Boss (see the comments of Gilbert in Chapter 9 and Lynch in Chapter 10).

Twain's Hank Morgan is the antithesis of the usual chivalric protagonist of medieval Arthurian romance, who is nobly born and good at fighting. A tendency in modern Arthurian fiction is to shift the focus from a hero central to the legend (Arthur, Lancelot, Gawain) to a more marginal character, thus allowing for criticism and even subversion. In the later twentieth century, in the wake of female emancipation and feminism, this protagonist has sometimes been a woman. Marion Zimmer Bradley's influential novel *The Mists of Avalon* (1982) is subversive in its choice of a female protagonist, Morgaine, who becomes her half-brother Arthur's implacable enemy. Bradley's omission of any episode which could not have been witnessed by a female character radically changes the nature of the story and draws attention to the male literary biases of the past – in *The Mists* battles and quests can only be reported second-hand. But the conflicts of love and honour are still present, albeit transformed in the struggle of Morgaine against Arthur and also against his very pious queen, and in the conflict between the matriarchal goddess worship of Avalon and the patriarchal Christianity which supersedes it. A more ferocious critique of the Arthurian world is offered in Haydn Middleton's Mordred Cycle, in which Arthur's rule is characterised as brutal and ruthless: he is 'the whirl-wind king, killing like a beast, fucking like a beast', and earns the implacable enmity of both Mordred and Morgan.[18] More recently, Philip Reeve's *Here Lies Arthur* (2007) presents Arthur as a minor warlord, selfish and brutal, whose often unheroic deeds are spun into the familiar legend of the national hero by the wily Merlin; he argues that people prefer stories of glory and marvels to the plain and often unpalatable truth – and perhaps this is indeed how the early legend grew.

Of course, subversive exploitations of the Arthurian legend can have targets other than the legend itself. Donald Barthelme's *The King*, set early in the Second World War, inverts Twain's strategy in *The Connecticut Yankee*: Arthur and his court are alive and well in twentieth-century Britain.[19] They are presented as worldly wise in dealing with problems such as the press (Lancelot successfully manipulates his obituarist and the paparazzi, Arthur deals with a *Spectator* columnist); racism (the Black Knight, Roger de Ibadan, really is black); fervent socialists (Walter the Penniless discourses to Lancelot on democracy); and superweapons (the Grail is the ultimate bomb – '"New problems demand new solutions"', explains the Blue Knight – but Arthur rejects it on the grounds that it is not '"a knightly weapon"').[20] The huge success of the film *Monty Python and the Holy Grail* and the spin-off musi-cal *Spamalot* derives in large part from witty, anachronistic and irreverent reworking of the familiar characters and stories, but this includes sophisti-cated comment on both medieval and modern politics and social conven-tions (see the discussions by Lynch and by Gilbert in this volume).

Erich Auerbach famously wrote that 'a self-portrayal of feudal knight-hood with its mores and ideals is the fundamental purpose of the courtly romance' (epitomised in his discussion by Chrétien's *Yvain*), and more recently Pearsall has seen in Chrétien 'the testing and confirmation of chivalric values'.[21] But other critics have found medieval Arthurian romance much more multi-faceted, and much less easy to sum up. Corinne Saunders argues about the romance genre generally that 'at their most sophisticated, romance narratives are characterised by irony, parody, self-consciousness and comedy – and sometimes by a deep sense of failure and loss', and this judgement seems to be applicable to many Arthurian romances.[22] Irony, parody and comedy need not necessarily indicate serious criticism of Arthurian ideals. In only a few medieval narratives do the protagonists actually turn their backs on Arthur's world (for instance in Marie's *Lanval* and some Grail texts). Post-medieval Arthurian narratives are often more openly critical of Arthurian practices and values. But as the chronologi-cal section of this volume demonstrates, the Arthurian legend is like a tall tree which bends with the prevailing wind. For nearly a thousand years writers have been criticising and mocking aspects of the legend, yet it is flexible enough to be still flourishing today; neither age nor Monty Python can wither it.

NOTES

1 Derek Pearsall, *Arthurian Romance: A Short Introduction*, Blackwell Introductions to Literature (Oxford: Blackwell, 2003), p. 21.
2 Pearsall, *Arthurian Romance*, p. 24.
3 O. J. Padel, *Arthur in Medieval Welsh Literature*, Writers of Wales (Cardiff: University of Wales Press, 2000), p. 123.
4 D. H. Green, *Irony in the Medieval Romance* (Cambridge University Press, 1979), p. 13; he cites Vinaver's comment on p. 390.
5 Peter Haidu, *Subject Medieval/Modern: Text and Governance in the Middle Ages* (Stanford University Press, 2004), p. 100.
6 *Medieval Latin Arthurian Literature*, ed. and trans. Mildred Leake Day, Arthurian Archives 11 (Cambridge: D. S. Brewer, 2005), pp. 56–121 (on the date, see p. 11).
7 *Andreas Capellanus on Love*, ed. and trans. P. G. Walsh (London: Duckworth, 1982). Peter Dronke has questioned much of the received wisdom about Andreas in 'Andreas Capellanus', *Journal of Medieval Latin*, 4 (1994), 51–63.
8 Siân Echard, *Arthurian Narrative in the Latin Tradition*, Cambridge Studies in Medieval Literature 36 (Cambridge University Press, 1998), pp. 112–21 (pp. 120–1).
9 *The Lais of Marie de France*, trans. Glyn S. Burgess and Keith Busby, 2nd edn (Harmondsworth: Penguin, 2003), pp. 73–81.
10 Thomas Chestre, *Sir Launfal*, ed. A. J. Bliss (London: Nelson, 1960), lines 790–2 and 809–10.
11 *Mantel et Cor: deux lais du XIIᵉ siècle*, ed. Philip Bennett, TLF 16 (University of Exeter Press, 1975). These stories recur in later Arthurian texts in various languages.
12 Guillaume le Clerc, *The Romance of Fergus*, ed. Wilson Frescoln (Philadelphia, PA: W. H. Allen, 1983), trans. D. D. R. Owen, *Fergus of Galloway, Knight of King Arthur*, Everyman's Library (London: Dent, 1991).
13 D. D. R. Owen, 'The Craft of *Fergus*: Supplementary Notes', *French Studies Bulletin*, 25 (1987–8), 1–5 (p. 4).
14 *Queste del Saint Graal*, trans. Lacy, III.8. Malory's Lancelot is less harsh: '"A, sir," seyde sir Launcelot, "comforte yourself! For hit shall be unto us a grete honoure, and much more than we dyed in other placis, for of deth we be syker"' (p. 867.10–12 [XIII.8]).
15 Laura Ashe, 'The Hero and his Realm in Medieval English Romance', in *Boundaries in Medieval Romance*, ed. Neil Cartlidge, Studies in Medieval Romance 6 (Cambridge: D. S. Brewer, 2008), pp. 129–47 (p. 139).
16 Elspeth Kennedy, 'Failure in Arthurian Romance', *Medium Ævum*, 50 (1991), 16–32 (p. 30), repr. in *The Grail*, ed. Mahoney, pp. 279–99.
17 Grantland Rice (1880–1954), 'Alumnus Football'.

18 Haydn Middleton, *The King's Evil* (London: Little Brown, 1995), p. 291; the cycle continues with *The Queen's Captive* (1996) and *The Knight's Vengeance* (1997).
19 Donald Barthelme, *The King* (New York: Harper & Row, 1990). For other examples of twentieth-century Arthurian satire, see Norris Lacy's essay in this volume.
20 Barthelme, *The King*, pp. 77 and 130.
21 Erich Auerbach, *Mimesis: The Representation of Reality in Western Literature*, trans. Willard R. Trask (Princeton University Press, 1953), p. 131; Pearsall, *Arthurian Romance*, p. 35.
22 Corinne Saunders, 'Introduction', in *A Companion to Romance: From Classical to Contemporary* (Oxford: Blackwell, 2004), pp. 1–9 (p. 3).

9

JANE GILBERT

Arthurian ethics

My topic is Arthurian ethics in the plural, for no single idea of the 'good' governs all Arthurian works. 'Ethics', as I understand the term here, concerns reflection on the ways in which particular fields of moral criteria are constituted. Ethical literary criticism analyses the moral organisation of texts, assessing internal consistency, noting what is endorsed, condemned, obscured or omitted. It examines both any specific precepts encouraged by a work and the ways in which readers are directed towards those precepts. In one famous account of authorial moral guidance, Oscar Wilde's Miss Prism, questioned about the novel she has composed, declares, 'The good ended happily, and the bad unhappily. That is what Fiction means'.[1] Apart from simplifying many comedies, Miss Prism's rule would outlaw tragedy – a genre in which the protagonist's punishment exceeds any crime or error committed – as well as many forms of satire; yet it is evident that characters' narrative fates are often morally charged. Works of ethical criticism are themselves inspired by different moral and critical principles which guide their investigation.

Can we, then, speak of distinctively 'Arthurian ethics'? In the long tradition of Arthurian works, Arthur's court may be depicted as good or bad, and individual characters as better or worse than that court. No figure is condemned or idealised beyond recall. Moreover, Arthurian works, like all others, dialogue with the historical moments in which they were – and still are – produced and consumed; dialogue with non-Arthurian works also necessarily influences their varying moral orientations. Arthurian works are nevertheless significantly aware of themselves as Arthurian, belonging to a specific ancient and ongoing tradition. We can therefore speak of an Arthurian discourse which retains consistency even as it changes with time and other factors, and whether the works present themselves as fact or fiction – or even as criticism. To write about Arthur is to accept the determinants of this discourse.

Ethically speaking, this means entering debates whose topics are, largely, the following: love in various forms, both between men and between men and women; tension between emotional and institutional bonds (as between heterosexual love and marriage, or between homosocial love and feudal ties); masculinity and femininity (primarily, as they mean for men);[2] allegiance and its conflicts; personal loyalty and betrayal; justified and unjustified violence; power and governance, with their rights, obligations and dangers; the nature of the court and the roles of courtier and overlord; social and moral hierarchies, viewed both positively as order and negatively as inequality. Arthurian discourse gives to these universal human problems specific inflections which allow for breadth of coverage and freedom of conclusion – within certain limitations. Many aspects of life are excluded or at best marginalised: from its medieval beginnings onwards the Round Table has been linked to the chivalric problems of an elite of knightly practitioners, clerkly theoreticians and admiring or critical readers. Even its popular strands appeal to this elitism. Although there are undoubtedly overlaps between Arthurian and other discourses, the parameters just indicated are not those of, for example, ancient Greek tragedy or the realist novel. Even within the broader discourse of medieval romance, the choice to write about Arthur determines available engagements and directions. Arthurian ethics as a field of study relates to and reflects on these moral debates and their constraints.

Neither now nor never

Arthurian ethics in the plural, then. But Arthurian discourse does have binding factors, one of which is that the Arthurian scene is never *now*. Arthurian chivalry always lies in a past discontinuous from the present or in some fantastical otherwhere, and is contemplated at a distance by a consciously 'modern' commentator. Arthurian discourse therefore incorporates two distinct moral spaces, one identified as Arthurian and another portrayed as that of the text's own present. This dual vision means that Arthurian discourse is inherently ethical. Some Arthurian texts try to privilege one moral space over the other in nostalgia, utopianism or celebration of modernity, yet it is a feature of the discourse that such hierarchies rarely remain stable. Each distinct 'world' retains the potential to reflect critically on the other. Thus, even if the Arthurian scene is never fully present in the present, it is not confined to the historical past or to an isolated fantasy space. *Quondam et futurus* ('once and future') does not adequately express the dynamic relationship between the represented Arthurian world and the time of the discourse. Somewhat like the Aboriginal Dreamtime, 'Arthurtime' exists in constant tension with the present, pressing upon it and on what it may imminently become: neither now nor never.

As its consumers and practitioners, we need to be aware that a writer may not turn to Arthurian discourse in order to convey an urgent message; the discourse itself imparts an imperative quality. This is further reason for caution when assessing an Arthurian work's ethical import in its real-life contexts. A second relevant analogy is with modern virtual environments (like the 'online 3D virtual world' Second Life: http://secondlife.com/), which, though avowedly not 'real life', exist in a complex relation to it, staging significant events and encounters. Our moral judgements on what we may term 'Arthur Life' and its actors are complicated by our perception of them as neither 'us' nor 'not-us' and neither real nor inconsequential. Our positions are compromised by our nearness to the Arthurian world as well as by our distance from it, both sources of potential ethical anxiety. In this essay I also use 'the Arthurian scene', evoking a third analogy: Freud's elaboration of the complex ways in which fantasy derives from and bears on life.[3] Whether situating themselves as 'historical' or as 'fantastical', Arthurian works always participate in 'fantasy' in this Freudian sense, whose political dimensions have been elaborated by such later commentators as Fredric Jameson, Julia Kristeva and Slavoj Žižek.

A second unifying factor of the discourse lies in this: if Arthurian writers and readers can never fully inhabit the Arthurian moment, neither can its residents. As Arthur himself says in *Monty Python and the Holy Grail* (dir. Terry Gilliam and Terry Jones, 1975) on first glimpsing the castle about which he and his knights have just made a literal song and dance: 'On second thoughts, let's not go to Camelot. It is a silly place.' An analogous disenchantment afflicts the court at the beginning of the final book of the Old French prose Vulgate Cycle, *La Mort le roi Artu* (c. 1215–30, hereafter *Mort Artu*), for the preceding Grail quest has eliminated the *raison d'être* of the Round Table and many of its best men. In Arthurian discourse, Arthurian ideals remain unrealisable and irreconcilable even for Arthurian heroes. In non-Arthurian courtly medieval literature, the court is not infrequently portrayed as the enemy of the courtly: the gossipy, back-biting rivalry of courtiers renders such virtues as loyalty, discretion and devotion impossible to live out. In Arthurian discourse, however, the problem cuts deeper. The characteristic Arthurian dilemmas can only be resolved in an elsewhere outside the court, a fantasy space receding within the works themselves. Thus the Grail is achieved in a distant castle, and knights love happily in far-flung domains. Alternatively, long-standing dilemmas are overcome just when collapse has already become unstoppable, as when Arthur at the height of his conquering glory hears that Mordred has seized his throne. Fulfilment is inseparable from breakdown. 'Mort' texts examine in detail this variant on the general impasse. 'Camelot', viewed as the conjunction of a set of ideals with a lived place, is an inaccessible object of desire and anxiety within the Arthurian world. It bears comparison with the Grail, which, however, as a religious phenomenon, is finally attainable through a transcendence which also exorcises it. Being strictly ethical, 'Camelot' puts pressure on the Arthurian characters within the works, as the Arthurian world itself presses on producers and audiences of Arthurian discourse. In the remainder of this essay I shall examine how some instances of Arthurian discourse position themselves in relation to the Arthurian scene, and how that positioning contributes to their ethics and aesthetics.

Playing the game: twelfth-century French romances and their legacy

In twelfth-century French verse romances, the Arthurian setting provides a place emphatically not the real, present world, in which to test principles of fundamental relevance to that world: principles moral, psychological, social and political. As in modern science fiction, real-world expectations are suspended in order for the testing to proceed unhampered. Protagonists and audiences discover together the laws of the somewhat different world that each romance presents. Like experienced computer game players encountering an unfamiliar game, we enter the romance armed with a number of alternatives for action. To caricature: when faced with a new creature, we can hit it, kiss it or ask it a question. In the course of this game-playing, the romances explore different notions of the 'good' and the tensions between them. Thus, though audience and hero enter the game with a number of precepts for determining the correct action (e.g. hit discourteous knights, kiss beautiful ladies, question hermits, show mercy to submissive, defeated enemies), these will be reconfigured; the audience expects this although the hero usually does not. When the hero inevitably makes a mistake he is eventually informed of it and given another 'life' in which to try again. Symbolic deaths abound.

The archetype of such romances is *Le Conte du Graal* (*The Story of the Grail*) by Chrétien de Troyes (*c.* 1180), the most influential Arthurian writer of the period. Chrétien's untutored hero attempts to negotiate chivalric life armed only with his mother's sketchy (and misunderstood) lessons. However, the sense of discovering a new world and the play with expectations are essential elements of any twelfth-century Arthurian romance. Individual narratives ring changes on preceding ones, expanding underdeveloped possibilities. Irony, comedy and parody are inherent aesthetic and ethical building blocks. Thus in Renaut de Beaujeu's *Le Bel Inconnu* (*c.* 1190), the hero is confronted by a hideous serpent.[4] Initially confident that this is a moment for hitting, he hesitates when the serpent mimes surrender. Suddenly it kisses him on the lips and flees from the room, to be replaced by a wonderful damsel, Blonde Esmeree, who introduces herself as the former serpent now rescued from enchantment. The hero accepts that he has won her but is unhappy because he loves another, the Damsel of the White Hands. Having instead to marry the Blonde turns his plight into a parody of Tristan's, for the latter marries Ysolt of the White Hands in a vain attempt to extricate himself from his affair with Ysolt the Blonde. Although Tristan's dilemma results from unlikely circumstances – a magic potion makes irresistible a treasonous, adulterous and incestuous love for his uncle's wife – it encapsulates a tragic universal: the ultimate incompatibility of passion with life in society. Twelfth- and thirteenth-century romances return repeatedly to Tristan's story, softening the conflicts that it calcifies in order to probe deeper into the partial satisfactions that social life offers. When the narrator promises to rescue the Bel Inconnu only if his own (the narrator's) lady consents to accept him, more stress is laid on frustration than on possible fulfilment. For protagonist, narrator and audience, the story can only remain incomplete.

Chrétien's later romances challenge the Arthurian courtly values established in his first, *Erec et Enide* (*c.* 1170). The choices that confront his protagonists are ethical, offering an opportunity to step outside one value-system in order to weigh the competing or complementary claims of another. Thus Lancelot in *Le Chevalier de la charrete* (*Knight of the Cart*) (*c.* 1177) learns that to obtain information about the abducted Guinevere he must ride in a cart which the text stresses is a symbol of unbearable shame:

> Reason, who does not follow Love's command, told him to beware of getting in, and admonished and counselled him not to do anything for which he might incur disgrace or reproach. Reason, who dared tell him this, spoke from the lips, not from the heart; but Love, who held sway within his heart, urged and commanded him to climb into the cart at once. Because Love ordered and wished it, he jumped in; since Love ruled his action, the disgrace did not matter.
> (lines 365–77, Kibler, p. 212)

Chivalric reason dictates that the knight pursue honour and avoid shame. Love is ideally correlated with this goal, spurring the knight to fight better so as to win his lady's affection and his community's esteem. In Lancelot's case, however, love opposes the rational norm and, further, the very logical structure which would oppose 'good' and 'bad'. Lancelot is therefore a problem: is he the superlative knight whose devotion to his lady enables him to transcend the usual rules, or a social outcast and abject criminal? If both, then how is the relationship between these conditions to be conceived? The text requires us to examine critically our ideas of good and evil potentially much beyond the confines of the literary work. The layering and ironies which make his texts' moral positions impossible to fix are one of Chrétien's major contributions to twelfth-century Arthurian romance.

For Chrétien and others, paradox is an opportunity to display social and academic skills in analyses which combine suave rhetorical elegance with virtuoso scholastic dialectic. The urbane, often light-hearted tone is linked to the works' ethical openness. In the thirteenth century, Arthurian romances distanced themselves from the intellectual playfulness and ethical experimentation of the early works. The Arthurian moral space becomes didactic, a place of lessons directed to the text's own present. Paradox and irony now signal a tragic mystery weighing on the human race. It is in this context that what we may call 'The Lancelot Question' looms over thirteenth-century French Arthurian writing in the Vulgate Cycle of prose romances (and is echoed in the Prose *Tristan* integrated into the Arthurian universe). Lancelot is, as the Demoiselle d'Escalot describes him in the *Mort Artu*, 'li plus vilains chevaliers del monde et li plus vaillanz' (Ch. 71, lines 26–28): not only 'the most uncourtly knight in the world and the worthiest', but a figure in whom *vilains* ('uncourtly') and *vaillanz* ('worthy') are near-indistinguishable. In context, this testimony to Lancelot's impossible status replaces Chrétien's ethical challenge with a moral statement reflecting humanity's fallen condition and the consequent inevitable failure of aspiration. The *Mort Artu* presents a Lancelot who is neither specially guilty nor unclassifiable but exemplarily symptomatic – a tragic hero. In the Vulgate *Queste del Saint Graal* (c. 1215–30), contrastingly, Lancelot is humiliated for his adultery and displaced in favour of his Christ-like son Galahad, representative of a new, strictly Christian chivalry. He is nonetheless redeemed for knightly virtues which set him apart from the Arthurian court, unlike Gawain, so often the bearer of that court's merits and limitations, who is damned in the *Queste* as an unenlightened sinner.

Although it establishes an eschatological framework which later Arthurian discourse will find hard to ignore, the Vulgate does not have the final word on the Lancelot Question. Malory in his fifteenth-century English prose compendium *Le Morte Darthur* (completed 1469–70) exposes the extraordinary political, social, moral and spiritual benefits that the Arthurian community gains by Lancelot's love of the queen. Malory further idealises Lancelot himself as a rare worthy in a corrupt world that includes the Round Table (witness his reworking of the ambiguous 'Cart' episode to celebrate Lancelot's moral independence of the court: p. 1154.3–11 [XIX.13]). The famous disclaimer 'And whether they were abed other at other maner of disportis, me lyste nat thereof make no mencion, for love that tyme was nat as love ys nowadayes' (p. 1165.11–13 [xx.3]), effectively dismisses the adultery charge; even if Lancelot and Guinevere did have a sexual relationship, modern norms cannot be permitted to constrain the behaviour of heroes in 'Arthurtime' (overtaking Chrétien's hint in the *Charrete* that infringement of rules is, if not positively a sign of the ideal, at any rate a stage on the road towards it). Idealisation definitively separates this heroic realm from the everyday world of the text's own present, which is played out in the failings and failures of the narrative's various courts. Malory's 'Arthur Life' incorporates real life at the price of divorce from what we should properly in this case call 'Lancelot Life', an exalted and unrealisable dream shared by the text's Arthurian and present worlds.

Out of 'old, corrupt language': late medieval romance rewriting

A revisionist urge dominates the writing of Arthurian fiction in court circles of England and France in the late Middle Ages. Although new romances were written, the preference, in the fifteenth century especially, was for updating earlier medieval works to suit modern tastes. Reworkers often justified their efforts by alleging that readers no longer understood the older idiom, which they termed 'corrupt' (*corrompu*). We need not examine the literal truth of this proposition to accept its symbolic value. Early Arthurian romances did not speak the same moral language as did the late medieval centuries. Note that the butt of criticism is not generally the Arthurian court. In a representative example, the Burgundian prose reworking of Chrétien's *Erec* (1450–60), Arthur's court and its inhabitants are presented as models for moderns to imitate. Refashioning focuses on the form and the style of the earlier works, as the prologue asserts:

> One may benefit much in various ways from the continual practice of recounting the histories containing the deeds of nobles of former days. And because I have been presented with the history in rhyme of Erec son of King Lac, I – at God's pleasure – shall turn my efforts [*occuperay mon estude*] for a short while to transforming it from rhyme into prose in the manner which follows, beseeching those who will henceforward read it that they excuse my uncultivated manner of speech.[5]

Given the elegant phrasing and the prestige attached to such prosifications, we can dismiss the term 'uncultivated' (*ruide*) as a conventional expression of humility (the 'modesty topos') encoding a claim to the virtues of plain-speaking. The modifications purport to clarify the alleged difficulties of the earlier works, in a project which bears significantly on the texts' ethical organisation. The new romance differs as much from the tragic paradoxes, dramatic ironies and pessimism of the morally intense thirteenth-century prose romances as it does from the ethical experimentation and play, conflicts and ironies for which it condemns the earlier verse romances as ambiguous, obscure and shallow. Instead an exemplary Arthurian court is matched with an aspiring present, the stress on utility emphasising that the fiction's ideals and values are to be carried into contemporary life. By this process of ideological harmonisation the rewritings attempt 'the deletion of the alterity of Chrétien's Arthurian kingdom', erasing the distance that earlier works inscribed between the Arthurian scene and the space of the Arthurian writer-audience.[6]

In fact, this distance is only re-located. When they depict the earlier verse tradition as suspect, these late romances retain the dual vision which divides Arthurian discourse between 'past' and 'present' moral frameworks. The self-alterity which once provided for ethical reflection is dismissed as linguistic and literary 'corruption'. Translating into 'proper' language will rescue the Arthurian world from this supposedly extraneous ethical ambiguity and allow its innate moral value to shine. All the same, the judgement implied in the reworkings expresses a typically Arthurian ambivalence troubling the new moral order. The reconstructed romances inevitably also preserve the archaic, thus at once testifying to desire for them and installing them as something against which the present must define itself in order to forge its own future more successfully. A superseded, rejected Arthurian past, here that of romance writing, haunts the present and threatens its efforts to build an ideal order. Thus the inherently ethical nature of Arthurian discourse reasserts itself against efforts to make it bear a straightforward moral message.

Against this background the late fourteenth-century English *Sir Gawain and the Green Knight* appears to be something of a throwback to the early French romances to which it is often compared. It presents its protagonist with classic disorienting and challenging situations, at first sight recalling those faced by Chrétien's heroes. The text is nevertheless of its time; the rather obvious way in which these 'games' (*gomnes*) are signalled suggests an audience no longer acclimatised to such patterns. Although this contemporary context has been neglected by scholars, *Sir Gawain* shares in the late medieval trend for morally corrective reworking. Instead of over-writing its predecessors with an improved and improving prosification, it imitates earlier verse romances while incorporating a judgemental attitude towards them. The most pressing ethical question facing Gawain in both the Beheading and Exchange of Winnings games is whether these and other courtly games are worth the playing or should properly not be played at all. These are issues that Chétien's heroes rarely confront in seriousness. Late medieval French discussions of chivalry within and outside romances prioritise *le bien publique* ('the common good') over individualistic pursuits and consider leadership to be the knight's vocation. Similar opinions are voiced by some members of Arthur's court as they watch Gawain ride to his doom (lines 674–83). The games thus appear to be instances of the frivolity of which late medieval writers accused early romances. *Sir Gawain* here misrepresents earlier works, at least where the Exchange of Winnings and the Seduction scenes are concerned. No Arthurian tradition approves the breaking of even minor oaths, or requires a knight to commit sexual treason out of good manners to a lady. (Not that different avatars might not act otherwise: other Gawains sleep with hosts' daughters, beloveds or wives without apparent scruple.) These dilemmas reflect instead contemporary efforts to minimise the role of love and females in chivalric identity and activity.[7]

Yet the poem is not unequivocally supportive of modern values. Once the avowedly childish Beheading Game is initiated, *Sir Gawain* presents unambiguously its hero's duty to keep his pledged word in the face of death, in accordance with established tradition and against the court's objections, which bespeak a certain short-sightedness. As in the French prose rewritings, past and present Arthurian discourses are shown not to speak the same moral language, although in this case the advantage is not all with the present. Taken seriously, early romance's juvenile games can produce transcendence, and present a knight with opportunities to excel beyond the bounds set by pragmatism. The text presents a double bind, for it seems that taking these games seriously, as Gawain does the Beheading Game, is an error; but so is treating them as inconsequential, as he ultimately does the Exchange Game. *Sir Gawain* thus portrays the earlier romance tradition as simultaneously unworthy and as the only worthy support, not so much of the Round Table as of the hero who insists on living out its ideals against its counsel. Gawain's exemplary chivalry shares much with earlier Arthurian romance, whereas his weaknesses are largely those of Arthur's seemingly more modern court. The poem's restrictive morality is shown by its conception of failure: in place of the perversity that afflicts twelfth-century and even some thirteenth-century Arthurian heroes, Gawain fails by falling short of a fully expounded ideal. The pentangle values that he bears on his shield are those of a perfected courtly chivalry reconciling all conflicts. According to this poem, such chivalry cannot survive within the world of Arthurian romance, whether at Camelot or at Hautdesert. Gawain, who attempts to adventure outside that world, finds himself caught within its coils when the apparent alterity of the Green Knight turns into Bertilak's homeliness. The ancient Arthurian universe can here only ever confront its own internal problems, materialised as Morgan le Fay. Such high ideals as Gawain pursues are achievable only by going quite beyond the terms of the Arthurian court – a familiar picture, but Gawain is not Galahad. His role remains that of representative of the court, with its strengths and its limitations.

The denouement follows the twelfth-century pattern in upsetting the hero's understanding of the moral structure of the romance and in awarding him a new 'life' in which to do better. Gawain undergoes the humiliation suffered by many of his predecessors, and that he learns is clear from his 'confession': 'Corsed worth [= be] cowarddyse and couetyse boþe' (line 2374). It is significant, though, that he chooses as his fault's emblem the green girdle – voluntarily adopted, infinitely re-signifiable and ultimately removable – rather than the scar on his neck, which, permanent and outside his field of vision, is not subject to his control. Even in the hero who partially transcends it, the Arthurian world is permitted little authentic moral insight. The narrative ends with the optimistic foundation of the Order of the Green Girdle. But this future is foreclosed as the entire Arthurian order is doomed. However, precisely insofar as the text casts doubt on the ability of Arthurian discourse to sustain worthwhile moral discussion and insists on the limitations imposed on its conclusions by the Arthurian framework, it raises in its audience's minds the major ethical issue of the validity of those conclusions beyond that framework. Its relentless closing down of the Arthurian world lays wide open the question of the relations between 'Arthur Life' and real life.

Not now but here: the 'historical' tradition

Arthurian romances vary in how they present their geography. Chrétien's locations, though named, remain 'elsewhere', while *Sir Gawain* situates the internal fantasy space, embodied by the conventional stunning otherworld castle in wild forest, in the north-west Midlands, source of the poem's own dialect. One of the features distinguishing the more 'historical' variants of Arthurian discourse is their emphasis on the Arthurian space as a geopolitical 'here' in relation to writer and audience. This 'here' is capable of different extension, partly because the Arthurian interest in adventure often correlates to an expansionist vision. In his letter to Henry II of England included in the Latin chronicle *Draco Normannicus* (c. 1167–70), Arthur (now living in the Antipodes) declares his intention to force Henry to renounce his campaign to conquer Brittany. Henry, though uncowed, offers in response to hold Brittany under Arthur's law.[8] Regardless of whether twelfth-century people 'believed' in this fiction, it lays out genuine alternatives facing some of them – resist Henry's claim or accede to it – and offers a solution via the Arthurian scene. Arthurian discourse sanctions Angevin empire-building by giving it a particular gloss: Henry will join the Breton empire, not vice versa. At the same time, Arthur is presented as bellicose and arrogant, Henry as law-abiding.[9] The Angevin present is better than the Arthurian past, even while the latter's legendary prestige is pressed into service to sketch out a desired future.

The late fourteenth-century Alliterative *Morte Arthure*, a Middle English romance with strong chronicle elements, concentrates on Arthur's European campaigns.[10] The Arthurian problems of power and governance are played out in the king's own conquests. Initially his presence on the Continent is rewarded by his heroic liberation of Normandy from a man-eating giant; thus should a king protect his people and enact justice in his domains. This same king will later bloodily sack the cities of Metz and Milan. Arthur's dream of the Wheel of Fortune (lines 3218–455) portrays this moral descent as inevitable and links it to the exercise of supreme power and superlative military prowess. The philosophers who interpret as Arthur himself the dragon of his earlier dream which comes to overwhelm his people (lines 760–831) point to the conclusion: great kings are ambiguous figures, dreadful and gracious. Once the endgame is included in the horizon of any Arthurian text a sense of fatality dominates, and culpability tends to become both generally distributed and diffuse. Arthur's sins in the Alliterative *Morte* are those of his estate, the proper response to them the personal one of almsgiving and confession leading to a good death.

The poem's 'historical' detail and 'chronicle' effects contribute as much to its ethical positioning as does its 'Mort' framework. Notably, the Arthurian characters and the narrator treat France, flower among kingdoms (line 556), as a homeland and cultural and political unity with Britain. Legally, too, Arthur is merely defending his own lands as laid out in lines 26–47, which linger lovingly on the territories of an expanded France, from Navarre to Provence, Burgundy to Hainault and Brittany to Bordeaux, adventuring more sketchily east and north into central Europe and Scandinavia. Moral alienation occurs only when Arthur enters the undisputed territory of the fourteenth-century Holy Roman Empire to attack Metz, then Italy. These incursions seem a step too far, even though they are arguably defensible within the poem because of the vast lands held by Arthur's predecessors and because of the unchristian and tyrannical behaviour imputed to the Romans, and even though the text celebrates Arthur as a conqueror and justifies conquest as legal title. Even if kings are dragons and power leads inexorably to moral degradation, nevertheless the poem draws a line between justified and unjustified violence, and draws it geopolitically. We can note, for the record, that its disposition of Arthurian and Imperial territories intertwines in typically convoluted manner with the organisation of late medieval Europe.

Thus contemporary French kings expanded their domain in all directions – including the lands in the west, south and north of France mentioned in the Alliterative *Morte* – but were broadly content with the north-eastern boundary at the Meuse, to the west of Metz (then a free, wealthy bourgeois city-state within the Empire and object of numerous predatory attacks by brigands and nobles).

Making knighthood grotesque and absurd

In Mark Twain's 1889 novel, *A Connecticut Yankee in King Arthur's Court*, Hank Morgan – self-assured, direct, rationalist, eminently practical – finds himself transported to sixth-century England, where he introduces 'the march of civilization'.[11] Arthur's time is a dark age of superstition and filth (conventional signifiers of the non-modern) in which the ruler is manipulated by a wily but equally benighted Merlin and where the virtuous characters appear only as big children. Morgan's outrage at economic, political and social inequality presents the Arthurian past as a mirror in which modernity can measure its undoubted moral progress. The tendency of the powerful to abuse their power may not change, but human consciousness does: Morgan is fired with the republican ideals of liberty, equality and fraternity and armed with the intellectual and practical tools appropriate to those moral goals. This aspect of the novel is well realised in Dan Beard's illustrations to the first American edition. One shows two female figures of Justice captioned '19th Century' and '6th Century' holding unequal balances (p. 211). Both lighter scales hold a mallet labelled 'Labor' whereas the heavier scale is filled in the present by a bag of many dollars ($1000000 – the zeros disappear out of sight) and in the past by a crown and medal inscribed 'Title'. The image's symmetry underlines the message 'plus ça change …', with the inequality between the scales significantly greater in the modern version. Another illustration presents three images all captioned '"Brother! – To Dirt Like This?"' (a phrase pronounced by Arthur in the text). On the left a shackled peasant bows his head to a king, in the middle a collared slave stands below an American Southern gentleman with a whip, and on the right a man in working clothes lower than a man in a formal suit. Beneath each pair is an emblem – respectively a sword, lawbook and moneybags – crushing fallen human figures and labelled 'Oppressor'. Again Beard's image distinguishes between past and present even as it insists on the parallel; the superior figures sneer identically but the inferiors (arguably) progress from broken submission to an upright stance and steady gaze that promises much (p. 160). According to Beard's presentation, therefore, contemporary problems stem from the survival of standards and behaviour that belong properly in the past; modernity must assume its own morality in the march towards a better future.

Twain's text engages more subtly with the Arthurian scene. Having introduced the industrial technology and modern bureaucracy which, to his mind, national prosperity requires, Morgan reflects on three years of his rule:

> Now look around on England. A happy and prosperous country, and strangely altered. Schools everywhere, and several colleges; a number of pretty good newspapers. ... Slavery was dead and gone; all men were equal before the law; taxation had been equalized. (p. 228)

The problems that Twain opens up in this promising situation are strongly Arthurian. The ellipsis in the above quotation contains the following lines:

> Even authorship was taking a start; Sir Dinadan the Humorist was first in the field, with a volume of gray-headed jokes which I had been familiar with during thirteen centuries. If he had left out that old rancid one about the lecturer I wouldn't have said anything; but I couldn't stand that one. I suppressed the book and hanged the author. (p. 228)

The joke has a serious side. Morgan, like the Arthur of the Alliterative *Morte*, himself enacts power's inevitable tendency to tyranny. Having intended to hand power to the people once he has educated them to wield it, Morgan will end by fighting for the king against a revolution, though hardly a popular one. Twain does not simply invert republican values. As Morgan pursues his Holy Grail of a free Protestant Church and democracy with universal adult suffrage (utopian goals in 1889), we face the familiar Arthurian scenario in which the highest achievements of a character associated with the Round Table take us beyond the ideological and moral setting of that order, and in fact point to its collapse. Morgan's role combines his namesake's with that of Galahad.

For all the realism with which he presents the medieval past, 'Arthur Life' provides Twain with an ahistorical space for an experiment in moral social reform. However, Arthurian discourse imposes its own history, and ultimately the narrative becomes a fatalistic 'Mort' drama of noble intentions gone tragically and ironically awry. Most bitingly, it dramatises the failure of knowledge to make a difference. Morgan, familiar with British history, knows power's corrupting influence. The short lifespan of the improvements that his science brings to sixth-century England is underlined by the nineteenth-century England, still fettered by monarchic rule and the class system, known to frame-narrator and audience. Arthurian history simply absorbs Yankee anachronism in taking its known course, with

Agravaine's and Mordred's decision to impel Arthur to confront Lancelot and Guinevere's adultery prompted by a fleecing on the stock-market. In spite of his profound, principled hostility towards the establishment, and indeed as a means of serving that hostility, Morgan becomes a knight and part of the Arthurian order, 'Sir Boss'. Although he does not appear to know it, his text is periodically invaded by Malory's when sixth-century courtiers take up the story, and increasingly in his own archaisms. Ultimately Morgan's narrative succumbs entirely to the medieval as Merlin – not such a charlatan after all – places him in enchanted sleep for thirteen centuries.

Unlike Beard, Twain does not diagnose the moral problems within the text as contagions from the past. Instead he uses 'Arthurtime' to predict pitfalls lurking in modernity's supposedly triumphal progress. The question of the positive and negative social effects of chivalric violence is reframed within modernity as Morgan converts knights-errant into travelling salesmen as part of his plan for 'extinguishing knighthood by making it grotesque and absurd' (p. 112): 'if they couldn't persuade a person to try a sewing machine on the instalment plan, … they removed him and passed on' (p. 228). Feudalism segues into equally violent and unenlightened capitalism. Grotesquery and moral extinction overtake also the nineteenth-century oppression derided by Beard but not by Morgan, for whom capitalism is a prerequisite for democracy. Twain's critical presentation of the Arthurian past – unlike those of Beard or Morgan – is not matched by a faith that modernity's morals will prevail, or even in those morals' superiority. His novel testifies to Arthurian discourse's ability to be a vehicle for modern utopian ideals while also showing its ability to interrogate and challenge modernity's moral framework.

This essay comes full circle with *Monty Python and the Holy Grail*, since to take this film seriously, as I propose to do here, is to accept it as an Arthurian game comparable to those of the twelfth century, though much less polished in execution. In a series of encounters that would be familiar to early romance audiences, the Arthurian heroes are repeatedly baffled both by events and by encounters with figures who offer alternative understandings of the textual universe. The opening scenes confront a visually familiar, knightly Arthur with a man-at-arms who challenges the king's claim to have ridden the length and breadth of the country, pointing out that he has no horse. A debate ensues about how the coconut shells with which Arthur's squire is making clopping sounds reached tenth-century Britain. Swallows are suggested as carriers, but a discussion about the air-speed velocity and weight-to-strength ratio of the different species exposes Arthur as lacking both scientific knowledge and logical habits of mind. The king then meets labourers whose filthy condition emphasises that his immaculate white surcoat denotes conspicuous wealth as well as moral idealism. Dennis the peasant derides Arthur's legendary investiture by the Lady of the Lake and offers a Marxist critique of the economic exploitation on which the Arthurian world-vision rests.

In its highlighting of actualities normally excluded from and incongruous with the Arthurian court, *Monty Python and the Holy Grail* bears comparison with Chrétien de Troyes's *Yvain* (*Le Chevalier au lion, Knight with the Lion*), where the knights encounter a herdsman whom they can only interpret as monstrous in spite – or because – of his practical utility, and who perceives them with equal disbelief and greater scepticism (lines 267–407, pp. 298–301).[12] In the film, the non-Arthurian voices align different orders of scientific, materialist 'realism': the portrayal of the lower orders in their historically authentic living conditions (signalled by superstition and filth, again), modernity's political critique of the Middle Ages, and physics. Against this conglomerate, Arthur appears an idealistic but comically deluded figure out of touch with the reality about him and pursuing goals which are no more than ideological cover for an inequitable distribution of wealth and power. Modernity's knowledge of the Arthurian world is much superior cognitively and morally to Arthur's own.

As the film continues, however, this ethical configuration changes. Not only the medieval characters are made 'grotesque and absurd'. 'Modern' visionaries are mocked for failing according to their own criteria, as when Herbert's pragmatic father insists on building his castle on a swamp in spite of observable practical disadvantages or the peasants declare themselves part of an 'anarcho-syndicalist collective', showing a grasp of medieval circumstance no better than Arthur's. It becomes increasingly evident that the Arthurian world-vision, though factually and morally wrong, wins out in the film. 'A Famous Historian' arrives to voice the scientific account only to be cut down by a passing knight, now actually on horseback. Medieval absurdities create narrative reality, as when the bunny of Caerbannog proves a killer. Although the knights find these phenomena surprising, they seek just such wonders, which therefore have a place in the Arthurian world; for the modern rationalist, however, the fantastical is inadmissible. The cinematography supports the Arthurian vision, rendering the scene of the Black Knight's first fight at the ford, for instance, darkly enjoyable. The film is with Arthur and his knights for all that they are mistaken, irrelevant or oppressive. Like the recurrent motif of characters who, being declared dead, riposte that they are 'feeling much better', the Arthurian order rejects the news of its demise. Faced with a threatened Arthurian takeover, modernity finally literally calls in the police, imposing its own version of reality by state-sanctioned violence. And we note that although the unceremonious

rebellion occurs during his absence, precipitating the beginning of the end of British greatness. At face value, Arthur's imperial ambition may seem either redundant to his status or fatally overweening. On the other hand, the fantasy of Arthur as emperor was of great importance to many medieval writers, especially in England. It is interesting to re-examine how Arthurian imperialism was conceived and represented in medieval literature, given that later developments have led to its apparent neglect. We can also ask whether changes to the ideological demands made on Arthurian stories brought the end of the imperial claim, or whether the legend's imperialist functions were continued by other means. What was and what has remained or become 'imperial' about Arthur?

As an early and most influential treatment of Arthurian imperialism, Geoffrey of Monmouth's *History* supplies a basic grammar of the topic. Its key term is 'conquest'. Arthur's argument for war on Rome is unashamedly acquisitive: '"Let him who comes out on top carry off what he has made up his mind to take"' (Thorpe, ix.16, p. 233). In effect, Geoffrey's Arthur seeks to 'carry off' Rome's prestige back to Britain, not to fill the emperor's shoes. The scene is never set in Rome itself. We do not see the Emperor Leo or the Roman Senate directly. The 'procurator' Lucius stands in for Leo so fully that in Wace's version Lucius himself simply becomes 'the emperor',[3] as he remains in the Alliterative *Morte* and in Malory. In the 'Galfridian' tradition (i.e. the tradition based on Geoffrey of Monmouth) the Roman Empire is represented by its generals, ambassadors and tributary kings, and objectified as a catalogue of possessions. It is a series of opponents to be browbeaten and defeated, and of rich pickings, as Arthur makes plain: '"Yours shall be its gold, silver, palaces, towers, cities, castles, and all the other riches of the vanquished!"' (x.7, p. 249). The thought of spoil supersedes imperial occupation and rule. 'Winning' Rome is to be a continuation of Arthur's previous successes as king, the ultimate trophy but no radical change of status. He cites the British rulers Belinus and Brennius as precedents, who occupied and 'held' Rome for a long time – by the Alliterative *Morte* it has become 160 years – but we are given no notion of how that arrangement has worked. In Geoffrey, Belinus, 'that most glorious of the Kings of the Britons' (ix.16, p. 233), has quickly returned home; Brennius has stayed on in Italy only to wreak more havoc (iii.10, p. 99). They look like successful raiders, not emperors.

As the climactic British king, Geoffrey's Arthur has implicitly been set up as a natural claimant to Rome by the narrative twinning of Britain's founder Brutus with Aeneas, a theme later reprised by comments from Julius Caesar and Cassivelanus (iv.2, pp. 108–9). Caesar's military victories in Britain, cited by the Romans as their authority to demand tribute, give

Arthur the same example and rationale (ix.16, p. 233). Yet Arthur admits that acquisition by force does not confer legal rights, though he is careful to claim these in Gaul, and jokes later that he is not interested in a Roman legal decision (ix.16 and 20, pp. 232, 236). Neither does the matter rest simply with the view that those who try unjustly to seize another's property deserve to lose their own (ix.16 and 20, pp. 233–4, 236). Rather, military conquests over Roman possessions are offered as a sign of Britain's prior attainment of cultural and moral superiority. As if Arthur were playing the computer game *Civilization*, the Roman ambassadors' demand for tribute is preceded by the statement that Britain now leads all other kingdoms in wealth, manners, culture and technology (ix.13–14, pp. 229–30). That assessment is backed up by a description of Caerleon's court ceremony and architecture as 'a match for Rome' (ix.12, p. 226; Wace lines 12009–10). Similarly, the first battles against Lucius follow Arthur's demonstration of righteous strength against the giant of St Michael's Mount. Figuratively, the 'right', first to Gaul and then to Rome, is founded on the attachment of a more than legal prestige to military prowess. Lucius' speech to his men (x.8, pp. 249–50) expresses a master pattern of the *History*, in which soldierly courage and integrity are seen to lead the will of God in deciding battles. But whereas Lucius can only appeal to the courage and integrity of Roman ancestors, Arthur tells his men to remember their *own* proven courage (x.7 and 11, pp. 248–9, 255) – 'Think of your own right hands' – and mentions only the *wrongs* done to their ancestors (x.11, p. 255). Providential history, appealed to first in prophecy (ix. 17, p. 234) and later in British victory (x. 12, p. 256) depends on the prior claims of current human agents.

Arthur wins an empire mainly, it seems, to give it away. Defeating Rome's might, he retains or creates a large number of client rulers, following on naturally from his continuing need to attract 'very distinguished men from far-distant kingdoms' (ix.11, p. 222). Norway is conquered to be given to Loth. Auguselus gets Scotland, Gawain Lothian, Bedivere Normandy, Kay Anjou, and so on. Given that Anjou was the hereditary enemy of Normandy, and Geoffrey was writing for Anglo-Norman patrons, Arthur's supposed control of this overlordship was significant, as was the claim to dispose of Scotland and Wales, often referenced by later monarchs. Overall, the concept of extended imperial citizenship is thoroughly lost in a feudal structure of kin, personal allegiance and sworn fealty. There is no respect for the Roman system of provinces and governors. Despite Frollo's efforts as governor, Geoffrey's Arthur can say that the 'Romans' 'made no effort to defend' Gaul (ix.16, p. 233). To Wace, though he appreciates Frollo's attempt to save Paris, Roman Gaul is a political blank with 'neither king nor over-lord' (Wace line 9906). Laʒamon, responding in a different way to the same problem, makes him 'King Frolle' who has come from Rome into France and sends back yearly tribute.[4] Wace expands on Geoffrey's suggestions that the empire is a distant and arrogant tax-master which, unlike Arthur's Britain, cannot command local loyalty in a crisis and must rely on unchristian allies (Wace lines 9914–54). There is no positive reference to Roman civic virtues, infrastructure, religious observance or customs. Brave military opponents like Frollo and Lucius are needed to maintain Arthur's prestige as their conqueror, but in itself the empire is effete, corrupt and ripe for replacement by manly feudal monarchies.

The shadowy 'Romanness' of the Continent provides some sense of cohesion for the lands that Geoffrey's Arthur takes over. It also distinguishes and naturalises as a unified non-Roman British 'home' the various insular territories earlier wrung from Saxons, Picts, Scots and Irish, and the cousin-kingdom of Brittany ('Little Britain'). Like the legend of the eponymous Brutus, the Roman wars help distract from the perception that 'Britain' is not a self-evident political entity but itself an empire won by conquest, which comes into being really as an expanded England. Especially in the final context of Arthur's sudden forced return from Gaul to Glastonbury, by way of Richborough, Winchester and Camblam, the effect of his time 'away' is more to define this 'home' than to unify a broader empire. The Galfridian tradition confers an imperial *cachet*; it 'seizes for England the symbolic capital of the great empires of the east',[5] but, it must be noted, without really incurring the responsibilities of wider imperial rule.

Roman *imperium* itself is an idea or a regnal style more than a territorial fact for Arthur. This is even so in Malory, who foregrounds Arthur's dealings with Rome early on, in a way that sets him apart from earlier writers. The Roman ambassadors in Caxton's Malory claim to represent 'that noble Empire whiche domyneth upon the unyversal world' (p. 186.13–14 [v.1]), but Emperor Lucius' own challenge to Arthur already acknowledges 'all thy realmys that thou weldyst' (p. 186.11 [v.1]), and the ambassadors marvel and tremble at the 'wysedome ... fayre speche ... royalté and rychesse' of Arthur and his court (p. 192.1 [v.2]). Malory's Arthur may be crowned in Rome, but we do not see him later losing the empire because there is no further reference to him possessing it. Lancelot seems to be king of most of France, and Arthur finally wages war on him there like a contemporary English campaigner, a liege lord only in Lancelot's mind. The point of the Roman wars is for Britain to have won a European empire so that a British (or English) successor may in the future claim a version of it again. It is not needed in the present, except as part of 'the mechanism for generating new stories'.[6] In his own lifetime, Malory's Arthur re-enacts the shift from a literal to a figural imperial status. Just as Britain's supremacy has preceded the almost redundant campaign against Lucius, the meaning of subsequent Arthurian imperialism has to be read in semi-detachment from actual conquests and possessions. Fifteenth-century stained-glass windows show Arthur in imperial guise along with the Emperor Constantine, who was regarded as British, and Henry IV, Henry V and Henry VI. These images were part of an attempt to 'exalt the Lancastrian dynasty though association with famed rulers of the past'.[7] John Lydgate in *Fall of Princes* (1430s) gives only four lines to the king's early insular and European conquests, but massively expands on the 'imperial' reputation they earn for Britain:

> Thus in Breteyne shon the cleere liht
> Of cheualrye and of hih prowesse,
> Which thoruh the world[e] shadde his bemys briht,
> Welle of worshep, conduit of al noblesse,
> Imperial court al wrongis to redresse.[8]

Arthur's supposed royal seal at Westminster Abbey, to which Caxton refers in his preface to Malory (1485), claimed him as Emperor of Britain, Gaul, Germany and Dacia. It was later used by Henry VIII as evidence of his right to be Holy Roman Emperor. Nevertheless, the imperial associations of Arthur in the later Middle Ages are still mainly based on his fame as a *conquestor* (conqueror) rather than as a Holy Roman Emperor.[9] International conquest gives him 'the powers of the Roman emperor within his own realm'.[10] Caxton patriotically calls Arthur 'a man borne wythin the royame and kyng and emperour of the same' (p. cxliv.7–8 [Preface]).

Arthurian writers in the Galfridian tradition are therefore more ambiguous propagandists for imperialist expansionism than they may seem. It is a complex situation: Rome embodies what is pre-eminently desirable but the Romans are enemies; the idea is for the British to beat them, not to be them. To become 'Romans' would be to become foreigners whose rule is arrogant oppression, so in that respect it may seem necessary as well as tragic for Arthur not to get over the Alps into Italy. Empire must exist in some form friendly to insular feeling, and supra-national ambitions need special justification. In the Alliterative *Morte* and Malory the Roman wars take on something of the feeling of Crusade; it has been suggested that the Saracen allies of Rome are invoked to encourage genocide,[11] whereas in Geoffrey it was war against the Saxons that most resembled Crusade, and the Romans themselves were more tainted with 'effeminacy' than with religious infidelity (Thorpe, x.11, p. 255). The later imposition of Crusade on Arthur's European territorial ambitions may reflect an anxiety that solely in themselves they are too much. In the Alliterative *Morte*, as the virtual conqueror of Rome, Arthur is suddenly censured as an oppressor, who has 'fremydly [as a hostile outsider] in Fraunce' killed Frollo and Feraunt, and many others 'in sere [many] kynges landis'.[12] The feudalist failure of the Galfridian tradition to appreciate Roman *imperium* means that outside his homeland, Arthur is more apt to be seen as a stranger in someone else's, and the closer he gets to Rome the more alienated he may seem from the legitimacy he enjoys at home.

Arthurian Englishness is easier to take for granted at home, and so more easily internationalised, whilst on their foreign campaign the king's men are more like a touring national team, 'oure noble knyghtes of mery Ingelonde' (Malory, p. 209.10 [v.6]). The later Round Table of Malory's *Morte* attracts international recruits – French knights like Lancelot and his kin, Saracens like Safir and Palomides, and Sir Urry from Hungary – and extends membership to many races and ethnicities, so that peace at home in Camelot feels more imperial than war away. Certainly, imperial supremacy is confirmed by territorial conquest, but its discursive registers – chivalric, courtly, religious, moral, masculine – and its political manifestations may vary considerably. And because the Galfridian empire is essentially a trophy, different in degree but not in kind from other honours, it can more easily find equivalent cultural substitutes. England's fifteenth-century loss of empire in France has been seen as the sub-text of Malory's later *Morte*, but we might rather read Malory as taking further a tendency in the Galfridian tradition to treat *imperium* independently of territorial possession. Malorian court scenes such as the Great Tournament, or the Healing of Sir Urry, with its mighty list of names, make an imperial equivalent to the splendid Caerleon feast in Geoffrey. The *imperium* Arthur subsequently loses is not land – he hands on 'this realm' territorially intact to Sir Constantine, foiling Mordred's plans to divide it with the Saxons – but the fullness, integrity and limitless potential of power expressed in those scenes at home, 'whan he helde the Rounde Table moste plenoure' (p. 293.1–2 [VII.1]).

The later medieval divorce of Arthur's *imperium* from European possessions may help explain why post-medieval traditions of Arthur have been able to remain imperialist while dispensing with the story of his wars abroad. Nineteenth-century Arthurianism became dominated by Alfred Tennyson's moral revision of Malory in the long-running series that became *Idylls of the King* (1830s–1880s). In the many subsequent Tennysonian retellings and selected editions of Malory, the Roman wars were usually the first item to be cut. That may not have been simply because the story seemed luridly unhistorical or culpably aggressive. What the Galfridians, without much of a real British empire, were originally moved to invent and aggrandise, Victorian and Edwardian writers of the imperial age were freer to downplay and transmute, especially as the empire was mainly situated far away, and Britain seemed mostly at peace with Europe. Empire is crucial to Tennyson's vision in the *Idylls* – without it, he says, Britain would be 'Some third-rate isle half-lost among her seas' ('To the Queen', line 25) – but its presence is registered obliquely, the word itself not uttered until the closing dedication to Queen Victoria. In Tennyson's scenario, Arthur never leaves home yet everything comes to him. Rome, 'The slowly-fading mistress of the world' ('The Coming of Arthur', line 504), has already deserted Britain, and Arthur's 'strife' with her about the tribute is passed over in five words. Rome, 'the old order', perhaps with an allusion to the 'old religion' of Roman Catholicism, is too 'weak and old' to defend civilisation ('The Coming of Arthur', line 510), so Arthur must take up the Christian fight. The scene is set locally, in a moralised war of liberation from the 'beast' and 'heathen'. Imperialism was not overtly part of nineteenth-century Arthurianism, but it is always covertly accommodated because the 'blameless' Arthur of Tennyson and his successors can have no legitimate opposition, so in theory his claim to power knows no boundaries. He is not simply fighting other monarchs and nations but is on a God-given mission to 'cleanse the world', bringing 'law' and 'light', and drawing 'all / The realms together' ('Guinevere', lines 458–9).

Just as the *Historia Brittonum* and Geoffrey of Monmouth based Brutus on Virgil's Aeneas, so Tennyson seems to have drawn up his general justification of Britain's *imperium* in sympathy with the underworld prophecies of Virgil's Anchises:

> 'But, Rome, 't is thine alone, with awful sway,
> To rule mankind, and make the world obey,
> Disposing peace and war by thy own majestic way;
> To tame the proud, the fetter'd slave to free:
> These are imperial arts, and worthy thee.'[13]

The vaguer the sense that imperial status is gained by conquest, the louder are its claims to be God-given and sempiternal. Empire is deeply inscribed in the allegorical fabric and ritual order of Tennyson's Camelot said to be 'built / To music, therefore never built at all, / And therefore built for ever' ('Gareth and Lynette', lines 272–4). In 'The Passing of Arthur', as in Geoffrey, the idea that loss of core race-values brings loss of imperial power underwrites the suggestion that those who have empires have them by right – in Geoffrey's case a right of conquest based on manly courage, in Tennyson's a vaguer moral right. The sad story of losing an empire may therefore seem for the home audience the happy prospect of keeping and extending their own. Nevertheless, it has been persuasively argued that the overt imperialism in Tennyson's final dedication of *Idylls* 'To the Queen' (1872) is a 'manifestation' of contemporary British 'political and economic anxieties', not a 'solution' to them: 'Although the occasionally feverish imperial sentiment of this period was largely couched in terms of Britain's providential role, it was directly fuelled by a decline in the nation's economic power relative to the United States and Germany.'[14] That may be why Tennyson, for all his moral justifications, also promises the empire will make Britain (or rather, 'ever-broadening England') – 'wealthier – wealthier – hour by hour!' ('To the Queen', line 23).[15]

Mark Twain in *A Connecticut Yankee in King Arthur's Court* (1889) might well seem Tennyson's opposite, because he writes polemically as an American against an English Arthurian ethos based on monarchy, tradition and the rejustification of class privilege. The novel is told through the persona of a modern democrat, the Yankee Hank Morgan, who is transported back through time to a notional sixth-century Camelot. Twain's Arthuriad anachronistically blends the outward trappings of Malory's fifteenth-century world with a bundle of other evils loosely associated with pre-modernity, including slavery, *droit de seigneur*, lack of free speech, and domination by 'the [Catholic] Church'. Twain had identified his audience as less cultured and literate than the normal patrons of bookshops and libraries. That influenced the nature of the book, with its short chapters, jokes, heavy pathos, many illustrations and informal style. Writing in fierce opposition to the imagined influence of romantic medievalism, especially the novels of Sir Walter Scott, Twain emphasised the modern benefits of capitalism, a free press, advertising, intellectual property rights, improved technology and transport. Nevertheless, his depiction of Hank Morgan, 'The Boss', is ambivalent. Morgan seems allowed to speak for all of Twain's pet beliefs, but he also figures as a ruthless coloniser invading an underdeveloped society, and introducing superior technology and free trade in order to gain despotic control. His initially progressive and well-meaning rule of England culminates in the slaughter of many thousands by means of machine-guns, dynamite and electrified fences. In effect, Morgan ends up close to the sentiments of the colonist Mr Kurtz in Joseph Conrad's *Heart of Darkness* (1899): ' "Exterminate all the brutes!" '

It has been argued that in *A Connecticut Yankee* 'Twain makes the equation between capitalist expansion and Euroamerican imperialism that did not enter the public debate until several decades later'.[16] How fully Twain was aware of that connection at the time is doubtful. He and his book were deeply implicated in the capitalist system. 'Mark Twain' was more than a pen name; it was a registered trade mark and an incorporated enterprise. Twain sold his books by subscription, and gave detailed instructions to his travelling salesmen:

> Keep the Book in Your Own Hands. Possession is power. Surrender the book, and you lose the power of showing it. ... Strive to 'keep the upper hand' all

through. As nearly as possible, do all the thinking, talking, deciding, that there is to be done, yourself. Aim to make your INFLUENCE a controlling one.[17]

As modern successors to Arthur, both Hank and Twain display an appetite for possession and control that seems to equal or outdo that of their original and rivals the conservative imperialism of Tennyson. Hank's fascination with total power reproduces the evils of medieval church and state which he set out to overcome. In different ways, both *A Connecticut Yankee* and *Idylls of the King* represent their Arthurian social experiments as brief triumphs of a new order which end in failure, as Tennyson's Arthur fears at the end:

> For I, being simple, thought to work His will,
> And have but stricken with the sword in vain;
> And all whereon I leaned in wife and friend
> Is traitor to my peace, and all my realm
> Reels back into the beast, and is no more.
> ('The Passing of Arthur', lines 22–6)

For all the celebration of moral or social progress in Tennyson and Twain, it is the death of the Arthurian world that finally dominates their imaginations. Both narratives speak for the notable ideological extremism within nineteenth-century appropriations of Arthurianism, veering between visions of total domination and total extinction.

As a version of cultural imperialism, Twain's treatment of Malory is typical of contemporary attitudes to *Le Morte Darthur* in its mixture of respect and condescension. He insists at best on the noble simplicity and 'quaintness' of the medieval text, its status as a child-like version of the modern. Sandy, the girl-wife of Morgan, loyal, nurturing and naïve, is the acceptable, spiritual face of the medieval to Twain. By contrast all his images of 'Church' *imperium* are male, mature, and either violent or greedy. As in Tennyson, whose feminisation of Arthurian virtue has been noted,[18] it seems that the medieval imaginary is less welcome in its overt masculine forms of military and clerical authority than as a feminised disguise for power or complement to it. At the same time, the maintenance of traditional gender hierarchy is essential even to this limited approval of the feminine. Throughout the *Idylls*, Guinevere's failure, unwomanly and un-'medieval' in nineteenth-century terms, to respond to the 'stainless' Arthur's idealism lies at the root of all his political problems, and brings about the end of his empire.

As has long been understood, Arthurianism and empire were fused in educational and exemplary versions of the legend in the later Victorian and Edwardian periods. Arthur's story provided a model of righteous power and of the formation of the English gentlemen who were called on to administer it.[19] Malory, mainly neglected in serious academic study, was a common school text, especially for boys, whilst Tennyson's version was highly influential generally. The major response to Arthurian imperialism in the mid-twentieth century fittingly came from a schoolteacher, T. H. White (1906–64), whose four-volume *The Once and Future King* (1958), whilst revealing some erotic attraction to violence, took up a strongly anti-militarist line. White was a child of Empire, born to English parents in India, and a patriot for English heritage and countryside. He was also deeply pessimistic about the aggressive tendencies of the human race, its 'incorrigible irrationality and wickedness'.[20] He loved Malory's work, but rejected the interpretation of it as a celebration of chivalric prowess, and had come to believe that ' "the central theme of Morte d'Arthur is to find an antidote for War" '.[21] The literary result was a half-nostalgic, half-despairing retelling of the medieval story as a challenge to the European legacy of violence and militarism: 'White ... constructs a social and political order which we are invited to compare with our own present-day systems.'[22] Totalitarian dictatorships of the twentieth century provided topical examples of the cult of power, and were satirised by White in his transformations of Malory's original. The giant Galapas is at once Mussolini, a sadistic boarding school housemaster, and a gangster who provides 'thousand-dollar wreaths at funerals'.[23] British versions of power get off more lightly. Merlin characterises them as more amateurish and less thorough: ' "A lot of brainless unicorns swaggering about and calling themselves educated just because they can push each other off a horse with a bit of stick! ... The trouble with the English Aristocracy is that they are games-mad, that's what it is, games-mad".'(p. 106). White's work is fundamentally about the socio-political and psychological effects of education and upbringing; his story treats Queen Morgawse's children Mordred (the eventual traitor) and Gaheris, who kills his mother, as case studies in psycho-pathology. Unlike Twain, White directs his satire not against an idea of the Middle Ages them-selves, but against a modern educative tradition of competitive aggression, in which medievalist models were routinely used to ennoble the idea of war and empire.

White's natural inheritors were not the Broadway composers of *Camelot*, the romantic musical based on his Arthuriad, but the makers of *Monty Python and the Holy Grail* (dir. Terry Gilliam and Terry Jones, 1975). This film was the second movie spin-off of a very popular television series of the early 1970s. Most of the Python team were products of the English public-school system and Oxbridge colleges. They were familiar with medievalist educational and religious models of manly behaviour, but also with actual medieval history and literature. Their humour, like White's, worked through a parodic connection of existing modern idioms to the medieval scene, including television history documentaries, movie 'swashbucklers', church ritual and musical comedy. Some of this satire works by obvious anachronism, while some has close medieval analogues. The thirteenth-century French comic romance *Aucassin and Nicolette* features a scene in the land of Torelore in which the hero has to be restrained from killing the king's enemies with his sword; it is explained that there they only fight with rotten eggs and fresh cheeses. In the Python film, Lancelot, who seems to have wandered in from an Errol Flynn 'swashbuckler', slaughters wedding guests in the same inappropriate way. He explains that 'when I'm in this idiom I sometimes get a bit ... carried away'. In Chrétien de Troyes' twelfth-century romance *Yvain*, we see an aristocratic woman made to marry the killer of her husband because her people need a strong knight to defend their castle. In Monty Python's *Grail*, Princess Lucky is treated rather similarly by her dead bridegroom's grasping father. The central theme of the film, if a centre can be said to exist in the deliberately random series of scenes, is to expose the self-interested imposition of meaning on life by various systems of power in state, church, media and education. The huge cartoon foot that regularly descended on Python action is the image of this arbitrary power. Military strength, satirically deprived of its connection with masculine virtue and right, is still understood as the enforcer of 'truth'. Arthur ('"King of the *who?*"') regularly resorts to force when persuasion fails. It is suggested that modern academic interest in the medieval may itself have a vicarious investment in violence, one that is punished when Lancelot impossibly rides into the television documentary shooting-set and kills its enthusiastic presenter. Terry Jones, one of the film's directors, would soon go on to write *Chaucer's Knight: The Portrait of a Medieval Mercenary* (1980). He argued there that previous academic readings of the 'verray parfit gentil knyght' as a true ideal had completely missed the connection between violence and money in Chaucer's depiction of his military career.

Tennyson had treated the source of Arthur's *imperium*, symbolised by Excalibur, as a sacred mystery. Excalibur is part of a heavenly mission bestowed on Arthur by the 'Lady of the Lake', 'Clothed in white samite, mystic, wonderful':

> She gave the King his huge cross-hilted sword,
> Whereby to drive the heathen out: a mist
> Of incense curled about her, and her face
> Well nigh was hidden in the minster gloom.
>
> ('The Coming of Arthur', lines 284–7)

In the Python film, made well after Britain's loss of empire and economic dominance, a socialist peasant treats the mystery as 'outdated imperialist dogma':

'Listen. Strange women lying in ponds distributing swords is no basis for a system of government. Supreme executive power derives from a mandate from the masses, not from some farcical aquatic ceremony.'

From the beginning, Arthurian prestige is violated by the film, subjected to empirical critique, unsympathetic ridicule and even police investigation. Cuts to police inquiries form a parallel version of the film's 'quest'. Lancelot and Arthur are finally arrested, and a policeman's hand stops the filming, indicating that a new 'force' has effectively replaced knighthood as the 'supreme executive power' of the state. Arthur's 'I order you to be quiet' becomes Officer 1's concluding line: '"All right, sonny. That's enough. Just pack that in".'

The Python film touches directly on the threat of nuclear war in the 'Holy Hand-Grenade of Antioch' scene, in which two farcical clerics bless a weapon of mass destruction. Their style satirises the modern high Church of England, but the episode has medieval counterparts. Antioch was the site of atrocious sieges in the First Crusade (1098) and generated its own controversial sacred weapon, the 'Holy Lance'. The historical parallel implies that religious ideology, now as in medieval times, confers a false legitimacy on imperialism, and wrongly justifies the slaughter of foreign nationals as enemies. Religion, or its equivalent in fear-politics, is seen to disguise the self-interest and aggression of conquest as righteousness, by painting the victims, in the film's words, as 'naughty in My [God's] sight'. Tennyson's suggestions that Arthur's imperial mission is primarily moral and divinely inspired, even Christ-like, are completely reversed here.

Many English-language Arthurian versions after the second World War forsook the high medieval ambience of Tennyson, and set their stories in a simple Romano-Celtic sub-national world, with a younger, more vulnerable, leather-clad King Arthur. Yet they continued to find new forms of what has been called the imperial 'fantasy of ... wholeness'.[24] The Cold War concern with Western unity based on alliance with the USA found several aspects of Arthurianism congenial: the political centrism of Camelot from which all adventures start and to which all return – the period of John F. Kennedy's presidency (1961–3) later became popularly known as 'Camelot'; the Round Table, symbolising political unity and the world itself (Malory, p. 906.15–17 [XIV.2]); the sword Excalibur, understood as a symbol that 'true' power belongs to one wielder alone, whom all good people will benefit from supporting. A children's King Arthur book of 1962 has the

British nobles exclaiming: 'Find us a king, Merlin. Only a strong and wise leader can defend us against our enemies, and give us happiness again.'[25] In John Boorman's film *Excalibur* (1981), Arthur is made central to the entire natural environment, symbolised through his possession of Excalibur. The sword draws its power from him, as the chosen ruler. Merlin teaches Arthur that all things in nature are one, making up a supreme earth-force called the 'Great Dragon'. In his anguish at Guinevere's love for Lancelot, Arthur plunges Excalibur deep into the earth between them, wounding the Dragon and devastating the environment. In consequence, he himself becomes the wounded, impotent king of the Waste Land: 'The king without his sword; the land without a king!' In a bold departure from medieval tradition, the Grail, achieved by Perceval, is used to heal Arthur and Britain. In Chrétien de Troyes' original story (1180s), Perceval failed to ask the question 'Whom does the Grail serve?' In *Excalibur* he is himself asked this question by a mysterious apparition and correctly answers 'You, my lord ... You and the land are one ... You are my lord and king. You are Arthur'. This treatment of Arthur seems to be aiming for a perfect, if fragile, relation between the natural environment, male sexual potency and the enjoyment of political and military power. It represents a more extreme endorsement of Arthur's regime than is found in the medieval Grail tradition. In the thirteenth-century French prose *Queste del Saint Graal* (*Quest of the Holy Grail*) Arthur and his court are largely humiliated by failure, and the Grail, once achieved by Galahad, leaves Britain forever as a rebuke to its unworthiness. Galahad enters Camelot only once, after being raised to the age of fifteen by nuns in a convent. There is no sense in which Arthur's *imperium* is upheld through him or the Grail quest. Even in Malory's fifteenth-century adaptation, which strives to reflect more credit on Camelot, Arthur understands that the coming of the Grail means the beginning of the end of his fellowship.

The Mists of Avalon by Marion Zimmer Bradley has been a bestselling and influential Arthurian novel.[26] Its story is set in the late fifth century. The Britons are struggling to cope with Saxon invasion, the onset of Christianity and disunion amongst themselves. On this scene Bradley projects the events of *Le Morte Darthur*, but as told by a hostile witness, Morgaine (Malory's Morgan le Fay). Morgaine's 'eye-witness' view re-emphasises and re-motivates the traditional plot, to give the impression that the classic version is itself ideologically loaded and unreliable. Through her narrative, ostensibly, readers go beyond and behind the patriarchal tradition of Arthur to see what really occurred. Like Boorman in *Excalibur*, Bradley vests the right to rule in a oneness with nature. As 'the land', Britain is both a natural and a political entity; although territorially the term refers only to Arthur's relatively modest and embattled realm, as a concept it takes in all things, all experience. Britain is devoted to an earth-goddess mystery religion which links the political system of hereditary monarchy to a fertility ritual, 'The Great Marriage', supervised by the priestesses of Avalon (Glastonbury) under their 'Lady'. The king owes his power to his allegiance to this rite. Faced with growing Christian intolerance, the leaders of Avalon plot to control the royal succession by the begetting of Arthur on Igraine, sister of the High Priestess and of Morgaine. The scheme unravels when Arthur, under the influence of his Christian wife Gwenhyfar, eventually forsakes the Goddess worship.

Bradley's Arthurian story celebrates the idea of a ruling feminine principle, a universal 'Mother', in opposition to a patriarchal Christianity dominated by male authority. In this context the struggle for religious *imperium*, the right to say what divine power underlies everything, is of more narrative significance than Arthur's fight for political control. The long-term historical triumphs of the Saxon invaders and of antifeminist Christianity are finally accommodated by an anthropological understanding that all religions are really one, and by an acceptance that all is the inscrutable will of the Goddess. Bradley is like Twain, and unlike most other post-medieval Arthurian retellers before her time, in allowing the possibility of a legitimate opposition to Arthur and in admitting his faults. And whereas Tennyson insists that Arthur is 'stainless', Bradley celebrates his incestuous union with Morgaine in the 'Great Marriage'. Yet while she strives against traditional barriers to female power, her story insists on a traditional gender essentialism based on reproductive functions, enforced by the dominant symbolism of penile Excalibur and its vaginal scabbard, made by Morgaine herself. The empire of masculinity seems mirrored, not countered, by the structure of Avalon with its 'royal blood' and 'Lady'. In narrative scope, *The Mists of Avalon* ventures outside the ranks of the nobility scarcely more than *Le Morte Darthur* or *Idylls of the King*. Arthur's personal career is rendered less important by the suggestion that he was merely fulfilling a convenient role in a plan he never fully understood. Yet even in this polemical revision, where the once-despised Morgaine replaces Arthur or Lancelot as protagonist, the story still seems attached to the idea that all things are meant to be as they are, that the course of worldly *imperium* is not merely subject to historical contingency, but providential and inevitable. In that, Bradley remains at one with her conservative Arthurian forebears. Tennyson's hints that Arthur's reign follows a solar cycle, or even the Christian calendar of Incarnation, Death and Resurrection – '"From the great deep to the great deep he goes"' ('The Coming of Arthur', line 410; 'The Passing of Arthur', line 445) – are matched by Bradley's totalising vision of a religious destiny inherent in nature, in the land itself.

Continuing possession of European dominions was never the major feature of Arthur the medieval emperor. It is not necessarily, therefore, a radical change that the modern Arthur has largely become a defensivist Romano-Celtic leader, striving only to rally his people against invading hordes and to bring peace. It might even be argued that the modern discarding of his Roman wars is more a means of preserving than abandoning the imperialist potential that they once realised. Arthur is allowed to make war without too many questions asked. The pressing Saxon threat and need for unity justify his will to dominate Britain. Without the further narrative of continental campaigns, he suffers less scrutiny of personal ambition and military aggression in many modern versions than in a later medieval text like the Alliterative *Morte Arthure*. For all its revisions, modern Arthurianism still seems wedded to the concept of a 'true' ruler, in whom *imperium* is vested by a superior and unquestionable right. However far from Rome, Arthur still claims the power to intuit the order of things and set global goals, on a destined mission to unite, control and justify his world.

NOTES

1 Rosamond McKitterick, *History and Memory in the Carolingian World* (Cambridge University Press, 2004), pp. 10–11.

2 Siân Echard, *Arthurian Narrative in the Latin Tradition*, Cambridge Studies in Medieval Literature 36 (Cambridge University Press, 1998), p. 5n.

3 Wace, *Roman de Brut*, ed. and trans. Judith Weiss, *Wace's 'Roman de Brut', a History of the British: Text and Translation*, Exeter Mediaeval English Texts and Studies (University of Exeter Press, 1999), lines 12451–58.

4 *Laȝamon's Arthur: the Arthurian Section of Laȝamon's 'Brut'*, ed. and trans. W. R. J. Barron and S. C. Weinberg (Harlow: Longman, 1989), lines 11690–94.

5 Meg Roland, 'From "Saracens" to "Infydeles": The Recontextualization of the East in Caxton's edition of Le Morte Darthur', in *Re-Viewing Le Morte Darthur: Texts and Contexts, Characters and Themes*, ed. Kevin Whetter and Raluca Radulescu, Arthurian Studies 60 (Cambridge: D. S. Brewer, 2005), pp. 65–77 (p. 73).

6 Felicity Riddy, 'Contextualising Le Morte Darthur: Empire and Civil War', in *A Companion to Malory*, ed. Elizabeth Archibald and A. S. G. Edwards, Arthurian Studies 37 (Cambridge: D. S. Brewer, 1996), pp. 55–73 (p. 63).

7 John Withrington, 'King Arthur as Emperor', *Notes and Queries*, 35 (1988), 13–15 (p. 14).

8 John Lydgate, *The Fall of Princes*, ed. H. Bergen, *Lydgate's Fall of Princes*, 4 vols., EETS, e.s. 121–4 (Oxford University Press, 1927), IV, lines 2850–4.

9 Withrington, 'King Arthur', p. 14.

10 Riddy, 'Contextualising Le Morte Darthur', p. 69.

11 David Wallace, '*Imperium*, Commerce and National Crusade', *New Medieval Literatures*, 8 (2006), 45–66 (p. 60).

12 *Morte Arthure: A Critical Edition*, ed. Mary Hamel, Garland Medieval Texts 9 (New York and London: Garland, 1984), lines 3399–3405.

13 Virgil, *The Aeneid*, trans. John Dryden, *Virgil's 'Aeneid'* (New York: P. F. Collier, 1913), VI.1133–7.

14 Ian McGuire, 'Epistemology and Empire in *Idylls of the King*', *Victorian Poetry*, 30 (1992), 387–400 (pp. 397–8).

15 *Ibid.*

16 J. Carlos Rowe, 'How the Boss Played the Game: Twain's Critique of Imperialism in *A Connecticut Yankee in King Arthur's Court*', in *The Cambridge Companion to Mark Twain*, ed. Forrest G. Robinson (Cambridge University Press, 1995), pp. 175–92 (p. 181).

17 Mark Twain, 'The Successful Agent', ed. H. Hill, *Mark Twain and Elisha Bliss* (Columbia: University of Missouri Press, 1964), online: http://etext.lib.virginia. edu/railton/marketin/salestlk.html [accessed March 2007].

18 E. L. Gilbert, 'The Female King: Tennyson's Arthurian Apocalypse', *PMLA*, 98 (1983), 863–878.

19 Mark Girouard, *The Return to Camelot: Chivalry and the English Gentleman* (New Haven, CT: Yale University Press, 1981).

20 Elisabeth Brewer, *T. H. White's 'The Once and Future King'*, Arthurian Studies 30 (Cambridge: D. S. Brewer, 1993), p. 28.

21 White, quoted in Brewer, p. 41.

22 *Ibid.*, p. 27.

23 T. H. White, *The Sword in the Stone* (London: Collins, 1938, repr. 1998), p. 295.

24 Patricia Clare Ingham, *Sovereign Fantasies: Arthurian Romance and the Making of Britain*, The Middle Ages (Philadelphia, PA: University of Pennsylvania Press, 2001), p. 10.

25 Clifton Fadiman, *The Story of Young King Arthur* (London: Frederick Muller, 1962), pp. 6–7.

26 Marion Zimmer Bradley, *The Mists of Avalon* (London: Sphere, 1982, repr. 1984).

11

PEGGY MCCRACKEN

Love and adultery: Arthur's affairs

The subject of love and adultery in Arthurian romances usually calls to mind the love triangle that unites King Arthur, his wife Queen Guinevere, and the knight Sir Lancelot. The great love affair of Guinevere and Lancelot is often celebrated as an enduring passion that overcomes all obstacles, including the queen's marriage. Lancelot is inspired to accomplish extraordinary feats of prowess because of his love for the queen, and his successes in adventures, tournaments and contests contribute to the chivalric brilliance that establishes the reputation of Arthur's court and the Round Table. Yet even though the knight does great acts of chivalry for his beloved queen, his love for her must remain secret because it betrays the king. And although the queen rewards her knight with public displays of favour, her passionate love for him must remain hidden. Secrecy never adequately hides the queen's love affair from her husband, however, and the lovers are inevitably discovered. Indeed, medieval versions of the story recount a series of repeated episodes in which the love affair is revealed and then covered up again. That is, Arthur sees evidence of his queen's adultery, but he finds a way not to believe what he sees. In the thirteenth-century Old French Vulgate Cycle (also called the *Lancelot-Grail* Cycle by modern scholars), which combines the story of Lancelot with that of the Holy Grail, the final section, the *Mort Artu* (*Death of King Arthur*), recounts that the king repeatedly refuses to believe that Lancelot and Guinevere could betray him.[1] Or rather, he refuses to believe that Lancelot would betray him with the queen. When his nephew Agravain first accuses Lancelot and the queen of adultery, Arthur claims that, even if Lancelot loved the queen, he would never shame the king:

> 'To be sure,' said the king, 'if it's true that Lancelot was in love with her, I wouldn't believe him capable of betraying me with my wife, for treason cannot penetrate such a valiant heart, unless the devil has outdone himself. ... Even if everyone told me that rumor every day, and even if I had seen more evidence than I have, I wouldn't believe it.'
>
> (*Mort Artu*, Ch. 30, p. 30; trans. Lacy IV. 98–9)

Arthur refuses to know the secret of the queen's adultery, and he even denies that such a secret is possible. In his praise of Lancelot's loyalty Arthur does not mention his queen's honour, nor does he consider her possible guilt of the charge of adultery. From the king's perspective, it is impossible that the queen could have betrayed him with Lancelot, because Lancelot would not have betrayed the king.

The queen and her lover do in fact betray the king, but the queen's adultery may also bring advantages to the king's court. It guarantees Lancelot's presence at court; King Arthur's reputation and prestige are enhanced by Lancelot's exploits; and Lancelot earns Arthur's affection through his skills in war. Those who seek to reveal the queen's adultery are those, like Agravain, who wish to displace Lancelot from the king's favour. Knowledge of Guinevere's adultery becomes the instrument of political contests between factions that compete for the king's favour. Stability is maintained in the court, at least for a while, because the secrecy surrounding the queen's transgression allows the king initially to believe the accusations against the queen and her lover made by Agravain, and then to regain his faith in the innocence of his wife and the loyalty of her knight. The king manages to satisfy his nephew and those who accuse Lancelot while still retaining him at court.

This dynamic is an invention of twelfth- and thirteenth-century French romances. Arthur and Guinevere appear in earlier chronicles and in Celtic tales, but although Guinevere is represented as an adulterous wife in some of these narratives (because of her union with the traitor Mordred), it is only with Chrétien de Troyes's *Chevalier de la charrete* (*The Knight of the Cart*, from around 1177) that Guinevere is linked with Lancelot. Chrétien's romance provides a model for later medieval developments of the story, and the most prominent of these is the early thirteenth-century Old French Vulgate Cycle (1215–30), which incorporates the *Charrete* into the story of Lancelot's entire life, from his birth to his death. In the Vulgate, Lancelot's story is merged with the story of the Grail, and the compilation ends with *La Mort le roi Artu* (*The Death of King Arthur*), which recounts the discovery of the queen's adultery and the fall of Arthur's kingdom. This is the version of the story that Malory works into his larger story of Arthur as he restructures his French source while translating it into English in the fifteenth century; most post-medieval Arthurian literature in English is influenced by Malory's romance.

The queen's adultery is a central element of most medieval versions of Arthur's story. Like Iseut, the other prominent example of an adulterous queen in medieval romance, Guinevere is portrayed as a woman of exemplary beauty and courtesy who betrays her marriage vows to pursue a liaison with a lover. Iseut and Guinevere are morally complex characters, and the constancy of their devotion to their lovers stands in uneasy juxtaposition to their disregard for marital fidelity. Their apparent lack of regret for the betrayal of their husbands is set against the all-consuming nature of their passion for the knights who return their love: both the queen and her lover are ruled by an impossible love and by a passion beyond their control. This is given literal form in the Tristan stories, where the love of Iseut and Tristan is caused by a magic potion. Guinevere and Iseut are guilty of a crime against the king, but they are also the subjects of a love that is rendered exemplary, even praiseworthy, by its enduring passion and inescapable force.

In romance narratives, the queen's adultery is a transgression against the king. To be sure, the king is not always a faithful husband – and the queen may suffer the consequences of the king's infidelity – but the status of the queen's adultery is different from that of the king's infidelity. First, to the extent that fictional monarchies are structured like those of medieval Europe, the queen's adultery is implicated differently from the king's in succession concerns. The queen's conception of an illegitimate child would threaten the proper succession of the throne in a way that the birth of a king's bastard would not, since the queen's child would be born into the royal family, whether or not her husband was the father. Medieval romance narratives about adulterous queens generally avoid this scenario and the succession complications it would involve. Guinevere is a barren queen; she never conceives a child with either Lancelot or Arthur in the Old French Vulgate, nor in most versions of the story that derive from the Vulgate, including Malory's. In the thirteenth-century French *Perlesvaus*, Guinevere and Arthur have a son called Loholt (also mentioned, once and never again, by Chrétien de Troyes in *Erec*), but his primary role in the story seems to be to die young.[2] We also see the difference between the queen's adultery and the king's infidelity in the prominence given to the queen's transgression in romance narratives. Guinevere's liaison with Lancelot, although interrupted, lasts her entire life and most of his. In the Vulgate Cycle, however, Arthur's adulterous relationships are recounted as relatively brief episodes, and are usually attributed to a woman's trickery. Arthur betrays his wife either because he is drugged or because he is duped.

What could a serious consideration of Arthur's marital transgressions add to our understanding of representations of love and adultery in the Arthurian tradition? The characterisation of King Arthur as betrayed by his beloved wife and friend is undermined in the Vulgate Cycle by the stories of Arthur's enduring love first for the Saxon enchantress Camille, and later for the queen's half-sister, who claims to be Arthur's lawful wife and queen. In both of these episodes Arthur is initially a victim of trickery. He is enchanted or drugged or deceived, and he is then seduced by Camille and by the so-called False Guinevere. However, in both episodes the king

acts decisively to initiate or prolong his liaison, and both episodes compli-
cate our understanding of the king's devotion to his unfaithful wife. If these
episodes offer a new understanding of Arthur's desires, what might this tell
us about the representation of love and adultery in Arthurian legend? Why
does the story of Guinevere's adultery dominate the Arthurian tradition
while Arthur's betrayals of his wife seem less important or disappear entirely
in later retellings of his story?

This is in fact a question that medieval texts also ask. That is, medieval
stories about Arthur also debate the importance of his sexual transgressions.
The narrator of the Vulgate Cycle stops late in his story to go backwards
in time and recount the conception of Mordred, who is known to Arthur's
court as King Lot's youngest son. The narrator explains that before
becoming king, Arthur saw King Lot's wife at court and loved her without
knowing that she was his half-sister. He watched her room, and when her
husband left it, he slipped into the lady's bed. She thought that Arthur was
her husband returning to bed, and she embraced him. Arthur made love to
her without identifying himself and engendered Mordred.[3] In this version of
the story the future treachery of Mordred is not mentioned, and the fact that
Mordred will kill his father is not revealed until close to the end of the cycle.
The so-called Post-Vulgate version of the story, composed shortly after the
Vulgate, recounts this story differently. In the Post-Vulgate version of the
Arthurian legend, the king's incestuous liaison with his sister is recounted
at both the beginning and the end of King Arthur's story, and we might
see this as an effort to make sense of the consequences of the king's sexual
transgression, or perhaps even as an effort to displace the queen's adultery
with the king's incest by identifying the king's transgression, rather than the
queen's, as the cause of the destruction of Arthur's kingdom.

The Post-Vulgate opens with the story of Arthur's incest with his half-
sister, which here takes place after his coronation, not before. As in the
Vulgate, he sees her at court and does not know that her father is also his
own father. He honours her greatly at court because she is a queen and
daughter of a king, and he loves her:

> He saw that the lady was beautiful and loved her passionately and kept her at
> his court for two whole months, until finally he lay with her and begat on her
> Mordred, by whom such great wrongs were later done in the land of Logres
> and in all the world. Thus the brother knew his sister carnally, and the lady
> carried the one who later betrayed and killed his father and put the land to tor-
> ture and destruction, about which you may hear toward the end of the book.[4]

The death of King Arthur at the hands of his illegitimate son Mordred is
announced at the very beginning of his story in the Post-Vulgate, and it is

announced as the consequence of his desire for his beautiful sister, the wife of King Lot. The romance insists on the incest as the cause of the future downfall of Arthur's kingdom and as the cause of his own future death. When Arthur's incest is rewritten in the Post-Vulgate version of his story, the narrator makes it more prominent and, by giving Arthur's sexual transgression heightened importance in the story's outcome, seems to offer an alternative reading of the centrality of the queen's adultery in the story.

The importance of Mordred in Arthur's story is a development that some modern Arthurian novels pursue – Marion Zimmer Bradley's *The Mists of Avalon* (1982) is a prominent example – but while Mordred's role in the destruction of the Arthurian world is undisputed, most medieval versions of Arthur's story, like later modern versions, neglect or excuse the king's incest (he did not know that Mordred's mother was his sister) in order to focus on the queen's adultery. Retellings of the legend of King Arthur rarely include the king's adulterous liaisons recounted in the Vulgate, and even in the Vulgate Arthur's adulteries are less prominent than those of the queen. In fact, the significance of the king's adulterous liaisons has been little explored, perhaps in part because Arthur's liaisons with the Saxon princess Camille and the False Guinevere are initiated by trickery, and Arthur may be seen as a victim of these seductions. A central canon of Arthur's story is that he loves Guinevere and he loves Lancelot. But the Old French Vulgate tells us that after he marries Guinevere, he also loves Camille and he loves the False Guinevere. If the adulterous liaison between Guinevere and Lancelot is significant in the story because of the threat it poses to the king's authority, what are the consequences of the king's adulterous loves, which are not hidden but promoted and protected by the king himself?

Arthur's loves

Camille is an enchantress who knows more magic spells than any other damsel in the land; she is very beautiful, she is of Saxon lineage, and, as the Vulgate Cycle tells us initially, she loves Arthur as much as she could love any man. Arthur meets Camille when he goes to Scotland to fight Saxon and Irish invaders. He asks for her love, but she refuses him; this seems to provoke him to love her exceedingly: 'And every day King Arthur spoke to the maiden of the castle, begging for her love, but she cared nothing for him, though she had so affected him that he loved her beyond all measure' (*Lancelot* VIII.436; Lacy II.226). The birth of the king's consuming love for Camille is recounted in tandem with the consummation of Lancelot's love for Guinevere. When the king's forces confront the Saxons, the king performs better in battle than he has ever done before because he knows that Camille is watching him from her tower: 'The king himself bore arms. They did battle with the Saxons and the Irish, but the king did not have many troops, so he had to acquit himself well. In fact, he did so better than ever before, and this was more for the maiden who was watching him from the Rock than for himself' (*Lancelot* VIII.436; Lacy II.236). This is also a battle in which Lancelot takes part, and Lancelot, too, fights better than he ever has before because the queen is watching him from her tower. The romance thus describes parallel scenes of prowess inspired by love – the king fights, Camille watches from her tower; Lancelot fights, Guinevere watches from her tower. It also recounts parallel scenes of lovemaking. Arthur's prowess earns a response from Camille: she descends from her tower and invites him to come lie with her there that evening. Arthur agrees, if she will '"promise I may do with you what a knight should do to his ladylove"' (*Lancelot* VIII.441; Lacy II.227). Lancelot, too, earns a summons from his lady: Guinevere commands him to come to her that evening with his companion Galehaut. So, that night, Arthur, accompanied by his nephew Guerrehés, slips away from his sleeping knights, just as Lancelot, accompanied by Galehaut, slips away from his sleeping squires.

Arthur goes to Camille, just as she instructed. He lies with Camille and Guerrehés lies with a beautiful damsel in another bed, and after they have been there for a while, forty armed knights force their way into the room and take the king captive (*Lancelot* VIII.443; Lacy II.227). At the same time, Lancelot and Galehaut go to the queen's chambers, and 'each of them, very much in love, lay with his beloved, and they had all the joys that lovers can have' (*Lancelot* VIII.444; Lacy II.228). This is in fact the first night Lancelot spends with the queen, and the queen's adultery is possible because of the king's adultery – Arthur is absent because he has gone to meet Camille. However, Camille does not love Arthur after all. She has seduced him in order to imprison him and help her brother take Arthur's lands. Her capture of Arthur opens a narrative sequence that ends with the liberation of Arthur, the defeat of the Saxons, and the destruction of Camille's books of magic. Faced with defeat, Camille lets herself fall from the top of her tower. Arthur regrets her death, for he loved her greatly:

> When Camille learned of this [that her books had been burnt], her grief was so great that she threw herself down from the Rock and was most gravely injured. King Arthur was greatly distressed by this, for he loved her dearly, but she would rather have lost any four castles than her books.
>
> (*Lancelot* VIII.482; Lacy II.236)

Arthur loves Camille, and Camille loves her books. In the narrator's first description of her, he says that she also loved Arthur, but then he says that she seduced the king in order to help her brother take the king's lands. The narrator also says that Arthur loved her, and Arthur's love seems to remain unchanged by the knowledge of Camille's betrayal.

Camille disappears at this point in the story, never to reappear, and the text does not speak any more about Arthur's love for her. But the episode escapes closure in its affirmation of Arthur's love for Camille. It suggests that a seduction that is also a betrayal can still lead to love, and that the discovery of betrayal does not destroy love. This is a conclusion familiar from Arthur's relationship with his wife, a relationship that endures despite recurring evidence of betrayal. But Arthur's love for Camille offers something else to the story, and that is the idea that Arthur might love somebody besides Guinevere. If Camille used her magic to make Arthur love her (this is not explicit in the romance, but it is suggested), Arthur's love still endures after Camille and her magic books are destroyed. And Arthur's adultery with Camille leads directly into the story of Arthur's bigamous marriage to the False Guinevere.

The woman whom the Vulgate text calls the False Guinevere is the queen's half-sister, the daughter of Guinevere's father and his seneschal's wife. A plot to substitute the sister for the king's wife failed on Guinevere's wedding night, and the imposter reappears later in the story with a plot to usurp Guinevere's place as Arthur's queen. She sends a messenger to Arthur's court bearing a letter in which she claims to be Arthur's lawful wife. She was kidnapped on her wedding night, she explains, and her place was taken by the imposter whom Arthur now recognises as his queen (*Lancelot* 1.22; Lacy 11.246). The first plan to kidnap the real Guinevere on her wedding night and substitute the False Guinevere failed, so the second plan is to act as though it had succeeded: the False Guinevere claims that she is Arthur's rightful wife, and that Guinevere unlawfully took her place.

The False Guinevere asks for justice against the king's wife, but when the real Guinevere demands the right to prove that she has not betrayed the king, the False Guinevere has King Arthur kidnapped and taken to her lands. There, Arthur falls in love with her:

> Thus King Arthur remained with the woman, and his people never found out what had become of him. She often came to see him, and he found her courteous and pleasant to speak with. At length, he forgot his love for the queen, and throughout the time he stayed in prison, the damsel slept with him every night.
>
> (*Lancelot* 1.107; Lacy 11.264)

Arthur wants to leave his prison, but he will do whatever the damsel wants because he loves her: 'I love you more now than any other woman alive', he says to the False Guinevere, 'and there is no doubt I truly loved the wife I had, but you have made me utterly forget her' (*Lancelot* 1.108; Lacy II.264). The False Guinevere wants Arthur to reinstate her as his wife and repudiate the other Guinevere, and he agrees on the condition that she swear an oath to confirm the truth of her claim to be his lawful wife. The king then repudiates the real Guinevere and lives with the False Guinevere, who has drugged him so that he does everything she asks. He will not be without her and takes her everywhere with him. The deception is eventually discovered; the False Guinevere is stricken with disease, and is exiled to her own lands after she admits her treachery. She dies soon after she leaves King Arthur's lands, and the narrator says that 'her dying brought the king the greatest woe that he had ever known, because he had never loved any other woman as much as her' (*Lancelot* 1.165; Lacy II.278).

Arthur sends for Guinevere to return to court as his wife, and when she meets the king, the narrator again reminds us of Arthur's love for the False Guinevere: 'When the king met them, his greeting to Galehaut and to the queen herself was full of joy, even though he had not forgot his longing for the other woman; but, because of his people, he made an effort to put on a good face' (*Lancelot* 1.168; Lacy II.279). Guinevere is reconciled with Arthur, but Arthur's lingering regret for the imposter whom he loved is never explained away. In a so-called 'short version' of this episode, possibly an earlier version, the king himself speaks his love for the imposter who has taken the queen's place. When Gauvain (Gawain) reproaches him for loving a traitor, the king claims that he cannot conquer his heart (*Lancelot* III.93; not in Lacy). Despite himself, Arthur remains at the mercy of his love for the False Guinevere.

The story of King Arthur is the story of the enduring love between his queen and the greatest knight in his court. In the Vulgate Cycle, it is also the story of Arthur's enduring love for several other women: the Saxon enchantress Camille, with whom he spends a single night and whom he continues to love even after she betrays him, and the False Guinevere, who takes his wife's place and whom he continues to regret because he loves her more than any living woman. But these stories do not dominate in the narrative; they are not shown to have the consequences that the queen's love affair has, and they do not have a prominent place in the Arthurian legend in its post-medieval development. And while Arthur's incest with his half-sister might seem harder to efface, because it produces a son, Arthur also has a second son whose story proves much less enduring than Mordred's. One version of the Vulgate Cycle recounts that before he meets Guinevere, the young King Arthur had a short liaison with Lisanor, a beautiful young woman who comes to pay homage at his court.

As soon as he saw the young woman, King Arthur was very attracted to her. He used the help of Merlin to speak with her alone, and from there he was able to spend a night with her. And at that time Loholt was engendered; he later became a good knight and a companion of the Round Table.

(*Livre du Graal*, p. 859; my translation)

Loholt appears later in the story only to die captive in a prison, and Lisanor does not reappear at all, except when she is described as the mother of Loholt (whom Malory calls Borre in his reworking of the episode).[5]

Loholt is a curious character. Unlike Mordred, King Arthur's other son, he has no significant role in his father's story. He is born, and then he dies. We never hear that Arthur meets him after his birth, or that his birth or his death has any particular effect on Arthur, though Loholt seems to have become a knight at his court. Moreover, Loholt is identified as the son of Arthur and Guinevere, not Lisanor, in the *Perlesvaus*, as mentioned above. It is possible that just as the importance of the queen's adultery in the story obscured the significance of the king's, so too the importance of the king's first illegitimate son, Mordred, came to obscure the role of his second, Loholt, to the extent that medieval authors rarely identified Loholt as Arthur's legitimate son.

If we compare Arthur's adulterous relationships with the queen's, one obvious difference between her love affair with Lancelot and the king's liaisons with Camille and the False Guinevere is that, although the queen's relationship with Lancelot is frequently disrupted by separations caused by misunderstandings or jealousy, it is an enduring relationship – it lasts a lifetime. Arthur's relationships with his lovers do not endure, but his love for them does, even after their deaths. If his love is initially won through magic, Arthur continues to love the women he has lost after the magic is no longer effective. He continues to love women who betrayed him, who seduced him with magic and drugs in order to take his land or his power. On the one hand, a love that endures even in the face of betrayal might further reveal Arthur's susceptibility to manipulation, his indecision, and his willingness to forgive transgression. But, on the other hand, it also reveals that Arthur is not faithful to the queen and that he can conceive of a great and enduring love for a woman who is not his wife. So how do we understand the importance of Arthur's infidelities in the story? If the queen's adultery may be seen as an integral part of the structure of Arthur's court – if for no other reason than that it retains Lancelot at court and guarantees Arthur's power through the alliance of the best knight in the world – what is the role of the king's adultery in the world of the court? What happens to our view of the long-suffering king who ignores his wife's infidelity in the interests of unity at the court when we acknowledge his enduring love for Camille and the False Guinevere?

Arthur's body

In most medieval romances about Arthur, he is not a particularly active king. In the Vulgate Cycle, he leads his vassals in war when he first takes the throne, but as his sovereign authority becomes established, the king is increasingly located in his court, as a spectator of battles rather than as a participant. The war against the invading Saxons is an episode in which Arthur is unusually active; he fights better than he has ever fought before to please Camille, who watches him from her tower. So once he becomes king, Arthur rarely risks his body in battle or in the adventures that occupy his knights. He waits at court for adventures to arrive or for the stories of adventures that his knights bring back. It seems that Arthur risks his body only in love.

This is one way to understand Arthur's vulnerability to the women who seduce him: Arthur's body is vulnerable to the women whom he loves. He is the prisoner of Camille, and the False Guinevere drugs him so that he cannot move without her and takes her everywhere he goes. This is different, it seems, from other kinds of vulnerability more readily associated with Arthur. He is vulnerable to accusations against the queen, for example – his standing in his own court is threatened when the queen is accused of adultery, but this is a vulnerability that focuses on the queen's body, not the king's. In his love affairs, Arthur's own body is at stake: it is shown to be vulnerable not just to treachery, but also to desire.

It is tempting here to turn to the body metaphors used to describe kingship in medieval political theory in order to explain Arthur's bodily vulnerability to seduction. In this kind of thinking, the immortal yet human nature of the royal sovereign is represented by the king's two bodies, one undying and transcendent, the other mortal and human.[6] So while the body of the man experiences the pleasures and vicissitudes of human existence, the corporate body of the king transcends them through its enduring symbolic power. Yet this distinction does not seem to apply in representations of Arthur's bodily vulnerability in love. In the case of Arthur, the transcendent value of the king's symbolic corporate body seems inseparable from the king's material body. In the Vulgate Cycle, Arthur's kingship is shown to be invested in his body and is coterminous with it. For both Camille and the False Guinevere, to possess the king's body and to control the king's body – through spells, with drugs, by love – is to control the kingdom. What would it mean to say that romance narratives locate kingship in the material body of the king? What would such a reading offer to our understanding of kingship, love and adultery in the Arthurian legend?

To focus on the location of Arthur's authority and power in the king's material body is to recognise that the king does not have a legitimate son and he does not have an heir. He has nephews, and Gauvain is a valued counsellor and beloved companion of the king. Gauvain is like the king's son in his proximity to Arthur, particularly if we can read the relationship in the context of the strong bond between a brother and his sister's son in Frankish culture. But Gauvain is not the only knight whom Arthur loves like a son. Arthur's affection for his nephew Gaheriet (the French version of Gareth) is demonstrated in his extravagant grief when this knight is killed during Lancelot's rescue of the queen from the execution Arthur has ordered. Earlier, Lancelot himself is described as the object of Arthur's paternal affection. In a rare idyllic moment in the story, Arthur, Lancelot and Guinevere live together happily in Arthur's court. Arthur shows great affection to Lancelot, and even if Lancelot were his own son, Arthur does not see how he could love him more (*Lancelot* VI.66; Lacy III.295). But although Arthur may love his nephews and his knight like sons, they are not his sons, nor are they identified as his heirs. Even when Mordred is invested with Arthur's kingdom at the end of the story, he assumes power as Arthur's regent, not as his heir. The lack of an evident succession locates kingship in Arthur's own personal body. That is, his corporate body does not extend to an heir; the symbolic, corporate body of the king is contained by, subsumed by, the king's material body. And in this, the king is like the queen.

The status of a medieval queen is grounded in her material body – in medieval monarchy, the role of a queen is to produce an heir. The queen has no symbolic body through which she exercises or claims authority. For a medieval queen, personal and political influence are gained through the birth of the king's heir. So, paradoxically, the queen might gain symbolic power only through her material body, as mother of the king's heir. She may claim authority based on a relationship with her son. Guinevere has no son – she has no children at all in the Vulgate Cycle – and her barrenness is surely a primary reason for her vulnerability to accusations by the king's vassals or his nephews. Guinevere is a queen consort: she is a queen because her husband is a king, and since she has no children, her status depends on her husband's favour. The insecurity of her position is demonstrated when Arthur repudiates her and puts the False Guinevere in her place.

If the location of King Arthur's power and authority in his material body makes him like the queen, he is also like the queen in his vulnerability to sexual intrigue. He is like the queen in that his status and authority are located in his body, and that body is vulnerable to seductions that threaten his status and authority. This is what a consideration of Arthur's adulterous desires may suggest. Arthur's liaisons demonstrate not just that Arthur can be manipulated, but that through manipulation he can be made to love. And if status in the king's court depends on the king's favour, that is, on the king's love, then the danger at the heart of the court is not so much that Arthur will be taken captive, but that Arthur will love his captor, not so much that Arthur will be seduced, but that Arthur will love his seducer.

Nowhere in post-medieval Arthuriana are the dangerous consequences of the king's adulterous love more fully represented than in Sir Walter Scott's *Bridal of Triermain* (published in 1813).[7] In this tripartite poem, the story of Arthur's seduction by Guendolen, the daughter of a genie and a woman, results in his isolation in her bower where his neglect of the hunt signals a royal impotence: 'And Caliburn, the British pride / Hangs useless by a lover's side' (Canto 2.v.1). In Scott's story Arthur is not saved from the seductress through her death, as in medieval stories about Arthur's adulteries. Rather, his affair produces a child, and the poem explores the potentially destructive consequences of the king's adultery. That is, although Scott preserves the queen's barren adultery in his story, he fully represents the disastrous threat of an illegitimate heir in the royal household – through the figure of a daughter, not a son.

Arthur's daughter Gyneth arrives at his court to claim her patrimony which is, of course, a worthy husband. The tournament in which Arthur's knights dispute the honour of the marriage ends in bloodshed and death when Gyneth, coached by her mother's black spells and glorying in the carnage, refuses to call an end to the violence. Merlin appears to stop the killing and puts Gyneth to sleep in a bower until she is woken into docile and repentant womanhood 500 years later by the worthy Roland de Vaux. Order is restored to Arthur's kingdom when the consequences of his adultery are contained: his illegitimate daughter is just as destructive as the absent illegitimate son Mordred, but the danger she poses to the court is cut short not through death, but through a sleep that allows her to be woken later to life as a beloved lady who is compliant to her lover. Arthur's vulnerability to the consequences of his own adultery is contained by a woman's acceptance of a wife's role.

A similar acceptance of marital love – though to quite different ends – is at stake in Tennyson's *Idylls of the King* (first published in 1859). When Lancelot's and Guinevere's adultery is discovered, the queen claims responsibility for the liaison with Lancelot, telling her lover that 'Mine is the shame, for I was wife, and thou / Unwedded' ('Guinevere', lines 118–19). Guinevere flees to sanctuary in an abbey where her abjection is represented not just in her shame, but also in a young novice's chattering gossip about 'the good King and his wicked Queen' (line 207), and it culminates in her prostration before the king when he arrives at the abbey. Guinevere 'grovell'd with her face against the floor' (line 412) as Arthur blames her for the war in terms that directly acknowledge the queen's barrenness: '"Well it is that no child is born of thee. / The children born of thee are sword and fire, / Red ruin, and the breaking up of laws"' (lines 421–3). Moreover, Guinevere's sexual transgression is countered by Arthur's purity and faithfulness: '"For I was ever virgin save for thee"', he claims (line 554). When at last Guinevere realises her love for Arthur, for his nobility and goodness, she is in some sense redeemed by this new-found love for her husband: 'her good deeds and her pure life' (line 687) earn her an abbess's rank.

Tennyson elides Arthur's own infidelities (including the incest that engendered Mordred) in order to portray Arthur as the victim of his beloved wife's betrayal. He thus repeats a pattern found in the Vulgate, and he represents Arthur's enduring love as focused on his wife, not on seductresses who betray him. But Tennyson's poem, like the medieval Vulgate Cycle, suggests Arthur's vulnerability to love and to the women he loves. In both the medieval and the modern texts, the danger at the heart of the court is that Arthur will love a dangerous woman. If Arthur is vulnerable, it is not – or not only – because he is betrayed by those he loves, but because he loves traitors.

NOTES

1 References to the text and translation of the *Lancelot* are given by volume and page number; I have occasionally modified the translation in Lacy slightly. On the Vulgate Cycle (often cited as the *Lancelot-Grail* Cycle), see *AoF* and *A Companion to the Lancelot-Grail Cycle*, ed. Carol Dover, Arthurian Studies 54 (Cambridge: D. S. Brewer, 2003).

2 *Le Haut Livre du Graal: Perlesvaus*, ed. W. A. Nitze and T. A. Jenkins, 2 vols. (University of Chicago Press, 1932–7), I. 272–3. The Welsh tradition also mentions a son (sometimes called Llacheu), but this was either not known or disregarded by mainstream chroniclers such as Geoffrey of Monmouth; see R. H. Fletcher, *The Arthurian Material in the Chronicles* (New York: Burt Franklin, 1904), p. 141, and Keith Busby, 'The Enigma of Loholt', in *An Arthurian Tapestry: Essays in Memory of Lewis Thorpe*, ed. Kenneth Varty (Glasgow: French Department of the University of Glasgow, 1981), pp. 28–36.

3 *Le Livre du Graal*, ed. and trans. (into modern French) Daniel Poirion *et al.* (Paris: Gallimard, 2001–), I.870–1; this episode is part of the Vulgate Cycle *Estoire de Merlin* (see Taylor, Chapter 3).

4 *La Suite du roman de Merlin*, ed. G. Roussineau, 2 vols., TLF (Geneva: Droz, 1996), I, pp. 1–2; Lacy, IV.167.

5 Malory, p. 38.27–30 [I.17]; *Lancelot* VII.347 and 356; Lacy II.84 and 86.

6 E. Kantorowicz, *The King's Two Bodies: A Study in Medieval Political Theology* (Princeton University Press, 1957).

7 Sir Walter Scott, *The Poetical Works of Sir Walter Scott with the Author's Introductions and Notes*, ed. J. Logie Robertson (Oxford University Press, 1951), p. 561.

12

CORINNE SAUNDERS

Religion and magic

The themes of religion and magic, interwoven in the supernatural, are crucial to the Arthurian legend. Many of its most resonant motifs, both secular and sacred, are linked to the supernatural (quest and adventure, magic and enchantment, prophecy and destiny, miracle and marvel, the search for the Holy Grail), as are some of its most powerful figures (Merlin, Morgan le Fay, the Fisher King). The leitmotif of the supernatural echoes through Arthurian romance from its origins in the twelfth century to its modern manifestations. Writers such as Chrétien de Troyes, the *Gawain*-poet, Malory, Tennyson, T. H. White and Marion Zimmer Bradley engage in vastly differing ways with the supernatural, but it remains a constant, fundamental to their narratives. While in some contemporary works the supernatural is reduced or floats free of Christianity, the intimate connection between magic, religion and romance, established over something approaching a millennium, is not readily lost. Magic and the supernatural more generally provide romance with its quality of the marvellous, but may also be treated with profundity and realism. Medieval Arthurian legend, the focus of this essay, reflects a Christian world view in which the supernatural is assumed to play a part, and in which religion does not negate the possibility of magic. Some of the central tensions in Arthurian romance, however, arise from the clash between different sorts of supernatural, in particular between the secular (with its origins in the pagan) and the sacred, and the ways that chivalric ideals engage with these.

The thought-world of the later Middle Ages included a complex mix of ideas of magic and the supernatural, which stretched back through classical and Judaeo-Christian as well as Germanic and Celtic belief and ritual. Classical thought was infused with a strong sense of the supernatural: this was a world of gods and daemons, spirits who could act for good or ill. Classical literature told of celebrated practitioners of magic such as Medea and Circe, and of the flesh-devouring, child-killing *strix* or witch. There was also a strong tradition of what would come to be termed natural magic: Pliny's *Natural History* ferociously condemns magic as dependent on the powers of demons, but also repeatedly refers to the extraordinary attributes of plants, stones and animal substances. The oppositions between secular and spiritual, natural and demonic, licit and illicit magic established within the classical period would remain crucial.

In the early Christian world magic was associated with the pagan. Augustine states categorically in *The City of God* that magic is demonic, whereas miracles occur through faith.[1] Yet, like Pliny, Augustine readily accepts as part of God's universe the marvellous in nature, such as the properties of plants and stones. Theologians of the early Middle Ages followed Augustine, identifying pagan superstition as demonic and heretical, although its endurance is clearly indicated by the many references to practices such as the use of amulets, love-magic, medical magic and divination in secular and canon laws, penitentials and sermons, as well as the existence of collections of charms and remedies.

The rise of the universities and new interest in natural philosophy occasioned a shift in attitudes to magic from the thirteenth century onwards. As Arabic works, including treatises on astrology and alchemy, were translated into Latin, the idea of natural magic gained in force. The concept of the universe as a single organism, governed by a sophisticated set of correspondences, underpinned the idea that natural powers could be harnessed – powers emanating from the stars and planets but contained, for instance, in plants or stones. Chaucer's Physician practises 'magyk natureel' in his knowledge of how the stars cause maladies and humours, and his conversance with drugs and medicines, which would include knowledge of when to gather them according to the place of the moon and stars (*Canterbury Tales*, 1.416). Such 'natural magic' fell within the Christian scheme of existence.

Understandings of religion and magic were further complicated by the idea of an otherworld of faery, perhaps rooted in Celtic myths of gods and goddesses, as well as in myths of the classical underworld. This parallel world, neither demonic nor divine, peopled by larger-than-life figures with supernatural powers, is a conventional feature of folk belief. Faeries could readily be rationalised by theologians, and identified as demons, fallen angels with the power to tempt and harm. Romance and folktale are ambivalent about such creatures, portraying the otherworld as one into which humans may slip from time to time, while its inhabitants may step into the human world. An association with the faery may explain the marvellous powers of objects, and natural magic and otherworldly forces can be difficult to disentangle. But there remains a powerful belief in necromancy or 'nigromancy', black magic, which is destructive and may draw upon the art of demons. The specific notion of necromancy as employing the bodies or spirits of the dead, particularly demons, does not tend to be made explicit in romance, though it is sometimes hinted at. It is the black or dark meaning suggested by the etymology of the form used, 'nigromancy', that is most pervasive. 'Nigromancy' and 'sorcery' often appear as near-similes, along with (less often) 'witchcraft'.

Magic, then, is part of the medieval Christian world view, and the supernatural occupies a sliding scale from demons to faeries to natural magic to miracle. The imaginative literature of the Middle Ages takes up and explores all these facets of the supernatural, and Arthurian legend comes to be an especially fruitful space in which to probe their ambiguity, promise and menace. The motifs of marvel, otherworld and magic recur in early Welsh poetry, which seems to look back at a Celtic, pagan past in which Arthur figures as folk hero, achiever of strange adventures. In 'Preiddeu Annwn' ('The Spoils of Annwfn', found in the late thirteenth-century *Book of Taliesin*, but perhaps dating back to the tenth century), Arthur and his men journey to a mysterious land across the water, to win the magical cauldron of regeneration, perhaps a precursor of the Grail.[2] In the enigmatic 'Beddau englynion' ('The Stanzas of the Graves', found in the late thirteenth-century *Black Book of Carmarthen*, but perhaps dating back to the ninth or early tenth century), Arthur's death is linked to the marvellous: 'the world's wonder is the grave of Arthur'.[3]

Writers from Geoffrey of Monmouth onwards adopt a more explicitly Christian perspective, weaving together the themes of marvellous or otherworldly adventure, prophecy and predestination, and drawing both on pagan and Christian notions of the supernatural. Geoffrey links legends of the poet and prophet Myrddin with those of Arthur by including in his *Historia Regum Britanniae* (*History of the Kings of Britain*) a series of 'Prophecies of Merlin' (also circulated separately), which tell of the eventual defeat of the Anglo-Saxons by the British. Geoffrey's later *Vita Merlini* (*The Life of Merlin*) draws on the Myrddin tradition and related Celtic stories of the wild man and prophet Lailoken to offer an account of Merlin's madness and exile. Although Geoffrey relishes the marvellous, he also offers an explanation for Merlin's supernatural powers within a Christian theological framework. Merlin is begotten on a nun, daughter of the king of Dimetia, by a demon or incubus, a spirit of the kind extensively discussed by theologians, identified with the fallen angels (Thorpe, vi.19, p. 168). Merlin combines both prophetic and practical abilities. He erects Stonehenge with stones brought from Ireland; and his innovative powers with drugs allow for the shape-shifting of the king into the form of Ygrainne's husband Gorlois (viii.20, p. 206). Merlin's marvels do not negate the strong sense of Christian destiny, retained throughout Geoffrey's *History*, and evident not only in the prophecies but also in divine signs such as the appearance of the great star with its dragon-shaped ball of fire at the death of Aurelius Ambrosius (viii.15, pp. 200–1).

Wace, in the *Roman de Brut*, takes up Geoffrey's narrative, but reduces the emphasis on the supernatural, omitting Merlin's prophecies, about which he is sceptical. Wace is evasive about whether Merlin's magic is Christian or pagan: in the account of the moving of the Giants' Dance to build Stonehenge, Wace depicts Merlin as walking round the stones, his lips moving, but remarks, 'I don't know if he said a prayer or not'. The shape-shifting is achieved by 'new potions'.⁴ Wace's English translator, Laȝamon, sets up an opposition between Merlin's Christian magic and the ineffectual pagan rituals of Vortiger's magicians.⁵ Merlin, by contrast to the magicians, possesses true wisdom and knowledge compatible with Christian belief: his mother is a pious nun and princess, and the clerk Magan's explanation of the *Incubi Daemones* places them (and thus Merlin's father) firmly within Christian cosmology: 'some of them are noble creatures, and some of them do evil' (line 7874). This Merlin is more orthodox: the shape-shifting of Uther is explained as 'lechecraft', natural, medical magic (line 9448). Yet Laȝamon also chooses to follow pagan folk tradition, identifying the child Arthur with the otherworld of faery:

> As soon as he came upon earth, fairies ['aluen'] took charge of him; they enchanted the child with magic most potent: they gave him strength to be the best of all knights; they gave him another gift, that he should be a mighty king; they gave him a third, that he should live long; they gave him, that royal child, such good qualities that he was the most liberal of all living men.
>
> (lines 9608–14)

Laȝamon's use of the term 'aluen' suggests that his notion of otherworldly protection perhaps finds its roots in Anglo-Saxon folk tradition: elves are mentioned in Old English remedies as the bearers and healers of disease.

Rather than emphasising Arthur's Christian death, Laȝamon returns to the notion of the otherworld of faery, building on Geoffrey's statement that Arthur is carried to the Isle of Avalon for his mortal wounds to be tended, and on Wace's reference to Arthur as the hope of the Britons. Again, Laȝamon employs the term 'aluen', with its suggestion of healing magic, and Arthur is borne away in a boat with two 'wondrously arrayed' ladies. Laȝamon's Arthur foretells his own return and this section of the *Brut* concludes with a reference to the popular belief that Arthur still dwells in Avalon, and to Merlin's promise that 'an Arthur should come again to aid the people of England' (lines 14285 and 14297). In these legendary histories, then, nearly all the ingredients of the Arthurian supernatural are already present. The depiction of Arthur as ideal Christian king is underpinned by a complex blend of Christian and pagan traditions – predestination, prophecy, magic, the otherworld and its association with Arthur's death, and the role of Merlin. While the supernatural endorses Arthur, the chroniclers, like some later romance-writers, limit Merlin's role by removing him early on from the narrative, perhaps uneasy about this potentially pagan figure who is connected with demons.

Whereas the dynastic chronicles emphasised the historical aspect of Arthur, twelfth-century romanciers, particularly Chrétien de Troyes, developed the motif of marvellous adventure so crucial to the fabulous aspect of Arthurian romance (see Chapter 2). Chrétien's narratives depict the knight-hero as mysteriously elect, guided by the invisible hand of destiny through strange adventures. One of the special delights of his narratives is the sense of enigma: we are never quite sure whether we are in an otherworld of faeries and demons, a human world of natural magic and technology, or somewhere in between, although a broadly Christian context and notion of providence are always assumed, and events are often marked by references to the Christian liturgical year. Adventure, frequently of a secular kind, is repeatedly associated with the major Christian feast days on which Arthur's knights gather, perhaps suggesting an inherent tension between worldly and spiritual. Some adventures place Arthur's knights as Christian avengers, defending the cause of right: in *Le Chevalier de la charrete* (*Knight of the Cart*), Lancelot releases the prisoners of the land of Gorre with its resonances of a Celtic otherworld or land of the dead, though these are never made explicit. In *Le Chevalier au lion* (*Knight with the Lion*), Yvain liberates the maidens held in the castle of Pesme Aventure, at once an infernal world ruled by two demons and a more realistic space evoking the predicament of women employed as weavers. But many adventures are less clear cut: Chrétien suggests the contradictions within the chivalric ideal, but also explores and delights in the dramatic possibility of marvellous adventure.

Chrétien's narrative of the naïf hero Perceval in his last romance, *Le Conte du Graal*, presents the most haunting and resonant of otherworldly adventures, taken up and shaped by later writers into the central religious strand of Arthurian legend. Celtic folk material provided the motif of the wounded Fisher King awaiting the Questioner who would heal him and restore his waste lands; Christianity provided the context. Chrétien's work is dedicated to a great Crusader knight, Philip of Flanders, and it explores the possibility of a chivalry that incorporates both secular and sacred ideals. Perceval is educated in prowess and love, but fails the test of spiritual awareness. In the suddenly-appearing Grail Castle, he watches the mysterious procession of the sword that can only be broken in one 'perilous circumstance' (line 3219, Kibler, p. 419), the white lance that drips blood, and the Grail, accompanied by candles that in its light 'lost their brilliance like stars and the moon when the sun rises' (lines 3215–7, Kibler, p. 420). Silent during the opulent feast, Perceval wakes to find the castle empty and himself named 'the wretched' (line 3568, p. 425), for he has failed to ask the meaning of the Grail and lance, and hence to heal the maimed king. The religious meaning is only elaborated later, when Perceval meets a penitential procession of knights and ladies on Good Friday, and is moved to weep for his sinfulness and neglect of God: the holy hermit to whom the penitents lead him explains that the Grail serves the Fisher King's father, who is sustained only by the Eucharistic host, and explains too the silencing nature of sin, urging penance. The romance, left unfinished at Chrétien's death, remains delicately enigmatic, however, about the lance that bleeds and the 'graal' itself, which seems to be a dish or platter made of fine gold decorated with precious stones, and perhaps finds its origins in Celtic stories of a horn or cauldron of plenty.

Wolfram von Eschenbach's version of the story, *Parzifal* (c. 1200), contains interesting alterations and developments. He rewrites the notion of natural magic in his representation of the Grail as a holy stone, its power instilled by a Eucharistic wafer brought by a dove every Good Friday. The Grail enables the regeneration of the phoenix, prevents illness, age and death, and provides food and drink of all kinds. Wolfram's narrative develops the idea of the Grail community as a Christian order of knights, perhaps modelled on the Knights Templar, and ends with the hero's return to the Grail Castle to complete his quest, healing the wounded Anfortas (who has sinned by fighting for love) and becoming the Grail King. The ultimate message is that true chivalry, though it may be inspired by love, must serve the ideals of the Grail.

The great prose romances of the thirteenth century took up the tradition of marvellous adventure of different kinds, but began to weave this into a more coherent history of Arthur and his kingdom (see Taylor's discussion in Chapter 3). Its direction was stimulated in particular by continuations of Chrétien's *Perceval*, which identified the Grail in explicitly Christian terms as the vessel used at the Last Supper, in which Joseph of Arimathea was said to have collected Christ's blood after the Crucifixion, and the lance as that of Longinus, which had pierced Christ's side, causing blood and water to flow out. Robert de Boron's *Joseph d'Arimathie* (written c. 1200) told how the Grail was brought to Britain by Joseph, from whom a line of Grail-keepers known as the Fisher Kings had descended, and how the maimed king Pelles waited to be healed and his lands made fertile through the successful achievement of the Grail by the perfect knight. A subsequent romance (perhaps only begun by Robert, extant in fragmentary form in verse, but also, like *Joseph* and a third part, *Perceval*, in a prose redaction) interwove the stories of Merlin and the Grail, explaining Merlin's strange birth as a demonic plot to destroy mankind through the creation of the Antichrist. Merlin, however, siding with the forces of good and protected by God, turns his magic towards the establishing of the Arthurian world and becomes the prophet of the Grail. The *Lancelot-Grail* or Vulgate Cycle brings together prose versions of the *Estoire del Saint Graal* and the *Estoire de Merlin* with *Lancelot*, adapting these to correspond with the *Queste del Saint Graal*. Spiritual chivalry casts into relief the tarnished nature of secular chivalry, and the new emphasis is on the monastic values of abstinence, asceticism and penance. The sinfulness of Arthur's court, emblematised by the adultery of Lancelot and Guinevere, prepares the ground for the turning of Fortune's wheel and the fall of the Arthurian knights in the final section of the cycle, the *Mort Artu*.

English romance writers of the thirteenth and fourteenth centuries, then, inherited a complex notion of the supernatural spanning the natural, demonic, divine and otherworldly, a tradition of marvellous adventure, and a fully developed Arthurian legend. Through the presence of Merlin, with his demonic origins but influence for good, and through the emphasis on the Grail, Arthurian legend was explicitly situated within a larger Christian history. Merlin's appeal, however, lay not least in his magical feats, and thirteenth-century French romance also depicted rival practitioners of magic, in particular, enchantresses such as Morgan le Fay. The variousness and ambiguity of the supernatural and its practitioners became powerful tools in the creation of drama and suspense. Magic and the supernatural could proffer significant challenges to individual Arthurian knights and to the ideals of the Arthurian court. Among Middle English romances, *Sir Gawain and the Green Knight* offers perhaps the most resonant example of a narrative of supernatural adventure constructed in order to probe Christian chivalric ideals (see Burrow in Chapter 4).

The *Gawain*-poet exploits the ambiguity of magic by interweaving romance and realism, pagan and Christian. The Christian context is made explicit from the start: the adventure occurs at Christmas as the knights and ladies of the Arthurian court feast at Camelot – perhaps having forgotten the deeper significance of Christmas, although in this poem no didactic meaning is ever certain. The Green Knight's demand for a 'Crystemas gomen [game]' is as ambiguous as his appearance, which evokes a range of natural and supernatural possibilities and is realised in striking physical detail (line 283). The descriptive terms chosen emphasise the difficulty of interpreting this supernatural phenomenon, and the court is awestruck and silenced by the marvel, thinking it 'fantoum and fayry3e [illusion and magic]' (line 240). The Green Knight's powers include the ability to overcome death itself: he rides away laughing with his own severed head. Like Christmas itself, and like the Yule log burned at the Midwinter Solstice, the power of the Green Knight to survive beheading evokes both the pagan celebration of regeneration of the seasons, and the Christian hope for salvation and resurrection. The court reduces the multivalent supernatural by laughing at this marvel, while Arthur conceals his wonder, courteously placing the event as a more comprehensible kind of magic, an illusion or 'laykyng of enterludez [playing of theatrical interludes]' (line 472) fitting for Christmas. The unease, however, remains, crystallised in Gawain's anxiety as the time of his journey approaches, and in the court's belief that he will never return. His shield, decorated with the pentangle and with the image of Mary on the inside, symbolises the interwoven spiritual and secular virtues that must protect him against the unknown, but that also provide the basis for his testing.

We are made acutely aware once again of the ambiguity of the supernatural in Gawain's experiences at Hautdesert. The castle appears suddenly, apparently in answer to Gawain's prayer on Christmas Eve. It shimmers and shines, seeming 'pared out of papure [cut out of paper]' (line 802), but it is also a highly fashionable medieval barbican, complete with towers and turrets, ornamented and painted pinnacles, and chalk-white chimneys. The status of Hautdesert is rendered still more mysterious by its apparently Christian ideals: here Gawain attends Mass and makes a confession. Yet it is also a place of temptation and heightened material delight, focused in the surpassing beauty of Bertilak's lady, who comes to seduce Gawain in his bedroom, where he is cocooned in a feminised world, sleeping on in his luxurious bed while Bertilak rises early to hunt. While Gawain's chastity is tested and found true, his spiritual integrity is less certain, for he departs from the castle encircled by the lady's protective girdle, a secular symbol more resonant of pagan binding magic than of the Christian virtues of the pentangle.

The end of the poem identifies the loathly old lady of Hautdesert as Morgan le Fay, who is said to have devised the enchantment to frighten Guinevere, yet interpretation remains problematic. The Green Chapel proves not to be a chapel at all, and indeed seems remarkably unmagical, 'nobot an olde cave' (line 2182); Gawain, however, suspects that he is the victim of demonic deception. While Gawain may be seen as projecting his fears onto a hostile natural landscape, the Green Chapel may also be identified as a pagan site associated with demonic magic, with its 'bal3 ber3 [smooth barrow]' (line 2172), perhaps a pagan burial mound, next to its boiling spring and waterfall. The Green Knight's nicking of Gawain's neck, and the final images of severed flesh and gushing blood, make real the threat to Gawain's life and to the chivalric ideal. When the Green Knight is revealed to be Sir Bertilak of Hautdesert, we remain unsure whether he is demonic in his role of orchestrating temptation, or linked to the divine in his role as arbiter and confessor, whether he is a force of wild nature and seasonal renewal, or whether he is the servant of Morgan le Fay, his shape shifted through her magical arts of illusion. He cannot be reduced to positive or negative, demonic or divine, pagan or Christian, but the poet's use of all these resonances suggests that this magic is meaningful in some powerful symbolic sense, so that we are drawn into the enigma of the poem.

Earlier narratives of individual Arthurian adventure are complemented by Sir Thomas Malory's *Morte Darthur*, which offers a grand retrospective on Arthurian legend (see Chapter 5). Malory's adaptation of the great Vulgate Cycle, a version of which formed his 'Frensshe booke', is distinctively English, drawing also on the Alliterative and Stanzaic *Morte Arthur* poems (p. 12 [1.3–5]). Malory employs the language and style of the prose chronicle, selecting from his sources to emphasise causality. Yet his matter-of-fact, pared-down use of sources and realist mode by no means indicate a lack of interest in the supernatural: rather, its different facets are interwoven to create a multilayered fictional world, and to probe the human predicament.[6] The individual is situated within a world of conflicting and sometimes confusing forces. Like *Sir Gawain and the Green Knight*, the *Morte* both reflects ambivalent cultural attitudes to magic and plays with romance conventions of the supernatural, and the work explores the tension between secular and spiritual ideals. In the course of the rise and fall of Arthur and his court, which is placed within the larger cycle of Christian history, the magic of humans and otherworldly beings, angels and demons, interweaves, and natural and black magic, demonic temptation and miracle are all treated as real possibilities.

Marvellous objects endowed with supernatural powers recur in the *Morte* as in its antecedents: these familiar aspects of the Arthurian world may be seen as within the domain of natural magic and hence invested with a potential realism. The narrative relies on a ready assumption that the occult forces of the cosmos may be contained in natural objects, in particular, stones and plants, which can achieve marvellous effects. The metal of the sword Excalibur possesses a distinctive bite and its scabbard prevents the loss of blood. The 'vertu' of the stone in Lyonesse's ring both changes Gareth's colours and prevents loss of blood, in a story very much of Malory's own making (p. 345.14–24 [vii.28]); the potion ensures that the love between Tristram and Isode 'never departed dayes of their lyff'

(p. 412.25 [VIII.24]); the drink prepared by Dame Brusen makes Lancelot 'so asoted and madde' that he sleeps with Elaine in the belief that she is Guinevere (p. 795.9 [XI.2]). As Helen Cooper has pointed out, such magic is often interesting for its loss or failure.[7] Arthur's sword and scabbard, which have special protective qualities, are stolen by Morgan le Fay to arm her lover Accolon in his battle against Arthur. Arthur regains Excalibur, a fitting gift for a king and symbolic of his great abilities in battle, but the scabbard is taken again, to be irretrievably lost when Morgan throws it into deep water. For Arthur to retain its protection would destroy the suspense and tragedy of the work. Gareth's magic ring too is returned to Lyonesse, replaced by 'a goodly and a ryche rynge' (p. 360.22–3 [VII.35]) given him by her on their marriage; we are unlikely to think back to the first, protective ring at Gareth's death. While magical objects may disappear from the narrative, however, they remain within its frame of possibility, to be treated with a kind of easy, practical acceptance.

Malory does not explicitly associate practitioners of magic with the otherworld, but leaves their identities vague. Their arts most often fit the context of natural magic, and medicine and magic can overlap, particularly in the skills of the women in the *Morte*.[8] La Beale Isode, 'a noble surgeon' (p. 385.3 [VIII.9]), heals Tristram from his poisoned wound; her mother's medicinal skill provides the love potion. Excalibur and its scabbard are the gifts of the Lady of the Lake, and the Damosel of the Lake, Nenyve, is also a practitioner of white magic: 'ever she ded grete goodnes unto kynge Arthure and to all his knyghtes thorow her sorsery and enchauntementes' (p. 1059.14–15 [XVIII.8]). She preserves Pelleas from Ettard, and reveals the truth of the poisoned apple. The practitioners of magic can, however, be ambiguous, their magic positive or negative according to its motivation, but often quite menacing, and sometimes shading into necromancy. Nenyve assists Arthur in his battle against Accolon by returning Excalibur to him, yet we are reminded in the same sentence that she is the damosel 'that put Merlyon undir the stone' (p. 142.20–1 [IV.9]). Similarly, Elaine's nurse, Dame Brusen, 'one of the grettyst enchaunters that was that tyme in the worlde' (p. 794.19–20 [XI.2]), seems to use deeply unfair methods to orchestrate the conception of Galahad.

Even Merlin, whose powers are key to the construction of the Arthurian world, is treated with some ambiguity, although he also voices and orchestrates the workings of Christian destiny. Malory omits any account of Merlin's origins, perhaps suggesting an unease about magic that strays into the pagan or demonic. Merlin's magic includes the arts of prophecy, illusion and shape-shifting, but these are presented with understated realism. Thus the begetting of Arthur is foretold through matter-of-fact dialogue with

Uther: 'This nyght ye shalle lye with Igrayne in the castel of Tyntigayll. And ye shalle be lyke the duke her husband' (p. 9.8–9 [1.2]). Merlin most often figures as a counsellor figure, guiding the direction of Arthur's army, for instance, in the battle against the eleven kings; but his magic also plays a crucial role in authorising Arthur's reign, and his role as shaper of Arthur's destiny is essential to the early books of the *Morte*. Prophecy is often linked to shape-shifting, most eerily in Merlin's coming first as a child, then as an old man, to foretell Arthur's doom: 'ye have done a thynge late that God ys displesed with you, for ye have lyene by youre syster and on hir ye have gotyn a childe that shall destroy you and all the knyghtes of youre realme' (p. 44.18–19 [1.20]). It is telling, however, that when Merlin orchestrates Arthur's taking of the sword from the stone to prove his right to the throne, unease about Merlin is expressed by the British kings: some laugh 'and mo other called hym a wytche' (p. 18.13–14 [1.8]). The fearful and sinister aspect of the demonic plays a part in Merlin's own 'shamefull dethe' (p. 44.29 [1.20]), brought about by his repeated attempts to seduce Nenyve of the Lake. Fearing him 'for cause he was a devyls son' (p. 126.19–20 [IV.1]), she turns his own magic back on him, and traps him under a stone. Demonic arts are dangerous arts, even when they function to shape the destiny of the greatest Christian king.

The negative aspect of magic is most fully explored in Morgan le Fay, who repeatedly threatens the order of the Arthurian world. As Arthur's half sister, Morgan has her own rival court, and is thus established as the great opponent of Arthur, empowered not by military force but by magic. Malory does not probe Morgan's identity as 'le Fay', but notes that she 'was put to scole in a nonnery, and ther she lerned so moche that she was a grete clerke of nygromancye' (p. 10.9–10 [1.2]). Morgan is connected with the dark, demonic side of magic. She is skilled in illusion and shape-shifting, changing herself into the shape of great stones when pursued, creating the false sword and scabbard, and sending destructive gifts to the court. Her jealous magic includes the lengthy imprisonment of a beautiful lady in boiling water, and the desire either to gain Lancelot for her own lover or to destroy him.

At the start of the 'Book of Sir Launcelot', Lancelot is placed as vulnerable only to 'treson other inchauntement' (p. 253.11–12 [VI.1]), and the book is focused on the feminine threat of enchantment. Malory presents magic as enabling women to practise violence, to abduct, imprison and possess male bodies. Thus Morgan le Fay and three queens put Lancelot to sleep and abduct him in order to demand his love, imprisoning him in a 'chambir colde' (p. 257.5 [VI.3]). The most sinister practitioner of black magic in the *Morte* also pursues Lancelot's body: the enchantress Hellawes, a figure not found in the French Prose *Lancelot*. The strange, otherworldly adventure of the Chapel Perilous, with its ghostly knights who grin and gnash their teeth, turns out to be a complicated snare for Lancelot, who, if he had not refused Hellawes' request for 'one kiss', would have lost his life, his corpse surrendered to the necrophiliac enchantress: '"Than wolde I have bawmed hit and sered hit, and so to have kepte hit my lyve dayes; and dayly I sholde have clypped the and kyssed the, dispyte of quene Gwenyvere"' (p. 281.18–20 [VI.15]). Sex and death are equated in a highly threatening way, and the enchantress is characterised as the predatory woman who desires the body at all costs, even the cost of life itself. Enchantment replaces physical force, and traditional gender roles are reversed, although, unlike female victims, Lancelot is ultimately able to save himself, and it is Hellawes who dies of unrequited love for him. Despite her magical powers, the woman becomes the victim. As in *Sir Gawain and the Green Knight*, preservation of chastity has become synonymous with preservation of life, and only when Lancelot's body is taken in adultery with the queen is he finally overcome by the treason hinted at in the opening of Book VI.

Malory's enchantresses remain ambiguous, their practices shading between natural magic and necromancy, but in the books recounting the quest of the Sankgreal the supernatural is explicitly divine or demonic. The world of the Quest is actively Christian: in it knights become caught up in the struggle of good and evil, which is constantly re-enacted in symbolic terms. Characteristic is Bors' vision of a pelican sitting in a dry, leafless tree (p. 956.5–13 [XVI.6]): as he watches, the bird pierces itself with its beak in order to feed its starving young with its blood, and we scarcely need a hermit to interpret the dying bird as an emblem of Christ. The scene conveys vividly the symbolic quality of this landscape marked by waste lands, stunted trees, hermitages, rudderless boats, and a strange sense of prescience and deep religious meaning.

The Grail landscape can also open onto a violent, demonic world, as in the adventures of Perceval, carried for miles on a great black horse which disappears into a flaming river when he crosses himself. Finding himself on a barren rocky mountain, he is tempted by a beautiful woman, only to see her disappear when he again makes the sign of the cross: she was a manifestation of the devil himself. Similarly, the seduction of Bors is attempted by a lady who disappears with 'a grete noyse and a grete cry as all the fyndys of helle had bene aboute hym' (p. 966.9–10 [XVI.12]). Literal and symbolic interweave as what appear to have been physical realities prove demonic illusions. The enchantress is rewritten as the demonic temptress, illusory yet representing the greatest danger to the knight, eternal damnation.

The supernatural becomes a means of testing and shaping individual chivalric identity in ways that go far beyond the physical. Within the landscape of the Grail quest all glimmers with the possibility of religious interpretation, and adventure opens onto divine vision. When the Grail knights at last reach Corbenic, the boundary between earthly and celestial worlds disappears altogether. Ultimately, however, 'the dedly fleysh' cannot be sustained when 'the spirituall thynges' are seen openly, and Galahad is assumed into heaven (p. 1034.22 [XVII.22]); Perceval dies a saintly death in a hermitage the following year. Only Lancelot is left: restrained at the door of the Grail Chamber, he experiences in his swoon 'grete mervayles that no tunge may telle, and more than ony herte can thynke' (p. 1017.11–12 [XVII.16]), but is permitted to go no further because of his adulterous love for the queen. He is the pattern of virtuous but flawed humanity, seeing only through a glass darkly or in a world of dreams.

In the last books of the *Morte*, the challenge is to maintain the ideals of the Grail quest within a very different, secular landscape. Adventure, quest and marvel are largely left behind, to be replaced by slander and strife as the cracks in the fellowship deepen. Yet Malory does not wholly turn away from the supernatural: Christian miracle opposes black magic in the episode of the healing of the poisoned wounds of Sir Urry, caused by a sorceress. The episode provides Malory with the occasion to list the 110 Arthurian knights in a final celebration of the glory of the court, and the miracle of Urry's healing proves Lancelot's surpassing virtue in one last resounding triumph just before all spirals downwards.

In ensuing events, human choice and error merge peculiarly with chance and destiny. The will of God seems clear in Arthur's dream of Gawain, who warns him not to fight the next day, but to await Lancelot's arrival. Yet this 'grete grace and goodnes that Allmyghty Jesu hath unto [Arthur]' (p. 1234.10–11 [XXI.3]) is disturbingly set aside when on 'this unhappy day' the last battle begins through the mischance of a knight drawing his sword to kill an adder (p. 1235.18–29 [XXI.4]). Malory's focus is not on punishment of sin, as in the French *Mort Artu*, but on tragedy, as fortune or chance intervenes to oppose human will and overturn moral choices. Like the earlier chroniclers, Malory returns to the non-Christian supernatural in depicting Arthur's death. As Arthur is borne away in a ship by the enchantresses, Morgan le Fay (with two other queens) and Nenyve of the Lake, the healing and black arts of magic are brought together. We are reminded of the Celtic folk legend of the once and future king: 'som men say in many partys of Inglonde that kynge Arthure ys nat dede' and that 'he shall com agayne'. Malory's own verdict is more ambiguous, yet not unhopeful, for it gestures towards an afterlife, whether this is heaven or Avalon: 'rather I wolde sey: here in thys worlde he chaunged hys lyff' (p. 1242.22–7 [XXI.7]).

Only individual spirituality can redeem the terrific sense of loss and waste. The final pages of the *Morte*, which include some of Malory's most striking changes to his sources, return to a firmly Christian perspective, as miracle manifests itself once more in the holy ends of Lancelot and Guinevere. Perhaps the recurrent emphasis across Arthurian legend on Guinevere's choice to become a nun marks the gravity with which adultery in women is treated: her mortal sin is balanced by her active repentance, which Lancelot follows in his retreat to the hermitage. In the narrative of their deaths, repentance is finally written as redemption: Guinevere (whose death is not elaborated in Malory's sources) foresees her own end two days earlier, and knows that it will be conveyed in divine vision to Lancelot; Lancelot's death soon after is that of a saint, marked by his own prayer and prophecy, and the Archbishop of Canterbury's vision of angels that bear Lancelot into heaven. Sanctity is made manifest in miracle as Lancelot's companions experience 'the swettest savour about him that ever they felte' (a detail aparently added by Malory, p. 1258.17 [XXI.12]). These last miracles allow for a redemptive ending, a return to the numinous promise of the Grail landscape as we are reminded once more of the celestial world glimmering beyond.

The great themes of magic and religion are taken in many directions, but later tellings remain inspired by or respond to medieval Arthurian romance, its interplay between natural and demonic, divine and otherworldly, and its tradition of marvellous adventure. The association between magic, prophecy and the shaping of Christian destiny is taken up by Spenser: Prince Arthur's quest for the Faerie Queene is justified by Merlin's assurance that he is 'sonne and heire vnto a king'. Merlin becomes the voice of English history: in his cave, Britomart learns of Artegall, stolen by fairies, whose line will lead to the reign of Elizabeth.[9] Black magic here is linked to the Roman Catholic Church (personified in the evil harlot Duessa and the magician Archimago), and opposed by the white, benign power of Una, the embodiment of true faith, assisted by the Red Crosse Knight of St George. Spenser develops the notion of marvellous allegorical adventure to tell of a quest for perfection, the bringing together of ideal and real in the unity of Arthur and Elizabeth and their mirroring pairs, and the attainment of spiritual chivalry.

For Tennyson in the late nineteenth century, the power of the story remains rooted in its vision of ideal, predestined Christian rule. The first *Idyll*, 'The Coming of Arthur', presents a series of narratives of origin for Arthur, most memorably that of the babe snatched by Merlin from the fiery waves, whose destiny is endorsed by the 'subtler magic' of the Lady of the Lake, 'mystic, wonderful' ('The Coming of Arthur', lines 283–84). In the final *Idyll*, 'The Passing of Arthur', the magnificent portrayal of 'that last weird battle in the west' returns to the notion of the predestined king, echoed in the image of the keening, black-hooded queens who bear Arthur to Avalon, and the rhyme Sir Bedivere hears, 'From the great deep to the great deep he goes' (lines 29, 445). For Tennyson, the rarefied, celestial world of the Grail is threatening, further separating the secular and sacred worlds that Arthur has the power to bring together. His active embodiment of Christian virtue is a version of the muscular Christianity so characteristic of the Victorian religious sensibility. Most destructive to the ideal of Camelot are the forces of sexual desire and adultery. For Tennyson, Merlin was the figure of the artist, ensnared by the carnal attraction of the imagination, and put to sleep by the enchantress Vivien, demonised in her sinister sexuality. Richard Wagner's music-drama *Parsifal* (1882) returns to the opposition of flesh and spirit in its haunting narrative of Parsifal's battle against the temptations of the magician Klingsor's castle, and the wiles of the fallen enchantress Kundry in the quest to heal the wound of sexual sin in Anfortas.

The motif of the wounded Fisher King and his barren lands resonated too with the very different preoccupations of the early twentieth century. New anthropological ideas, memorably treated in James Frazer's *The Golden Bough*, challenged the separation of primitive and civilised, and a new richness and energy was discovered in other and early cultures. Jessie Weston's *From Ritual to Romance* placed the story of the Fisher King as an ancient, pagan fertility myth, providing the grounds for later imaginative literature. Such ideas inspired modernist writing, most famously T. S. Eliot's *The Waste Land*, in which the remnants of art and culture become fragments to shore against the poet's ruins, and perhaps against the ruins of Western civilisation. There is no Grail in Eliot's poem: rather, it is haunted by the image of the waiting, barren land where dry bones whisper in the wind. The silenced Questioner comes to stand for the modern human predicament, and the poem ends with the image of the Fisher King searching to set his arid lands in order.

Eliot's poem concerns the loss of faith, the absence of spiritual vision, and twentieth-century retellings of Arthurian legend sustain this emphasis in their tendency to detach magic from Christianity. T. H. White takes up the proto-realist aspect of magic in the wonderfully eccentric, schoolmaster Merlin of *The Sword in the Stone*, whose foreknowledge is explained by the fact that he travels backwards through time. His magic is specifically related to the animal world, though it has a strong political and pacifist agenda, which White pursued more and more seriously in the later novels of his five-volume sequence, *The Once and Future King*. Other novelists have taken an historical perspective associating magic with Celtic religion. Mary Stewart's trilogy, *The Crystal Cave*, *The Hollow Hills* and *The Last Enchantment*, recreates the pre-Christian world of fifth-century

Britain, centring on Merlin, the Celtic seer. Christianity is absent too from Stewart's last Arthurian novel, *The Wicked Day*, which takes Mordred as its protagonist, to narrate the enactment of a destiny partly shaped by the magic of Morgause, warned against by Merlin and the benign enchantress Nimue, but inexorable. In Marion Zimmer Bradley's *The Mists of Avalon*, magic again belongs to the Celtic world, in particular to the priestesses of the ancient cult of the Earth Mother, and its powers are opposed to a harsh, patriarchal Christianity. Bernard Cornwell's *Warlord Chronicles* also play on the opposition between Druidic and Christian religions, though he reduces Merlin's magic to a combination of shrewdness, disguise and deceit. Cornwell's series *The Grail Quest* takes a similarly cynical, realist approach in its weaving together of politics, battles, corruption and heresy in the period of the Hundred Years War.

In the world of medieval romance, however, the Celtic otherworld is integrated with the Christian supernatural. Magic is treated as a real force – dangerous if misused, but also with positive virtues. Supernatural powers can be wielded by both God and devil in the battle over men's souls, and romance can open onto the other worlds of heaven, hell or faery. It is not always clear whether the mysterious forces of destiny that shape adventure and the marvellous are to be understood as divine, demonic or otherworldly. Destiny can seem a battleground between good, evil and ambiguous forces, in which free will must blindly enact itself. Yet it is significant that the menace of otherworldly forces is repeatedly set aside in tellings of the final, seminal episode of Arthurian legend. Again and again, we are left with a reminder of the promise of the supernatural, as Arthur is carried in the barge with its mourning queens to Avalon. Thus in the image that closes Tennyson's *Idylls*, Bedivere looking out from the cliffs

> saw,
> Straining his eyes beneath an arch of hand,
> Or thought he saw, the speck that bare the King,
> Down that long water opening on the deep
> Somewhere far off, pass on and on, and go
> From less to less and vanish into light.
> And the new sun rose bringing the new year.
> ('The Passing of Arthur', lines 463–9)

NOTES

1 See St Augustine, *Concerning the City of God Against the Pagans*, x.ix, trans. Henry Bettenson, *Saint Augustine: City of God* (Harmondsworth: Penguin, 1984), p. 383.

2 Ceridwen Lloyd-Morgan, 'The Celtic Tradition', in *AoE*, pp. 1–9 (p. 3). See also *AoW* and *AoF*.

3 Lloyd-Morgan, 'The Celtic Tradition', p. 3.

4 *Wace's 'Roman de Brut: A History of the British', Text and Translation*, ed. and trans. Judith Weiss, Exeter Medieval English Texts and Studies (University of Exeter Press, 1999), lines 7539–42, 8150, 8702–6.

5 Laȝamon, *Brut or Hystoria Brutonum*, ed. and trans. W. R. J. Barron and S. C. Weinberg (Harlow: Longman, 1995), lines 7738–41.

6 Corinne Saunders, 'Violent Magic in Middle English Romance', in *Violence in Medieval Courtly Literature: A Casebook*, ed. Albrecht Classen, Routledge Medieval Casebooks (New York and London: Routledge, 2004), pp. 225–40 (pp. 232–6).

7 Helen Cooper, 'Magic that Doesn't Work', Ch. 3 of *The English Romance in Time: Transforming Motifs from Geoffrey of Monmouth to the Death of Shakespeare* (Oxford University Press, 2004), pp. 137–72.

8 See Geraldine Heng, 'Enchanted Ground: The Feminine Subtext in Malory', in *Courtly Literature: Culture and Context*, ed. Keith Busby and Erik Kooper (Amsterdam and Philadelphia, PA: Benjamins, 1990), pp. 283–300; Catherine La Farge, 'The Hand of the Huntress: Repetition and Malory's *Morte Darthur*', in *New Feminist Discourses: Critical Essays on Theories and Texts*, ed. Isobel Armstrong (London and New York: Routledge, 1992), pp. 263–79; and Elizabeth Edwards, 'The Place of Women in the *Morte Darthur*', in *A Companion to Malory*, ed. Elizabeth Archibald and A. S. G. Edwards, Arthurian Studies 37 (Cambridge: D. S. Brewer, 1996), pp. 37–54.

9 Edmund Spenser, *The Faerie Queene*, ed. A. C. Hamilton, Longman Annotated English Poets (London and New York: Longman, 1977), I.ix.5, III.iii.49.

13

ROBERT ALLEN ROUSE AND CORY JAMES RUSHTON

Arthurian geography

The true shape of Arthurian Britain was and remains a contentious battleground: even in our 'enlightened' modern age the search for sites and objects associated with Arthur continues, producing periodic 'amazing' discoveries – such as that of the 'Artognou' stone found at Tintagel in 1998 – that are met with a seemingly inextinguishable degree of enthusiasm from the contemporary media. However, for medieval writers, the locating of Arthurian geography within the actual landscape of the British Isles was not merely of antiquarian interest: rather, it was often a serious matter of political, cultural and institutional importance. Authors writing in numerous languages and hailing from a variety of courts looked towards Britain for indelible signs of that ancient conqueror who could validate the regimes of their own day, interpreting Arthur's actions through their own contemporary lens: for this was Logres, the legendary Britain of the past over which Arthur had once reigned so gloriously. The Arthurian tales of medieval Europe imagined this landscape as a place of marvels and conflicts, marked with tragic tales of loss and recovery, of the quest for the Grail and of the love of the French knight Lancelot for the British Queen Guinevere. The countryside of medieval Britain was littered with reminders of the past presence of Arthur and his knights, relics of a time of perfect chivalry and overwhelming imperial power. Tom Shippey has argued that 'England has a kind of mythical geography, a network of associations and oppositions, now dwindled largely to humour and tourism, but once a vital part of the country's being: a geography which accords special roles to Oxford and Cambridge, to Stratford and Glastonbury, to Wigan and Jarrow'.[1] The Arthurian tradition plays an important role in the construction and articulation of this mythical landscape, interweaving the aura of the age of Camelot into the palimpsest that is the British landscape.

Arthurian scholars have increasingly begun to read the Arthurian history of Britain as a post-colonial narrative, as a story of multiple ruptures through conquest and repeated attempts to rewrite both history and the landscape in order to legitimatise the invader or to provide consolation to the invaded. Within this malleable historiography Arthur stands as an associative figure of great utility: numerous English kings sought to appropriate his legacy for political and propaganda purposes, including Henry II, Edward I (particularly in his wars on the Scots), Edward III and Henry VII. These efforts all derived, albeit at some remove, from Geoffrey of Monmouth's foundational *History of the Kings of Britain*. While Geoffrey appears to have possessed a sound grasp of British geography, his successors were only sporadically interested in maintaining his conception of the shape of Arthur's kingdom: more often, they would exploit gaps in his geography just as they would exploit gaps in his chronology. The cosmopolitan nature of Arthur's court – which takes on something of the aspect of a chivalric United Nations – creates connections with a large number of different geographical locations, some real and some entirely fictional. Through this accretive process, Arthurian geography becomes a complex grafting of fictional, sometimes allegorical, places onto the real topography of the British Isles.

Even when an Arthurian site really existed, there could be no guarantee that the author in fact knew anything about its geographical reality; for every Chrétien de Troyes (who seems to have a remarkable knowledge of even rather obscure British places) or Guillaume le Clerc (who knows Scotland passably well, as attested by *Fergus*), there is a Wolfram von Eschenbach, whose geography in *Parzival* is idiosyncratic at best. Importantly for the English Arthurian tradition, Thomas Malory adds a significant layer of realism to his text when he mentions places he knows from his own career and times (e.g. Winchester, Alnwick), but such realism complicates the multiple layers of ill-understood names which he inherited from centuries of conflicting tradition. Attempts to map Arthur's Britain as it appears in texts such as the *Morte Darthur* or the Vulgate Cycle depend almost entirely on vague guesswork once the major historical sites such as London and Bath have been identified.

The literary understanding of Arthurian geography also fractures along language lines. The location of Camelot, for example, in the major medieval Arthurian texts is neatly, although not perfectly, divided between insular and continental texts: French texts consistently associate the major events of Arthur's reign with Camelot, while English texts are more likely to posit Carlisle as the site of Arthurian courtly life. Both the major Middle English exceptions to the Carlisle tradition – *Sir Gawain and the Green Knight* and *Le Morte Darthur* – are arguably more influenced by French antecedents than by the insular geographical traditions. French authors seem generally content to keep their Arthurian geography loose and indistinct, typically placing Arthur's court at some central but vaguely located Camelot, a mysterious place suiting a king whose own reality was often questioned. In contrast, many of the anonymous authors of English Arthurian texts ignore the mysterious Camelot altogether, instead locating Arthur's court in real places of historical political importance: Carlisle, given its importance on the border with Scotland, makes frequent appearances. When the French Vulgate's Lancelot flees England, he does so from an unnamed port, whereas when the English Lancelot goes into exile, he leaves from Caerleon in the Stanzaic *Morte Arthur*, or from Cardiff in *Le Morte Darthur*.

Medieval Arthurian geography is a complicated mixture of real places and mythic sites, and is shaped and reshaped in often idiosyncratic ways by successive authors and competing narrative traditions. However, within this constantly changing matrix of locations and events there are certain important places which seem to demand identification or explanation, a search manifested in both the textual tradition and in the wider context of medieval geography. Not all of the places discussed below have a strong role in Arthurian romance (Westminster, for example), but as we shall see, Arthur's impact upon the geography of medieval Britain was not limited to the world of romance.

Seeking Camelot

Camelot has always been a kind of British Troy for the many archaeologists seeking to be Arthur's Schliemann, but as we have seen, the fabled city's historicity has been long been questionable: even from the beginning of the tradition there have been at least two contenders, Caerleon and Carlisle. However, by the late-fifteenth century, and for one man in particular, Camelot's location can be determined exactly: 'the cité of Camelot, that ys in Englysh called Wynchester' (Malory, p. 92.1–2 [11.19]). Malory makes real the site of Camelot for his readers, and for late-medieval English culture, claiming once and for all a centralising English (as opposed to a more problematic and nebulous British) provenance for Arthur's legacy. But why Winchester? What leads Malory to make this identification? Malory is the first Arthurian authority to identify Winchester explicitly as Camelot. Prior to the *Morte Darthur*, Winchester is presented in the tradition merely as one of the many sites of Arthur's peripatetic court. Various explanations have been put forward to explain Malory's privileging of Winchester, but the most compelling remains the argument that the presence of the Round Table itself in Winchester's Great Hall determined Malory's identification. The first historical account of what seems to be the Winchester table is that of the fifteenth-century chronicler John Hardyng. In 1464 Hardyng wrote the revised version of his *Chronicle*, in which he records that 'The Rounde Table at Wynchestre beganne, and ther it ende and ther it hangeth yet'.[2]

While Malory seems to have used the Table as evidence of Winchester's status as the site of Arthur's Camelot, the question of why the Round Table was placed there in the first place remains an important aspect of the creation of fifteenth-century Arthurian geography. The Table itself, as Martin Biddle has convincingly argued, seems likely have been constructed on the orders of Edward I for a grand Arthurian themed tournament in the year 1290.[3] For Edward, this was no whimsical entertainment; rather, the king chose the Arthurian theme for the tournament because he knew what it represented – power, grandeur, and most importantly, imperial ambition. For in Arthur, Edward must have seen reflected his own desires: Arthur had been King of the Britons, and had conquered and ruled not only England, but also the rest of Britain. Arthur had conquered Edward's old enemies the Scots, had overrun the Welsh, and had forced the Irish to pay homage. Arthur had conquered and ruled all of Britain, and this too was Edward's goal. Thus, by publicly taking on the role of Arthur at the Winchester tournament, Edward was presenting himself, both to his own lords and to his important foreign guests, as equal to Arthur, as not just a king of England, but a *Rex Britanniae*, demonstrating to the world that just as Arthur had conquered all the peoples of Britain, so would he.

Prior to Malory's version of the legend, Winchester does not seem to have been widely considered to have once been Camelot, which raises the question of Edward's motivations for having a specifically Arthurian tournament there. We know that Edward shared his age's widespread enthusiasm for the Arthurian story, and that he participated in both the consumption and production of Arthurian texts: Rusticiano da Pisa received Edward's copy of *Guiron le Courtois* in the early 1270s directly from the king so that he might combine it with other Arthurian tales to create a huge anthology of the legends.[4] Edward was not the only member of the royal household to take part in the creation of Arthurian legend: his queen, Eleanor of Castile, commissioned the Arthurian verse romance *Escanor* from Gerard d'Amiens. The court's familiarity with the Matter of Britain, and its participatory role in the creation of texts which combined characters and motifs from earlier works, confirm that Edward could well have known a story in which Arthur did hold a tournament at Winchester. In the thirteenth-century French Vulgate *La Mort le roi Artu*, Arthur declares that a great tournament should be held at Winchester for the entertainment of his knights.[5] This establishes Winchester as an important site in Arthurian geography, and upon the authority of Arthur himself, who had chosen the city as a tournament site. The narrative feeds cannibalistically upon itself: Winchester is a city associated with English kings since the Anglo-Saxon period, when it acted as King Alfred's chief city and the traditional burial place of the Wessex kings, and therefore the *Mort Artu* describes Arthur holding a tournament there; this textual description then provides a later English king with the idea of holding an Arthurian-themed tournament there, and the memory of this reenactment reinforces the idea that Winchester was Camelot. The significance of the place is registered in a text which in turn endows the original place with a new signification. By such often complex processes Arthurian locations came into being.

Rivers and battles

While Camelot lay at the conceptual heart of Arthur's realm, its margins are often marked – in a characteristically medieval fashion – by rivers, and its scope (both in the landscape and in time) is marked by battle sites. When the ninth-century *Historia Brittonum* attributed to Nennius provides a list of twelve battle sites associated with Arthur's campaign against foreign invaders, the intention is clearly to suggest something about the scope of Arthur's activities and the breadth of his effective power: this is a man who fights invaders in every corner of the land he protects as *dux bellorum* (see Hutton, Chapter 1). That we cannot determine precisely where those battle sites were only adds to the mystery surrounding Arthur. In a strange sense, we are on firmer ground when we are discussing the manner in which Britain's rivers provide a locus for the Arthurian story, and set the limits of Arthur's reign. Even here, there can be fundamental disagreements amongst Arthurian scholars: the battles can be located in the south and south-west, the most common theory; or they can be located in the north, in the borderlands between England, Scotland and ancient Galloway – the adherents of the Scottish Arthur will prefer northern locations for Arthur's traditional battles.

Michelle Warren notes that the divisions within the British Isles were often delineated by watery boundaries, a trend which begins with the sons of Brutus in Geoffrey of Monmouth and continues throughout the insular tradition: the Humber dividing England/Logres from Scotland, the Severn dividing England/Logres from Wales, and the Channel dividing England from France.[6] Rivers, as liminal spaces that both demarcate and lie between, often function as sites of contact or transition between the mundane world and the fantastical, between here and there. 'As all authorities have recognized', wrote Loomis, 'the Celts believed the blissful abodes of the gods to be hidden from the eyes of normal man in a wide variety of places – behind a wall of mist, under ground, beyond a river, on a remote island, beneath a lake, under the sea.'[7] Even a cursory knowledge of Arthurian narrative confirms the importance of water, and land somehow bounded by water, to the Matter of Britain from its origins: Arthur's sword coming from and being returned to some mysterious watery realm, Lancelot and Gawain attempting to cross dangerous bridges into a kingdom that seems not quite mortal, the knights in numerous texts who defend less-unearthly bridges as a point of honour. Non-Arthurian romance does not share this omnipresent focus on rivers and lakes, and although the tradition continually renews itself by insisting on some relationship between Arthur's realm and Britain as each generation knew it, this merely produces a bewildering mix of the real and the fictional.

Nennius perhaps sets the tone. Where Geoffrey maintains a sharp interest in actual British geography, important for making his political and thematic points, Nennius provides a list of battles which seems to delight in being obscure, with seven battles along or near rivers (Glein, Bassas, Tribruit, and four along the Dubglas in the district of Linnuis), and five more in various locations: the Caledonian Wood (Cat Coit Celidon), Fort Guinnion, the City of the Legions, Mount Agned and, finally, the culminating conflict at Mount Badon (a name Nennius inherits from Gildas, who did not associate the battle with Arthur).[8] Geoffrey Ashe thinks that two of the battle locations are 'reasonably certain, Celidon and Chester', but according to P. J. C. Field, even identifying the City of the Legions requires an examination of three possible candidates: Caerleon-on-Usk (Geoffrey's choice), Chester or York (Field's choice).[9] Badon is even more difficult, not least because of this battle's importance in the chronology of Anglo-Saxon settlement in the British Isles; all that is certain is that Badon was in the south, with some of the most prominent candidates being Bath (an identification made by Geoffrey and maintained by some modern scholars), Badbury Rings in Dorset and the village of Badbury near Liddington Castle in Wiltshire.[10]

Arthur's final battle with Mordred, first mentioned in the tenth century *Annales Cambriae*, takes place at the equally mysterious Camlann, most often identified (again thanks to Geoffrey of Monmouth) with the river Camel near Camelford in Cornwall. The sixteenth-century antiquarian John Leland records that a battle did take place there, evidenced by finds of discarded armour and weapons in a field near the tantalisingly named Slaughter Bridge, although these are most probably remains from a recorded later battle between the West Saxons and the Cornish which took place in 823.[11] Those who prefer a northern Arthur believe that Camlann was at the Roman Fort at Birdoswald on Hadrian's Wall, called Camboglanna by the Romans.[12]

Another prominent example of such uncertainty is the castle of Dolorous Garde on the banks of the Humber, a place of deadly enchantment conquered by Lancelot early in the French prose Vulgate *Lancelot*, and the place where the young knight discovers his identity.[13] He renames the castle Joyous Garde and makes it his principle residence in England. The Vulgate describes this castle as being on an island, a feature it shares with other Humber communities in the Arthurian tradition, notably the Delectable Isle in the story of Palomides and the Red City (Malory, pp. 711–22 [x.61]). One might assume that this implies that there actually are islands in the Humber, but one would be wrong. The Humber is another example of life imitating art, like Winchester becoming Camelot. In 1299 Edward I – a noted Arthurian enthusiast – founded King's Town (now Kingston-upon-Hull, or simply Hull) on its banks. As a striking manifestation of his politically motivated belief in the historicity of the Arthurian legends, Edward endowed the newly established town with the same heraldic device that was often associated with Arthur: three gold crowns on a blue field. In doing so Edward sought once more – as with his construction of the Round Table in Winchester – to give material existence to the Arthurian legacy of England. Edward's motivations for founding King's Town were primarily military, as the site was ideal for launching both land and naval attacks against the Scottish enemy, and Arthur's device flying over the new city was a clear statement of the connection between the ancient king and his successors.

In the context of the prolonged Scottish conflict, the medieval English deployment of Arthur's reputation as a conqueror is witnessed in a material sense across the British north. Malory makes a link between Dolorous/ Joyous Garde and two Northumbrian castles, Alnwick and Bamburgh, although he refuses to decide between these two possibilities (p. 1257.24–8 [xxi.12]). It has long been noted that Malory is likely to have personally participated in a military campaign that brought him into contact with these fortresses. Although Malory may well have had a contemporary political motivation to make the topographical identifications that he does, he is also transmitting a textual tradition associating Lancelot's castle with Bamburgh that is found in one of his sources, John Hardyng's *Chronicle*. The confusion arises from Geoffrey of Monmouth, who claimed that a minor king, Ebrauke, founded both York and Mount Dolorous; Geffrei Gaimar later links Mount Dolorous to Bamburgh, and Hardyng links this place to Dolorous Garde in the first version of his chronicle. Richard Moll argues that while we cannot draw a 'coherent stemma of transmission' from these details, they do 'point to a tradition which circulated in a variety of formats' – in other words, the tendency to draw links between places with similar names, or to associate historical places with legendary figures, was widespread. For Malory this particular transmission 'furthers his own thematic aims' and helps him 'to strengthen the resonance between Arthurian discord and contemporary events'.[14] For example, Malory throughout his book evinces a distrust of the Scots and a keen awareness of the need for strength along the northern border, a strength historically associated with the Wardens of the March.[15]

The association of Lancelot with Ebrauke and Joyous Garde is potentially even more complex: just as Gaimar had added Bamburgh to Ebrauke's foundations, so Rauf de Boun added Nottingham in his *Le Petit Bruit* (*c.* 1309), which may have prompted an otherwise unattested identification of Joyous Garde with Nottingham in the Auchinleck manuscript version of the *Short English Metrical Chronicle* (*c.* 1330).[16] This link was first explored by Thorlac Turville-Petre, who argued that Lancelot's rescue and protection of the queen at Joyous Garde could be used by the chronicler to comment on 'a much more recent memory of Roger Mortimer and Queen Isabella in 1330 barricading themselves into Nottingham Castle' against the forces of her son Edward III.[17] Although the historical episode ended badly for Mortimer, the Auchinleck text allows for a reconciliation between Arthur and Lancelot at Glastonbury (where they hold a Round Table), which may be influenced by yet another geographical tradition – the reconciliation between Arthur and Guinevere's abductor Melwas in Caradoc of Llancarfan's *Vita Gildae* (*c.* 1130).[18]

Numerous British sites were imbued with enduring Arthurian connotations through the influence of Geoffrey's *History*, and it is often these same places which maintain such an association throughout the centuries, frequently resurfacing in modern Arthurian literature and on the ever-popular Arthurian tourist trail.

Origins and endings: Tintagel Castle and Glastonbury Abbey

While topographical boundaries such as the Humber mark the physical limits of Arthurian Britain (as opposed to his wider European empire), the bounds of Arthur's life were also celebrated in the physical environment of medieval Britain. Tintagel Castle is well known today as the legendary site of Arthur's conception, and this fictional history has prompted intense archaeological interest which, somewhat perversely, has obscured an already murky historical reality. Tintagel seems to have been inhabited in the years following withdrawal of the Roman legions from Britain, and was connected through trade with the continent and the Mediterranean: however, it remains something of a mystery why Geoffrey identifies Tintagel as the site of Arthur's conception. Regardless of his motivations, Geoffrey's narrative of Uther's cuckolding of Gorlois marks the beginning of Tintagel's significance as an Arthurian place: Henry Fitzcount, who administered the Earldom of Cornwall on behalf of King John, granted the castle of Tintagel to Gervase de Hornacot, who immediately changed his name to Gervase de Tintagel. At some point between the Domesday Book in 1086 and Geoffrey's *History*, a castle was constructed at Tintagel, and this castle became known as the place where Arthur was conceived.

The family of de Hornacot only held the castle until 1233, before it passed into the hands of Richard, a brother of Henry III, who had been given the Earldom of Cornwall in 1227, the year after having lost possession of the French lands of Poitou.[19] As an outsider Richard may have felt the need to ingratiate himself with his Cornish subjects. Cornwall, although no longer widely considered one of the British nations alongside England, Wales, Scotland and Ireland (at least in the devolutionary sense), maintained a strong sense of independence throughout the Middle Ages, and it was only following Henry VII's victory at Bosworth Field that Cornish culture began to be fully absorbed into the English nation. In 1235 the Cornish could still view their new Earl, the King's brother, as a foreign interloper – and although Cornish rebellions never met with any marked success, they were nonetheless common occurrences. Furthermore, in addition to his interests in strengthening his hold over Cornwall, Richard also had wider ambitions within England and, indeed, across continental Europe. The legendary significance of the castle at Tintagel must have seemed like a potential goldmine of symbolic potential for an ambitious noble like Richard.

Richard lost no time in obtaining the estates around Tintagel, acquiring them at great cost from the de Hornacot family. Once he had possession of the lands he rebuilt much of the castle, producing the bulk of that which still stands on the site today. It seems likely that Richard's interest in Tintagel was very much of an antiquarian and symbolic nature, as there would have been little practical reason for him to rebuild the castle at such great expense. The location had little strategic purpose, and it was expensive to build, maintain and provision: indeed, the headland itself was far from ideal terrain for the kind of grand-scale building Richard intended. Major engineering was required to level the land, and the castle itself seemed to hang from the cliffs. The castle was built in an antiquated style, with none of the modern features that Richard incorporated into the castle that he rebuilt at nearby Launceston. Presenting himself as the heir to Arthur in a ready-made fantasy castle seems to have been much more about his political image rather than any practical need. Richard's ambition to link himself to and thereby exploit the legendary Arthur could not be any plainer, and what is more, it seems to have worked. His brother-in-law Frederick II was the Holy Roman Emperor, ruler of Germany, and Richard had high hopes of being named as his successor: in 1256, while he was still in Cornwall, this personal dream came true, and he was named 'King of the Romans', although the political realities of the time never allowed him to be crowned thus by the Pope. Richard's rebuilding of the castle at Tintagel transformed it from a minor coastal stronghold into a conscious historical statement about Arthur, about Cornwall, and about Richard himself. Just as Edward I's Round Table helped to identify Winchester as Camelot, the walls of Richard's Tintagel Castle soon became the very walls that had witnessed the machinations of Merlin and the conception of Arthur. In trying to associate himself with the aura of King Arthur, Richard helped to fix one Arthurian story firmly to a specific historical place.

While the site of Arthur's conception became attached to Tintagel, the location of Arthur's final resting place has always been one of the most debated of issues within the Arthurian legends: what did happen to Arthur, and if he did die, then where was he buried? Geoffrey of Monmouth established the basic outline for Arthur's defeat and destiny, recounting that Arthur was mortally wounded and carried off to the Isle of Avalon, in order that his wounds might be attended to (Thorpe, ix.2, p. 261). He then passes on the crown of Britain to his cousin Constantine, and disappears from Geoffrey's history. This sparse narrative is later embellished by Geoffrey in his *Life of Merlin* (c. 1150), where he relates how the wounded Arthur is entrusted to the care of nine sisters, led by their leader Morgan, who inhabit the blessed Isle of Apples (Avalon).[20] Geoffrey here transmits the Celtic tradition that Arthur did not in fact die, but rather was carried off to some kind of otherworld, an earthly paradise. The story of Arthur's withdrawal to Avalon serves to create a sense of lasting ambiguity as to his final fate, and lies at the heart of the tradition that he would recover and lie in wait until his people needed him once more. This aspect of the legends shapes Arthurian geography: the sleeping Arthur is placed in a variety of specific locales: he is said to remain in Avalon; to sleep in a cave under Snowdonia; or even to rule in the Antipodes. The common factor in all these stories is a strongly held belief in his eventual return – a return that is often linked to a revival of the British nation. The wide dispersal of the legend across the British Isles suggests a competitive sense of local pride that became attached to such stories. However, for the English kings, the persistence of rumours of Arthur's return presented a continuing problem, in that it seemed to create a focus for rebellions and uprisings in the Celtic territories in which they increasingly wished to assert their political control. The myth of Arthur's return is repeatedly associated with Welsh rebellions of the 1130s, and even if the English did not themselves believe in such superstitious folklore, they clearly felt that it had a significant unsettling effect upon their Welsh subjects. Faced with such a troublesome legend, surely the following thought must have crossed their minds: if only it could be demonstrated that Arthur was in fact dead, preferably in some highly visible and incontrovertible fashion.

In 1191, the monks of Glastonbury Abbey made a discovery that seems to have been tailor-made to solve this very problem. In the grounds of their abbey they came across the long-lost grave of King Arthur himself. Gerald of Wales in his *Speculum Ecclesiae* (*c.* 1215) relates the finding and exhumation of the king's body in the graveyard of the abbey, lying with his wife in a grave that the monks discovered between two ancient inscribed pyramids in the abbey grounds.[21] The remains were raised from the grave and transferred by the monks to a magnificent tomb in the great church itself. Along with the two bodies, a vital piece of evidence was also found: a lead cross, engraved in ancient Latin characters, which declared that 'Here lies buried the renowned King Arthur, with Guinevere his second wife, in the Isle of Avalon'. This relic of the Arthurian past, Arthur's own grave marker, proved to the monks that this was indeed the grave for which they had been searching for so long.

Just why the monks decided to search for the grave of Arthur has long been debated, but the chronicler Gerald of Wales attributes their explorations to the desires of King Henry II.[22] Henry, Gerald tells us, had received secret information from a Welsh bard as to the location of Arthur's final resting place. Henry's interest in finding the grave of Arthur is a complex issue. We have only Gerald of Wales' account to tell us that Henry was behind the search, and it is entirely possible that this was a story that was invented either by the Glastonbury monks, in order to place a royal seal of approval on their discovery, or even by Gerald himself. If, on the other hand, the record of Henry's interest is authentic, then we have to ask what benefit he may have been seeking in encouraging the monks to find the grave. For Henry, the benefits would have been two-fold. First, the discovery would have quashed the persistent rumours of Arthur's return, thus, so Henry hoped, greatly diminishing value of Arthur as a symbol of Celtic national feeling. Second, the prestige involved in being the custodian of such remains as those of the legendary Arthur would have aided Henry's cause both at home in Britain and on the Continent. If the European kings and princes were impressed with the Round Table, then how much more impressed would they have been by Arthur's tomb and bones? As a legendary king of England and of a wider empire, Arthur acted as a symbol through which Henry could have glorified his identity as an English king of a British empire, in a similar fashion to the propaganda use that had been made of Charlemagne by the French Capetian kings.

What made Glastonbury such a convincing location for Arthur's grave? The answer lies in a tradition linking Arthur and Glastonbury, the origins of which can be found in Caradoc of Llancarfan's *Vita Gildae*, which first established the Arthurian provenance of Glastonbury. In Caradoc's narrative, Glastonbury is besieged by Arthur after his wife Gwenhwyfar has been abducted imprisoned there by King Melwas. When the abbot of Glastonbury discovers this, he intervenes between the two forces and negotiates the peaceful return of the queen. In return, the two kings then endow numerous lands upon the abbey. One important motivation that seems to lie behind Caradoc's account is an attempt to provide an origin story for the traditional wealth and privileges of the abbey. Such tales are commonplace in the *Vitae* of saints, and were used to add the weight of history to the claims of a particular monastic house. In Caradoc's case, his Glastonbury anecdote in the *Vita Gildae* had the added effect of establishing a lasting link between the abbey and Arthur. From this brief beginning, Glastonbury's Arthurian connections proliferated during the medieval period. The discovery of his grave was only the first such link that was made. During the next few hundred years Glastonbury became increasingly linked with Joseph of Arimathea and the Holy Grail, as well as with other Arthurian objects such as Craddok's mantle and the bones of Mordred.

Although the 1191 discovery and exhumation of Arthur's body may likely appear to be an obvious fraud to a modern interpreter of the events, the story seems to have been largely accepted by the chroniclers of the time, and quickly became established as part of the Arthurian chronology. Gervase of Canterbury, writing in 1205, demonstrates the belief in this addition to the legend, as can be seen by the changes that he makes to it in composing his own *Chronicle of the Kings*.[23] Taking his narrative from Geoffrey of Monmouth, Gervase follows his source faithfully except when it comes to the location of Arthur's burial, which he places firmly in the abbey at Glastonbury. From this first integration of the Glastonbury grave into the Arthurian legends, the event becomes a standard feature of many retellings of the myths. However, if the intention of the discovery of the grave had been to completely stamp out all stories of Arthur's possible return, then its success is questionable. Tales of Arthur as 'the sleeping king' continued to be told, especially in the Celtic regions of Britain, a narrative that Malory integrates into his version of the final days of Arthur. Malory's Arthur, attended by Sir Bedivere, is led away in a ship by a company of women including Morgan le Fay and Nimue. The next morning Bedivere, having wandered disconsolate all the long night, arrives at a chapel, which is later identified as Glastonbury. Inside this chapel he finds a hermit who is grovelling in tears next to Arthur's newly constructed tomb.

Later, however, Malory records the uncertainty that still exists regarding Arthur's true fate:

> yet som men say in many partys of Inglonde that kynge Arthure ys nat dede, but had by the wyll of oure Lorde Jesu into another place; and men say that he shall com agayne, and he shall wynne the Holy Crosse. Yet I woll nat say that hit shall be so, but rather I wolde sey: here in thys worlde he chaunged hys lyff. And many men say that there ys wrytten uppon the tumbe thys: HIC IACET ARTHURUS, REX QUONDAM REXQUE FUTURUS.
>
> (p. 1242.22–9 [XXI.7])

Despite the persistence of such doubts about whether Arthur had in fact died, the 'discovery' of Arthur's grave had established Glastonbury firmly in the popular consciousness as the location of his grave. Furthermore, the exhumation had reinforced the abbey's reputation as an Arthurian site. Glastonbury's place within Britain's 'mythical geography' has a great deal to do with its reputation as an Arthurian site, and the 1191 excavation can be seen to have played an important part in the construction of this reputation.

The success of Glastonbury's Arthurian programme has lasted well beyond the specific historical context which produced it, and continues to exert an influence in subcultures which are actively disengaged from traditional Christianity or patriarchal empire-building. The twentieth-century new-age movements of Wicca and women's spirituality have found an Arthurian culmination in, and in turn were strongly influenced by, the success of Marion Zimmer Bradley's novel *The Mists of Avalon*: Glastonbury is once again the historical Avalon, in Bradley's view co-opted by an intolerant and fundamentalist Christianity. Recent depictions of Glastonbury Tor in Arthurian texts are rarely exclusively Christian, but the links between Arthur and the place remain strong, attracting new forms of spirituality which understand Arthur and the Celtic world in a fluid manner which would surely alarm the monks and kings who originally claimed Arthur's body for themselves.

Material remains

If medieval English authors were eager to associate Arthur and his mythical geography with real places in the British landscape, other Englishmen were similarly interested in providing smaller but no less arresting proofs of the king's historical existence. While Caxton, in his preface to Malory's *Morte Darthur*, mentions Glastonbury as the first proof of Arthur's historicity, he moves on to list how 'in dyvers places of Englond many remembraunces ben yet of hym and shall remayne perpetually' (p. cxliv). Caxton's promise of perpetuity has turned out to be somewhat optimistic: Winchester's Round Table can still be seen, but the other items have all long since disappeared.

There seem to have been many more 'proofs' in existence than those Caxton records, as he himself indicates when he states that there were 'many other thynges'. No mere curiosities, many of these tangible Arthurian proofs were deployed as historical evidence in the construction of a precedent for medieval English imperial power, and – as we have seen in the case of Glastonbury – such objects often accumulated at sites of royal or institutional importance.

The shrine of Edward the Confessor in Westminster Abbey was one such site, and held at least one of these pieces of evidence: a cracked piece of red wax which appeared to hold the imprint of Arthur's own imperial signet ring, complete with a majestic and bearded portrait of Arthur himself. The antiquarians John Leland and John Rastell both witnessed the seal in the sixteenth century (c. 1529 and c. 1540 respectively, although the first reference to it appears to be Caxton's in 1485).[24] The wide-spread importance of the seal was such that in the early seventeenth century an Oxford historian named Brian Twyne could make reference to the seal in one of the period's frequent debates concerning Arthur's historicity, as Caxton had done over a century earlier. Although the object itself is now lost, the words recorded on the seal have been preserved in slightly different forms by both Caxton and Leland: the seal claims imperial power for Arthur over a variety of territories, some expected (Britain, Gaul) and some surprising (Germany, Dacia). That this object could be found at the heart of English power should not surprise us, even if it probably had more to do initially with Westminster's ambitions than with those of the English monarchs; Rastell was told that the seal had adorned a charter granted to the monastic community at Westminster, which they claimed to have received from Arthur. The seal seems to have played an important role in Westminster endeavours to embellish the institution's importance, lending it some of the aura of the legendary king.

Arthur's seal was not the only Arthurian relic that was associated with Westminster during the medieval period: the abbey also once seems to have held that most significant piece of Arthur's regalia, his crown. The story of the acquisition of such a wondrous item is one of translation – in a geographical sense – and transformation. In 1282, the last native Welsh prince, Llywelyn ap Gruffydd, was defeated and slain in battle at Builth, and soon afterwards his crown found its way into the hands of King Edward I. Royal records indicate that two years later a goldsmith named Matthew de Columbariis was paid to gild the crown, transforming it into a visually impressive emblem of Edward's victory. In a ceremony later that same year, Edward's heir Alphonso presented the golden crown to the shrine of Edward the Confessor in Westminster. This crown, claims Edward's chronicler Pierre de Langtoft, was not just that of a defeated Welsh prince, but had in fact once been the crown of the legendary King Arthur.[25] Westminster Abbey would, within a few years, also hold the Stone of Scone, used for the coronation of the Scottish kings, and therefore of great propaganda value; it entered English possession when John Balliol, the King of Scots, surrendered himself and the rest of the Scottish regalia to Edward I in 1296. Arthur's crown, wrested from the hands of the last independent Welsh prince, would be a fitting companion to these other proofs of England's power over her Celtic neighbours. The ultimate fate of Arthur's crown is unknown: it disappears from Westminster Abbey's records by the middle of the fifteenth century.

Arthur's sword Excalibur, for many modern enthusiasts the pre-eminent symbol of his military prowess and royal power, also makes a number of appearances in the historical record, but oddly enough it appears only outside of Britain. Most famously, a 'Sword of Arthur' is said to have been in Henry V's baggage during the victory against the French at Agincourt, perhaps magically accounting for the overwhelming nature of Henry's victory. Excalibur also makes an earlier appearance in Sicily, when Richard the Lionheart presents the sword to King Tancred as a gift in exchange for a silver ring, as a sign of peace and reconciliation between the two monarchs after a brief period of armed conflict. The true nature of this sword remains unknown: the chronicler Pierre de Langtoft claimed that it had been found at Arthur's side when his body was first exhumed at Glastonbury, but contemporary records of that event do not seem to bear this out.[26] In the case of Excalibur, it seems likely that the Arthurian story itself acted to prevent a proliferation of Excaliburs, as the return of the sword to the lake is an essential feature of many romance accounts of Arthur's death.

Conclusion

The desire to locate Arthur in the landscape did not end with the Middle Ages, nor with the Tudor dynasty's efforts to imbue itself with an Arthurian aura. Archaeologists have linked various sites with the legendary Camelot: Colchester, and most famously Cadbury Castle hill fort. Arthur himself is an object of regional dispute: while some scholars now believe that a 'historical' Arthur may have held power somewhere in lowland Scotland – on the basis of the early testimony of his name in the northern poem *The Gododdin* (possibly ninth century) – most still consider Wales or Cornwall to be the likeliest stage for his activities.[27] The discovery of the 'Artognou' stone at Tintagel, which tantalisingly locates an Arthur-like name from the sixth century in a site traditionally associated with Arthur, excited much international interest. Even today, this need to claim Arthur for a particular region can have political echoes. Alan Wilson, the owner of the remains of yet another sacred spot claiming Arthur's grave (St Peter's Super Montem Church in Bridgend, in south-east Wales), criticised Jerry Bruckheimer's film *King Arthur* (2004) for ignoring Arthur's historical connections with Wales when they chose to film in Somerset. Wilson's complaint reached the British House of Commons through the Member of Parliament for Newport, near Caerleon, who argued that there would be a substantial loss of Welsh pride and tourism prospects should their connection with Arthur be severed in the eyes of the public. Arthur – and Arthurian geography – still matters, even if the issue has become more a matter of tourism than of royal power.

NOTES

1 T. A. Shippey, 'Winchester in the Anglo-Saxon Period and After', in *Winchester: History and Literature*, ed. Simon Barker and Colin Haydon (Winchester: King Alfred's College, 1992), pp. 1–21 (p. 18).

2 Quoted in Andrea Hopkins, *Chronicles of King Arthur* (London: Collins and Brown, 1993), p. 35.

3 Martin Biddle, 'The Making of the Round Table', in *King Arthur's Round Table*, ed. Biddle (Woodbridge: Boydell Press, 2000), pp. 337–92 (pp. 361–4).

4 Donald L. Hoffman, 'Rusticiano da Pisa', in *The New Arthurian Encyclopedia*, ed. Norris J. Lacy (New York: Garland, 1986, rev. edn 1991), p. 392.

5 *Mort Artu*, ch. 3, p. 3; Lacy IV, p. 91.

6 Michelle Warren, *History on the Edge: Excalibur and the Borders of Britain, 1100–1300* (Minneapolis, MN: University of Minnesota Press, 2000), *passim* (esp. pp. 36–9).

7 Roger Sherman Loomis, *Arthurian Tradition and Chrétien de Troyes* (New York: Columbia University Press, 1949), p. 224.

8 The foundational article on Nennius is Kenneth Jackson, 'Once Again Arthur's Battles', *Modern Philology*, 43.1 (1945), 44–57. The subject has been revisited often, most recently and convincingly by N. J. Higham, *King Arthur: Myth-Making and History* (London and New York: Routledge, 2002).

9 Geoffrey Ashe, *The Discovery of King Arthur* (London: Guild Publishing, 1985), pp. 116–17; P. J. C. Field, 'Gildas and the City of the Legions', *The Heroic Age*, 1 (Spring/Summer, 1999), www.mun.ca/mst/heroicage/issues/1/hagcl.htm.

10 Geoffrey Ashe, 'Extending the Map', in *The Quest for Arthur's Britain*, ed. Ashe (London: Paladin Books, 1968), pp. 149–62 (pp. 150–1).

11 Ashe, *Discovery*, p. 120.

12 As first suggested by O. S. G. Crawford, 'Arthur and his battles', *Antiquity*, 9 (1935), 277–91.

13 *Lancelot*, VII.xxiva–xxva; trans. Lacy, II.75–85.

14 Richard J. Moll, 'Ebrauke and the Politics of Arthurian Geography', *Arthuriana*, 15.4 (2005), 65–71 (p. 68–9).

15 Cory J. Rushton, '"Of an uncouthe stede": The Scottish Knight in Middle English Arthurian Romances', in *The Scots and Medieval Arthurian Legend*,

ed. Rhiannon Purdie and Nicola Royan, Arthurian Studies 61 (Cambridge: D. S. Brewer, 2005), pp. 109–19 (pp. 118–19).

16 Moll, 'Ebrauke', p. 66. The passage is found in *An Anonymous Short English Metrical Chronicle*, lines 1071–90, ed. Ewald Zettl, EETS, o.s. 196 (Oxford University Press, 1935).

17 Thorlac Turville-Petre, *England the Nation: Language, Literature, and National Identity, 1290–1340* (Oxford: Clarendon Press, 1996), p. 111.

18 *Short English Metrical Chronicle*, lines 1085–102; Richard J. Moll, *Before Malory: Reading Arthur in Later Medieval England* (University of Toronto Press, 2003), pp. 28–9; *Two Lives of Gildas by a monk of Ruys and Caradoc of Llancarfan*, trans. Hugh Williams (London, 1899; Felinfach: Llanerch, 1990).

19 Robert Rouse and Cory J. Rushton, *The Medieval Quest for Arthur* (Stroud: Tempus, 2005), pp. 120–3.

20 *Life of Merlin: Vita Merlini*, ed. and trans. Basil Clarke (Cardiff: University of Wales Press, 1973), lines 916ff.

21 James P. Carley, 'Arthur in English History', in *AoE*, pp. 47–58.

22 *Giraldi Cambrensis Opera, scilicet, Speculum Ecclesiae*, ed. J. S. Brewer, Rolls Series 21 (London, 1873; 1964), vol. 4, pp. 47–51.

23 R. H. Fletcher, *The Arthurian Material in the Chronicles, especially those of Great Britain and France* (Boston: Ginn and Company, 1906), p. 202.

24 E. M. R. Ditmas, 'The Cult of Arthurian Relics', *Folklore*, 75 (1964), 19–33 (pp. 29–30); Rouse and Rushton, *Medieval Quest*, pp. 98–100.

25 Rouse and Rushton, *Medieval Quest*, pp. 92–98, 100–5.

26 *Ibid.*, p. 79.

27 Aneirin, *Y Gododdin*, ed. and trans. A. O. H. Jarman, *Y Gododdin: Britain's Oldest Heroic Poem*, The Welsh Classics 3 (Llandysul: Gomer, 1989).Figure 1 *The Sleep of King Arthur in Avalon* by Edward Burne-Jones. By permission of the Museo De Arte De Ponce, Puerto Rico.

FURTHER READING

This bibliography contains suggestions for further reading for each chapter. The suggested reading for the introduction focuses on reference works, studies of broad Arthurian themes, and studies of the literary, historical and cultural background; it also includes a list of recommended websites. More detailed information about editions and critical studies of individual texts can be found in the indispensable volumes in the series *Arthurian Literature in the Middle Ages* (see below).

REFERENCE BOOKS

Ackerman, R.W., *An Index of the Arthurian Names in Middle English*, Stanford University Press and Oxford University Press, 1952.

The Arthurian Annals: The Tradition in English from 1250 to 2000, ed. Daniel P. Nastali and Phillip C. Boardman, 2 vols., Oxford University Press, 2004.

Arthurian Bibliography I and II, ed. C. Pickford and R. Last, Arthurian Studies 3 and 6, 2 vols., Cambridge: D. S. Brewer, 1981–3.

Arthurian Bibliography III: 1978–1992, ed. Caroline Palmer, Arthurian Studies 31, Cambridge: D. S. Brewer, 1998.

Arthurian Bibliography IV: 1993–1998, ed. Elaine Barber, Arthurian Studies 49, Cambridge: D. S. Brewer, 2002.

Bruce, Christopher W., *The Arthurian Name Dictionary*, Garland Reference Library of the Humanities 2063, New York: Garland, 1998.

Flutre, Louis-Ferdinand, *Table des noms propres avec toutes leurs variantes, figurant dans les romans du Moyen Age écrits en français ou en provençal*, Poitiers: Centre d'études supérieures de civilisation médiévale, 1962.

Guerreau-Jalabert, Anita, *Index des motifs narratifs dans les romans arthuriens en vers des XXe et XIIIe siècles*, Publications romanes et françaises 202, Geneva: Droz, 1992.

Lacy, Norris J., ed., *A History of Arthurian Scholarship*, Arthurian Studies 65, Cambridge: D. S. Brewer, 2006.

ed., *Medieval Arthurian Literature: A Guide to Recent Research*, Garland Reference Library of the Humanities 1055, New York and London: Garland, 1996.

ed., *New Arthurian Encyclopedia*, expanded and revised edn, New York: Garland, 1991, and London: St James's Press, 1993.

ed., *The New Arthurian Encyclopedia, Updated Paperback Edition*, Garland Reference Library of the Humanities 931, New York: Garland, 1996. [Reissue of *The New Arthurian Encyclopedia*, with supplement for years 1990–5.]

Lacy, Norris J. and Geoffrey Ashe, eds., *The Arthurian Handbook*, 2nd edn, Garland Reference Library of the Humanities 765, New York: Garland, 1997.

Lacy, Norris J. and Raymond H. Thompson, eds., with Marianne E. Kalinke, Geoffrey Ashe, and Sandra Ness Ihle, 'The New Arthurian Encyclopedia, Supplement 1', *Arthurian Yearbook*, 3 (1993), 227–69.

eds., 'Arthurian Literature, Art, and Film, 1995–99', *Arthurian Literature*, 18 (2001), 193–255.

Mediavilla, Cindy, *Arthurian Fiction: An Annotated Bibliography*, Lanham, MD: Scarecrow, 1999.

Olton, Bert, *Arthurian Legends on Film and Television*, Jefferson, NC: McFarland, 2000.

Reiss, Edmund, Louise Horner and Beverly Taylor, *Arthurian Legend and Literature: An Annotated Bibliography*, vol. 1, Garland Reference Library of the Humanities 415, New York: Garland, 1984.

Ruck, E. H., *An Index of Themes and Motifs in Twelfth-Century French Arthurian Poetry*, Arthurian Studies 25, Cambridge: D. S. Brewer, 1991.

Thompson, Raymond H. and Norris J. Lacy, eds., 'The Arthurian Legend in Literature, Popular Culture, and the Performing Arts, 1999–2004', *Arthurian Literature*, 22 (2005), 100–75.

eds., 'Arthurian Literature and Film, 2004–7', forthcoming in *Arthurian Literature*, 26.

West, G., *Index of Proper Names in French Arthurian Prose Romances*, University of Toronto Press, 1978.

Index of Proper Names in French Arthurian Verse Romances 1150–1300, University of Toronto Press, 1982.

JOURNALS

Arthurian Yearbook [published 1991–3].

Arthurian Literature, annual volume published by Boydell & Brewer.

Arthuriana, official journal of the International Arthurian Society; amalgamated *Quondam et Futurus* and *Arthurian Interpretations*.

Bulletin bibliographique de la société internationale Arthurienne / Bibliographical Bulletin of the International Arthurian Society (BBIAS).

SERIES

Arthurian Archives: medieval Arthurian texts with facing page translations, Boydell & Brewer.

Arthurian Poets, Boydell & Brewer.

Arthurian Studies, Boydell & Brewer.

Studies in Arthurian and Courtly Cultures, Palgrave MacMillan.

Studies in Medievalism, Boydell & Brewer.

Monographs and collections of essays:

Arthurian Literature in the Middle Ages, series editors †W. R. J. Barron and Ad Putter, Cardiff: University of Wales Press. Volumes published so far:

The Arthur of the Welsh: The Arthurian Legend in Medieval Welsh Literature, ed. Rachel Bromwich, A. O. H. Jarman and Brynley Roberts, Arthurian Literature in the Middle Ages 1 (1991).

The Arthur of the English: The Arthurian Legend in Medieval English Life and Literature, ed. W. R. J. Barron, Arthurian Literature in the Middle Ages 2 (1999).

The Arthur of the Germans: The Arthurian Legend in Medieval German and Dutch Literature, ed. W. H. Jackson and S. A. Ranawake, Arthurian Literature in the Middle Ages 3 (2000).

The Arthur of the French: The Arthurian Legend in Medieval French and Occitan Literature, ed. Glyn S. Burgess and Karen Pratt, Arthurian Literature in the Middle Ages 4 (2006).

Forthcoming volumes:

The Arthur of the Iberians, ed. David Hook.

The Arthur of the Italians, ed. Gloria Allaire and Regina Psaki.

The Arthur of the Latin Tradition, ed. Siân Echard.

The Arthur of the Northmen, ed. Marianne Kalinke.

Arthurian Characters and Themes, series editor Norris J. Lacy:

King Arthur: A Casebook, ed. Edward Donald Kennedy, Arthurian Characters and Themes 1, New York and London: Garland, 1996.

Tristan and Isolde: A Casebook, ed. Joan Tasker Grimbert, Arthurian Characters and Themes 2, New York and London: Garland, 1995.

Arthurian Women: A Casebook, ed. Thelma Fenster, Arthurian Characters and Themes 3, New York and London: Garland, 1996.

Lancelot and Guinevere: A Casebook, ed. Lori J. Walters, Arthurian Characters and Themes 4, New York and London: Garland, 1996.

The Grail: A Casebook, ed. Dhira Mahoney, Arthurian Characters and Themes 5, New York and London: Garland, 2000.

Perceval/Parzifal: A Casebook, ed. Arthur Groos and Norris J. Lacy, Arthurian Characters and Themes 6, New York and London: Routledge, 2002.

Merlin: A Casebook, ed. Peter H. Goodrich and Raymond H. Thompson, Arthurian Characters and Themes 7, New York and London: Routledge, 2003.

Gawain: A Casebook, ed. Raymond H. Thompson and Keith Busby, Arthurian Characters and Themes 8, New York and London: Routledge, 2006.

COMPANIONS

A Companion to Arthurian Literature, ed. Helen Fulton, Oxford: Wiley-Blackwell, 2008.

A Companion to Chrétien de Troyes, ed. Norris J. Lacy and Joan Tasker Grimbert, Arthurian Studies 63, Cambridge: D. S. Brewer, 2005.

A Companion to the Gawain Poet, ed. Derek Brewer and Jonathan Gibson, Arthurian Studies 38, Cambridge: D. S. Brewer, 1997.

A Companion to Gottfried von Strassburg's 'Tristan', ed. Will Hasty, Studies in German Literature, Linguistics and Culture, Rochester, NY: Camden House, 2003.

A Companion to the Works of Hartmann von Aue, ed. Francis G. Gentry, Studies in German Literature, Linguistics and Culture, Rochester, NY: Camden House, 2003.

A Companion to the Lancelot-Grail Cycle, ed. Carol Dover, Arthurian Studies 54, Cambridge: D. S. Brewer, 2003.

A Companion to Malory, ed. Elizabeth Archibald and A. S. G. Edwards, Arthurian Studies 37, Cambridge: D. S. Brewer, 1996.

The Cambridge Companion to Medieval French Literature, ed. Simon Gaunt and Sarah Kay, Cambridge University Press, 2008.

The Cambridge Companion to Medieval Romance, ed. Roberta L. Krueger, Cambridge University Press, 2000.

A Companion to Romance: From Classical to Contemporary, ed. Corinne Saunders, Oxford: Blackwell, 2004.

A Companion to Wace, ed. Françoise H. M. Le Saux, Cambridge: D. S. Brewer, 2005.

A Companion to Wolfram's 'Parzival', ed. Will Hasty, Columbia, SC: Camden House, 1999.

CRITICAL STUDIES

Archibald, Elizabeth, 'Lancelot as Lover in the English Tradition before Malory', in *Arthurian Studies in Honour of P. J. C. Field*, ed. Bonnie Wheeler, Arthurian Studies 57, Cambridge: D. S. Brewer, 2004, pp. 199–216.

Ashe, Geoffrey, *Arthurian Britain*, Glastonbury: Gothic Image, 1997.

Auerbach, Erich, *Mimesis: The Representation of Reality in Western Literature*, trans. Willard R. Trask, Princeton University Press, 1953.

Barber, Richard, *The Arthurian Legends: An Illustrated Anthology*, Woodbridge: Boydell, 1979; repr. 1987.

The Holy Grail: Imagination and Belief, London: Allen Lane, 2004.

King Arthur: Hero and Legend, 3rd edn revised and extended, Woodbridge: Boydell Press, 1986.

The Knight and Chivalry, revised edn, Woodbridge: Boydell Press, 1995.

ed., *King Arthur in Music*, Arthurian Studies 52, Cambridge: D.S. Brewer, 2002.

Barber, Richard and Juliet Barker, *Tournaments: Jousts, Chivalry and Pageants in the Middle Ages*, Woodbridge: Boydell Press, 1989.

Barczewski, Stephanie, *Myth and National Identity in Nineteenth-Century Britain: The Legends of King Arthur and Robin Hood*, Oxford University Press, 2000.

Baswell, Christopher and William Sharpe, eds., *The Passing of Arthur*, New York and London: Garland, 1988.

Besamusca, Bart, *The Book of Lancelot: The Middle Dutch 'Lancelot' Compilation and the Medieval Tradition of Narrative Cycles*, Arthurian Studies 53, Cambridge: D. S. Brewer, 2003.

ed., *Cyclification:The Development of Narrative Cycles in the Chansons de gestes and the Arthurian Romances*, Amsterdam: North Holland, 1994.

Biddle, Martin, ed., *King Arthur's Round Table*, Woodbridge: Boydell, 2000.

Brewer, Elisabeth, *T. H. White's 'The Once and Future King'*, Arthurian Studies 30, Cambridge: D.S. Brewer, 1993.

Bruce, James D., *The Evolution of Arthurian Romance from the Beginnings Down to the Year 1300*, 2 vols., Göttingen: Vandenhoeck & Ruprecht, and Baltimore: Johns Hopkins University Press, 1923.

Bryden, Inga, *Reinventing King Arthur: The Arthurian Legends in Victorian Culture*, Aldershot: Ashgate, 2005.

Bumke, Joachim, *Courtly Culture in the High Middle Ages*, trans. Thomas Dunlap, Berkeley and Oxford: University of California Press, 1991.

Busby, Keith, *Codex and Context: Reading Old French Verse Narrative in Manuscript*, 2 vols., Amsterdam: Rodopi, 2002.

Gauvain in Old French Literature, Amsterdam: Rodopi, 1980.

ed., *Word and Image in Arthurian Literature*, New York: Garland, 1996.

Carley, James P., ed., *Glastonbury Abbey and the Arthurian Tradition*, Arthurian Studies 44, Cambridge: D. S. Brewer, 2001.

Chambers, E.K., *Arthur of Britain*, London: Sidgwick and Jackson, 1927; repr. 1966.

Chênerie, Marie-Luce, *Le Chevalier errant dans les romans arthuriens en vers des XIIe et XIIIe siècles*, Publications romanes et françaises 172, Geneva: Droz, 1986.

Claassens, Geert H.M. and David F. Johnson, eds., *King Arthur in the Medieval Low Countries*, Leuven: Leuven University, 2000.

Cooper, Helen, *The English Romance in Time: Transforming Motifs from Geoffrey of Monmouth to the Death of Shakespeare*, Oxford University Press, 2004.

Dean, Christopher, *Arthur of England: English Attitudes to King Arthur and the Knights of the Round Table in the Middle Ages and the Renaissance*, University of Toronto Press, 1987.

Delcorno Branca, Daniela, *Tristano e Lancilotto in Italia: Studi di letteratura arturiana*, Ravenna: Longo, 1998.

Echard, Siân, *Arthurian Narrative in the Latin Tradition*, Cambridge University Press, 1998.

'"Hic est Artur": Reading Latin and Reading Arthur', in Lupack, *New Directions*, pp. 49–67.

Entwistle, William J., *The Arthurian Legend in the Literatures of the Spanish Peninsula*, London and New York: Dent, 1925.

Faral, Edmond, *La Légende arthurienne: études et documents*, 3 vols., Paris: Champion, 1929.

Finke, Laurie and Martin Shichtman, *King Arthur and the Myth of History*, Gainesville: University of Florida, 2004.

Fletcher, R.H., *The Arthurian Material in the Chronicles especially those of Great Britain and France*, Boston: Ginn, 1906.

Gardner, Edmund G., *The Arthurian Legend in Italian Literature*, London: Dent, 1930.

Gaunt, Simon, *Gender and Genre in Medieval French Literature*, Cambridge University Press, 1995.

Girouard, Mark, *The Return to Camelot: Chivalry and the English Gentleman*, New Haven, CT, and London: Yale University Press, 1981.

Glencross, Michael, *Reconstructing Camelot: French Romantic Medievalism and the Arthurian Tradition*, Arthurian Studies 36, Cambridge: D.S. Brewer, 1995.

Gowans, Linda, *Cei and the Arthurian Legend*, Arthurian Studies 18, Cambridge: D. S. Brewer, 1988.

Green, D.H., *The Beginnings of Medieval Romance: Fact and Fiction, 1150–1220*, Cambridge University Press, 2002.

Guerin, M. Victoria, *The Fall of Kings and Princes: Structure and Destruction in Arthurian Tragedy*, Stanford University Press, 1995.

Harty, Kevin J., ed., *Cinema Arthuriana: Essays on Arthurian Film*, Jefferson, NC: McFarland, 1991.

The Reel Middle Ages: American, Western and Eastern European, Middle Eastern and Asian Films About Medieval Europe, 2nd rev. edn, Jefferson, NC: McFarland, 2006.

ed., *King Arthur on Film: New Essays on Arthurian Cinema*, Jefferson, NC: McFarland, 1999.

Higham, N.J., *King Arthur: Myth-Making and History*, New York: Routledge, 2002.

Howey, Ann F., *Rewriting the Women of Camelot: Arthurian Popular Fiction and Feminism*, Westport, CT, and London: Greenwood, 2001.

Hutton, Ronald, *Witches, Druids and King Arthur: Studies in Paganism, Myth and Magic*, London: Hambledon & London, 2003.

Ingham, Patricia, *Sovereign Fantasies: Arthurian Romance and the Making of Britain*, Philadelphia, PA: University of Pennsylvania, 2001.

Kaeuper, Richard W., *Chivalry and Violence in Medieval Europe*, Oxford University Press, 1999.

Kalinke, Marianne E., *King Arthur North by North-West: The 'Matière de Bretagne' in Old Norse-Icelandic Romances*, Copenhagen: Reitzel, 1981.

Keen, Maurice, *Chivalry*, New Haven, CT: Yale University Press, 1984; repr. 2005.

Kelly, Douglas and Keith Busby, eds., *The Legacy of Chrétien de Troyes*, 2 vols., Amsterdam: Rodopi, 1987–8.

Kendrick, T. D., *British Antiquity*, London: Methuen, 1950.

Kennedy, Elspeth, 'Failure in Arthurian Romance', *Medium Ævum*, 50 (1991), 16–32; reprinted in *The Grail: A Casebook*, ed. Mahoney, pp. 279–300.

Knight, Stephen, *Arthurian Literature and Society*, London: Macmillan, 1983.

Lacy, Norris J., 'Arthurian Research in a New Century: Prospects and Projects', in Lupack, *New Directions*, pp. 1–20.

ed., *The Fortunes of Arthur*, Arthurian Studies 64, Cambridge: D.S. Brewer, 2005.

ed., *The Grail, the Quest, and the World of Arthur*, Arthurian Studies 72, Cambridge, D. S. Brewer, 2008.

ed., *Text and Intertext in Medieval Arthurian Literature*, Garland Reference Library of the Humanities 1997, New York: Garland, 1996.

Lacy, Norris J. and Raymond H. Thompson, eds., 'Arthurian Literature, Art, and Film, 1995–1999', *Arthurian Literature*, 18 (2001), 193–255.

Lagorio, Valerie and Mildred Leake Day, eds., *King Arthur through the Ages*, 2 vols., Garland Reference Library of the Humanities 1269 and 1301, New York: Garland, 1990.

Larrington, Carolyne, 'The Enchantress, the Knight and the Cleric: Authorial Surrogates in Arthurian Romance', *Arthurian Literature*, 25 (2008), 43–65.

King Arthur's Enchantresses: Morgan and her Sisters in Arthurian Tradition, London: I. B. Tauris, 2006.

Loomis, R.S., ed., *Arthurian Literature in the Middle Ages: A Collaborative History*, Oxford: Clarendon Press, 1959.

Loomis, R.S. and Laura Hibbard Loomis, *Arthurian Legends in Medieval Art*, New York: Modern Language Association of America and Oxford University Press, 1938.

Lupack, Alan, ed., *New Directions in Arthurian Studies*, Arthurian Studies 51, Cambridge: D. S. Brewer, 2002.

Lupack, Alan and Barbara Tepa Lupack, *King Arthur in America*, Arthurian Studies 41, Cambridge: D. S. Brewer, 1999.

Lupack, Barbara Tepa, ed., *Adapting the Arthurian Legends for Children: Essays on Arthurian Juvenilia*, New York: Palgrave MacMillan, 2004.

Lupack, Barbara Tepa with Alan Lupack, *Illustrating Camelot*, Cambridge: D. S. Brewer, 2008.

McCracken, Peggy, *The Romance of Adultery: Queenship and Sexual Transgression in Old French Literature*, Philadelphia, PA: University of Pennsylvania Press, 1998.

Mancoff, Debra N., *The Return of King Arthur: The Legend through Victorian Eyes*, New York: Harry N. Abrams, 1995.

ed., *King Arthur's Modern Return*, Garland Reference Library of the Humanities 2022, New York: Garland, 1998.

Marino, John B., *The Grail Legend in Modern Literature*, Arthurian Studies 59, Cambridge: D. S. Brewer, 2004.

Mathis, Andrew E., *The King Arthur Myth in Modern American Fiction and Culture*, Jefferson, NC: McFarland, 2002.

Ménard, Philippe, *De Chrétien de Troyes au Tristan en prose: Etudes sur les romans de la Table Ronde*, Publications romanes et françaises 224, Geneva: Droz, 1999.

Merriman, James Douglas, *The Flower of Kings: A Study of the Arthurian Legend in England Between 1485 and 1835*, Lawrence, KA: University Press of Kansas, 1973.

Mertens, Volker, *Der deutsche Artusroman*, Stuttgart: Reclam, 1998.

Moll, Richard, *Before Malory: Reading Arthur in Later Medieval England*, University of Toronto, 2003.

Morris, Rosemary, *The Character of King Arthur in Medieval Literature*, Arthurian Studies 4, Cambridge: D. S. Brewer, 1982.

Oergel, Maike, *The Return of King Arthur and the Nibelungen: National Myth in Nineteenth-Century English and German Literature*, Berlin and New York: Walter de Gruyter, 1998.

Padel, O. J., *Arthur in Medieval Welsh Literature*, Cardiff: University of Wales Press, 2000.

Pearsall, Derek, *Arthurian Romance: A Short Introduction*, Oxford: Blackwell, 2003.

Poulson, Christine, *The Quest for the Grail: Arthurian Legend in British Art 1840–1920*, Manchester and New York: Manchester University Press, 1999.

Purdie, Rhiannon and Nicola Royan, eds., *The Scots and Medieval Arthurian Legend*, Arthurian Studies 61, Cambridge: D.S. Brewer, 2005.

Putter, Ad, 'Finding Time for Romance: Medieval Arthurian Literary History', *Medium Ævum*, 63 (1994), 1–16.

'Sir Gawain and the Green Knight' and French Arthurian Romance, Oxford: Clarendon Press, 1995.

Rouse, Robert and Cory J. Rushton, *The Medieval Quest for Arthur*, Stroud: Tempus, 2005.

Schmolke-Hasselmann, Beate, *The Evolution of Arthurian Romance: The Verse Tradition from Chrétien to Froissart*, trans. Margaret and Roger Middleton, Cambridge University Press, 1998.

Shichtman, Martin and James Carley, eds., *Culture and the King: Social Implications of the Arthurian Legend*, Albany: State University of New York, 1994.

Simpson, Roger, *Camelot Regained: The Arthurian Revival and Tennyson 1800–1849*, Arthurian Studies 21, Cambridge: D. S. Brewer, 1990.

Sklar, Elizabeth S. and Donald L. Hoffman, eds., *King Arthur in Popular Culture*, Jefferson, NC: McFarland & Company, 2002.

Stones, Alison, 'Arthurian Art after Loomis', in van Hoecke, *Arturus Rex*, II, pp. 21–78.

'Illustrating Lancelot and Guinevere', in *Lancelot and Guinevere: A Casebook*, ed. Walters, pp. 125–57.

'Seeing the Grail: Prolegomena to a Study of Grail Imagery in Arthurian Manuscripts', in *The Grail: A Casebook*, ed. Mahoney pp. 301–66.

Sweeney, Michelle, *Magic in Medieval Romance: A Study of Selected Romances from Chrétien de Troyes to Geoffrey Chaucer*, Dublin: Four Courts, 2000.

Taylor, Beverly and Elisabeth Brewer, *The Return of King Arthur: British and American Arthurian Literature since 1900*, Arthurian Studies 9, Cambridge: D. S. Brewer, 1983.

Thompson, Raymond H., *The Return from Avalon: A Study of the Arthurian Legend in Modern Fiction*, Westport, CT, and London: Greenwood, 1985.

Tolhurst, Fiona, 'The Once and Future Queen: The Development of Guenevere from Geoffrey of Monmouth to Malory', *BBIAS*, 50 (1998), 272–308.

Torregrossa, Michael, 'Camelot 3000 and Beyond: An Annotated Listing of Arthurian Comic Books Published in the United States, c. 1980–1998', *Arthuriana*, 9.1 (1999), 67–109.

Trachsler, Richard, *Clôtures du cycle Arthurien: étude et textes*, Publications romanes et françaises 215, Geneva: Droz, 1996.

Turville-Petre, Thorlac, *England the Nation: Language, Literature and National Identity, 1290–1340*, Oxford: Clarendon Press, 1996.

van Hoecke, Willy, *et al.*, eds., *Arturus Rex: Acta conventus Lovaniensis*, 2 vols., Leuven: Leuven University Press, 1991.

Vinaver, Eugène, *The Rise of Romance*, 1971; repr. Cambridge: D. S. Brewer, 1984.

Warren, Michelle R., *History on the Edge: Excalibur and the Borders of Britain, 1100–1300*, Minneapolis, MN: University of Minnesota, 2000.

Wheeler, Bonnie, ed., *Arthurian Studies in Honour of P. J. C. Field*, Arthurian Studies 57, Cambridge: D.S. Brewer, 2004.

Wheeler, Bonnie and Fiona Tolhurst, eds., *On Arthurian Women: Essays in Memory of Maureen Fries*, Dallas: Scriptorium, 2001.

Whitaker, Muriel, *The Legends of King Arthur in Art*, Arthurian Studies 22, Cambridge: D. S. Brewer, 1990.

Wolfzettel, Friedrich, ed., *Arthurian Romance and Gender: Selected Proceedings of the XVIIth International Arthurian Congress*, Amsterdam: Rodopi, 1995.

ed., *Artusroman und Intertextualität*, Giessen: Schmitz, 1990.

ed., *Das Wunderbare in der Arthurischen Literatur: Probleme und Perspektiven*, Tübingen: Niemeyer, 2003.

Wood, Juliette, 'The Selling of Arthur: Popular Culture and the Arthurian Legend', *Folklore in Use*, 2 (1994), 115–29.
Eternal Chalice: The Enduring Legend of the Holy Grail, London: I. B. Tauris, 2008.

KING ARTHUR ON THE WEB

The Camelot Project, 'Arthurian Texts, Images, Bibliographies and Basic Information' www.lib.rochester.edu/camelot. This site, maintained at the University of Rochester (USA), offers much reliable information and links to other useful sites; it also includes valuable bibliographies, for instance on Gaelic material.

Arthurian Resources, www.arthuriana.co.uk, is maintained by Dr Thomas Green. It focuses on the Welsh Arthurian tradition, and also includes links to other reliable sites.

Britannia History, www.britannia.com/history/h12.html, includes useful timelines and bibliography.

Heroic Age is an on-line journal for the history of Early Medieval North-Western Europe, maintained at Memorial University, Newfoundland: http://mun.ca/mst/heroicage.

THE EARLY ARTHUR: HISTORY AND MYTH

Anderson, Graham, *King Arthur in Antiquity*, London: Routledge, 2004.
Bachrach, Bernard S., 'The Questions of King Arthur's Existence, and of Romano-British Naval Operations', *Haskins Society Journal*, 2 (1990), 13–28.
Bromwich, Rachel and D. Simon Evans, eds., *Culhwch and Olwen*, Cardiff: University of Wales Press, 1992.
Dark, Ken, *Britain and the End of the Roman Empire*, Stroud: Tempus, 2000.
'Changing Places? 5th and 6th Century Culture in Britain and Ireland', *Minerva*, 13.6 (2002), 38–40.
Dumville, David, '"Nennius" and the "Historia Brittonum"', *Studia Celtica*, 10–11 (1975–6), 78–95.
Field, P. J. C., 'Nennius and his History', *Studia Celtica*, 30 (1996), 159–65.
Fulford, Michael J., 'Byzantium and Britain', *Medieval Archaeology*, 33 (1989), 1–5.
Green, Thomas, *Concepts of Arthur*, Stroud: Tempus, 2007.
Henig, Martin, 'Roman Britons after AD 410', *Archaeology*, 68 (2002), 9–12.
Higham, Nicholas, *King Arthur: Myth-Making and History*, London: Routledge, 2002.
Hutton, Ronald, 'Arthur and the Academics', in Ronald Hutton, *Witches, Druids and King Arthur: Studies in Paganism, Myth and Magic*, London: Hambledon & London, 2003, pp. 39–58.
Isaac, G. R., 'Readings in the History and Transmission of the "Gododdin"', *Cambrian Medieval Celtic Studies*, 37 (1999), 55–78.
Jackson, Kenneth Hurlstone, *The International Popular Tale and Early Welsh Tradition. The Gregynog Lectures 1961*, Cardiff: University of Wales Press, 1961.
Koch, John T., ed. and trans., *The Gododdin of Aneirin*, Cardiff: University of Wales Press, 1997.

Lapidge, Michael and David Dumville, eds., *Gildas: New Approaches*, Studies in Celtic History 5, Cambridge: Boydell Press, 1984.

Littleton, C. Scott, and A. C. Thomas, 'The Sarmatian Connection: New Light on the Origin of the Arthurian and Holy Grail Legends', *Journal of American Folklore*, 91 (1978), 512–27.

Morris, Christopher, 'Tintagel', *Current Archaeology*, 159 (1998), 84–8.

Ó hÓgáin, Dáithí, *Fionn Mac Cumhaill: Images of the Gaelic Hero*, Dublin: Gill and Macmillan, 1988.

Padel, O. J., *Arthur in Medieval Welsh Literature*, Cardiff: University of Wales Press, 2000.

'The Nature of Arthur', *Cambrian Medieval Celtic Studies*, 27 (1994), 1–31.

'A New Study of the *Gododdin*', *Cambrian Medieval Celtic Studies*, 35 (1998), 45–56.

Thomas, Charles, *English Heritage Book of Tintagel*, London: Batsford, 1993.

THE TWELFTH-CENTURY ARTHUR

Barber, Richard, *The Holy Grail: Imagination and Belief*, London: Allen Lane, 2004.

Bromwich, Rachel and D. Simon Evans, eds., *Culhwch and Olwen: An Edition and Study of the Oldest Arthurian Tale*, Cardiff: University of Wales Press, 1992.

Burgess, Glyn S., *Chrétien de Troyes: Erec et Enide*, Critical Guides to French Texts 32, London: Grant & Cutler, 1984.

Duggan, Joseph J., *The Romances of Chrétien de Troyes*, New Haven, CT: Yale University Press, 2001.

Echard, Siân, *Arthurian Narrative in the Latin Tradition*, Cambridge Studies in Medieval Literature 36, Cambridge University Press, 1998.

Frappier, Jean, *Chrétien de Troyes: The Man and His Work*, trans. Raymond Cormier, Athens, OH: Ohio University Press, 1982.

Hanning, Robert W., *The Individual in Twelfth-Century Romance*, New Haven, CN: Yale University Press, 1977.

Lacy, Norris J. and Joan Tasker Grimbert, eds., *A Companion to Chrétien de Troyes*, Arthurian Studies 63, Cambridge: D. S. Brewer, 2005.

Lacy, Norris J., Douglas Kelly and Keith Busby, eds., *The Legacy of Chrétien de Troyes*, 2 vols., Amsterdam: Rodopi, 1987–8.

Le Saux, F. H. M., ed., *A Companion to Wace*, Cambridge: D. S. Brewer, 2005.

Schmolke-Hasselman, Beate, *The Evolution of Arthurian Romance: The Verse Tradition from Chrétien to Froissart*, trans. Margaret and Roger Middleton, Cambridge University Press, 1998.

Wright, Neil, 'Introduction', in *Historia Regum Britannie I: Bern, Burgerbibliothek, MS. 568*, ed. Neil Wright, Cambridge: D. S. Brewer, 1985.

THE THIRTEENTH-CENTURY ARTHUR

Baumgartner, E., *Le Tristan en prose; essai d'interprétation d'un roman médiéval*, Publications romanes et françaises 133, Geneva: Droz, 1975.

Besamusca, Bart, ed., *Cyclification: The Development of Narrative Cycles in the Chansons de Geste and the Arthurian Romances*, Amsterdam: North-Holland, 1994.

Bogdanow, Fanni, *The Romance of the Grail*, Manchester University Press, 1966.

Bruckner, Matilda Tomaryn, *Chrétien Continued: A Study of the 'Conte du Graal' and its Verse Continuations*, Oxford University Press, 2009.

Busby, Keith, *Codex and Context: Reading Old French Verse Narrative in Manuscript*, 2 vols., Faux Titre 222, Amsterdam and New York: Rodopi, 2002.

Gauvain in Old French Literature, Amsterdam: Rodopi, 1980.

Dover, Carol, ed., *A Companion to the Lancelot-Grail Cycle*, Arthurian Studies 54, Cambridge: D. S. Brewer, 2003.

Frappier, J. and R.R. Grimm, *Le Roman jusqu'à la fin du XIIIe siècle, 1: Partie historique* (1978); *2. Partie documentaire* (1984), *Grundriss der romanischen Literaturen des Mittelalters*, Heidelberg: C. Winter, 1972–, vol. 4.

Hasty, Will, ed., *A Companion to Wolfram's 'Parzival'*, Columbia, SC: Camden House, 1999.

Kelly, Douglas, *The Art of Medieval French Romance*, Madison, WI, and London: University of Wisconsin Press, 1992.

Kennedy, Elspeth, *Lancelot and the Grail: A Study of the Prose 'Lancelot'*, Oxford: Clarendon Press, 1986.

Lacy, Norris J., ed., *Medieval Arthurian Literature: A Guide to Recent Research*, Garland Reference Library of the Humanities 1955, New York and London: Garland, 1996.

Lacy, Norris J., Douglas Kelly and Keith Busby, eds., *The Legacy of Chrétien de Troyes*, 2 vols., Amsterdam: Rodopi, 1987.

Lot, Ferdinand, *Etude sur le Lancelot en prose*, 2nd edn, revised by Myrrha Lot-Borodine, Paris: Champion, 1954.

Schmolke-Hasselmann, Beate, *The Evolution of Arthurian Romance: The Verse Tradition from Chrétien to Froissart*, trans. Margaret and Roger Middleton, Cambridge University Press, 1998.

Vinaver, Eugène, *The Rise of Romance*, Oxford: Clarendon Press, 1971.

Walters, Lori J., ed., *Lancelot and Guinevere: A Casebook*, Arthurian Characters and Themes 4, New York and London: Garland, 2002.

THE FOURTEENTH-CENTURY ARTHUR

Barron, W. R. J., *English Medieval Romance*, Longman Literature in English, London: Longman, 1987.

Brewer, Derek and Jonathan Gibson, eds., *A Companion to the Gawain-Poet*, Arthurian Studies 38, Cambridge: D. S. Brewer, 1997.

Burrow, J. A., *A Reading of 'Sir Gawain and the Green Knight'*, London: Routledge, 1965; repr. 1966.

Dembowski, Peter F., *Jean Froissart and His 'Meliador': Context, Craft, and Sense*, Lexington, KY: French Forum, 1983.

Gardner, Edmund, *The Arthurian Legend in Italian Literature*, New York: Dutton, 1930.

Matheson, Lister M., *The Prose 'Brut': The Development of a Middle English Chronicle*, Tempe, AZ : Medieval and Renaissance Texts and Studies, 1998.

Moll, Richard, *Before Malory: Reading Arthur in Late Medieval England*, Toronto University Press, 2003.

Putter, Ad, *An Introduction to the Gawain-Poet*, Longman Medieval and Renaissance Library, London: Longman, 1996.

Trachsler, Richard, *Clôtures du cycle Arthurien: étude et textes*, Publications romanes et françaises 215, Geneva: Droz, 1996.

Turville-Petre, Thorlac, *England the Nation: Language, Literature, and National Identity*, 1290–1340, Oxford: Clarendon Press, 1996.

THE FIFTEENTH-CENTURY ARTHUR

Alexander, Flora, 'Late Medieval Scottish Attitudes to the Figure of King Arthur: A Reassessment', *Anglia*, 93 (1975), 17–34.

Anglo, Sydney, *Spectacle, Pageantry and Early Tudor Policy*, Oxford: Clarendon Press, 1969.

Archibald, Elizabeth and Edwards, A. S. G., eds., *A Companion to Malory*, Arthurian Studies 37, Cambridge: D. S. Brewer, 1996.

Benson, L. D., *Malory's 'Morte Darthur'*, Cambridge, MA: Harvard University Press, 1976.

Besamusca, Bart, *et al.*, eds., *Cyclification: The Development of Narrative Cycles in the Chansons de gestes and the Arthurian Romances*, Koninklijke Nederlandse Akademie van Wetenschappen 159, Amsterdam: North Holland, 1994.

Bastert, Bernd, 'Late Medieval Summations: *Rappoltsteiner Parzifal* and Ulrich Füetrer's *Buch der Abenteuer*', in *AoG*, pp. 166–80.

Bogdanow, Fanni and Richard Trachsler, 'Rewriting Prose Romance: The Post-Vulgate Roman du Graal and Related Texts', in *AoF*, pp. 370–92.

Carley, James P., ed., *Glastonbury Abbey and the Arthurian Tradition*, Arthurian Studies 44, Cambridge: D. S. Brewer, 2001.

Dean, Christopher, *Arthur of England: English Attitudes to King Arthur and the Knights of the Round Table in the Middle Ages and the Renaissance*, University of Toronto Press, 1987.

Hughes, Jonathan, *Arthurian Myths and Alchemy: The Kingship of Edward IV*, Stroud: Sutton, 2002.

Ingham, Patricia Clare, *Sovereign Fantasies: Arthurian Romance and the Making of Britain*, Philadelphia, PA: University of Pennsylvania Press, 2001.

Kennedy, Edward Donald, 'John Hardyng and the Holy Grail', *Arthurian Literature*, 8 (1989), 185–206; reprinted in Carley, ed., *Glastonbury Abbey*, pp. 249–68.

Kipling, Gordon, *The Triumph of Honour: Burgundian Origins of the Elizabethan Renaissance*, Publications of the Sir Thomas Browne Institute, Leiden and The Hague: Leiden University Press, 1977.

Lagorio, Valerie M., 'The Evolving Legend of St Joseph of Glastonbury', in Carley, ed., *Glastonbury Abbey*, pp. 55–82.

Moll, Richard J., *Before Malory: Reading Arthur in Later Medieval England*, University of Toronto Press, 2003.

Pickford, C. E., *L'Evolution du roman arthurien en prose vers la fin du Moyen Age d'après le manuscrit 112 du fonds français de la Bibliothèque nationale*, Paris: Nizet, 1960.

Radulescu, Raluca L., *The Gentry Context for Malory's 'Morte Darthur'*, Arthurian Studies 55, Cambridge: D. S. Brewer, 2003.

Trachsler, Richard, *Clôtures du cycle Arthurien: étude et textes*, Publications romanes et françaises 215, Geneva: Droz, 1996.

Withrington, John, 'The Arthurian Epitaph in Malory's *Morte Darthur*', *Arthurian Literature*, 7 (1987), 103–44; repr. in Carley, ed., *Glastonbury Abbey*, pp. 211–47.

THE ARTHUR OF THE SIXTEENTH TO NINETEENTH CENTURIES

Barczewski, Stephanie L., *Myth and National Identity in Nineteenth-Century Britain: The Myths of King Arthur and Robin Hood*, Oxford University Press, 2000.

Brinkley, Roberta Florence, *Arthurian Legend in the Seventeenth Century*, Johns Hopkins Monographs in Literary History 3, Baltimore, MD: The Johns Hopkins University Press, 1932.

Brooks, Chris, and Inga Bryden, 'The Arthurian Legacy', in *AoE*, pp. 247–64.

Bryden, Inga, *Reinventing King Arthur: The Arthurian Legend in Victorian Culture*, Aldershot: Ashgate, 2005.

Jones, Ernest, *Geoffrey of Monmouth 1640–1800*, University of California Publications in English 5, no. 3, Berkeley and Los Angeles, CA: University of California Press, 1944.

Kendrick, T. D., *British Antiquity*, London: Methuen, 1950.

Knight, Stephen, *Arthurian Literature and Society*, London: Macmillan, 1983.

Lupack, Alan, *The Oxford Guide to Arthurian Literature and Legend*, Oxford University Press, 2005.

Lupack, Alan and Barbara Tepa Lupack, *King Arthur in America*, Arthurian Studies 41, Cambridge: D. S. Brewer, 1999.

MacCallum, M. W., *Tennyson's 'Idylls of the King' and Arthurian Story from the XVIth Century*, Glasgow: James Maclehose and Sons, 1894.

Merriman, James Douglas, *The Flower of Kings: A Study of The Arthurian Legend in England between 1485 and 1835*, Lawrence, KA: University of Kansas Press, 1973.

Millican, C. B., *Spenser and the Round Table: A Study in the Contemporaneous Background for Spenser's Use of the Arthurian Legend*, Harvard Studies in Comparative Literature 8, Cambridge, MA: Harvard University Press, 1932.

Simpson, Roger, *Camelot Regained: The Arthurian Revival and Tennyson, 1800–1849*, Arthurian Studies 21, Cambridge: D. S. Brewer, 1990.

Taylor, Beverly and Elisabeth Brewer, *The Return of King Arthur: British and American Arthurian Literature Since 1800*, Arthurian Studies 9, Cambridge: D. S. Brewer, 1983.

Whitaker, Muriel, *The Legends of King Arthur in Art*, Arthurian Studies 22, Cambridge: D. S. Brewer, 1990.

THE ARTHUR OF THE TWENTIETH AND TWENTY-FIRST CENTURIES

Grimbert, Joan Tasker and Norris J. Lacy, 'Arthur in Modern French Fiction and Film', in *AoF*, pp. 546–70.

Harty, Kevin J., ed., *Cinema Arthuriana: Twenty Essays*, revised edn, Jefferson, NC: McFarland, 2002.

Lacy, Norris J. and Geoffrey Ashe, *The Arthurian Handbook*, 2nd edn, Garland Reference Library of the Humanities 765, New York: Garland, 1988; 2nd edn, 1997.

Lacy, Norris J., *et al.*, eds., *The New Arthurian Encyclopedia*, expanded and revised edn, New York: Garland, 1991.

Lupack, Alan, *The Oxford Guide to Arthurian Literature and Legend*, Oxford University Press, 2005.

ed., *New Directions in Arthurian Studies*, Arthurian Studies 51, Cambridge: D. S. Brewer, 2002.

Lupack, Alan and Barbara Tepa Lupack, *King Arthur in America*, Arthurian Studies 41, Cambridge: D. S. Brewer, 1999.

Müller, Ulrich and Werner Wunderlich, 'The Modern Reception of the Arthurian Legend', in *AoG*, pp. 303–23.

Nastali, Daniel P., and Phillip C. Boardman, eds., *The Arthurian Annals: The Tradition in English from 1250 to 2000*, 2 vols., Oxford University Press, 2004.

Thompson, Raymond H., *The Return from Avalon: A Study of the Arthurian Legend in Modern Fiction*, Contributions to the Study of Science Fiction and Fantasy, Westport, CT: Greenwood, 1985.

QUESTIONING ARTHURIAN IDEALS

Archibald, Elizabeth, 'Latin Arthurian Romance', in *The Arthur of the Latin Tradition*, ed. Siân Echard, Cardiff: University of Wales Press, forthcoming 2009.

Bloomfield, Morton, 'The Problem of the Hero in the Later Medieval Period', in *Concepts of the Hero in the Middle Ages and the Renaissance*, ed., Norman T. Burns and Christopher Reagan, London: Hodder, 1976, pp. 27–48.

Cigman, Gloria, 'The Medieval Self as Anti-Hero', in *Heroes and Heroines: A Festschrift Presented to André Crépin on the Occasion of his Sixty-Fifth Birthday*, ed. Leo Carruthers, Cambridge: D. S. Brewer, 1994, pp. 161–70.

Comedy in Arthurian Literature, Special issue: *Arthurian Literature* 19 (2002).

Echard, Siân, *Arthurian Narrative in the Latin Tradition*, Cambridge Studies in Medieval Literature 36, Cambridge University Press, 1998.

Green, D. H., *The Beginnings of Medieval Romance: Fact and Fiction, 1150–1220*, Cambridge University Press, 2002.

Haidu, Peter, *Aesthetic Distance in Chrétien de Troyes: Irony and Comedy in 'Cligés' and 'Perceval'*, Histoire des idées et critique littéraire, Geneva: Droz, 1968.

Jaeger, C. Stephen, *The Origins of Courtliness: Civilizing Trends and the Formation of Courtly Ideals 939–1210*, Philadelphia, PA: University of Pennsylvania Press, 1985.

Kennedy, Edward Donald, ed., *King Arthur: A Casebook*, Arthurian Characters and Themes 1, New York and London: Garland, 1996.

Kennedy, Elspeth, 'Failure in Arthurian Romance', *Medium Ævum*, 50 (1991), 16–32; repr. in *The Grail*, ed. Mahoney, pp. 279–99.

Lacy, Norris J. and Joan Tasker Grimbert, eds., *A Companion to Chrétien de Troyes*, Arthurian Studies 63, Cambridge: D. S. Brewer, 2005.

Mahoney, Dhira B., ed., *The Grail: A Casebook*, Arthurian Characters and Themes 5, New York and London: Garland, 2000.

Ménard, Philippe, *Le Rire et le sourire dans le roman courtois en France au moyen âge 1150–1250*, Publications romanes et françaises 105, Geneva: Droz, 1969.

Morris, Rosemary, *The Character of King Arthur in Medieval Literature*, Arthurian Studies 4, Cambridge: D. S. Brewer, 1982.

Taylor, Beverly and Elisabeth Brewer, *The Return of King Arthur: British and American Arthurian Literature since 1900*, Arthurian Studies 9, Cambridge: D. S. Brewer, 1983.

Thompson, Raymond H. and Keith Busby, eds., *Gawain: A Casebook*, Arthurian Characters and Themes 8, London: Routledge, 2006.

Walters, Lori J., ed., *Lancelot and Guinevere: A Casebook*, Arthurian Characters and Themes 4, New York and London: Garland, 1996.

ARTHURIAN ETHICS

Bloch, R. Howard, *Medieval French Literature and Law*, Berkeley and Los Angeles, CA: University of California Press, 1977.

Bogdanow, Fanni, 'The Changing Vision of Arthur's Death', in *Dies Illa: Death in the Middle Ages*, ed. by Jane H. M. Taylor, Liverpool: Cairns, 1984, pp. 107–23.

Brown-Grant, Rosalind, *French Romance of the Later Middle Ages: Gender, Morality and Desire*, Oxford University Press, 2008.

Cannon, Christopher, 'Malory's Crime: Chivalric Identity and the Evil Will', in *Medieval Literature and Historical Enquiry: Essays in Honour of Derek Pearsall*, ed. David Aers, Cambridge: D. S. Brewer, 2000, pp. 159–83.

Dinshaw, Carolyn, *Getting Medieval: Sexualities and Communities, Pre- and Postmodern*, Durham, NC: Duke University Press, 1999.

Gaunt, Simon, *Gender and Genre in Medieval French Literature*, Cambridge University Press, 1995.

Love and Death in Medieval French and Occitan Courtly Literature: Martyrs to Love, Oxford University Press, 2006.

Griffin, Miranda, *The Object and the Cause in the Vulgate Cycle*, Oxford: Legenda, 2005.

Haidu, Peter, *The Subject Medieval/Modern: Text and Governance in the Middle Ages*, Stanford University Press, 2004.

Heng, Geraldine, *Empire of Magic: Medieval Romance and the Politics of Cultural Fantasy*, New York: Columbia University Press, 2003.

Kaeuper, Richard W., *Chivalry and Violence in Medieval Europe*, Oxford University Press, 1999.

Kay, Sarah, *Courtly Contradictions: The Emergence of the Literary Object in the Twelfth Century*, Stanford University Press, 2001.

Krueger, Roberta L., *Women Readers and the Ideology of Gender in Old French Verse Romance*, Cambridge University Press, 1993.

Putter, Ad, *'Sir Gawain and the Green Knight' and French Arthurian Romance*, Oxford University Press, 1995.

Vitz, Evelyn Birge, *Medieval Narrative and Modern Narratology: Subjects and Objects of Desire*, New York University Press, 1989.

IMPERIAL ARTHUR: HOME AND AWAY

Brewer, Elisabeth, *T. H. White's 'The Once and Future King'*, Arthurian Studies 30, Cambridge: D. S. Brewer, 1993.

Echard, Siân, *Arthurian Narrative in the Latin Tradition*, Cambridge Studies in Medieval Literature 36, Cambridge University Press, 1998.

Gilbert, Elliot L., 'The Female King: Tennyson's Arthurian Apocalypse', *PMLA*, 98 (1983), 863–78.

Girouard, Mark, *The Return to Camelot: Chivalry and the English Gentleman*, New Haven, CT: Yale University Press, 1981.

Ingham, Patricia Clare, *Sovereign Fantasies: Arthurian Romance and the Making of Britain*, The Middle Ages, Philadelphia, PA: University of Pennsylvania Press, 2001.

Jones, Terry, *Chaucer's Knight: The Portrait of a Medieval Mercenary*, London: Weidenfeld and Nicolson, 1980.

Leckie, R. William, Jr, *The Passage of Dominion: Geoffrey of Monmouth and the Periodization of Insular History in the Twelfth Century*, University of Toronto Press, 1981.

Lupack, Alan and Barbara Tepa Lupack, *King Arthur in America*, Arthurian Studies 41, Cambridge: D. S. Brewer, 1999.

McGuire, Ian, 'Epistemology and Empire in *Idylls of the King*', *Victorian Poetry*, 30 (1992), 387–400.

Riddy, Felicity, 'Contextualising *Le Morte Darthur*: Empire and Civil War', *A Companion to Malory*, ed. E. Archibald and A. S. G. Edwards, Arthurian Studies 37, Cambridge: D. S. Brewer, 1996, pp. 55–73.

Roland, Meg, 'From "Saracens" to "Infydeles": The Recontextualization of the East in Caxton's edition of *Le Morte Darthur*', *Re-Viewing 'Le Morte Darthur': Texts and Contexts, Characters and Themes*, ed. Kevin Whetter and Raluca Radulescu, Arthurian Studies 60, Cambridge: D. S. Brewer, 2005, pp. 65–77.

Rowe, J. C., 'How the Boss Played the Game: Twain's Critique of Imperialism in *A Connecticut Yankee in King Arthur's Court*', *The Cambridge Companion to Mark Twain*, ed. Forrest G. Robinson, Cambridge Companions to Literature, Cambridge University Press, 1995, pp. 175–92.

Wallace, David, '*Imperium*, Commerce and National Crusade', *New Medieval Literatures*, 8 (2006), 45–66.

Withrington, John, 'King Arthur as Emperor', *Notes and Queries*, 35 (1988), 13–15.

Wood, Juliet, 'Where Does Britain End? The Reception of Geoffrey of Monmouth in Scotland and Wales', *The Scots and Medieval Arthurian Legend*, ed. Rhiannon Purdie and Nicola Royan, Arthurian Studies 61, Cambridge: D. S. Brewer, 2005, pp. 9–24.

ARTHUR'S AFFAIRS

Armstrong, Dorsey, *Gender and the Chivalric Community in Malory's* Morte Darthur, Gainesville, FL: University of Florida Press, 2003.

Burns, E. Jane, *Arthurian Fictions: Rereading the Vulgate Cycle*, Columbus, OH: Ohio State University Press for Miami University, 1985.

Cherewatuk, Karen, *Marriage, Adultery and Inheritance in Malory's 'Morte Darthur'*, Arthurian Studies 67, Cambridge: D. S. Brewer, 2006.

Dover, Carol, ed., *A Companion to the Lancelot-Grail Cycle*, Arthurian Studies 54, Cambridge: D. S. Brewer, 2003.

Edwards, Elizabeth, 'The Place of Women in the *Morte Darthur*', in *A Companion to Malory*, ed. Elizabeth Archibald and A.S.G. Edwards, Arthurian Studies 37, Cambridge: D. S. Brewer, 1996, pp. 37–54.

Kennedy, Edward Donald, ed., *King Arthur: A Casebook*, Arthurian Characters and Themes 1, New York and London: Garland, 1996.

Larrington, Carolyne, *King Arthur's Enchantresses: Morgan and Her Sisters in Arthurian Tradition*, London: I. B. Tauris, 2006.

McCracken, Peggy, *The Romance of Adultery: Queenship and Sexual Transgression in Old French Literature*, Philadelphia, PA: University of Pennsylvania Press, 1998.

Rockwell, Paul V., 'The Falsification of Resemblance: Reading the False Guenièvre', *The Arthurian Yearbook*, 1 (1991), 27–42.

Walters, Lori J., ed., *Lancelot and Guenevere: A Casebook*, Arthurian Characters and Themes 4, New York: Garland, 1996.

RELIGION AND MAGIC

Chandès, Gérard, *Le Merveilleux et la magie dans la littérature*, C.E.R.M.E.I.L. 2, Amsterdam and Atlanta, GA: Rodopi, 1992.

Clark, Stuart, *Thinking with Demons: The Idea of Witchcraft in Early Modern Europe*, Oxford University Press, 1997.

Cooper, Helen, *The English Romance in Time: Transforming Motifs from Geoffrey of Monmouth to the Death of Shakespeare*, Oxford University Press, 2004.

Duffy, Maureen, *The Erotic World of Faery*, 1972; London: Cardinal–Sphere Books, 1987.

Flint, Valerie I.J., *The Rise of Magic in Early Medieval Europe*, Oxford: Clarendon, 1991.

Jolly, Karen, Catharina Raudvere and Edward Peters, *Witchcraft and Magic in Europe: The Middle Ages*, Athlone History of Witchcraft and Magic in Europe 3, London and New York: Continuum Press, 2001.

Kieckhefer, Richard, *Magic in the Middle Ages*, Cambridge University Press, 1989; Canto edn, 2000.

Larrington, Carolyne, *King Arthur's Enchantresses: Morgan and her Sisters in Arthurian Tradition*, London: I. B. Tauris, 2006.

Lecouteux, Claude, *Fées, sorcières et loups-garous au moyen âge: histoire du double*, Paris: Imago, 1992.

Magie et illusion au moyen âge, Centre Universitaire d'Etudes et de Recherches Médiévales d'Aix, Senefiance 42, Aix-en-Provence: CUERMA, Université de Provence, Centre d'Aix, 1999.

Saunders, Corinne, *Magic and the Supernatural in Medieval English Romance: Ideas and Imaginings*, Studies in Medieval Romance, Cambridge: D. S. Brewer, 2009.

Sweeney, Michelle, *Magic in Medieval Romance from Chrétien de Troyes to Geoffrey Chaucer*, Dublin: Four Courts Press, 2000.

Thomas, Keith, *Religion and the Decline of Magic: Studies in Popular Beliefs in Sixteenth and Seventeenth Century England*, 2nd edn, London: Weidenfeld & Nicolson, 1977.

Whitaker, Muriel, *Arthur's Kingdom of Adventure: The World of Malory's Morte Darthur*, Arthurian Studies 10, Cambridge: D. S. Brewer, 1984.

ARTHURIAN GEOGRAPHY

Ashe, Geoffrey, ed., *The Discovery of King Arthur*, London: Guild Publishing, 1985.

ed., *The Quest for Arthur's Britain*, London: Paladin Books, 1971.

Biddle, Martin, ed., *King Arthur's Round Table*, Woodbridge: Boydell, 2000.

Ditmas, E. M. R., 'The Cult of Arthurian Relics', *Folklore*, 75 (1964), 19–33.

'More Arthurian Relics', *Folklore*, 77 (1966), 91–104.

Dumville, David N., 'Sub-Roman Britain: History and Legend', *History*, 62.205 (1977), 173–92.

Higham, N. J., *King Arthur: Myth-Making and History*, London and New York: Routledge, 2002.

Jackson, Kenneth, 'Once Again Arthur's Battles', *Modern Philology*, 43.1 (1945), 44–57.

Moll, Richard J., *Before Malory: Reading Arthur in Later Medieval England*, University of Toronto Press, 2003.

Rouse, Robert and Cory J. Rushton, *The Medieval Quest for Arthur*, Stroud: Tempus, 2005.

Vermette, Rosalie A., 'Terrae Incantatae: The Symbolic Geography of Twelfth-Century Arthurian Romance', in *Geography and Literature: A Meeting of the Disciplines*, ed. William E. Mallory and Paul Simpson-Housley, New York: Syracuse Press, 1987, pp. 144–60.

Warren, Michelle, *History on the Edge: Excalibur and the Borders of Britain*, Minneapolis, MN: University of Minnesota Press, 2000.

INDEX

Cambridge Companions to ...

AUTHORS

Edward Albee edited by Stephen J. Bottoms

Margaret Atwood edited by
Coral Ann Howells

W. H. Auden edited by Stan Smith

Jane Austen edited by Edward Copeland and
Juliet McMaster

Beckett edited by John Pilling

Aphra Behn edited by Derek Hughes and
Janet Todd

Walter Benjamin edited by David S. Ferris

William Blake edited by Morris Eaves

Brecht edited by Peter Thomson and
Glendyr Sacks (second edition)

The Brontës edited by Heather Glen

Frances Burney edited by Peter Sabor

Byron edited by Drummond Bone

Albert Camus edited by Edward J. Hughes

Willa Cather edited by Marilee Lindemann

Cervantes edited by Anthony J. Cascardi

Chaucer second edition edited by
Piero Boitani and Jill Mann

Chekhov edited by Vera Gottlieb and
Paul Allain

Kate Chopin edited by Janet Beer

Coleridge edited by Lucy Newlyn

Wilkie Collins edited by Jenny Bourne Taylor

Joseph Conrad edited by J. H. Stape

Dante edited by Rachel Jacoff
(second edition)

Daniel Defoe edited by John Richetti

Don DeLillo edited by John N. Duvall

Charles Dickens edited by John O. Jordan

Emily Dickinson edited by Wendy Martin

John Donne edited by Achsah Guibbory

Dostoevskii edited by W. J. Leatherbarrow

Theodore Dreiser edited by Leonard Cassuto
and Claire Virginia Eby

John Dryden edited by Steven N. Zwicker

W. E. B. Du Bois edited by Shamoon Zamir

George Eliot edited by George Levine

T. S. Eliot edited by A. David Moody

Ralph Ellison edited by Ross Posnock

Ralph Waldo Emerson edited by Joel Porte
and Saundra Morris

William Faulkner edited by
Philip M. Weinstein

Henry Fielding edited by Claude Rawson

F. Scott Fitzgerald edited by Ruth Prigozy

Flaubert edited by Timothy Unwin

E. M. Forster edited by David Bradshaw

Benjamin Franklin edited by Carla Mulford

Brian Friel edited by Anthony Roche

Robert Frost edited by Robert Faggen

Elizabeth Gaskell edited by Jill L. Matus

Goethe edited by Lesley Sharpe

Günter Grass edited by Stuart Taberner

Thomas Hardy edited by Dale Kramer

David Hare edited by Richard Boon

Nathaniel Hawthorne edited by
Richard Millington

Seamus Heaney edited by
Bernard O'Donoghue

Ernest Hemingway edited by
Scott Donaldson

Homer edited by Robert Fowler

Ibsen edited by James McFarlane

Henry James edited by
Jonathan Freedman

Samuel Johnson edited by Greg Clingham

Ben Jonson edited by Richard Harp and
Stanley Stewart

James Joyce edited by Derek Attridge
(second edition)

Kafka edited by Julian Preece

Keats edited by Susan J. Wolfson

Lacan edited by Jean-Michel Rabaté

D. H. Lawrence edited by Anne Fernihough

Primo Levi edited by Robert Gordon

Lucretius edited by Stuart Gillespie and
Philip Hardie

David Mamet edited by Christopher Bigsby

Thomas Mann edited by Ritchie Robertson

Christopher Marlowe edited by
Patrick Cheney

Herman Melville edited by Robert S. Levine

Arthur Miller edited by Christopher Bigsby

Milton edited by Dennis Danielson
(second edition)